# Lecture Notes in Computer Science 8788

*Commenced Publication in 1973*
Founding and Former Series Editors:
Gerhard Goos, Juris Hartmanis, and Jan van Leeuwen

T0213751

More information about this series at http://www.springer.com/series/7410

Karin Bernsmed · Simone Fischer-Hübner (Eds.)

# Secure IT Systems

19th Nordic Conference, NordSec 2014
Tromsø, Norway, October 15–17, 2014
Proceedings

 Springer

*Editors*
Karin Bernsmed
SINTEF ICT
Trondheim
Norway

Simone Fischer-Hübner
Karlstad University
Karlstad
Sweden

ISSN 0302-9743
ISBN 978-3-319-11598-6
DOI 10.1007/978-3-319-11599-3

ISSN 1611-3349 (electronic)
ISBN 978-3-319-11599-3 (eBook)

Library of Congress Control Number: 2014949561

LNCS Sublibrary: SL4 – Security and Cryptology

Springer Cham Heidelberg New York Dordrecht London

Printed on acid-free paper

Springer is part of Springer Science+Business Media (www.springer.com)

# Preface

This volume contains the papers presented at NordSec 2014: The 19th Nordic Conference on Secure IT Systems held during October 15–17, 2014 in Tromsø, Norway.

The NordSec conferences were started in 1996 with the aim of bringing together researchers and practitioners within computer security in the Nordic countries–thereby establishing a forum for discussions and cooperation between universities, industry, and computer societies. NordSec addresses a broad range of topics within IT security and privacy, with special emphasis on applied security that could encourage interchange and cooperation between the research community and the industrial/consumer community. In 2014, the conference had a special focus on "Security and Privacy for Cloud Computing and Big Data."

NordSec 2014 received 42 submissions, which were reviewed by at least three members of the international Program Committee (PC). Based on discussions among the reviewers and other PC members, 15 papers were finally accepted for presentation at the NordSec and inclusion in this volume.

In addition to the main conference, the NordSec 2014 Poster Session that aims at facilitating discussions on research and cooperation between young Nordic researchers was coorganized by the Swedish IT Security Network for PhD students, SWITS, and the Norwegian Research School of Computer and Information Security, COINS. Short abstracts of 10 poster submissions were selected by the Poster Section Program Committee and are included in this volume.

Further highlights of NordSec 2014 are two invited keynote presentations by high-ranked IT-Security and Privacy experts: Dr. Siani Pearson (HP Labs), who presented "Accountability in Cloud Service Provision Ecosystems" and Prof. David Sands, who talked about "Differential Privacy: Now it's Getting Personal." The keynote paper by Dr. Siani Pearson is also included in this proceedings.

We would like to thank all authors, especially those who presented their work selected for the program. Moreover, we are very grateful to all PC members and additional reviewers, who contributed with thorough reviews and who actively participated in the PC discussions, ensuring a high quality of all accepted papers and posters.

We gratefully acknowledge the special contributions of the General Conference Chair, Ragnar Soleng (University of Tromsø, Norway), who has very professionally helped with all local arrangements. Finally, we warmly thank the University of Tromsø (UiT), The Arctic University of Norway, which generously sponsored NordSec 2014.

August 2014

Karin Bernsmed
Simone Fischer-Hübner

# Organization

## General Conference Chair

Ragnar Soleng                     University of Tromsø, Norway

## Programme Committee Co-chairs

Karin Bernsmed                    SINTEF ICT, Norway
Simone Fischer-Hübner             Karlstad University, Sweden

## Program Committee

Magnus Almgren                    Chalmers University of Technology, Sweden
Tuomas Aura                       Aalto University, Finland
Stefan Axelsson                   Blekinge Institute of Technology, Sweden
Fredrik Björck                    Stockholm University, Sweden
Sonja Buchegger                   KTH – Royal Institute of Technology, Sweden
Bengt Carlsson                    Blekinge Institute of Technology, Sweden
Rafik Chaabouni                   University of Tartu, Estonia
Mads Dam                          KTH – Royal Institute of Technology, Sweden
Lothar Fritsch                    Norwegian Computing Center, Norway
Kristian Gjøsteen                 Norwegian University of Science and
                                  Technology, Norway
Danilo Gligoroski                 Norwegian University of Science and
                                  Technology, Norway
Dieter Gollmann                   Hamburg University of Technology, Germany
Martin Gilje Jaatun               SINTEF ICT, Norway
Christian Damsgaard Jensen        Technical University of Denmark, Denmark
Audun Josang                      University of Oslo, Norway
Niels Christian Juul              Roskilde University, Denmark
Ella Kolkowska                    Swedish Business School, Örebro University,
                                  Sweden
Stewart Kowalski                  Stockholm University, Sweden and Gjøvik
                                  University College, Norway
Hanno Langweg                     Gjøvik University College, Norway
Peeter Laud                       Cybernetica AS, Estonia
Felix Leder                       Blue Coat Systems, Norway
Katerina Mitrokotsa               Chalmers University of Technology, Sweden
Simin Nadjm-Tehrani               Linköping University, Sweden

| | |
|---|---|
| Tomas Olovsson | Chalmers University of Technology, Sweden |
| Jakob Illeborg Pagter | Centre for IT Security, The Alexandra Institute Ltd., Denmark |
| Ebenezer Paintsil | Point Transaction Systems AS, Norway |
| Willard Rafnsson | Chalmers University of Technology, Sweden |
| Hanne Riis-Nielson | Technical University of Denmark, Denmark |
| Chunming Rong | University of Stavanger, Norway |
| Sini Ruohomaa | University of Helsinki, Finland |
| Andrei Sabelfeld | Chalmers University of Technology, Sweden |
| Einar Snekkenes | Gjøvik University College, Norway |
| Bart van Delft | Chalmers University of Technology, Sweden |
| Rose-Mharie Åhlfeldt | University of Skövde, Sweden |

## Additional Reviewers

| | |
|---|---|
| Aslanyan, Zaruhi | Hausknecht, Daniel |
| Balliu, Musard | Li, Ximeng |
| Ding, Jiangio | Rafnsson, Willard |
| Dollar, Piotr | Schwarz, Oliver |
| Guanciale, Roberto | Vigo, Roberto |

# Contents

## Attacks and Defenses

## Security in Healthcare and Biometrics

## Poster Papers

# Keynote Paper

# Accountability in Cloud Service Provision Ecosystems

Siani Pearson

Security and Cloud Lab, Hewlett Packard Labs, Bristol, UK
Siani.Pearson@hp.com

**Abstract.** In data protection regulation since the 1980s, accountability has been used in the sense that the 'data controller' is responsible for complying with particular data protection legislation and, in most cases, is required to establish systems and processes which aim at ensuring such compliance. This paper assesses this notion in the context of cloud computing, and describes how better and more systematic accountability might be provided.

**Keywords:** Accountability, cloud computing, non-functional requirements, security.

## 1 Introduction

In this paper the concept of accountability will be discussed in the context of cloud service provision. Accountability is a type of non-functional requirement, that is, a quality that defines how a system is supposed to be, as opposed to functional requirements, which define what a system is supposed to *do*. First we will consider how accountability, and closely related non-functional requirements such as privacy, security and compliance, are of considerable interest to potential cloud users. We will then focus on this important non-functional requirement of accountability, and examine how it can be provided in the cloud, especially in relation to the data protection domain. In this context we will explain the approach of the Cloud Accountability project (A4Cloud) [1], which is a European Community collaborative research project funded under the 7th Framework Programme for Research that focuses on accountability as a critical prerequisite for effective governance and control of corporate and personal data processed by cloud-based information technology (IT) services.

The National Institute of Standards and Technology (NIST) defines cloud computing as "*a model for enabling ubiquitous, convenient, on-demand network access to a shared pool of configurable resources (e.g., networks, servers, storage, applications, and services) that can be rapidly provisioned and released with minimal management effort or service provider interaction*" [2]. The service models defined by NIST are: *Software as a Service (SaaS)*, where consumers use cloud service providers' (CSPs') applications running on a cloud infrastructure; *Platform as a Service (PaaS)*, where consumers deploy (onto a cloud infrastructure run by a CSP) applications that have been created using programming languages and tools supported by that provider; *Infrastructure as a Service (IaaS)*, where consumers deploy and run software, with a CSP controlling the underlying cloud infrastructure. Deployment models encompass

K. Bernsmed and S. Fischer-Hübner (Eds.): NordSec 2014, LNCS 8788, pp. 3–24, 2014.
DOI: 10.1007/978-3-319-11599-3_1, © Springer International Publishing Switzerland 2014

private, community, public and hybrid clouds [2]. The combination of such cloud computing features enables different business models, and hence different types of cloud ecosystem.

Although cloud computing can bring many benefits for different parties, including for example decreased initial capital expenditure for cloud users and increased capacity for handling spikes in business demand, it can also bring new risks and vulnerabilities [3-5]. These increased risks are largely due to de-localisation and subprocessing (which of course may also happen in non-cloud environments), and there can be resultant worries from potential cloud users about lack of control and transparency, as well as about confidentiality (see further discussion in Section 2). As a result, organisations may be reluctant to let data flow outside their boundaries into the cloud, especially for public cloud, and are especially concerned in cloud environments with data breaches and data loss [6].

However, the perceptions of risk by organisations change over time: based on analysis carried out within different versions of the Cloud Security Alliance (CSA) top threats reports [7,8], there have been significant changes in ordering, including data breaches moving from fifth to the overall top threat between 2010 and 2013, and introduction of new threats, such as denial of service, which moved to be the fifth highest listed in 2013. And since then, fears about surveillance by foreign governments have had a big effect on customers' fears, making this issue rise up the list [8]. This was triggered by the Snowden revelations that the United States (US) National Security Agency (NSA) ran a surveillance programme known as PRISM, which collected information directly from the servers of big technology companies such as Microsoft, Google and Facebook [9].

Many of the requirements that need to be addressed in cloud environments are non-functional, as can be seen in Figure 1, which shows the top ranking of key actions to improve cloud adoption by business users, based on information from a recent International Data Corporation (IDC) report [10]. 80% of respondents nominated accountability, portability, connection or security certification within the top three proposed actions. Accountability was seen in this survey as the most important action of all to help improve cloud adoption [10].

Accepting responsibility and giving and holding to account are central to what is meant by accountability, and its meaning will be discussed in more detail in the following section. In Section 3, data protection, which is one of the biggest drivers of non-functional requirements, will be considered, particularly as legal restrictions on processing of personal data mean that it can be very hard to be compliant in cloud service provision ecosystems, even for those companies that put significant effort into this. There can be a tension between addressing these concerns and realising the benefits of cloud computing, as discussed further in Subsection 3.1, which examines data protection issues related to cloud computing, with explanation of the European context given in Subsection 3.2. Section 4 considers accountability relationships within cloud service provision ecosystems, and Section 5 moves on to consider what is involved in being accountable. In this context some of the work being carried out within the Cloud Accountability Project (A4Cloud) [1] is positioned. Finally, conclusions are given.

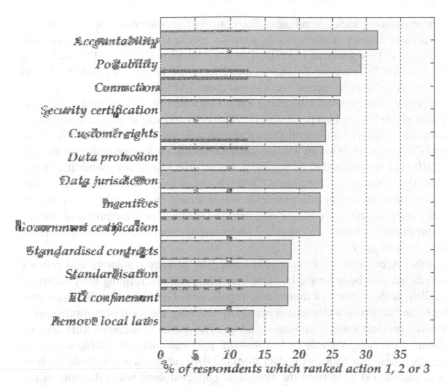

Fig. 1. Business Users' Ranking of Key Actions to Improve Cloud Adoption (based on data obtained from [7])

## 2    The Concept of Accountability

Although it is a complex notion, it could be argued that at its core, accountability is a very simple idea. It says that not only should an organisation do everything necessary to exercise good stewardship of the data under its control, it should also be able to demonstrate that it is doing so. Good stewardship is achieved by designing systems appropriately, so that they reflect privacy principles and security expectations from partners, regulators and data subjects, as well as by the organisation living up to its promises and ensuring responsible behaviour. The core of accountability, and indeed, the root word of accountability, is 'account', which must include descriptions and explanations of the organisation's actions [11]. The demonstration – via provision of an account to supervisory authorities – is an essential aspect, but can be challenging to provide. Furthermore, if there is a data protection breach, organisations need to pro-vide a means of remediation and demonstrate reasonable efforts to prevent a repeat occurrence.

Accountability has been used in data protection regulation since the 1980s in the sense that the data controller is responsible for complying with particular data protec-tion legislation and, in most cases, is required to establish systems and processes which aim at ensuring such compliance. The notion of accountability appears in several international privacy frameworks in addition to the Organisation for Economic Co-operation and Development (OECD) Privacy Guidelines (1980) [12], including Canada's Personal Information Protection and Electronic Documents Act (PIPEDA) (2000) [13], Asia Pacific Economic Cooperation (APEC)'s Privacy Framework (2005), papers by the Article 29 Working Party (launched in 1996 to give expert advice on data protection to European states) (2010) [14,15] and some elements of the draft European Union (EU) General Data Protection Regulation (GDPR) [16]. Notably, the EU's Article 29 Working Party recommendation on accountability to the EC in July 2010 [15] recommended inclusion of a new principle of accountability in the revised EU Data Protection Directive (GDPR). It stated (p2): *"this Opinion puts forward a concrete proposal on accountability which would require data controllers to put in place appropriate and effective measures to ensure that principles and obligations set out in the Directive are complied with, and to demonstrate so to supervisory authorities upon request."*

The Global Accountability Project [17] started by privacy regulators and privacy professionals has also been for the last few years defining and refining the concept of accountability in the context of these latest regulations. Guidance has also been produced by Canadian Privacy Commissioners [18] outlining the form of comprehensive accountability programs that organisations adopt. The notion of accountability utilised by regulators is evolving towards an 'end-to-end' personal data stewardship regime in which the enterprise that collects the data from the data subject is accountable for how the data is shared and used from the time it is collected until when the data is destroyed. This extends to onward transfer to third parties. For a broader analysis of the notion of accountability, see [19].

An example of the evolution of the concept is the development of governance models which incorporate accountability and responsible information use. Frameworks such as the EU's Binding Corporate Rules (BCRs) [20] and APEC's Cross Border Privacy Rules (CBPRs) [21] are being developed by legislative authorities to try to provide a cohesive and more practical approach to data protection across disparate regulatory systems, and can be viewed as operationalising accountability, as regulators increasingly require that companies prove they are accountable. Thus, BCRs require organisations to demonstrate that they are, and will be, compliant with EU Data Protection Authorities' (DPAs) requirements for transferring data outside the EU.

## 3      Data Protection in the Cloud

Data protection is one of the biggest drivers of non-functional requirements for cloud computing. Not only can huge amounts of data be moved around, but there can be increased risks and correspondingly there are increased concerns from regulators. Data protection is about the processing of personal data, which involves a whole range of activities. For personal data, the framing is in terms of identifiability rather than ownership: personal data is information that can be traced to a particular individual. Sensitive information is a special category of personal data for which there are stricter handling requirements.

At this point it is useful to explain some terminology commonly used in data protection. A *data controller* (DC) essentially determines the purposes for which and the manner in which personal data is processed. A *data processor* (DP) processes personal data upon the instructions of the data controller. The *data subject* is the living person that can be identified by personal data, and the *data protection authority* (DPA) is the supervisory body. See further discussion in [22], as well as [23], which provides the definitions used in the current European data protection directive.

In the cloud context, the organisational cloud customer is in general considered to be the DC, and is regulated by the DPA. The cloud service provider (CSP) is nearly always a DP, but could be a DC. They may need to assume co-controllership responsibilities, but may now know who the users are or what their services are being used for. These relationships are explored further in Section 4.

The core principles that form the basis of most worldwide data protection and privacy legislation are the OECD data privacy principles [12] (which were updated in 2013 [24]). These encompass collection limitation, data quality, purpose specification, use limitation, security, openness, individual participation and accountability. The security principle relates to protection of personal data. The accountability principle is about the obligation of the DC to put measures in place that satisfy the other principles, as discussed in the previous section. CSPs acting as DCs will be responsible for this, but it can be a challenge to meet these requirements in the cloud, as considered in the following subsection.

## 3.1    Core Issues

Data protection is a big challenge in the cloud for a number of reasons, but especially because of the complexity within service provision networks, the dynamic nature of cloud and legal restrictions on data crossing jurisdictional boundaries. The current system includes an inconsistent and often divergent matrix of regulations, which adds layers of complexity and administrative burden for cloud providers, and makes it hard for businesses to ensure full compliance. One aspect is that transborder flow of personal information (including access to this information) is restricted by some of these laws. For example, the EU data protection directive [23] restricts the movement of data from the EU to non-EU countries that do not meet the EU 'adequacy' standard for privacy protection. In practice contractual mechanisms like Binding Corporate Rules (BCRs) or model contracts might need to be put in place in such cases. However, putting a model contract in place and having it approved within the EU could take several months and so is not well suited to cloud environments, and BCRs also need to be set up in advance and only apply to outsourcing within the same corporate group.

| Cloud features | Potential data protection issues |
|---|---|
| Multi-tenancy | • Data of co-tenants may be revealed in investigations<br>• Isolation failure<br>• Proper deletion of data and virtual storage devices |
| Elasticity | • Multiplies attack surfaces<br>• De-anonymisation facilitated |
| Abstraction | • Cannot rely upon physical security controls |
| Automation | • Ensuring appropriate data protection when data flows are dynamic<br>• Decrease in human involvement in data protection |
| Data duplication | • Detecting and determining who is at fault if privacy breaches occur<br>• Difficulty in knowing geographic location and which specific servers or storage devices will be used |
| Easy data access from multiple locations | • Data access from remote geographic locations subject to different legislative regimes, and transborder data flow compliance issues<br>• Potential for risky usage by employees without due consideration |
| Subprocessing | • Potential complexity of cloud service delivery chains, both horizontally and vertically<br>• Lack of transparency or compliance by subprocessors<br>• Unauthorized data access from employees of CSPs<br>• Risks to confidentiality from subpoenas or access by foreign governments<br>• Overlapping responsibilities in data management<br>• Unauthorized secondary usage and profiling<br>• Vendor demise |

**Fig. 2.** Cloud Features and Issues

There are a variety of data protection concerns related to cloud computing that include ongoing questions of jurisdiction and exacerbation of privacy risk through subprocessing and de-localisation [3-5], as well as legal uncertainty [26]. Figure 2 highlights key issues by means of illustrating how many of the features that characterise the cloud can enhance data protection risks. A categorization of risks from an EU perspective has been made according to lack of transparency or control by the Article 29 Working Party in their Opinion on Cloud Computing [27], which is summarized in Figure 3. Similar risks were highlighted by the French data protection authority [27], with the addition of ineffective or non-secure destruction of data, or excessive data retention periods, and of takeover of the CSP by a third party. A more detailed analysis of cloud computing risks has been provided by European Union Agency for Network and Information Security (ENISA) [3].

The situation is further complicated because increasingly there is inherent complexity in the way that services are provided, which can be difficult or indeed inappropriate to convey to end users. In addition, transparency and control are not just an issue with regard to collection of data, but also with regard to data sharing and data inferences made about people based upon the data.

| Lack of transparency | Cause |
| --- | --- |
| Lack of appropriate action by DC or by DS | Insufficient knowledge about potential threats and risks |
| Lack of knowledge by DC about chain processing | Increased risk involving multiple processors and subcontractors |
| Lack of knowledge about law applicable to data protection disputes | Personal data processed in different geographic locations within EEA |
| Lack of knowledge about inadequate levels of data protection or illegality of transfers | Personal data transferred outside EEA without appropriate measures |
| Lack of control | Cause |
| Lack of availability | Vendor lock-in |
| Lack of integrity | Sharing of resources |
| Lack of confidentiality | Law enforcement requests made directly to a CSP, or without valid EU legal basis |
| Lack of intervenability | Complexity and dynamics of outsourcing chain |
| Lack of data subjects' rights | Lack of tools for access, deletion and correction of data |
| Lack of isolation | Cloud admins with privileged access rights might link info across clients |

**Fig. 3.** Data Protection Risks of Cloud Computing, from a European Perspective

## 3.2 European Context

The European Union (EU) is often viewed on a global stage as a normative leader and this is especially true on data protection as the EU is recognized as a thought leader in this domain to protect individual privacy while preserving business dynamics. For example, the ePrivacy Directive [28] outlaws spam, and mandates opt-in for use of cookies and location based services). This, and other ongoing developments (as listed below) collectively create a pull for accountability and the closely related notions of breach notification and other forms of transparency, security, privacy by design, certification and sanctions.

— *EU General Data Protection Regulation (GDPR) [16]:* problems with the 1995 EU Data Protection Directive [23] as a harmonisation measure and in relation to new technologies including cloud computing led the European Commission in January 2012 to publish a draft of replacement GDPR that is currently being discussed and revised [16], in which accountability features and privacy by design take greater precedence. Amongst other things, this imposes new obligations and liabilities for DPs, new requirements on data breach notification and stricter rules on international data transfers. It also empowers National Regulatory authorities to impose significantly higher fines.

— *European Cloud Computing Strategy [29]*: this was launched in September 2012, aiming at more clarity and knowledge about the applicable legal framework and making it easier to verify compliance with the legal framework (for example, through standards and certification). One result is that in June 2014, the Cloud Select Industry Group set up by the European Commission issued guidelines on the standardisation of service level agreements for CSPs [30], focusing on security and data protection in the cloud.

— *Cybersecurity Strategy [31]*: published in February 2013 by the EC, alongside a draft directive on network and information security [32]. Once implemented, many service providers will be covered by a range of data security obligations including adopting risk management practices and reporting major security incidents.

## 4     Accountability Relationships in the Cloud

In this section we will consider the relationship of accountability to privacy and security, explain the roles involved in cloud service provision and analyse accountability relationships across these.

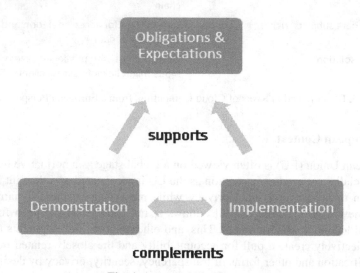

**Fig. 4.** Accountability Context

It is important to realise that accountability complements privacy and security, rather than replacing them. If organisations are accountable, they need not just to define and implement privacy and security controls where appropriate, but also define and accept responsibility for so doing, show that they are in compliance with privacy and security requirements, and provide remediation and redress in case of failure. As shown in Figure 4, businesses operate under many obligations, and these can be normative (derived from social norms), regulatory or contractual. Here, we are using obligation in the sense of being a requirement, agreement or promise for which there are certain consequences if it is breached. In this paper we are concerned with organisations that are accountable for obligations in relation to the treatment of data. The organisations need to implement appropriate measures to meet these obligations and manage risks. Furthermore, they need to demonstrate how their obligations are met and risks are managed. This is a central part of accountability, and increases trust.

Hence, accountability in the cloud should complement the usage of appropriate cloud privacy and security controls [33, 34] in order to support democratically determined principles that reflect societal norms, regulations and stakeholder expectations. Governance and oversight of this process is achieved via a combination of data protection authorities (DPAs), auditors and Data Protection Officers within organisations, the latter potentially supplemented by private accountability agents acting on their behalf. Accountability and good systems design (in particular, to meet privacy and security requirements) are complementary, in that the latter provides mechanisms and controls that allow implementation of principles and standards, whereas accountability makes organisations responsible for providing an appropriate implementation for their business context, and addresses what happens in case of failure (i.e. if the account is not provided, is not adequate, if the organisation's obligations are not met e.g. there is a data breach, etc.).

Before we consider the accountability relationships further between these actors, first we shall clarify the roles involved. The cloud supply chain taxonomy defined by NIST [35] has been almost universally adopted by industry and academia to describe cloud supply chains in terms of consumers, providers, brokers, auditors and carriers. Some actors may hold more than one role: for example, cloud customers may also act as cloud providers. This taxonomy defines a cloud customer as an entity that both has a business relationship with and uses the services of a cloud provider.

However, this taxonomy has shortcomings in regard to describing cloud accountability roles because parties that may be affected, own or be identified via data – and indeed the relevant supervisory authorities for a particular regulatory domain – may not be reflected in this taxonomy. For example, a data subject may have a business relationship with a cloud customer rather than a cloud provider, or a business could provide confidential data to another business, which itself uses the service of a cloud provider. And although DPAs or telecom regulators could be viewed as cloud auditors in the NIST model [35], they in addition hold enforcement powers. Hence the *cloud subject* and *cloud supervisory authority* have been added as distinct actors within the A4Cloud cloud taxonomy [36], resulting in the following cloud roles:

— **Cloud Subject:** An entity whose data are processed by a cloud provider, either directly or indirectly.
— **Cloud Customer:** An entity that maintains a business relationship with and uses services from a cloud provider.
— **Cloud Provider:** An entity responsible for making a service available to cloud customers
— **Cloud Carrier:** The intermediary entity that provides connectivity and transport of cloud services between cloud providers and cloud customers.

- **Cloud Broker:** An entity that manages the use, performance and delivery of cloud services, and negotiates relationships between cloud providers and cloud customers.
- **Cloud Auditor:** An entity that can conduct independent assessment of cloud services, information system operations, performance and security of the cloud implementation, with regards to a set of requirements, which may include security, data protection, information system management, regulations and ethics.
- **Cloud Supervisory Authority:** An entity that oversees and enforces the application of a set of rules (in a similar way to the competent authority defined by EC that should be designated in all Member States [32]).

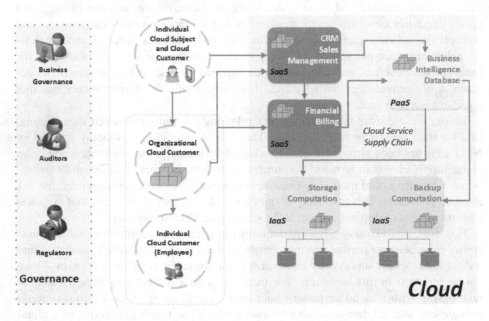

**Fig. 5.** Example Cloud Ecosystem

In a given scenario, and from a data protection perspective, entities may take on data protection roles as appropriate. For example, cloud subjects may be data subjects, cloud customers and cloud providers would be DCs or DPs, and cloud carriers and cloud brokers may be DPs, or possibly DCs or else fall outside the controller/processor distinction, depending upon their function. The organisational cloud customer (which is a business or a legal person) is considered to be a DC. Even though in most cases cloud customers are not in a position to negotiate with CSPs, they may still choose amongst offerings and hence are still considered a DC [26]. An individual cloud customer (who is a natural person) is likely to be considered to be a data subject, although there are situations where they would be considered as a DC, for example where they use a cloud service for professional purposes involving processing data of other data subjects. Cloud providers can be considered to be DPs or DCs. If they process personal data which is not provided by a cloud customer, acting autonomously to define the means and the purpose of the processing, the cloud provider is a DC. On the other hand, the cloud provider is a DP if it processes personal data to provide a service requested by a cloud customer and does not further process the data for its own purposes. There are also cases where the cloud provider can be a joint DC, namely when it processes data to provide a service requested by a cloud customer but in addition further processes the data for its own purposes (e.g. advertising). In the EU General Data Protection Regulation (GDPR) [16], DPs who process data beyond the DC's instructions would be considered as a joint DC, and this case might include changing security measures or data handling practices. For more detailed analysis, see for example [25].

Let us now consider the accountability relationships between the various actors in an example cloud ecosystem such as those illustrated by Figure 5. Every party of the cloud service is called to be accountable to other parties. There are different obligations according to the roles that apply in a given scenario. The DC is accountable for applicable data protection measures, as we discussed earlier. The CSPs as DPs must provide security measures, and their responsibilities will vary according to the combination of cloud service and deployment models. For example, PaaS providers are responsible for the security of the platform software stack and SaaS providers are responsible for security applications delivered to end users. The lower down the stack the CSP stops, the more security the consumer is tactically responsible for implementing and managing.

The liabilities involved are expressed within contracts as there can be ramifications of failure within cloud ecosystems, affecting other parties. The DPs are accountable for co-operation with the DC to meet data subjects' rights, assist the DC in providing security measures, and should act only on the DC's behalf. Thus, there are chains of accountability through the cloud service supply chains to the cloud customer. In addition, cloud providers and customers are accountable to the actors involved in governance and enforcement, as shown on the left hand side of Figure 5. These include regulators, stakeholders and society, as well as auditors and business governance. These are especially interested in monitoring and measuring non-functional aspects, leaving it to the service providers to determine how they actually want to achieve those. The cloud customer is in general accountable to these governance entities for applicable data protection measures. All actors in the supply chain are ultimately accountable to the cloud subject. Moreover, extending the accountability relationship between cloud providers and cloud consumers to the provider's responsibility to society at large provides a broader perspective on the need for accountability in the cloud.

## 5    From Accountability to Being Accountable

In this section some potential solutions for an improved approach to accountability in cloud environments are explored and suggested and a framework is proposed in which these can be modelled and categorized.

## 5.1   Model of Accountability

In Figure 6 a model of accountability is presented that shows how accountability can be captured at different layers of abstraction, ranging from conceptual to organisational to operational. The top layer of the pyramid shown in Figure 6 corresponds to the definition of accountability in cloud environments, namely:

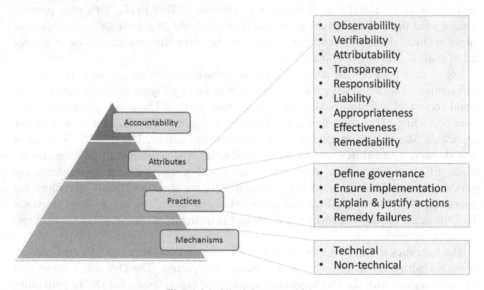

**Fig. 6.** Model of Accountability

**Definition of Accountability for Data Stewardship in the Cloud:** Accountability for an organization consists of accepting responsibility for the stewardship of personal and/or confidential data with which it is entrusted in a cloud environment, for processing, storing, sharing, deleting and otherwise using the data according to contractual and legal requirements from the time it is collected until when the data are destroyed (including onward transfer to and from third parties). It involves committing to legal and ethical obligations, policies, procedures and mechanisms, explaining and demonstrating ethical implementation to internal and external stakeholders and remedying any failure to act properly. [36]

Moving down the model in terms of becoming less abstract, the other layers correspond in turn to the following aspects:

1. *Accountability attributes.* These are the central conceptual components of accountability, namely: observabililty, verifiability, attributability, transparency, responsibility, liability, appropriateness, effectiveness and remediability. Further details are given in [36, 37].
2. *Accountability practices.* These define the central behaviour of an organisation adopting an accountability-based approach, which in a general sense are defining governance, ensuring implementation of appropriate actions, explaining and justifying those actions and remedying any failure to act properly. More specifically, an accountable organisation must commit to responsible stewardship of other people's data. It should define and deploy policies regarding its data practices that link to

relevant external criteria (such as best practice or codes of conducts), meet regulatory, contractual and normative obligations that apply to the context and are supported by senior management. It should deploy mechanisms to put these policies in place, which are represented in the bottom layer of the diagram. It should also monitor data practices (and keep records), including internal review to provide assurance that the mechanisms are working. It should also correct policy violations, which includes informing appropriate stakeholders, putting in place remedies and improving mechanisms. Finally, it needs to demonstrate that it is using appropriate and effective measures to ensure policy compliance, which involves being open to enforcement agency oversight and provision of an account. These map to the Global Accountability Project's 'essential elements' of accountability [17] and other opinions influenced by that [18]. But in addition, two other important aspects need to be emphasised: first, accountable organisations must ensure that accountability extends through across their service supply chains, in other words ensuring that the services and partners they use are accountable too, which involves amongst other things proper allocation of responsibilities and provision of evidence about satisfaction of obligations along the service provision chain; second, there are implications in terms of the way that the enforcement and verification mechanisms for accountability will operate, the scope of risk assessment and the ways in which other stakeholders are able to hold an organisation to account. For example, verification could involve a party being certified against specific criteria to meet the accountability level needed, with this mechanism including auditing and in some cases even continuous monitoring of this accountability level.

3. *Accountability mechanisms and tools.* These tools and mechanisms offer enhanced accountability; organisations in addition will need to use privacy and security controls appropriate to the context, as described in previous sections. Some of the tools may form a toolbox from which organisations can select as appropriate. They can be (extensions of) existing business processes like auditing, risk assessment and the provision of a trustworthy account, or non-technical mechanisms like formation of appropriate organisational policies, remediation procedures in complex environments, contracts, certification procedures, and so on. Or they can be technical tools, which would include tracking and transparency tools, detection of violation of policy obligations, notification of policy violation, increased transparency without compromising privacy, and so on. Some mechanisms may be mandatory, such as means to make uses transparent to individuals and assure their rights are respected. The proposed GDPR [16] already includes many accountability elements including, in Article 22, a list of a DC's accountability instruments, namely:

— Policies
— Documenting processing operations
— Implementing security requirements
— Data Protection Impact Assessment
— Prior authorisation/consultation by Data Protection Authority
— Data Protection Officer
— If proportional, independent internal or external audits

**5.2     Proposed Characteristics of an Accountability Approach**

Accountability measures have to be appropriate and effective in a verifiable way. In order to avoid charges of 'privacy whitewashing', whereby apparent accountability encourages a false basis for trust in DCs by data subjects, in this paper we argue that an accountability approach should have the following characteristics:

1. *Supporting externally agreed data protection approach*: Accountability should be viewed as a means to help organisations be accountable for the personal and confidential information that they collect, store, process and disseminate, not as an alternative to reframing basic privacy principles or legal requirements. Thus, the accountability elements in the GDPR provide a certain assurance of compliance with the data protection principles, but do not replace them.
2. *Trust in the verification process*: There needs to be a strong enough verification process to show the extent to which commitments have been fulfilled. Missing evidence can pose a problem, and guarantees are needed about the integrity and authenticity of evidence supporting verification. In addition, the actor carrying out the verification checks needs to be trusted by the data subject and to have the appropriate authority and resources to carry out spot checking and other ways of asking organisations to demonstrate compliance with regulatory and contractual obligation by providing accounts that may take various forms (e.g. certificates, seals and audit reports). This is why the DPAs will need to play a key role in the trust verification, for example in data protection certification. Data protection impact assessments, codes of conduct and certifications can be used to increase trust in CSPs who adhere to them. It is thus of the utmost importance that regulatory and supervisory bodies have a primary role in the verification of the level of compliance of these tools. Furthermore, to give data subjects back some control the data subjects' comments and needs could receive a response and ideally even show some fundamental development in the application or organisational data processing [38]. This form of feedback to the data subjects (in response to their feedback) is another form of verification. There are further related aspects supporting this approach in terms of responsibility and transparency, as listed below.
3. *Enforcement*: Strong enforcement strategies, not only in terms of verification, but also in terms of increasing the likelihood of detection of unlawful practices and strong penalties if caught, seem to be a necessary part of accountability.
4. *Clarity and acceptance of responsibility*: The relationship between controllers and processors in cloud service provision chains can sometimes be complex, as considered within Section 3. The commitments of the DC need to be well defined – this is (part of) the aspect of responsibility, that is an element of accountability. The respective responsibility of cloud customers and CSPs will need to be defined in contracts and the definition of standard clauses by the industry, as validated by regulators, will help cloud customers with lower negotiation capabilities. The commitments of the DC should include all applicable legal obligations, together with any industry standards (forming part of the external criteria against which the organisation's policies are defined) and any other commitment made by the DC in privacy statements. Once again, the responsibilities of the entities along the CSP chain

need to be clearly defined, including relative security responsibilities. On the other hand, certain tasks will need to be jointly carried out to be effective, such as risk assessment and security management. In this case there is a clear need for cooperation and coordination. As discussed in Section 4, the extent to which CSPs should be considered as controllers or processors remains questionable.

5. *Transparency*: A main goal of accountability is to go beyond regulation through fostering transparency about actual practices and thus enabling promotion of good privacy practices, in a proactive sense. The commitments of the DC(s) need to be expressed in an understandable language by the data subjects affected and other parties as appropriate – this is a key transparency aspect. In addition, the mechanisms used and relevant properties of the service providers in the provision chain need to be clarified as appropriate to cloud customers and regulators. It would also be beneficial to integrate social interaction between data subjects and the cloud infrastructure and service providers, for example via feedback mechanisms that enable comments on privacy policies and data usage reports. Furthermore, data protection impact assessments and privacy impact assessments are forms of verification for accountability (that should be used in conjunction with others) that can be used to help provide transparency about the nature of the risks, including the criteria used in the risk assessment, how decisions are made to mitigate risk, and whether the mechanisms to be used and implemented are appropriate for the context. Comprehensive obligations for controllers to inform supervisory authorities and data subjects of personal data breaches would further increase transparency.

6. *Avoidance of increased risk*: Technical security measures (such as open strong cryptography) can help prevent falsification of logs, and privacy-enhancing techniques and adequate access control should be used to protect personal information in logs. Note however that data that is collected for accountability might be itself data that can be abused and hence needs to be protected as much as the processed data. The potential conflict of accountability with privacy is somewhat reduced as the focus in data protection is not on the accountability of data subjects but rather of DCs, which need to be accountable towards data subjects and trusted "intermediaries".

7. *Avoidance of increased burden*: Accountability must deliver effective solutions whilst avoiding where possible overly prescriptive or burdensome requirements.

8. *Avoidance of social harm*: Accountability should have democratic and ethical characteristics. Transparency should be as high as possible, in balance with other interests, as considered above in 5. Mechanisms should also be developed to help regulators do their job, notably with respect to enhancement of the verification process as discussed above.

As considered already in Figure 4, appropriate security and privacy design (for instance, to provide anonymity and confidentiality) needs to be used in conjunction with accountability, which focuses on demonstrating that and providing remediation if things go wrong. Inclusion of privacy provisions and liability assignment within security requirements is a good start, but more can be done. The organizational commitment to accountability is according to external standards that include practical guidance such as guidance about data protection and cloud security [39-42]. Each organization should assess the relevance of risks for its own situation and study the measures put in place by itself and by its service provider(s) to reduce these risks [27,43,44].

Butin *et al* have introduced a notion of strong accountability [45] that applies not only to policies and procedures, but also to practices, so that the effectiveness of the processing of personal data can be overseen (this stresses a distinction between 'reporting' and 'demonstrating'). It is supported by precise binding commitments enshrined in law and involves regular audits by independent entities. They assert that this should not be contradictory with the need for flexibility that is required by the industry. The A4Cloud project approach also addresses accountability at the practices level, as described in the previous and following section, and operates in line with, or aims to satisfy, the characteristics given above. Example mechanisms being developed within the A4Cloud project that can be used to support accountability include data protection impact assessment, automated evidence collection to be provided within accounts, tools to support contractual transparency, clear definition of responsibilities within policies that are then enforced, and incidence response and remediation tools.

Accountability is particularly hard to achieve in the cloud context, but that is actually a context where it is strongly needed. The main factors contributing to this difficulty are government surveillance, potential weak links in dynamically formed CSP chains and the current shallowness of transparency and verifiability in the cloud context. Of these, addressing surveillance is out of scope for the A4Cloud project, although accountability might help to provide a solution to the state surveillance issue, but only in a limited sense as confidentiality is the core issue in that case. Regarding the potential shallowness of transparency and verifiability, technical and organisational measures embedding transparency and verifiability by design are key for effective accountability. The model proposed in the previous section includes such tools. Without this, accountability-based approaches in the cloud can only be relatively weak. Most of the risks considered in Section 3.1 should be reduced by contractual provisions that can include penalties for the service provider, and by technical and organisational measures for the customer and the service provider. If the DC is ultimately made accountable for meeting obligations right along the service provision chain, they should try to obtain contractual assurances that lessen the risk of potential weak links in dynamically formed CSP chains. That is, contractual agreements between the series of actors taking part in the cloud chain should provide for the accountability obligations of DCs ultimately owed to DSs.

Accountability can be achieved via a combination of *public accountability* that is derived from transparent interaction (between subjects of personal data, supervisory authorities, regulatory bodies and DCs), legislation, soft regulation, on-going Privacy Impact Assessments (PIAs), certification, audit, public policy, etc. and *private accountability*, that is derived from interactions between DCs and data processors (premised on contract law, technological processes and practical internal compliance requirements) [46]. Furthermore, we advocate the combination of a strong and soft approach to support accountability provision. The strong approach involves supporting accountability of practice, provision and analysis of trusted evidence to show whether or not data protection obligations have been fulfilled, verification by independent, trusted entities and certification based on such verification. The soft approach relates to addressing how accountability can be achieved in a socially beneficial way, including ethical governance and the democratic aspect.

## 5.3    How Can We Implement Accountability in Cloud and Complex Service Provision Environments?

In this section the approach of the A4Cloud project [10, 47] is described at a high level, giving an explanation of the tools and mechanisms that are being developed in the project to try to tackle the issues discussed above.

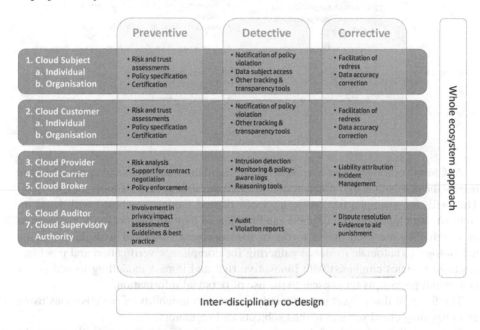

**Fig. 7.** Accountability Framework

The project aims to assist holding cloud (and other) service providers accountable for how they manage personal, sensitive and confidential information 'in the cloud' and how they deliver services. This will be achieved by an orchestrated set of mechanisms: preventive (mitigating risk, for example, to assess and reduce privacy harm before personal data is collected), detective (monitoring and identifying risk and policy violation) and corrective (managing incidents and providing redress). Used individually or collectively, these should make the Internet in the short- and longer-term more transparent and trustworthy for:

- *prospective users of cloud services* who have to balance innovation with legal obligations and the expectations of individuals
- *their customers*
- *suppliers* within the cloud eco-system, who need to be able to differentiate themselves in the ultimate commodity market.

| Practice | Function | Mechanisms |
|---|---|---|
| Define governance | Policy definition | • Clear definition of responsibilities within policies<br>• Enhancement of policies to include ethical aspects reflecting social values<br>• Machine readable policies |
| Ensure implementation | Policy implementation | • Automated policy enforcement |
| | Risk assessment | • Data protection impact assessment |
| Explain & justify actions | Transparency | • Tool to support contractual transparency<br>• Tool to support data subject access and correction |
| | Evidence for verifiability (e.g. within provision of accounts or for certification) | • Automated monitoring and collection of evidence tools<br>• Assurance about accountability tools deployed |
| | Detection of policy violation | • Assessment of satisfaction or violation of obligations |
| Remedy failure | Remediation | • Remediation tool<br>• Attribution of failure |
| | Exception notification | • Incident response tool |

**Fig. 8.** A4Cloud Accountability Mechanisms

A4Cloud combines socio-economic, legal, regulatory and technical approaches and brings these together into a coherent and interoperable system of tools and services. This will, for example, involve using sophisticated models combined with legal insight so that cloud service contracts can be selected that are appropriate to the context in which they are used, novel forms of measurement combined with data tracking technology to automate evidence gathering for compliance verification and machine-readable policies combined with innovative risk and impact modelling to add richer contextual provisions for consent to the use of personal information.

The focus of this project is particularly on the accountability of organisations using and providing cloud services to data subjects and regulators.

The overall framework of the project is shown in Figure 7, which illustrates the main stakeholder groups targeted by the project as rows of a matrix, and shows example accountability tools that may be provided for such users, according to the categories described above. Figure 8 shows the tools currently being developed within A4Cloud, which can be used in a standalone way or else in combination with other tools being developed internal or external to the project.

Let us consider briefly just one example. As illustrated in Figure 8, one aspect of accountability is how to make the differences between cloud offerings more transparent to cloud customers. Examples of properties that vary across CSPs from a more fine-grained perspective (and that are reflected in cloud contracts) include subcontracting, location of data centres, use restriction, applicable law, data backup, encryption, remedies, storage period, monitoring/audits, breach notification, demonstration of compliance, dispute resolution, data portability, law enforcement access and data deletion from servers. The tool that we are developing within the A4Cloud project to do this is the Cloud Offerings Advisor, which performs a comparison of cloud offerings, helping make the various non-functional requirements listed above more transparent to cloud customers, offering advice and guidance about the implications and thereby helping them choose what is most appropriate.

## 6    Conclusions

In an effort towards a comprehensive and better approach to address the issues raised in Subsection 3.1 and satisfy the characteristics presented in Subsection 5.2, the A4Cloud project aims to develop a framework for addressing these problems, together with example tools that may be used individually or in combination with these or other accountability mechanisms in order to support an approach that is a mixture of a strong and a soft accountability approach.

The aim is that actors within cloud ecosystems may select, beyond what is mandatory by law, mechanisms and tools to support accountability practices, and thereby help them to comply with relevant regulatory regimes within specific application domains and possibly offering also an added value. Accountability aims to entrust organisations with the practical aspects of complying with data protection obligations, and so there is this element of choice to help facilitate compliance, but also the necessity for proof that what has been done is both appropriate and is operating effectively. The legal and contractual context defines obligations, responsibilities and liabilities of actors in a given cloud ecosystem. Businesses need to meet these obligations, as well as obligations and requirements imposed by other stakeholders that include customers and data subjects. Accountability mechanisms can help them to mitigate risk and uncertainty in dynamic and global environments, clarify what their obligations are and help them meet these. The mechanisms also help provide transparency, including an account that is trusted in the sense that it provides improved evidence about the degree of compliance with these obligations. However, achieving this is a challenging problem especially where service provision chains are complex and this is still research in progress.

**Acknowledgements.** This work has been partly funded from the European Commission's Seventh Framework Programme (FP7/2007-2013) under grant agreement no: 317550 (A4CLOUD – http://www.a4cloud.eu/) Cloud Accountability Project. I would like to acknowledge the various members of the A4Cloud project who contributed to the approach and technologies described in Sections 4 and 5, and to Rehab Alnemr for reformatting Figure 5.

## References

1. Pearson, S., et al.: Accountability for Cloud and Other Future Internet Services. In: Proc. CloudCom 2012, pp. 629–632. IEEE (2012)
2. Mell, P., Grance, T.: The NIST Definition of Cloud Computing, NIST Special Publication 800-145 (September 2011)

3. Catteddu, D., Hogben, G. (eds.): Cloud Computing: Benefits, Risks and Recommendations for Information Security. ENISA Report (November 2009)
4. Gellman, R.: Privacy in the Clouds: Risks to Privacy and Confidentiality from Cloud Computing. World Privacy Forum (2009)
5. Pearson, S.: Privacy, Security and Trust in Cloud Computing. In: Pearson, S., Yee, G. (eds.) Privacy and Security for Cloud Computing, Computer Communications and Networks, pp. 3–42. Springer (2012)
6. Cloud Security Alliance: The Notorious Nine: Cloud Computing Top Threats in 2013, Top Threats Working Group (February 2013)
7. Cloud Security Alliance (CSA): Top Threats to Cloud Computing. v1.0, Cloud Security Alliance (March 2010)
8. European Parliament: Fighting Cyber Crime and Protecting Privacy in the Cloud, Directorate-General for Internal Policies (2012), http://www.europarl.euopa.eu/RegData/etudes/join/2012/475104/IPOL-IMCO_ET(2012)475104_EN.pdf
9. Landau, S.: Making Sense from Snowden: What's Significant in the NSA Surveillance Revelations. IEEE Security & Privacy 11(4), 66–75 (2013)
10. International Data Corporation (IDC): Quantitative Estimates of the Demand of Cloud Computing in Europe (2012)
11. Raab, C.: The Meaning of 'Accountability' in the Information Privacy Context. In: Guagnin, D., et al. (eds.) Managing Privacy through Accountability, pp. 15–32. Macmillan (2012)
12. OECD: Guidelines for the Protection of Personal Data and Transborder Data Flows (1980)
13. PIPEDA (2000), http://laws-lois.justice.gc.ca/eng/acts/P-8.6/
14. European DG of Justice (Article 29 Working Party): The future of privacy: joint contribution to the consultation of the European Commission on the legal framework for the fundamental right to protection of personal data (WP168), paragraphs 74-79 (December 2009)
15. European DG of Justice (Article 29 Working Party): Opinion 3/2010 on the principle of accountability (WP 173) (July 2010), http://ec.europa.eu/justice/policies/privacy/docs/wpdocs/2010/wp173_en.pdf
16. European Commission (EC): Proposal for a directive of the European Parliament and of the council on the protection of individuals with regard to the processing of personal data by competent authorities for the purposes of prevention, investigation, detection or prosecution of criminal offences or the execution of criminal penalties, and the free movement of such data (January 2012)
17. Center for Information Policy Leadership (CIPL): Accountability: A compendium for stakeholders. The Galway Project (2011)
18. Office of the Information and Privacy Commissioner of Alberta, Office of the Privacy Commissioner of Canada, Office of the Information and Privacy Commissioner for British Colombia: Getting Accountability Right with a Privacy Management Program (2012)
19. Papanikolaou, N., Pearson, S.: A Cross-Disciplinary Review of the Concept of Accountability. In: Proceedings of the DIMACS/BIC/A4Cloud/CSA International Workshop on Trustworthiness, Accountability and Forensics in the Cloud (TAFC) (May 2013)
20. Information Commissioner's Office (ICO): Binding corporate rules (2012)
21. APEC Data Privacy Sub-Group: Cross-border privacy enforcement arrangement, San Francisco (2011)
22. Van Alsenoy, B.: Allocating responsibility among controllers, processors, and "everything in between": the definition of actors and roles in Directive 95/46/EC. Computer Law & Security Review 28, 25–43 (2012)

23. European Commission (EC): Directive 95/46/EC of the European Parliament and of the Council of 24 October 1995 on the protection of individuals with regard to the processing of personal data and on the free movement of such data (1995)
24. OECD: Guidelines Concerning the Protection of Privacy and Transborder Flows of Personal Data (2013)
25. Millard, C. (ed.): Cloud Computing Law. Oxford University Press (2013)
26. European DG of Justice (Article 29 Working Party): Opinion 05/12 on Cloud Computing (2012)
27. CNIL: Recommendations for Companies Planning to Use Cloud Computing Services (2012)
28. EC: Electronic Communications Sector Directive 2002/58 EC (E-Privacy Directive) (2002)
29. EC: Unleashing the Potential of Cloud Computing in Europe (2012), http://eur-lex.europa.eu/LexUriServ/LexUriServ.do?uri=COM:2012:0529:FIN:EN:PDF
30. Select Industry Group SLA Subgroup: Cloud Service Level Agreement Standardisation Guidelines, Brussels, June 24 (2014)
31. EC: Cybersecurity Strategy of the European Union: An Open, Safe and Secure Cyberspace (2013), http://ec.europa.eu/information_society/newsroom/cf//document.cfm?doc_id=1667
32. EC: Directive on Network and Information Security (2013), http://ec.europa.eu/digital-agenda/en/news/eu-cybersecurity-plan-protect-open-internet-and-online-freedom-and-opportunity-cyber-security
33. Cloud Security Alliance (CSA): Security Guidance for Critical Areas of Focus in Cloud Computing, v3.0, Cloud Security Alliance (2011)
34. Pearson, S.: On the Relationship between the Different Methods to Address Privacy Issues in the Cloud. In: Meersman, R., Panetto, H., Dillon, T., Eder, J., Bellahsene, Z., Ritter, N., De Leenheer, P., Dou, D. (eds.) OTM 2013. LNCS, vol. 8185, pp. 414–433. Springer, Heidelberg (2013)
35. Liu, F., et al.: NIST Cloud Computing Reference Architecture, NIST Special Publication 500-292 (September 2011)
36. Felici, M., Pearson, S. (eds.): Conceptual Framework Final Report, D:C-2.1, A4Cloud Project (2014)
37. Felici, M., Koulouris, T., Pearson, S.: Accountability for Data Governance in Cloud Ecosystems. In: Proc. IEEE CloudCom 2013, vol. 2, pp. 327–332. IEEE (2014)
38. Guagnin, D., Hempel, L., Ilten, C.: Bridging the gap: We need to get together. In: Guagnin, D., et al. (eds.) Managing Privacy Through Accountability, pp. 102–124. Palgrave (2012)
39. Information Commissioner's Office: Guidance on the Use of Cloud Computing (2012), http://www.ico.org.uk/for_organisations/guidance_index/~/media/documents/library/Data_Protection/Practical_application/cloud_computing_guidance_for_organisations.ashx
40. UK government's National Technical Authority for Information Assurance (CESG): Cloud Security Guidance (2014), http://www.gov.uk/government/collections/cloud-security-guidance
41. Jansen, W., Grance, T.: Guidelines on Security and Privacy in Public Cloud Computing. Special Publication 800-144, NIST (December 2011)

42. Radack, S. (ed.): Guidelines For Improving Security And Privacy In Public Cloud Compu-ting. ITL Bulletin (March 2012), http://csrc.nist.gov/publications/nistbul/march-2012_itl-bulletin.pdf
43. CNIL: Methodology for Privacy Risk Management (2012), http://www.cnil.fr/fileadmin/documents/en/CNIL-ManagingPrivacyRisks-Methodology.pdf
44. Horwath, C.: Enterprise Risk Management for Cloud Computing, COSO (June 2012), http://www.coso.org/documents/Cloud%20Computing%20Thought%20Paper.pdf
45. Butin, D., Chicote, M., Le Métayer, D.: Strong Accountability: Beyond Vague Promises. In: Gutwirth, S., Leenes, R., de Hert, P. (eds.) Reloading Data Protection: Multidiscipli-nary Insights and Contemporary Challenges, pp. 343–369. Springer (2014)
46. Charlesworth, A., Pearson, S.: Developing Accountability-based Solutions for Data Priva-cy in the Cloud. Innovation, Special Issue: Privacy and Technology. European Journal of Social Science Research 26(1), 7–35 (2013)
47. Pearson, S., Wainwright, N.: An Interdisciplinary Approach to Accountability for Future Internet Service Provision. International Journal of Trust Management in Computing and Communications (IJTMCC) 1(1), 52–72 (2013)

# Information Management
# and Data Privacy

# Information Classification Issues

Erik Bergström and Rose-Mharie Åhlfeldt

Informatics Research Centre
University of Skövde, 541 28 Skövde, Sweden
{erik.bergstrom,rose-mharie.ahlfeldt}@his.se

**Abstract.** This paper presents an extensive systematic literature review with the aim of identifying and classifying issues in the information classification process. The classification selected uses human and organizational factors for grouping the identified issues. The results reveal that policy-related issues are most commonly described, but not necessarily the most crucial ones. Furthermore, gaps in the research field are identified in order to outline paths for further research.

**Keywords:** information classification, systematic literature review, information security management systems.

## 1    Introduction

Information security is achieved by implementing, for example, policies, processes, organizational structures, and technical measures. To control these activities, an Information Security Management System (ISMS) is used. As mentioned in [1], one example of a widespread ISMS is the ISO 27000-series [2], that amongst others offer best-practice recommendations for initiating, implementing and maintaining ISMS. In ISMS, asset management is a central activity since it establishes ownership of all organizational assets. The assets are identified by doing an inventory of all assets such as software, physical assets (for example, computers, and network equipment), services (for example, power, and air-condition), people and their skills and experience, intangibles such as the reputation and image of the organization, and the information in the organization [3]. The information can be found in many places in the organization, and take different shapes. After the inventory, ownership or responsibility is designated to all assets, and guidelines are set up for acceptable use of the assets. The objective of doing information classification is to *"ensure that information receives an appropriate level of protection in accordance with its importance to the organization"* [3 p. 15]. The information classification also serves as a major input for the risk analysis that also need to be performed as a part of the ISMS [1].

The information identified as an asset should be classified according to its value, and criticality to the organization, and be protected accordingly. Normally, a classification scheme uses categories in a hierarchical model, where each category is associated with procedures for how to handle the information, and what protection mechanisms it requires. An organization should not use too many classification categories as

K. Bernsmed and S. Fischer-Hübner (Eds.): NordSec 2014, LNCS 8788, pp. 27–41, 2014.
DOI:10.1007/978-3-319-11599-3_2, © Springer International Publishing Switzerland 2014

complex schemes may become harder and uneconomic to use, and a typical organiza-tion might have between three and five categories in a hierarchy [4]. The probably most well-known information classification scheme comes from the US military, and includes the three levels: top secret, secret and unclassified [5]. In a company setting, the equivalent could be public, proprietary and proprietary restricted [4].

The information classification can also change over time, for example, an annual report from a stock market company contains very sensitive information before it is publicized, but the information classification changes at the point of publication.

In a study by Park, et al. [6], ISMS were investigated in five large hospitals. From a checklist compiled from the complete ISO/IEC 27001 (including, for example, hu-man-resource security, physical security, communications and operation's manage-ment, and access control), reveals that asset management in general, and information classifications, in particular, were the most vulnerable part of the ISMS. Problems included lack or weak descriptions of classification guidelines, insufficient inventory of assets, and unclear ownership. Hospitals were also investigated in a study by Luethi and Knolmayer [7], where organizational capabilities such as responsibility for assets and information classification was labelled as they lacked some capabilities. Overall, it was found that organizational rather than technical measures and capabili-ties were lacking.

Several studies highlights the fact that information classification is not a new con-cept, but still many organizations struggle to complete their information classification [8-12].

To summarise, it is apparent that there are broad issues with applying a widely ac-cepted technique for valuing and classifying information. The aim of this study is to narrow down and identify the issues that occur when information classification is performed, and provide a comprehensive and structured overview of the problems identified in the research field. The analysis is conducted using a systematic literature review (SLR) that contributes to the field primarily by (1) reviewing and summarizing what is known about the issues in the information classification process, and (2) by offering directions for future research.

In this work, the guidelines of Kitchenham and Charters [13] have been followed to elaborate a research question (RQ).

RQ: *What are the main issues in the information classification process?*

To the best of our knowledge, no literature surveys have focused on identifying the issues in the information classification process. Although information classification is a central, and in many cases, a mandatory activity for many organizations, not much attention has been directed at understanding the underlying issues in the process and how they can be reduced or eliminated. Information classification research in general is limited [1] with few research contributions focusing on the classification process itself. Some notable exceptions are Virtanen [14] that proposes a solution for reclassi-fication where previous data is used to recalculate the classification automatically. An approach with the same intent is presented by DuraiPandian and Chellappan [15] and Hayat, et al. [16]. Several authors [17-20], provide guidelines, frameworks or models with varying degree of detail for how to classify information. Fernando and Zavarsky [21] propose a categorization with thresholds to enable an organization to handle parts of the information lifecycle such as the disposal of data. Fibikova and Müller [22] describe two alternative approaches to classifying information, a process-oriented approach and an application-oriented approach. Several of the contributions predate the commonly used ISO 27000-series standard where many organizations take their stance from today, but they still contribute to the overall understanding of the information classification process and its related issues. There are also some studies describing how to handle issues in the classification process [10], practical tips for implementing classification [8], and why it needs to be done [23], but it is unclear whether these studies are scientifically verified.

In the following section, the research methodology and the classification factors are explained. In section 3, the classification and analysis of the literature according to the factors are presented. This is followed by section 4 where the results are discussed and section 5 where the conclusions and directions for future research are outlined.

## 2    Method

The research question will be answered using an SLR following the guidelines from Kitchenham and Charters [13]. SLRs aim to provide a synthesis of the knowledge in an area [24]. The authors are aware of critique against SLRs [25], and acknowledge that the actual search is not the most important step, but the reading and understanding of the area.

Information classification is a term used, for instance, in the ISO 27000 series, and it is a well-established term. However, after surveying a number of publications in research databases and Google Scholar, a number of synonyms were found. The found synonyms to information classification were *"information security classification"*, *"data classification"*, and *"security classification"*. Especially the term *"data classification"* gives many false positives when used as a search string, but the decision was taken to be inclusive and filter manually. The following search query (("security classification" OR "information classification" OR "data classification") AND "information security") was used. The query aims only to limit the classification terms to an *"information security"* context, but otherwise to be inclusive.

The following databases were used for full-text or all-field's searches without any limitations; IEEE Xplore, The ACM Guide to Computing Literature, ScienceDirect (Elsevier), Springer Link and Inspec (Ovid). In total, the searches generated 1545 hits, distributed as shown in Table 1. The reason to choose full-text search and not only search title and abstract were taken after the initial pilot study where initial searches were performed. This initial study revealed several results in publications mentioning information classification where the main focus was something else than information classification. That full-text search makes it more likely to find relevant articles are also consistent with the results from a study performed by Lin [26].

The searches were performed in the weeks of 50-51, 2013, and all results were thereafter downloaded and aggregated into a reference manager. A first rough sorting was performed by looking at the title, abstract and searches in the full text in order to find out where the word classification was used. Exclusion criteria used in this first sorting was duplicate hits in databases, if the publication were not available, if the same chapter appeared in several books, the result was in another language than English, the search terms only appear in author biography or in the reference list, faulty results as for instance "...information, classification of....", and if the result was in a completely other context than the aim of the study. After this initial sorting, 254 papers remained in focus of the study. Thereafter, a more detailed full-text sorting was performed and where the context was taken into consideration. Then 152 papers remained, and after a final full-text review, 70 papers describing issues with information classification remained.

**Table 1.** Results of the literature search

| Database | Number of results |
|---|---|
| IEEE Xplore | 541 |
| Inspec (Ovid) | 42 |
| ScienceDirect (Elsevier) | 394 |
| Springer Link | 308 |
| The ACM Guide to Computing Literature | 290 |

Kraemer, et al. [27] identify nine thematic categories of human and organizational factors in information security; *external influences, human error, management, organization of CIS* (computer and information security), *performance management, policy, resource management, technology, training.* The selected factors have been selected as they are broad and inclusive, and should be seen as a starting point for further research. In this work, these factors have been used, but *management* and *organization of CIS* have been merged to one factor, and *training* has been excluded. The merge of *management* and *organization of CIS* was done as a consequence of the results found in the literature study. The mention of management related problems were few, and so intertwined no separation were meaningful. *Training* was removed as a category since none of the papers explicitly mentioned training as a problem but rather as an enabler. When the results were classified into the factors, 18 additional papers were left out of scope as it became apparent that they rather described the consequences of issues with information classification rather than an issue such as for instance over- and underclassification of information as elaborated in section 3.7. In total, 52 papers were classified according to the classification factors.

The analysis performed was descriptive (non-quantitative) as described by Kitchenham and Charters [13], and the analysis used coding techniques as described by Strauss and Corbin [28]. The first step was to use open coding [28] to break down all the data extracted from the literature review into discrete parts to see similarities and differences. The next step was to use axial coding [28] to connect the data to the categories from Kraemer, et al. [27].

# 3     Classification and Analysis of Literature

The selected literature has been classified according to the factors described by Kraemer, et al. [27]. By categorizing the issues identified in areas, it is possible to better see and understand which factors are the most commonly referred to as problematic. It also serves as a tool for labelling issues that are not necessarily, or naturally referred to as a specific factor explicitly.

In the following sub-sections, we elaborate on the issues found for the respective factors.

## 3.1     External Influences

Information classification has been around for a long time in the military sector. Several authors believe one of the problems with information classification is its military roots and that the confidentiality model cannot be transferred directly from a military to a corporate setting [5, 19, 29-34]. The underlying reasons for this belief are that it is originally developed as a process for controlling information flow on paper that has moved to electronic ones [9, 35], and that when the business world adopted the process, they only adopted the multilevel concept but not the routines for staff clearance and authorization [19]. In the commercial world, generally different categories for information classification apply, but they tend to not be hierarchical according to Winkler [36].

## 3.2     Human Error

Humans are many times seen as a weak link when it comes to information security, and when it comes to information classification, these are some human related issues identified. The main problem is that all information in an organization has to be classified, and that all staff in an organization that handles the data or has access to it needs to understand and apply classification. Several authors acknowledge a problem with subjective judgement, including [8, 19, 37-39] and consistency in the classifications [17]. This might be due to too complex schemes [19], schemes that do not fit business people´s needs [33], or a lack of skills [40].

## 3.3     Management and Organization of CIS

Collette [10] identifies that there is often a lack in the authority of leaders (for example, the chief information security officer) that can drive through a whole classification program from planning to implementation. This can be because of a lack of political power in the organization of information security [10]. There can also be a lack of centralized asset control and a need to better define ownerships and asset responsibilities [41].

## 3.4    Performance Management

Several issues are related to the information lifecycle management (ILM) in which information is identified and classified after what value the information possesses. The value of information can change over time, and it is possible that cost and resources are wasted if information, for example, is classified as more important than it is. The fundamental problem for an organization is to identify their information capital [35, 39], and decide its value [42, 43]. From an ILM perspective, also information provenance, where the source and modification history of the information is included needs to be considered [44]. The information provenance and preservation or curation of data is important, especially from a governmental viewpoint to prevent information leakage [44]. There might, however, be a drawback with the introduction of more sophisticated models for evaluating the value of information, because it can in turn lead to more sophisticated information classification models [45].

From an ILM perspective, information can reside in different stages such as in use or archived, and have different value at different points in time. For this to happen, information needs to be reclassified to keep an up-to-date classification which is another issue identified by several authors [14, 22, 35]. The underlying problems why reclassification can be problematic are connected to, for instance, changes in organizations, where users shift domains and projects [15], no well-defined automated mechanisms, leaving the job to humans [34], and a tendency to refrain from declassification [46].

## 3.5    Policy

Some authors describe the process of developing a classification scheme as problematic in a general way [33, 37], but also the usage, and the enforcement of the classification schemes and policies governing information classification are problematic. Several authors relate the problematic situation of information classification to the standard or framework publishers. Bayuk [5] describes the generic guidelines provided in standards as too generic to cover system characteristics for many systems used in enterprises. Janczewski and Xinli Shi [41] argue that there is a lack of specific standards for health information classification. The lack of more detailed guidelines creates a difficulty of developing robust schemes that cover the requirements from the organization, but still provide flexibility without being too cumbersome [9]. This leads to a situation where people find it difficult to classify information because the scheme does not fit their needs [33]. Many times, the classification schemes turn out to be too complex, which leads to disuse [33, 47] or that new classifications are developed in different business organization units [33]. Examples of the creation of new categories to better suit the organizations needs come mainly from the governmental sector where, for instance, the usage of "sensitive but unclassified" [46, 48] has been introduced. This kind of undefined categories raises the question of both the legitimate use of the information and the category itself [46].

The security policy of an organization has a direct relationship with information classification [45], and when the organization classifies information according to a classification scheme, it automatically classifies according to a hierarchical model. This leads to an assumption that the organization uses a similar hierarchy for responsibility and for accessing the information among the users [45], which is not necessarily the case.

The policy might be extra critical when placing data in the cloud [36, 49, 50], or when outsourcing [51]. The central problem is that if the policy is not clearly defined, or correct information values are defined, it is possible that highly sensitive data are migrated [52]. The policy might need to be extra fine-grained [53], and passed to the cloud providers [54] to avoid some of the problems. The problem is similar even if the information is not placed in a cloud, but rather shared with other organizations. The usage of organization specific policies and classification schemes, combined with the sharing of data is described as one of the biggest obstacles, especially in the governmental and military sectors. The main issues here are to align what equals one category in one organization to another organization's categories, and to align the rules for handling the information [55]. Just the fact that the many ways of implementing the classifications, which in turn leads to increased difficulties of sharing information are described by [56-58].

Finally, many organizations use data privacy policies, but there are interdependencies to the information classification process. When data is consolidated, privacy breaches might arise as a result of the consolidation [59, 60].

## 3.6     Resource Management

Resource management issues are primarily related to costs of classifying information. The costs of information classification are twofold [10]: the cost and effort of developing the classification scheme with appropriate controls [9, 17, 47, 61, 62] and the cost of training all staff [10]. For organizations required by law to classify information, costs can be more easily motivated, but for non-regulated organizations, it can be difficult to justify the efforts as they don't directly lead to revenue generation [10]. Hayes [11] captures the resource management issues as *"it can prove difficult to get colleagues excited about a business case for valuing data. There's just too much of the stuff, and the task is too daunting"* [11, p. 61].

## 3.7     Technology

Several tools for automatic information classification exist, but there are many questions about what kind of information or data they can manage, and how the information is classified. One of the fundamental problems within autonomous systems is to automatically evaluate the information and classify it [16]. There are also issues with overclassification when data is taken from several sources and automatically consolidated [63]. Overclassification and underclassification for that matter are not an information classification problem per se, but rather a consequence of the usage of the information classification scheme, regardless if it is manual or automated. There are consequences with over- and underclassification of information, such as unintended operational consequences that are hindering people from doing their job when metadata is used to label information that in turn hinders them from accessing the information [52], or when information is overclassified to protect the asset owners [64].

Everett [52] believes it is not possible to just solve the problem of information classification by adopting technology since it is very much a human and process problem, and that even if a tool existed, automatic classification based on key words and phrases without the need for manual intervention are not available anyway.

Due to characteristics such as decentralized storage, ad-hoc relationships with other data sources, and the volatility of the data itself, makes it very challenging to enforce information classification [61]. Wei, et al. [65] describe a situation where many platforms, different development languages and static and dynamic content became an insurmountable obstacle.

In order to be able to enforce the classification it is important to point out that after a piece of information has been classified according to the classification scheme, it needs to be labelled accordingly. This labelling or tagging has several issues. Firstly, there are issues with the representation on a binary level, because computer systems normally do not enforce labelling [36]. Furthermore, not all kinds of information allow direct labelling [22], for example, if high granularity on the classified information exist, potentially each cell in a database needs to be labelled which makes it almost impossible to establish and maintain the protection when information is aggregated [66]. The implementation of labels also causes issues in orthogonal systems, where it is hard to trace classifications outside a single application [67], and when implementing the authorization runtime in access control systems [68]. Finally, there are also challenges when labelling in virtualized systems and in cloud computing [17].

One big question raised by many is on what level of granularity the information classification needs to be performed. This might, to some extent, be organizational specific, but it is clear that many are struggling with granularity and the implications of it. It is normally quite easy to protect, for instance, an entire database if all included data have the same classification [66]. If the granularity is on a lower level, e.g. an individual cell in a database or every email, every file or even sentences in a text document, it can enable access to information [69, 70], but it can also inhibit it. This is especially true when information is combined and the aggregated information automatically gets assigned the highest classification of the combined data [69]. In parallel to the discussion of increasing granularity, there is also a question of decreasing the granularity to reduce the amount of classifications [28].

# 4    Discussion

An overview of the findings is presented in Table 2, where publications are classified according to the corresponding factors. It is important to point out that the issues found should not be measured in a quantitative way, but rather be seen as a more frequently mentioned issue. The *policy* factor, for example, is not more important or a more severe inhibitor than *management and organization of CIS* even though it has a greater number of publications mentioning the issue. If, for instance, there is a lack of leadership in the organization, there might be no information classification at all, regardless of how suitable and applicable the policy is.

It should also be mentioned that most of the publications only appear in Table 2 once, which means that they only discuss one of the factors. This is because most of the publications does not describe information classification issues, but rather mentions it in relation to something other, that is in focus of their work.

**Table 2.** Overview of findings

| Factors | Publications |
| --- | --- |
| External influences | [5], [9], [19], [29], [30], [31], [32], [33], [34], [35], [36]. |
| Human error | [8], [17], [19], [33], [37], [38], [39], [40]. |
| Management and organization of CIS | [10], [41]. |
| Performance management | [14], [15], [22], [34], [35], [39], [42], [43], [44], [45], [46]. |
| Policy | [5], [9], [33], [36], [37], [41], [45], [46], [47], [48], [49], [50], [51], [52], [53], [54], [55], [56], [57], [58], [59], [60]. |
| Resource management | [9], [10], [11], [17], [47], [61], [62]. |
| Technology | [16], [22], [36], [52], [54], [61], [63], [64], [65], [66], [67], [68], [69], [70]. |

*Policy* turns out to be a very widely used term to depict several different things. The literature mixes the use of policy, guideline, scheme, matrix and model for describing the information classification process and its associated documentation. In this work, the original terms used by the respective authors have been used to a great extent, both to highlight the issue itself, but also to keep the accuracy in the classification. There are not necessarily any correct term to use, but ISO/IEC uses the term *information classification scheme* to describe the classification scheme and its associated meta-information [3]. It is recommended that an organization use the policy term with care as it otherwise might reduce the influence of the information security policy, but also to limit confusion when referring to the policy. Clearly, the information security policy is a managerial document that in turn can mandate the use of information classification as a part of the asset management. To support in the classification, an information classification scheme with guidelines should be used. This also highlights the connection to *management and organization of CIS*, since the lack of a clear scheme and guidelines is a management issue. In turn, this affects several of the other factors since they are intertwined and depend on clear guidelines. The external influences are affected if the classification scheme is not adapted to the organization, and if the guidelines are hard to interpret, human *error* can lead to subjective judgement and consistency issues. The lack of an information lifecycle management perspective in the guidelines might affect archiving of information and inhibit reclassification, and therefore, also affect the *performance management*. Finally, a lack in *resource management* might also connect to the management since if too few resources are invested into creating the guidelines and the classification scheme, the classification process can suffer.

The lack of a formalized process description for information classification might be one of the answers to why it is a problematic task to perform. For example, both ISO and COBIT uses information classification as a part of their asset management, but the processes are described very generally, which is because of the general nature of the standards. If the standards are to fit all, they need to be on a general level, but we firmly believe that the processes could be explained more in detail to avoid some of the problems identified in this paper. There are some process descriptions trying to describe the information classification process, for example [71], but we strongly believe an even more detailed process model is needed to facilitate information classification in practice.

It is of course not possible to develop generic guidelines that fit exactly for all organizations, and each individual organization needs to develop their own scheme with their own classification categories. This leads to a situation where more or less compatible classification schemes need to co-exist and be mapped together every time data is to be outsourced, put in a cloud or shared. More detailed guidelines and a process description will, at least, provide a common language and a common view that will decrease the tensions in such situations.

Furthermore, there is a notable lack of papers describing the use of information classification in ISMS. To a certain extent, this is explainable by a low adoption rate, combined with a low interest from academia in studying ISMS [72].

From another perspective, it is possible to ask if information classification and the ISMS are the wrong way for organizations to take as a part of their information security work. Siponen and Willison [73] agree with the previously mentioned results about the issues of being too generic in the guidelines from the standards issuer, but also adds that the standards have not been validated but rather fostered to an appeal to common practice and authority which is an unsound basis for a true standard. Furthermore, it is added that the ISMS process is likely to be fallible because of this [73].

Much research is performed in the areas that relate to, or make an impact on the information classification process. Automatic classification, using, for instance, different techniques from machine learning and linguistics seem to be a growing field. Access control mechanisms and models are researched in a number of ways, for example, on giving access to more fine-grained data, which it is important since it enforce the information classification when access is to be granted to a specific piece of information. There is also research about the labelling part of the information classification process, and topics include, for instance, how labelling inside a text document, individual cells in a database or individual emails are to be labelled. Not all the issues identified in the SLR will be solved by technology, but clearly it will play an increasingly important role in decreasing the impact in some of the issues.

Finally, the factors selected for classification could be developed further. There are possibilities to increase the granularity of the respective factors to create a more detailed view over the issues. The fundamental problems of classifying issues in this domain are the lack of common terms and the lack of a clear process description. If a well-accepted and well-used process description existed, this literature survey would have used it as a framework for classifying the issues.

# 5    Conclusions and Further Research

In this work, a comprehensive review of the current status of issues in the information classification process is presented and classified into human and organizational factors. Although the SLR returned a large amount of publications, few focus on the issues of the information classification process itself. It is very evident that more research is needed in this field, so that issues can be better understood and avoided or have their impact decreased when implementing ISMS in an organization. Furthermore, in the light of the found issues, it is essential to investigate the enablers to information classification.

Additionally, it is obvious that the management factor is more important than portrayed in the existing body of literature and that more research is needed to understand the roles and effects of the *management and organization of CIS*. Partly, this problem is due to the lack of a common formalized process description of information classification, but also to a lack of using a common language to describe the process.

There are many other aspects of the classification process that needs further investigation. The connection to information lifecycle management (ILM) could be investigated from many perspectives. Firstly, one can explicitly connect the information classification process to the ILM, and secondly, will that alleviate the work with the classifications?

Finally, there are few examples of papers describing the empirical work with information classification, especially in relation to ISMS. Mainly, the literature is focused on theoretic work, for instance, automatic classification, and how to achieve finer granularity and labelling. If the information classification process is going to expand from a need in most organizations to something comprehensible and performed, more real-world examples are needed.

# References

1. Oscarson, P., Karlsson, F.: A National Model for Information Classification. In: AIS SIGSEC Workshop on Information Security & Privacy (WISP 2009), Phoenix, AZ, USA (2009)
2. ISO/IEC 27000: Information technology – Security techniques – Information security management systems – Overview and vocabulary. ISO/IEC (2014)
3. ISO/IEC 27002: Information technology – Security techniques – Code of practice for information security controls. ISO/IEC (2013)

4. Axelrod, C.W., Bayuk, J.L., Schutzer, D.: Enterprise Information Security and Privacy. Artech House (2009)
5. Bayuk, J.: The utility of security standards. In: 2010 IEEE International Carnahan Conference on Security Technology (ICCST), pp. 1–6 (2010)
6. Park, W.-S., Seo, S.-W., Son, S.-S., Lee, M.-J., Kim, S.-H., Choi, E.-M., Bang, J.-E., Kim, Y.-E., Kim, O.-N.: Analysis of Information Security Management Systems at 5 Domestic Hospitals with More than 500 Beds. Healthc. Inform. Res. 16, 89–99 (2010)
7. Luethi, M., Knolmayer, G.F.: Security in Health Information Systems: An Exploratory Comparison of U.S. and Swiss Hospitals. In: 42nd Hawaii International Conference on System Sciences, HICSS 2009, pp. 1–10 (2009)
8. Glynn, S.: Getting To Grips With Data Classification. Database and Network Journal 41, 8–9 (2011)
9. Ghernaouti-Helie, S., Simms, D., Tashi, I.: Protecting Information in a Connected World: A Question of Security and of Confidence in Security. In: 14th International Conference on Network-Based Information Systems (NBiS), pp. 208–212 (2011)
10. Collette, R.: Overcoming obstacles to data classification [information security]. Computer Economics Report (International Edition) 28, 8–11 (2006)
11. Hayes, J.: Have data will travel - [IT security]. Engineering & Technology 3, 60–61 (2008)
12. Kane, G., Koppel, L.: Information Protection Function One: Governance. In: Kane, G.K., Lorna (eds.) Information Security, ch. 1, pp. 1–11. Elsevier, Boston (2013)
13. Kitchenham, B., Charters, S.: Guidelines for performing Systematic Literature Reviews in Software Engineering. Keele University and Durham University Joint Report (2007)
14. Virtanen, T.: Design Criteria to Classified Information Systems Numerically. In: Dupuy, M., Pierre, P. (eds.) Trusted Information. IFIP, vol. 65, pp. 317–325. Springer, Boston (2001)
15. DuraiPandian, N., Chellappan, C.: Dynamic information security level reclassification. In: 2006 IFIP International Conference on Wireless and Optical Communications Networks, Bangalore, India (2006)
16. Hayat, Z., Reeve, J., Boutle, C., Field, M.: Information security implications of autonomous systems. In: Proceedings of the 2006 IEEE Conference on Military Communications, pp. 897–903. IEEE Press, Washington, D.C. (2006)
17. Eloff, J.H.P., Holbein, L.R., Teufel, S.: Security classification for documents. Computers & Security 15, 55–71 (1996)
18. Feuerlicht, J., Grattan, P.: The role of classification of information in controlling data proliferation in end-user personal computer environment. Computers & Security 8, 59–66 (1989)
19. Parker, D.B.: The classification of information to protect it from loss. Information Systems Security 5, 9–15 (1996)
20. Kwo-Jean, F., Shu-Kuo, L., Chi-Chun, L.: A study on e-Taiwan information system security classification and implementation. Computer Standards & Interfaces 30, 1–7 (2008)
21. Fernando, D., Zavarsky, P.: Secure decommissioning of confidential electronically stored information (CESI): A framework for managing CESI in the disposal phase as needed. In: 2012 World Congress on Internet Security (WorldCIS), pp. 218–222 (2012)
22. Fibikova, L., Müller, R.: A Simplified Approach for Classifying Applications. In: Pohlmann, N., Reimer, H., Schneider, W. (eds.) ISSE 2010 Securing Electronic Business Processes, pp. 39–49. Vieweg+Teubner (2011)
23. Everett, C.: Building solid foundations: the case for data classification. Computer Fraud & Security 2011, 5–8 (2011)

24. Wohlin, C., Runeson, P., da Mota Silveira Neto, P.A., Engström, E., do Carmo Machado, I., de Almeida, E.S.: On the reliability of mapping studies in software engineering. Journal of Systems and Software 86, 2594–2610 (2013)
25. Boell, S., Cezec-Kecmanovic, D.: Are systematic reviews better, less biased and of higher quality? In: European Conference on Information Systems (2011)
26. Lin, J.: Is searching full text more effective than searching abstracts? BMC Bioinformatics 10, 1–15 (2009)
27. Kraemer, S., Carayon, P., Clem, J.: Human and organizational factors in computer and information security: Pathways to vulnerabilities. Computers & Security 28, 509–520 (2009)
28. Strauss, A., Corbin, J.: Basics of Qualitative Research: Techniques and Procedures for Developing Grounded Theory. Sage Publications, Inc., Thousand Oaks (1998)
29. Gantz, S.D., Philpott, D.R.: Federal Information Security Fundamentals. In: Gantz, S.D.P., Daniel, R. (eds.) FISMA and the Risk Management Framework, ch. 2, pp. 23–52. Syngress (2013)
30. Grandison, T., Bilger, M., O'Connor, L., Graf, M., Swimmer, M., Schunter, M., Wespi, A., Zunic, N.: Elevating the Discussion on Security Management: The Data Centric Paradigm. In: 2nd IEEE/IFIP International Workshop on Business-Driven IT Management, BDIM, pp. 84–93 (2007)
31. Jafari, M., Fathian, M.: Management Advantages of Object Classification in Role-Based Access Control (RBAC). In: Cervesato, I. (ed.) ASIAN 2007. LNCS, vol. 4846, pp. 95–110. Springer, Heidelberg (2007)
32. Lindup, K.R.: A new model for information security policies. Computers & Security 14, 691–695 (1995)
33. Parker, D.B.: The strategic values of information security in business. Computers & Security 16, 572–582 (1997)
34. Ramasamy, H.V., Schunter, M.: Multi-Level Security for Service-Oriented Architectures. In: Military Communications Conference, MILCOM 2006, pp. 1–7. IEEE (2006)
35. Bunker, G.: Technology is not enough: Taking a holistic view for information assurance. Information Security Technical Report 17, 19–25 (2012)
36. Winkler, V.: Chapter 3 - Security Concerns, Risk Issues, and Legal Aspects. In: Winkler, V. (ed.) Securing the Cloud, pp. 55–88. Syngress, Boston (2011)
37. Baškarada, S.: Analysis of Data. In: Information Quality Management Capability Maturity Model, pp. 139–221. Vieweg+Teubner (2009)
38. Booysen, H.A.S., Eloff, J.H.P.: Classification of objects for improved access control. Computers & Security 14, 251–265 (1995)
39. Ku, C.-Y., Chang, Y.-W., Yen, D.C.: National information security policy and its implementation: A case study in Taiwan. Telecommunications Policy 33, 371–384 (2009)
40. Puhakainen, P., Siponen, M.: Improving employees' compliance through information systems security training: an action research study. MIS Q. 34, 757–778 (2010)
41. Janczewski, L., Xinli Shi, F.: Development of Information Security Baselines for Healthcare Information Systems in New Zealand. Computers & Security 21, 172–192 (2002)
42. Al-Fedaghi, S.: On Information Lifecycle Management. In: Asia-Pacific Services Computing Conference, APSCC 2008, pp. 335–342. IEEE (2008)
43. Aksentijevic, S., Tijan, E., Agatic, A.: Information security as utilization tool of enterprise information capital. In: MIPRO, 2011 Proceedings of the 34th International Convention, pp. 1391–1395 (2011)
44. Ager, T., Johnson, C., Kiernan, J.: Policy-Based Management and Sharing of Sensitive Information Among Government Agencies. In: Military Communications Conference, MILCOM 2006, pp. 1–9. IEEE (2006)

45. Arutyunov, V.V.: Identification and authentication as the basis for information protection in computer systems. Sci. Tech. Inf. Proc. 39, 133–138 (2012)
46. Seifert, J.W., Relyea, H.C.: Do you know where your information is in the homeland security era? Government Information Quarterly 21, 399–405 (2004)
47. Saxby, S.: News and comment on recent developments from around the world. Computer Law & Security Review 24, 95–110 (2008)
48. Feinberg, L.E.: FOIA, federal information policy, and information availability in a post-9/11 world. Government Information Quarterly 21, 439–460 (2004)
49. Velev, D., Zlateva, P.: Cloud Infrastructure Security. In: Camenisch, J., Kisimov, V., Dubovitskaya, M. (eds.) iNetSec 2010. LNCS, vol. 6555, pp. 140–148. Springer, Heidelberg (2011)
50. Wilson, P.: Positive perspectives on cloud security. Information Security Technical Report 16, 97–101 (2011)
51. Freeman, E.: Information and Computer Security Risk Management. In: Ghosh, S., Turrini, E. (eds.) Cybercrimes: A Multidisciplinary Analysis, pp. 151–163. Springer, Heidelberg (2011)
52. Everett, C.: Building solid foundations: the case for data classification. Computer Fraud & Security 2011(6), 5–8 (2011)
53. Adiraju, S.K.: Security Considerations in Integrating the Fragmented, Outsourced, ITSM Processes. In: 2012 Third International Conference on Services in Emerging Markets (ICSEM), pp. 175–182 (2012)
54. Chaput, S., Ringwood, K.: Cloud Compliance: A Framework for Using Cloud Computing in a Regulated World. In: Antonopoulos, N., Gillam, L. (eds.) Cloud Computing, pp. 241–255. Springer, London (2010)
55. Hilton, J.: Improving the secure management of personal data: Privacy on-line IS important, but it's not easy. Information Security Technical Report 14, 124–130 (2009)
56. Wang, W., Peng, G., Lu, G.: Agricultural Informationization in China. In: Ordóñez de Pablos, P.L., Miltiadis, D. (eds.) The China Information Technology Handbook, pp. 271–297. Springer US (2009)
57. Boonstra, D., Schotanus, H.A., Verkoelen, C.A.A., Smulders, A.C.M.: A methodology for the structured security analysis of interconnections. In: Military Communications Conference - MILCOM 2011, pp. 1267–1272 (2011)
58. Wrona, K., Hallingstad, G.: Controlled information sharing in NATO operations. In: Military Communications Conference - MILCOM 2011, pp. 1285–1290 (2011)
59. Karat, J., Karat, C.-M., Brodie, C., Feng, J.: Privacy in information technology: Designing to enable privacy policy management in organizations. International Journal of Human-Computer Studies 63, 153–174 (2005)
60. Vrhovec, G.: Beating the privacy challenge. Computer Fraud & Security 2011, 5–8 (2011)
61. Kulkarni, A., Williams, E., Grimaila, M.R.: Mitigating Security Risks for End User Computing Application (EUCA) Data. In: 2010 IEEE Second International Conference on Social Computing (SocialCom), pp. 1171–1176 (2010)
62. Tsai, W.T., Wei, X., Chen, Y., Paul, R., Chung, J.-Y., Zhang, D.: Data provenance in SOA: security, reliability, and integrity. SOCA 1, 223–247 (2007)
63. Newman, A.R.: Confidence, pedigree, and security classification for improved data fusion. In: Proceedings of the Fifth International Conference on Information Fusion, vol. 2, 1402, pp. 1408–1415 (2002)
64. Taylor, L.P.: Chapter 8 - Categorizing Data Sensitivity. In: Taylor, L.P. (ed.) FISMA Compliance Handbook, 2nd edn., pp. 63–78. Syngress, Boston (2013)

65. Wei, W., Shengzhong, Y., Hong, H.: Design of Portal-Based Uniform Identity Authentication System in Campus Network. In: 2010 International Conference on Multimedia Communications (Mediacom),, pp. 112-115 (2010)
66. Blyth, A., Kovacich, G.L.: IA and Software. Information Assurance, pp. 191–212. Springer, London (2006)
67. Demsky, B.: Cross-application data provenance and policy enforcement. ACM Trans. Inf. Syst. Secur. 14, 1–22 (2011)
68. Ashley, P., Vandenwauver, M., Siebenlist, F.: Applying authorization to intranets: architectures, issues and APIs. Computer Communications 23, 1613–1620 (2000)
69. Burnap, P., Hilton, J.: Self Protecting Data for De-perimeterised Information Sharing. In: Third International Conference on Digital Society, ICDS 2009, pp. 65–70 (2009)
70. Alqudah, B.I., Nair, S.: Toward Multi-Service Electronic Medical Records Structure. In: Suh, S.C., Gurupur, V.P., Tanik, M.M. (eds.) Biomedical Engineering, pp. 243–254. Springer, New York (2011)
71. Etges, R., McNeil, K.: Understanding data classification based on business and security requirements. ISACA Information Systems Control Journal 5 (2006)
72. Fomin, V.V., de Vries, H.J., Barlette, Y.: ISO/IEC 27001 information systems security management standard: exploring the reasons for low adoption. In: EUROMOT 2008 Conference, Nice, France (2008)
73. Siponen, M., Willison, R.: Information security management standards: Problems and solutions. Information & Management 46, 267–270 (2009)

# DEICS: Data Erasure in Concurrent Software

Kalpana Gondi, A. Prasad Sistla, and V.N. Venkatakrishnan

Department of Computer Science, University of Illinois, Chicago

A well known tenet for ensuring unauthorized leaks of sensitive data such as passwords and cryptographic keys is to erase ("zeroize") them after their intended use in any program. Prior work on minimizing sensitive data lifetimes has focused exclusively on sequential programs. In this work, we address the problem of data lifetime minimization for concurrent programs. We develop a new algorithm that precisely anticipates when to introduce these erasures, and develop an implementation of this algorithm in a tool called DEICS. Through an experimental evaluation, we show that DEICS is able to reduce lifetimes of shared sensitive data in several concurrent applications (over 100k lines of code combined) with minimal performance overheads.

## 1 Introduction

Improper handling of data in C programs can often lead to its disclosure to unauthorized principals. This is because such sensitive data can often be stolen through various low-level attacks that C programs are prone to. The recent Heartbleed vulnerability [6] in OpenSSL is one such example. This security hole rendered millions of organizations on the Internet vulnerable to data theft attacks as it facilitated the risk of sensitive data being read from a OpenSSL connection through a buffer over-read. Such risks of sensitive data being stolen can be minimized if the program erased sensitive data that remained in memory beyond its intended use in the program.

**Prior Work:** The security issues in not erasing sensitive data in C programs are well documented in the systems community [17,18,23]. As documented in these works, a number of online and offline attacks could result from sensitive data that is resident in memory beyond its lifetime. In [23], authors had proposed an approach to minimize such disclosure of data in applications written in C through program analysis and transformation. The main idea is to identify the "first no use" points ( First-No-Use) for any piece of sensitive data and introduce a zeroing instruction immediately before those points. The implementation of their approach was tested on several C programs and was demonstrated to work on large applications. One main limitation of their approach is that it cannot handle concurrent applications.

**Problem Setting:** In this paper, we consider the problem of sensitive data-lifetime minimization for concurrent applications. Implementing and understanding a concurrent application is relatively more difficult for a programmer due to the added complexity of programming such applications. While programming such applications, it is possible that a programmer may ignore other security considerations such as zeroing sensitive data after their intended use in the program. A recent low-level vulnerability (CVE-2011-0992) [1] in the popular Mono application (which implements the Silverlight API

K. Bernsmed and S. Fischer-Hübner (Eds.): NordSec 2014, LNCS 8788, pp. 42–58, 2014.
DOI: 10.1007/978-3-319-11599-3_3, © Springer International Publishing Switzerland 2014

for Linux) allows remote attackers to obtain sensitive information that is unauthorized. Specifically, threads in Mono were not properly cleaned up upon finalization, so if one thread was resurrected, it would be possible to observe the pointer to freed memory, leading to unintended information disclosure.

Such risk of disclosure would have been minimized by zeroing sensitive data values after use. Since a significant number of programmers are not aware [26] of these subtle security issues, we consider the problem of retrofitting a concurrent program with zeroing instructions that minimizes the lifetime of sensitive data used by that application.

**Challenges:** In order to minimize data lifetime, one must analyze the lifetime of sensitive data in concurrent programs. The non-determinism involved in thread interleavings leaves a challenge for a static analysis to precisely reason the order of shared memory accesses by different threads. In general, programmers try to make use of locks to access any shared data to avoid conflicts in updating and accessing the data. Thus, any analysis should also keep track of all such synchronization constructs used in the program while accessing any shared data (i.e., the number of locks used for accessing a shared data). The erase instructions that would be introduced by our analysis should also be well guarded by such locks. The number of threads that may access a shared data could be dynamic in nature. Often, it is not feasible to assume the number of threads statically. For example, if a thread is invoked within a loop, our analysis should also consider a possible interleaving of a thread with itself.

**Our Approach:** Our approach is to transform concurrent applications with zeroing instructions (`memset` instructions in C) to erase shared data so that the exposure of data is minimized. The main challenge in doing this is to determine whether an erase instruction for a shared data object can be safely introduced at a given program point, by considering all possible concurrent executions of threads. The main contribution of this paper is to address the abovementioned challenge by introducing a formal notion of *RacyPairs*, which assists in determining whether a given erasure for a shared object is safe or not. In addition, we give an algorithm to effectively compute *RacyPairs*, by leveraging existing work [19] on concurrent dataflow analysis using a race-detection engine. Our approach is implemented in a tool called DEICS, which transforms given concurrent C program into an equivalent C program with reduced lifetime of sensitive data used in the program. DEICS exclusively handles shared data and minimizes its lifetime by inserting erase instructions in a conservative way. By conservative we mean that any piece of shared data will not be erased by our approach if there can be a potential access by some thread in the program.

To the best of our knowledge, DEICS is the first known approach in the literature to bring data lifetime reduction technique to the realm of concurrent programs. This paper makes the following contributions:

- A formal notion of *RacyPairs* that suggests when a given erasure is safe
- An algorithm to effectively compute *RacyPairs* using race detection engines
- Implementation of the algorithm in the form of a tool called SWIPE
- A detailed evaluation of our approach by transforming over 100k lines of C applications (combined, with the largest application consisting of 57k LOC).

The rest of the paper is organized as follows: Section 2 presents the challenges of introducing erase instructions for data lifetime minimization in concurrent applications with an illustrative example. We explain our approach in section 3. The main algorithm behind our transformation scheme is described in section 4. Section 5 provides a detailed evaluation of our approach on set of real-life concurrent applications written in C. Section 6 presents the related work and we conclude in section 7.

## 2 Running Example

**Example:** Figure 1 gives a simplified version of producer-consumer example implemented using threads. In this program, the server thread accepts the connection from the client and collects the *Request* and places it in a shared memory (here the *request* variable declared at line 2) for the worker thread to process the same.

Threads are created in the $main$ function (which is the main thread) at lines 40 and 41 and all the three threads run in parallel starting from line 42. Shared variable, $request$ (defined at line 2) is accessed by server and worker threads and its access is protected by a lock variable $lockv$ for synchronization purpose. After receiving the request from client, the server thread, puts it in $request$ at line 9 and logs the $request$ at line 10. The worker thread reads the same data on line 25. (Let us ignore line 25a for the moment as it is not part of the original but belongs to the transformed program that we will explain shortly). After processing $request$ on line 25, it is no longer required in the program, but remains available in the rest of the worker thread and may be to other threads (lines 26-37 in worker, lines 12-21 in server, and lines 42-53 in main). Note that the actual execution at line 25 will depend on thread interleavings in general.

```
1   DEFINE LENGTH 20;
2   char *request;
3   mutex_type lockv;
    /* Server thread  accepts
    connection
    and collects  client  HTTP requests
    */
4   int  server ( ){
5   char * localdata ;
6     lock(&lockv);
7     request = malloc(LENGTH);
8     localdata = getRequestfromUser();
9     strcpy ( request ,  localdata ,  LENGTH);
10    log( request );   // read( request )
11    unlock(&lockv);
12    // do other work : Lines 12- 20
21  }
```

```
22   int  worker(){
     /* Worker thread  to process
     request */
23     lock(&lockv);
24     if ( request != NULL){
25       process ( request );
       // read( request )
25a:   memset( request ,  0,  LENGTH );
26     }
27     unlock(&lockv);
28   // generating response : Lines 28 − 36
37   }
38   int  main(){
39     mutex_init (&lockv);
40     thread_create ( server );
41     thread_create (worker);
42     // do some other work : Lines 42 − 52;
53   }
```

**Fig. 1.** Running example with erase instructions introduced for shared data

## 3  Approach

**Transformed Example:** We first show how our approach transforms the original program given in figure 1. Our transformation simply introduces an erase for the shared variable *request* after line 25 since *request* is no longer required after line 25 in worker thread. This is accomplished using the call to memset introduced by our approach in line 25a. Note that, here we only highlight the erasure of shared data. Erasures for local variables within each function / thread could be introduced using the approach from existing work [23], and we do not discuss the erasure of locals further in our technical approach.

**Main Idea:** Our approach to minimize lifetime of shared data in concurrent applications is to identify a location in the application, after which a particular definition of shared data is no longer required. If a shared definition is available at a location in a thread and is no more required further in that thread or any other thread running in parallel, we can safely erase such data after that location. Since execution of threads is not predictable statically, we adopt a conservative approach that, for each definition of a variable, identifies program locations after which no other thread accesses that definition. Note that, we use the word *definition*, to differentiate between a variable and its values at different times during the program execution. A shared variable can hold multiple definitions in a program. Our analysis treats each definition of a shared variable separately and tries to erase the contents of each definition after its intended use in the program (and thereby minimizes the exposure of data between definitions).

Introduction of an erase operation is safe only when the erase (which is a write operation) does not influence a read in another thread. Consider the running example given in figure 1. If we introduce an erase for *request* in worker thread after line 25, we can clearly see that there is no parallel read that is influenced by it and is therefore safe. On the other hand, if the *request* is erased in server thread after line 10, the worker thread may get a zero value for access at line 25, and is therefore not safe.

One may be tempted to identify parallel reads that may get influenced by the write we introduce by checking for data-races [1] caused by our write. However, absence of such data-races does not guarantee that our writes do not influence a parallel read. For example, in the running example given in 1, there was a last access for the *request* in the server thread at line 10. Even though, the *request* is last accessed at line 10 in server thread, it may still be required in worker thread based on the execution order. However, a race-detector may not identify the write we may introduce (before line 11) as a data-race, as all the accesses are protected by the locks. This leaves us with a challenge to keep track of all the accesses to shared variable irrespective of the program being data-race free.

Alternatively, mere presence of parallel reads should not prevent the introduction of erasures. In the running example given in figure 1, there is a definition for the shared variable *request* inside the worker thread at line 9. Introducing erasure for the shared data *request* in the worker thread before line 26 does not influence the value read

---

[1] There are various types of races as explained in [35], but we use a fairly general notion of a data-race which simply happens when two threads that access and modify shared data at the same time without any protection mechanism.

in server thread at line 10 (because of the definition at line 9), irrespective of thread interleavings. Therefore our analysis should be more precise to check if the parallel reads in other threads are actually influenced by our erasure.

## 3.1 Approach Overview

Given two threads $T1$ and $T2$ (and the non-determinism in their interleaving during execution), we need to ensure that for a shared data, the erasure point identified in thread $T1$ is safe, i.e., thread $T2$ will not need this data anymore. One simple way is to analyze thread $T2$ to check if there are any *read* operations on the shared data. As observed earlier, it is not sufficient to check for parallel reads, we should also consider other writes which may actually influence those reads (in the running example given in figure 1, the read for *request* in server thread at line 10 depends only on the definition at line 9 and does not get influenced by any write in worker thread ). However, if we can identify a location $l$ in thread $T2$ which would get influenced by our write in thread $T1$, and an actual read operation in $T2$ is reachable from $l$ without another write operation in between, then the actual read is influenced by our write. To identify such locations that would get influenced by our erasure (i.e., write operations), we can make use of a *pseudo-read* at those locations and check for a data-race (in particular, Write (our erasure)-Read (pseudo-read) races). We use the term pseudo-reads for imaginary reads, which are just used to query the race-detection engine, but are not actual reads in the program. Then, our analysis can be reduced to the problem of identifying critical pairs of locations $(l, l')$ specified as follows - $l$ is location in a thread where a pseudo-read of the shared data is in race with the write we introduced, and $l'$ is another location which consists of an actual read operation on the same shared variable, and $l'$ is reachable from $l$ without another definition to this shared variable in between. Absence of such critical pairs confirm that we can safely introduce erasures.

We explain our approach with the help of the running example given in figure 1. Consider the erase of the shared variable *request* in *worker* thread at new line 25a as shown in the figure 2.

```
22    int worker(){
      /* Worker thread processing   request */
23      lock(&lockv);
24      if ( request != NULL){
25        process( request );    // read( request )
      25a: memset( request , 0, LENGTH ); // write( request )
26      }
27      unlock(&lockv);
28      // generating response : Lines 28 - 36
37    }
```

**Fig. 2.** Erasing shared data *request* in worker thread

We now introduce pseudo-reads for the shared variable *request* after line 5 and line 11 in the *server* thread as shown in the figure 3. Querying a race-detection engine identifies the pseudo-reads after lines 5 and 11 in *server* thread to be in race with the write at line 25a in *worker* thread. Note that we show pseudo-read instructions only

```
4   int  server (){
5   char * localdata ;
    pseudo−read(request );
6     lock(&lockv);
7     request  = malloc(LENGTH);
8     localdata  = getRequestfromUser ();
9     strcpy ( request ,  localdata ,  LENGTH);
10    log( request );       // read( request )
11    unlock(&lockv);
    pseudo−read(request );
11    // do other  work : Lines  12 − 20
21  }
```

**Fig. 3.** Erasing shared data *request* in server thread

after lines 5 and 11. Pseudo-reads after lines ranging from 6-10 will not be in race with the write we introduced at line 25a as these lines are inside a lock region (The number of pseudo-read instructions to be considered in a thread can be optimized as explained in section 4).

There is an actual read for the shared data *request* inside the *server* thread at line 10, which is reachable from the pseudo-read after line 5. However, it cannot generate a critical pair as there is a definition for *request* at the line 9 that is on the control flow path from line 5 to line 10. Also, for the pseudo-read after line 11, there is no actual read on *request* in *server* thread reachable from it. In this scenario, the set of critical pairs is empty for the write at line 25. Therefore, we can introduce the erase instruction for the shared variable *request* inside the thread *worker*.

Now let us consider the introduction of an erasure for the shared data *request* in *server* thread immediately after line 10. However, a pseudo-read after line 22 in the *worker* thread will be in race with this write on *request* after line 10, furthermore there is an actual read at line 25 that is reachable from line 22 without any re-definition of *request* in between. Hence, the pair $(22, 25)$ forms a critical pair and we cannot introduce erase for *request* in the *server* thread after line 10.

### 3.2  Technical Description

***System Model.***   We formalize the intuitive description given before using a subset of C language with concurrency constructs given in Table 1. Table 1 gives the syntax of the executable part a program or a function. Declaration of a function is given by specifying the function name, return type, the formal parameters, and the function body specified using the syntax of table 1. The labels of statements in all the functions including the main function are assumed to be distinct. We use $sv$ to represent a typical shared variable and $lckv$ to represent a typical lock variable used for synchronization.

In a program $P$, threads (represented using $t$ in the language shown in Table 1) are created by invoking the call $thread(t)$. Thread invocations are different from normal function calls. They represent a parallel execution during runtime. Functions in the program are classified into two distinct sets called *ordinary functions* and *thread*

**Table 1.** A small subset of C language with concurrency constructs

| | |
|---|---|
| $P ::= S;$ | [PROGRAM] |
| $S ::= \, ^*px := E$ | [ASSIGN1] |
| $\mid \; l: \; x := E$ | [ASSIGN2] |
| $\mid \; l: \; px := E$ | [ASSIGN3] |
| $\mid \; l: \; \text{if } E \text{ then } S \text{ else } S \text{ endif}$ | [IF-ELSE] |
| $\mid \; l: \; \text{while } E \text{ do } S \text{ done}$ | [LOOP] |
| $\mid \; l: \; S \; ; \; S$ | [LIST] |
| $\mid \; l: \; \text{exit}$ | [EXIT] |
| $\mid \; l: \; \text{return } [\text{x} \mid \text{px}]$ | [RETURN] |
| $\mid \; l: \; \text{lock (lckv)}$ | [LOCK] |
| $\mid \; l: \; \text{unlock (lckv)}$ | [UNLOCK] |
| $\mid \; l: \; \text{thread (t)}$ | [THREAD-CREATE] |
| $E ::= \, \text{x} \mid \&\text{x} \mid \, ^*px \mid E \text{ bop } E$ | |
| $\mid \quad \text{call } f(E, \dots, E)$ | [EXPRESSION] |

*functions.* A thread function is only invoked when a thread is created (i.e., using the call $thread(t)$). Whereas an ordinary function is not invoked in a thread creation statement. Inside a function, ordinary functions or other thread functions can be invoked.

**Assumptions:** We assume that ordinary functions invoked in distinct thread functions are different, i.e., the same ordinary function is not invoked in more than one thread function. We assume that there is no recursion. In this model by inlining all the ordinary function invocations, we can convert the program into a form that contains only the main function and thread functions. (The inlining of functions is assumed only for simplicity of presentation. Our actual algorithm does not do this. Instead it computes function summaries as in SWIPE [23] and uses them wherever a function is invoked.) The bodies of the main function and the thread functions invoke only thread functions.

We treat all the global variables as shared variables (similar to [39]). Authors of [23,38,10,9,40] assume that a pointer variable in the program accesses the data within its allocated memory bounds. We make similar assumptions about pointer variables for our analysis.

A definition is a statement that updates the value of a variable, such as an assignment statement or a library call that reads external values and assigns it to a parameter. A definition is denoted by a unique identifier $id$. Standard definitions of *Aliases*, *must_definitions*, *may_aliases*, *succ*, and *preds* are adopted from SWIPE [23]. A definition of a variable $x/sv$ at location $l$ is a *must_definition* if the left hand side of the assignment consists of $x/sv$ or $*p$ for a pointer variable $p$ where $*p$ aliases only to $x/sv$ at location $l$.

In our analysis, we treat a shared variable $sv$ as a formal parameter. Throughout our analysis we differentiate between local data and shared/global data. We also identify different definitions of $sv$.

***Intra-procedural Analysis:*** DEICS first computes a control flow graph (CFG) for each thread function in the program. The CFG represents each instruction of the program as a node. For each definition (including the definitions of shared variables which are added as formals) denoted by $id$, DEICS computes all the nodes where the definition $id$ is reachable inside the function. We call this set as Reachability($id$) (as defined in [23]). We split the Reachability($id$) set into three different sets named UsePoints($id$), NoUse($id$) and ErasePoints($id$). UsePoints($id$) is the set of nodes where a definition $id$ is required and NoUse($id$) is the set of nodes where the definition $id$ is available but not required. For a given definition $id$, a transition from UsePoints($id$) to NoUse($id$) is the place where we can introduce erase instructions for $id$. We call this set of nodes as ErasePoints($id$) before which we may be able to safely introduce erase instructions (similar to [23]).

During our analysis, we identify each local variable $x$ of each thread function. For each definition $id$ of this local variable $x$, at each location $l$ in ErasePoints($id$) we can safely introduce erase instructions before $l$ provided there is no global pointer $p$ pointing to $x$, i.e., for each global pointer variable $p$, $*p$ does not alias $x$.

From here onwards, we describe the approach for erasures of definitions of shared variables. As explained earlier, in the running example of figure 1, we treat the shared variable $request$ as an implicit formal parameter to each of the functions ($server$, $main$, and $worker$). There is exactly one definition, which is at line 9, for the location pointed to by $request$. We let $request\_id$ denote this definition. Our analysis as given by SWIPE [23] for the $server$ thread, computes ErasePoints($request\_id$) = 11 and for the $worker$ thread it computes, ErasePoints($request\_id$) = 26.

Once the ErasePoints($id$) is computed for shared variables in each thread, our analysis needs to check that if introducing these erasures before the lines in ErasePoints($id$) would effect the reads in other threads. For each definition of a shared variable $sv$ denoted by $id$, we consider the introduction of dummy writes (i.e., erasures) for $sv$, before each location in the set ErasePoints($id$) of a thread function. For each such dummy write, denoted by DummyWrite($id$), our analysis computes the set RacyPairs(DummyWrite($id$)) defined below, of critical pairs discussed earlier.

**Definition 1.** *For each dummy write DummyWrite($id$) of a definition of a shared variable $sv$, denoted by $id$, RacyPairs(DummyWrite($id$)) is the set of all pairs $(l, l')$ of locations in some thread function $t$ such that a pseudo-read immediately after location $l$ would be in race with the dummy write DummyWrite($id$), and there is a path from $l$ to $l'$ in the CFG of $t$ such that there is no must_definition of $sv$ on this path, and there is a read of $sv$ at $l'$.*

Existence of at least one element in RacyPairs(DummyWrite($id$)) indicates that it may not be safe to introduce DummyWrite($id$). However, absence of such pairs guarantee that we can safely introduce $Erase(id)$ for shared data at the location of DummyWrite($id$).

As explained in section 3.1, for the running example of Figure 1, the set RacyPairs(DummyWrite($request\_id$)) is empty if DummyWrite($request\_id$) denotes the dummy write on the variable $request$ just before line 26 in the worker thread. Hence this erase statement for $request$ can be safely introduced before line 26. On the other hand, if DummyWrite($request\_id$) denotes the dummy write before the line 11 in the server thread then the pair $(22, 25) \in$ RacyPairs(DummyWrite($request\_id$)). Thus an erase statement for $request$ cannot be introduced just before line 11.

*Inter-procedural Analysis:* When ordinary functions are involved we use the summary of the function at each invocation. We follow the approach given in SWIPE to compute summaries of ordinary functions. For thread functions, we do not require the computation of such summaries since we use RacyPairs(DummyWrite) for determining whether erase instructions for shared variables can be safely introduced in thread functions.

## 4 Algorithm and Implementation

### 4.1 Algorithm

Algorithm 1 shows the outline of our approach which we have implemented into the tool DEICS. The algorithm is divided into four major steps. For simplicity of presentation the algorithm is given assuming that there is no recursion and all ordinary functions are inlined as explained in section 3 (the algorithm can be easily modified to avoid inlining the ordinary function and also to handle recursion by using function summaries as given in [23]).

---

**Algorithm 1.** DEICS Implementation

---

**Notation:** $f$ - thread function, $id$ - unique identifier for a definition $\phi$ - empty set

**for** *each f* **do**

    attach shared variable to formals set;

    **for** *each definition id* **do**

1         Compute Reachability($id$);

        Spilt Reachability($id$) into UsePoints($id$) and NoUse($id$) ;

        Compute ErasePoints($id$) ;

        introduce $Erase(id)$ for all local variables;

    **end**

**end**

**for** *each definition id of shared variable* **do**

    **for** *each* ErasePoints($id$) **do**

2         introduce DummyWrite($id$) before;

    **end**

**end**

**for** *each* DummyWrite($id$) **do**

3     Compute RacyPairs(DummyWrite($id$));

**end**

**for** *each function f* **do**

    **for** *each definition id of shared variable* **do**

        **if** RacyPairs(DummyWrite($id$)) $= \phi$ **then**

4             introduce $Erase(id)$;

        **end**

    **end**

**end**

---

**Step 1:** As mentioned in the approach, the first step is to treat each global variable as formal variable. We then identify definitions and aliases using fix-point computation. For each definition of local variables and formal variables, the set Reachability is computed considering aliases. The Reachability is then split into two sets UsePoints and NoUse. Note that the UsePoints set consists of all the locations where the definition is actually used and also the locations, which need to retain the definition for an actual use at later point in the program. Summaries of ordinary functions are used wherever they are invoked in the program to cover the inter-procedural analysis. The ErasePoints set is computed for the locations where the definitions can be erased. All the local definitions can be erased at the appropriate ErasePoints if there is no global pointer $p$ such that $*p$ aliases to the variable of definition.

**Step 2:** For each definition $id$ of shared variable, or a definition whose alias is a shared variable, we introduce $DummyWrite(id)$ before each location in the set ErasePoints$(id)$ computed in step 1. Dummy writes are introduced first and actual erases are introduced based on our analysis on the changed program with dummy writes.

**Step 3:** We compute RacyPairs(DummyWrite$(id)$) using the technique outlined in approach section 3. For each shared variable corresponding to definition $id$, pseudo-reads are inserted and race-detection engine is invoked to identify racy pseudo-reads and RacyPairs(DummyWrite$(id)$) is computed.

**Step 4:** We then transform the program by introducing erase instructions in place of those DummyWrite$(id)$ whose corresponding set RacyPairs(DummyWrite$(id)$) is empty. We provided a discussion on how one can prevent the compiler from optimizing our erasing instructions in [23].

### 4.2 Implementation

In our implementation, we assume that all global variables are shared variables, treated as additional formal variables to any function. We perform a sequential analysis to compute Reachability sets for all the definitions within each function along with the definitions of shared variables in the form of formal variables. Following the method explained in section 3, we then compute UsePoints and NoUse points by splitting the reachability set. We compute ErasePoints for all definitions inside each function and erase all the local data that is not being pointed to by any of the global/shared variables.

Our implementation captures the effect of introducing erasures for the shared data at ErasePoints by leveraging on existing concurrent data flow analysis. In particular, we use and build on the RADAR [19] framework for concurrent program analysis. RADAR is a data-flow analysis framework which converts a sequential analysis into the one that is sound for concurrent programs. This framework has a built-in race-detection engine (RELAY), which identifies racy accesses on shared data.

A straightforward use of RADAR approach does not suffice for our purpose of data erasure. This is because, in RADAR, the main focus is on *writes* performed by all the threads. Whereas, our analysis introduces *writes*. RADAR considers write-write races in addition to write-read races. However, we only need to consider the later type of races, more specifically, races between dummy writes and pseudo-reads that are introduced.

**Dummy Writes for Potential Erasures:** We modified the RADAR framework to introduce dummy writes for shared data before the set ErasePoints$(id)$ as indicated earlier.

In addition, pseudo-reads are introduced. These dummy writes are treated as original writes during the analysis inside RADAR. For each definition $id$ of shared variable, instead of computing the set RacyPairs(DummyWrite($id$)), our analysis computes a superset of RacyPairs which we call $WeakRacyPairs$ that we explain below.

**WeakRacyPairs:** $WeakRacyPairs$ is a set of pairs of locations $(l, l')$ specified as follows : $l$ is location in a thread where a pseudo-read of the shared data is in race with the write we introduced, and $l'$ is another location which consists of an actual read operation on the same shared variable, and $l'$ is reachable from $l$. Note that, the original criterion of the absence of redefinition of shared variable in the path between $l$ and $l'$ for $RacyPairs$, is relaxed for the computation of $WeakRacyPairs$.

Emptiness of the set $WeakRacyPairs$ confirms that we can safely introduce erasures and therefore is still sound.

**Reducing Invocations of Race-detection Engine:** Instead of introducing pseudo-reads at each program location, the program can be divided into race equivalence regions. A representative program location is chosen from each region to introduce pseudo reads. A race equivalence region is a region in the program where the raciness behavior is same throughout the region. For the running example given in figure 1, instead of introducing pseudo-reads at each location in the $server$ thread, it is sufficient to introduce pseudo-reads after lines 5, 6 and 11. For each definition of shared variable inside a function, after identifying a representative location for each race equivalence region, a pseudo read is introduced for that definition using the modified RADAR framework.

We give a detailed evaluation of this implementation by transforming various concurrent applications in next section.

## 5   Evaluation

We implemented our tool DEICS in Ocaml using the CIL [34] and RADAR.

**Applications:** Using our tool, we transformed five multi-threaded applications written in C. The common feature of all these applications is that they use Pthreads library for the multi-threading functionality. Of the five, three of the applications (zebedee [5], retawq [41], mtdaapd [2]), handle sensitive data such as ftp passwords and database records. In order to further illustrate the precision and performance aspects of DEICS, we chose two additional applications (pfscan [3], knot [11]) from the RADAR benchmarks suite [4].

**Table 2.** Application size and transformation time taken

| Application | Size (LOC) | no.of funcs | Xfrmtion time(sec) |
|---|---|---|---|
| pfscan | 1259 | 24 | 15 |
| knot | 2255 | 56 | 21 |
| zebedee | 11682 | 220 | 55 |
| mtdaapd | 57102 | 637 | 3150 |
| retawq | 38750 | 638 | 2753 |

**Table 3.** Effect of transformation on Applications

| Application | #of globs | #of thrds | erasures globs | #of locals | erasures locals |
|---|---|---|---|---|---|
| pfscan | 18 | 2 | 11 | 156 | 114 |
| knot | 43 | 6 | 10 | 62 | 160 |
| zebedee | 61 | 3 | 928 | 3776 | 2465 |
| mtdaapd | 326 | 5 | 176 | 5359 | 3755 |
| retawq | 444 | 2 | 342 | 3511 | 4387 |

Table 2 shows the application sizes and transformation time taken. The largest application consists of 57K lines of code (LOC). Column 2 in table 2 shows how DEICS scales well to transform applications from 1K LOC to 57K LOC, whose sum of lines of code is more than 100K. Total number of functions in each application is given in column 3 and the transformation time taken for each application is shown in column 4. We observed a correlation between the number of functions and transformation time. The transformation time includes the time taken by race-detection engine as well.

## 5.1 Effectiveness

Table 3 shows the effect our transformation. For each application (shown in column 1), we identified the number of global variables (excluding pthread mutex variables) which is shown is column 2 of the table 3. Minimum number of threads required to run each application is also shown (column 3). The effect of our approach is given in column 4 as the number of erases introduced for globals. For a given global, there can be more than one definition and for each definition there can be more than one erase point as the size of ErasePoints set can be greater than one. For example, in *zebedee* application, there are only 61 globals, but number of erasures are 928. We observed that, there is a switch case in the program with different cases and the globals are getting erased in each case of the switch statement. Also, DEICS introduces erases for globals before all termination points in the program, covering all possible paths an execution can take. The number of local variables in each application is shown in column 5. The number of erasures DEICS introduced for definitions of local variables is shown in column 6 of table 3.

We also evaluated the effectiveness of our tool to check if the erasures are introduced for sensitive information in local and shared global variables. For the application *zebedee*, DEICS erased sensitive information such as keys used for data encryption. In the text-based browser application *retawq*, most of the global data has already been erased by the developer. For the sensitive data like, *FTP_login_password* and *current_keymap_keystr*, the application has erase instructions. DEICS also introduced erases at the same location. This clearly shows that, by introduction of such erase instructions in an application, DEICS reduces the data exposure by introducing erases automatically. The audio media server application *mtdaapd*, uses the database to store the music information which is retrieved by the users connected to the server. DEICS introduced erasures for the global shared variables, which contain sensitive information. After analyzing each application, it is clear that, most of the applications do handle sensitive data in local and shared variables and erasure of such data is important.

**Precision:** We illustrate the utility and precision of DEICS using *pfscan* and *knot* applications. The *pfscan* application already had *free* instructions for some sensitive objects. DEICS introduced erase instructions for these objects much before these free instructions, thus reducing the exposure of the data. For the *knot* application, DEICS our manual review of certain key program variables indicates that DEICS is precise in identifying the erase points for data held in these variables.

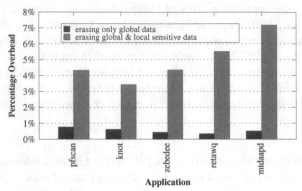

**Fig. 4.** Performance overhead of concurrent applications

## 5.2  Performance

We measured the performance overhead of transformed applications (shown is figure 4). We ran our experiments on x86 Linux platform with configuration of 8 GB of memory and a 3 GHz AMD Phenom processor. To capture the execution time, we ran each application multiple times with the same input and using same number of threads. For each application, we used minimum set of required threads during the execution of original and transformed program (this varied between 2 and 6 threads).

The overhead caused due to the erase instructions for sensitive data in global variables as well as local variables of individual functions In this case, the maximum runtime overhead is less than 8% and average is around 5%.

Another set of experiments are conducted to measure the overhead due to erasing only shared / global data (without erasing local data) (measuring only the overheads of the work reported in this paper). In this case, the runtime overhead ranged from 0.3% to 0.7%, averaging 0.5%. We show this in Figure 4 (black bars). We observe that transforming applications with a tool like SWIPE would also have the overhead of around 5%. Our transformation in DEICS to erase shared data adds only an additional performance overhead of 0.5% to minimize the lifetime of shared data.

## 6  Related Work

**Data Lifetime Minimization.** There have been various works in this area of data lifetime minimization in the systems community by employing techniques from operating systems  [24,25,13,8,31,18]. Our approach uses program transformation techniques. In addition, we handle concurrent programs which is not handled by prior work.

**Static Analysis of Concurrent Applications:** There are tools and frameworks developed to perform dataflow analysis  [20,19]. In  [32,22,39,20], a graph to represent the parallelism is built and a modified version of sequential analysis is performed.  [21,14] provide a generic approach for static analysis of concurrent programs. Qadeer et. al. proposed a technique to transform concurrent programs to sequential programs  [36] for finding errors in concurrent programs. All these works mainly focus on identifying bugs in programs. Our objective of minimizing sensitive data lifetimes is different from all of the above works.

**Garbage Collection and Region-Based Management.** Our approach for reducing sensitive data-lifetimes is related to approaches for garbage collection. A key difference between our approach and garbage collection is that our approach uses a tight, dynamic criterion for erasing sensitive data whereas garbage collectors use a more relaxed criteria. We could augment such a garbage collector with memory erasing routines to ensure that freed objects are erased in memory. However, such a solution may still be imprecise in addressing our goal, namely to erase contents of sensitive memory *immediately* after their lifetime. By calling the garbage collector more often, this gap can be narrowed, however, this frequent calling can introduce overheads that are unpredictable. Free-me [27] aims to insert deallocation instructions by conservatively estimating object lifetimes.

Extensive work in the area of region-based memory management has been performed [37,7,28,12,42]. The main goal of these works is to have an economic usage of memory and reduce the need for invoking garbage collector. A region based approach could be used for erasing sensitive data, however it might result in poor precision.

**Data Erasure and Memory Safety.** Chong et.al [16,15] provide a formal treatment to information erasure in their paper. Their approach is targeted towards new applications, whereas our approach can transform existing applications as well. Memory management techniques have been proposed to minimize the risk of data exposure [8,31]. However data lifetime minimization is not achieved with these approaches.

**Privilege Separation.** Approaches such as [29,33,30,43] rely on changes at operating system and hardware level to maintain the sensitive data separately so that there are no privilege escalation attacks. Our approach focuses on modifying applications to have built-in mechanisms for minimizing data exposure.

## 7 Conclusion

In this paper, we presented an approach to minimize lifetime of data in concurrent applications. Our approach is implemented as a tool called DEICS, which automatically transforms concurrent programs with instructions to erase data after its intended use. Our tool is based on static analysis to minimize the runtime overhead. We have evaluated a set of real world concurrent applications written in C to show its effectiveness.

**Acknowledgements.** This material is based on research sponsored in part by DARPA under agreement number and by National Science Foundation under grants FA8750-12-C-0166, CCF-0916438, CNS-1035914, CCF-1319754, CNS-1314485, CNS-0845894, DGE-1069311, and NSF-1241685. The U.S. Government is authorized to reproduce and distribute reprints for Governmental purposes notwithstanding any copyright notation thereon. The views and conclusions contained herein are those of the authors and should not be interpreted as necessarily representing the official policies or endorsements, either expressed or implied, of DARPA, NSF or the U.S. Government.

## References

1. Common vulnerability exposures, https://cve.mitre.org/
2. Mtdaapd, http://sourceforge.net/projects/mt-daapd/

3. Pfscan, http://freecode.com/projects/pfscan
4. Radar, http://cseweb.ucsd.edu/~lerner/radar.html
5. Zebedee, http://www.winton.org.uk/zebedee/index.html
6. Heartbleed (2014), http://en.wikipedia.org/wiki/Heartbleed
7. Aiken, A., Fahndrich, M., Levien, R.: Better static memory management: improving region-based analysis of higher-order languages. In: Proceedings of the ACM SIGPLAN 1995 Conference on Programming Language Design and Implementation, New York, NY, USA (1995)
8. Akritidis, P.: Cling: A Memory Allocator to Mitigate Dangling Pointers. In: USENIX Security Symposium, Washington, DC (2010)
9. Andersenm, L.O.: Program Analysis and Specialization for the C Programming Language. Technical report (1994)
10. Avots, D., Dalton, M., Benjamin Livshits, V., Lam, M.S.: Improving Software Security with a C Pointer Analysis. In: International Conference on Software Engineering, St. Louis, MO (2005)
11. von Behren, R., Condit, J., Zhou, F., McCloskey, B., Brewer, E., Necula, G.: Knot, http://capriccio.cs.berkeley.edu/
12. Birkedal, L., Tofte, M., Vejlstrup, M.: From region inference to von neumann machines via region representation inference. In: Proceedings of the 23rd ACM SIGPLAN-SIGACT Symposium on Principles of Programming Languages, POPL 1996, pp. 171–183. ACM, New York (1996)
13. Boehm, H.-J.: A Garbage Collector for C and C++ (2002), http://www.hpl.hp.com/personal/Hans_Boehm/gc
14. Bouajjani, A., Esparza, J., Touili, T.: A generic approach to the static analysis of concurrent programs with procedures. In: Proceedings of the 30th ACM SIGPLAN-SIGACT Symposium on Principles of Programming Languages, POPL 2003, pp. 62–73. ACM, New York (2003)
15. Chong, S., Myers, A.C.: Language-Based Information Erasure. In: Computer Security Foundations Workshop, Aix-en-Provence, France (2005)
16. Chong, S., Myers, A.C.: End-to-End Enforcement of Erasure and Declassification. In: Computer Security Foundations Symposium, Pittsburgh, PA (2008)
17. Chow, J., Pfaff, B., Garfinkel, T., Christopher, K., Rosenblum, M.: Understanding Data Lifetime via Whole System Simulation. In: USENIX Security Symposium, San Diego, CA (2004)
18. Chow, J., Pfaff, B., Garfinkel, T., Rosenblum, M.: Shredding Your Garbage: Reducing Data Lifetime through Secure Deallocation. In: USENIX Security Symposium, Baltimore, MD (2005)
19. Chugh, R., Voung, J.W., Jhala, R., Lerner, S.: Dataflow analysis for concurrent programs using datarace detection. In: Proceedings of the 2008 ACM SIGPLAN Conference on Programming Language Design and Implementation, PLDI 2008, pp. 316–326. ACM, New York (2008)
20. De, A., D'Souza, D., Nasre, R.: Dataflow analysis for datarace-free programs. In: Barthe, G. (ed.) ESOP 2011. LNCS, vol. 6602, pp. 196–215. Springer, Heidelberg (2011)
21. Duesterwald, E., Soffa, M.L.: Concurrency analysis in the presence of procedures using a data-flow framework. In: Proceedings of the Symposium on Testing, Analysis, and Verification, TAV4, pp. 36–48. ACM, New York (1991)

22. Dwyer, M.B., Clarke, L.A.: Data flow analysis for verifying properties of concurrent programs. In: Proceedings of the 2nd ACM SIGSOFT Symposium on Foundations of Software Engineering, SIGSOFT 1994, pp. 62–75. ACM, New York (1994)

23. Gondi, K., Bisht, P., Venkatachari, P., Prasad Sistla, A., Venkatakrishnan, V.N.: Swipe: eager erasure of sensitive data in large scale systems software. In: Proceedings of the Second ACM Conference on Data and Application Security and Privacy, CODASPY 2012, pp. 295–306. ACM, New York (2012)

24. Gutmann, P.: Secure Deletion of Data from Magnetic and Solid-state Memory. In: USENIX Security Symposium, San Jose, California (1996)

25. Gutmann, P.: Data Remanence in Semiconductor Devices. In: USENIX Security Symposium, Washington, DC (2001)

26. Guttman, P.: Software Leaves Encryption Keys, Passwords Lying around in Memory. Security Focus Vuln Dev Mailing List (2002), http://www.securityfocus.com/archive/82/298001/30/0/threaded

27. Guyer, S.Z., McKinley, K.S., Frampton, D.: Free-Me: A Static Analysis for Automatic Individual Object Reclamation. In: Programming Language Design and Implementation, Ottawa, Ontario, Canada (2006)

28. Hallenberg, N., Elsman, M., Tofte, M.: Combining region inference and garbage collection. In: Proceedings of the ACM SIGPLAN 2002 Conference on Programming Language Design and Implementation, PLDI 2002, pp. 141–152. ACM, New York (2002)

29. Khatiwala, T., Swaminathan, R., Venkatakrishnan, V.N.: Data Sandboxing: A Technique for Enforcing Confidentiality Policies. In: Annual Computer Security Applications Conference, Miami Beach, FL (2006)

30. Krohn, M., Yip, A., Brodsky, M., Cliffer, N., Frans Kaashoek, M., Kohler, E., Morris, R.: Information Flow Control for Standard OS Abstractions. In: Symposium on Operating Systems Principles, Washington, WA (2007)

31. Lattner, C., Adve, V.: Automatic Pool Allocation: Improving Performance by Controlling Data Structure Layout in the Heap. In: Programming Language Design and Implementation, Chicago, IL (2005)

32. Lee, J., Padua, D.A., Midkiff, S.P.: Basic compiler algorithms for parallel programs. In: Proceedings of the Seventh ACM SIGPLAN Symposium on Principles and Practice of Parallel Programming, PPoPP 1999, pp. 1–12. ACM, New York (1999)

33. McCune, J.M., Li, Y., Qu, N., Zhou, Z., Datta, A., Gligor, V., Perrig, A.: TrustVisor: Efficient TCB Reduction and Attestation. In: IEEE Symposium on Security and Privacy, Oakland, CA (2010)

34. Necula, G.C., McPeak, S., Rahul, S.P., Weimer, W.: CIL: Intermediate Language and Tools for Analysis and Transformation of C Programs. In: Nigel Horspool, R. (ed.) CC 2002. LNCS, vol. 2304, pp. 213–228. Springer, Heidelberg (2002)

35. Netzer, R.H.B., Miller, B.P.: What are race conditions?: Some issues and formalizations. ACM Lett. Program. Lang. Syst. 1(1), 74–88 (1992)

36. Qadeer, S., Wu, D.: Kiss: keep it simple and sequential. SIGPLAN Not. 39(6), 14–24 (2004)

37. Ruggieri, C., Murtagh, T.P.: Lifetime analysis of dynamically allocated objects. In: Proceedings of the 15th ACM SIGPLAN-SIGACT Symposium on Principles of Programming Languages, POPL 1988, pp. 285–293. ACM, New York (1988)

38. Rugina, R., Rinard, M.: Symbolic Bounds Analysis of Pointers, Array Indices, and Accessed Memory Regions. In: Programming Language Design and Implementation, Vancouver, British Columbia, Canada (2000)

39. Sinha, N., Wang, C.: Staged concurrent program analysis. In: Proceedings of the Eighteenth ACM SIGSOFT International Symposium on Foundations of Software Engineering, FSE 2010, pp. 47–56. ACM, New York (2010)
40. Steensgaard, B.: Points-to Analysis in Almost Linear Time. In: Principles of Programming Languages, St. Petersburg Beach, FL (1996)
41. Thomaßen, A.: Retawq, http://retawq.sourceforge.net/
42. Tofte, M., Talpin, J.-P.: Implementation of the typed call-by-value λ-calculus using a stack of regions. In: Proceedings of the 21st ACM SIGPLAN-SIGACT Symposium on Principles of Programming Languages, POPL 1994, pp. 188–201. ACM, New York (1994)
43. Zeldovich, N., Boyd-Wickizer, S., Kohler, E., Mazières, D.: Making Information Flow Explicit in HiStar. In: Symposium on Operating Systems Design and Implementation, Seattle, WA (2006)

# A Practical Analysis of Oblivious Sorting Algorithms for Secure Multi-party Computation*

Dan Bogdanov[1], Sven Laur[2], and Riivo Talviste[1,2]

[1] Cybernetica, Mäealuse 2/1, 12618 Tallinn, Estonia
{dan,riivo}@cyber.ee
[2] University of Tartu, Institute of Computer Science, Liivi 2, 50409 Tartu, Estonia
swen@math.ut.ee

**Abstract.** Cryptographic secure computing methods like secure multi-party computation, circuit garbling and homomorphic encryption are becoming practical enough to be usable in applications. Such applications need special data-independent sorting algorithms to preserve privacy. In this paper, we describe the design and implementation of four different oblivious sorting algorithms. We improve two earlier designs based on sorting networks and quicksort with the capability of sorting matrices. We also propose two new designs—a naive comparison-based sort with a low round count and an oblivious radix sort algorithm that does not require any private comparisons. For all these algorithms, we present thorough complexity and performance analysis including detailed breakdown of running-time, network and memory usage.

**Keywords:** privacy, algorithms, sorting, implementation, performance analysis, secure multi-party computation.

## 1 Introduction

In many cases, we need to aggregate data from different sources and thus explicitly address the privacy concerns of individual data donors. For that we need a solution that allows controlled data mining that preserves the privacy of the data owners. Standard textbook solutions are based on anonymization like $k$-anonymity [24], $\ell$-diversity [20] and others [11]. These transform data by adding noise so that certain statistical properties remain, but individual records do not disclose private information. However, statistical deanonymization is an efficient counter-measure against anonymization, especially if auxiliary information is present [21]. Threats caused by deanonymization through auxiliary information can be estimated and mitigated using the notion of differential privacy [9]. Differential privacy can be achieved by also adding noise to the output of algorithm.

* This research was supported by the European Regional Development Fund through Centre of Excellence in Computer Science (EXCS); the European Social Fund Doctoral Studies and Internationalisation programme DoRa; the European Union Seventh Framework Programme (FP7/2007-2013) under grant agreement no. 284731; and by the Estonian Research Council under Institutional Research Grants IUT2-1 and IUT27-1.

K. Bernsmed and S. Fischer-Hübner (Eds.): NordSec 2014, LNCS 8788, pp. 59–74, 2014.
DOI: 10.1007/978-3-319-11599-3_4, © Springer International Publishing Switzerland 2014

It is an efficient method for building private data analysis tools when initialized with correct threshold parameters.

However, the privacy analysis only specifies how much does a desired output leak information about the individual data records but does not provide any mechanism for computing these outputs. The task of computing outputs while hiding inputs and all intermediate values can be solved with secure multi-party computation. Secure multi-party computation (SMC) has gained popularity as it has become more efficient. Initial cryptographic protocols were tailored for particular tasks like the scalar product [13], but programmable SMC has gained efficiency and has become as fast or even faster. Some of the fastest SMC systems [5,4,8] are based on secret sharing and share-computing. Secret sharing [23] is a cryptographic primitive for securely sharing confidential information among several parties. Share-computing protocols allow secret-shared data to be processed without reconstructing the original secrets. There are also encryption schemes that allow such processing known as crypto-computing [22,12], but these solutions are less efficient at this time.

Sorting is an important operation in privacy-preserving data analysis and data mining. In addition to its obvious use in ordering data, sorting is used for finding ranked elements (top-k, quantiles), performing group-level aggregations and implementing statistical tests. There are two principal ways how an oblivious sorting algorithm can be implemented. First, we can use secret sharing and share-computing to hide how the values are propagated in sorting networks [18]. This leads to practical solutions [17,25] with complexity $\mathcal{O}(nlog^2n)$, as no *practically* efficient construction for sorting network of size $\mathcal{O}(nlogn)$ is known. The second alternative is to use sorting algorithms as a basis. The latter is more difficult, as the behaviour of a sorting algorithm depends on the input. However, this problem can be removed by obliviously shuffling the input before sorting. In [15], Hamada *et al.* propose a generic blueprint for converting any comparison-based sorting algorithm into an oblivious sorting algorithm. Recently, Hamada *et al.* have published a manuscript describing oblivious version of radix sort [14].

In [26], Zhang proposes multiple constant-round sorting schemes for secret sharing schemes. These include counting sort, arrayless bead sort and sorting key-indexed data. These schemes assume a known range of inputs and the author proposes to use radix sort on top of these protocols to deal with larger ranges.

**Our Contribution.** We would like to have a secure sorting algorithm that has low round count for short inputs and low communication complexity for large inputs. Towards this goal we propose two new sorting algorithms starting with a naive comparison-based sorting algorithm with a low round count that is suitable for sorting short vectors. Secondly, as an independent work (see [3]) we have also constructed an oblivious version of radix sorting algorithm that is very similar to the one proposed in [14]. Radix sort does not declassify comparison results and works in data-independent time. Additionally, it does not require oblivious comparisons, which are usually complex protocols with high running-time. We also show how to extend any sorting algorithm for sorting matrices based on the values of one or more columns.

Most importantly, we implement all of the mentioned sorting algorithms and give a thorough analysis of their running time, network communication complexity and memory consumption. We also provide component break-down graphs for all of the implemented sorting algorithms to point out possible bottlenecks for future improvement. Our benchmark results are measured on implementation developed for the SHAREMIND secure computation platform [1]. The algorithms are implemented using the SECREC programming language [2]. We implemented all the algorithms on the same platform to perform a fair comparison.

## 2    Requirements for Oblivious Sorting Algorithms

Most oblivious sorting algorithms in this paper are not designed for a particular secure computation technology. However, we analyze the efficiency of the algorithms in an SMC environment based on secret sharing. We focus on solutions based on secret sharing, as they currently provide the fastest practical implementations. In this setting, $n$ parties evaluate a function $f(x_1, \ldots, x_n) = (y_1, \ldots, y_n)$ so that party $i$ will learn its input $x_i$, output $y_i$ and nothing else.

Secret sharing [23] allows us to hide secret values by splitting them into random shares that are distributed among the parties. In additive secret sharing, a secret value $x$ is split into $n$ random addends $x_1, \ldots, x_n$ held by parties $\mathcal{P}_1, \ldots, \mathcal{P}_n$ so they add up to the original value (modulo some $p$):

$$x = x_1 + x_2 + \ldots + x_n \mod p.$$

A bitwise secret-sharing scheme works similarly, except instead of sum we use the bitwise exclusive or operation to calculate and reconstruct the shares:

$$x = x_1 \oplus x_2 \oplus \ldots \oplus x_n.$$

In this paper, we denote a secret-shared value $x$ by $[\![x]\!]$.

Arguing about the security of secure multi-party computation protocols often includes demonstrating that an adversary cannot distinguish between the secure processing of actual inputs from the similar evaluation of random inputs. We suggest that the reader studies the work of Canetti on proving the security of SMC protocol suites [6]. It is important that the SMC protocols are *universally composable*, so they could be used to build algorithm implementations.

Algorithms must fulfill the following requirements to be *data-independent*. First, the intermediate and output values of the algorithm must not leak anything about the secret inputs. This prevents information leakage through observing the memory during execution. Second, for a fixed number of private inputs, the algorithm's execution time should not depend on the input values. This prevents information leakage through observations of the algorithm's running time.

Hiding the number of inputs is rarely required in practice. While this is possible, such techniques still require an upper bound for the number of inputs, resulting in a leak of information on the maximum number of records and a waste of computing resources on unused elements. Therefore, we explicitly allow oblivious sorting algorithms that leak the size of the input.

---

**Algorithm 1.** NaiveCompSort

---

**Data:** Input array $[\![x]\!] \in \mathbb{Z}_{2^k}^n$
**Result:** Sorted array $[\![x']\!]$
1 Let $[\![x]\!] = \mathsf{Shuffle}([\![x]\!])$
2 Compute in parallel values $[\![g_{i,j}]\!] = [\![x_i]\!] \leq [\![x_j]\!]$ for $1 \leq i < j \leq n$.
3 Declassify the values $[\![g_{i,j}]\!]$ and sort $[\![x]\!]$ according to them, obtaining $[\![x']\!]$
4 **return** $[\![x']\!]$

---

## 3  Oblivious Sorting Techniques

### 3.1  Constructions Based on Oblivious Shuffling

It is possible to run any comparison based sort algorithm on the vector of shared inputs $[\![x_1]\!], \ldots, [\![x_n]\!]$ by using share-computing protocols to evaluate comparisons $g_{i,j} = [\![x_i < x_j]\!]$. Although this hides the individual values $x_i$, it leaks information about the initial order of elements. Hence, the data must be obliviously shuffled before we run the comparison based algorithm [15]. As a result, we get a randomized algorithm which running time does not depend on the input and which is provably secure provided that there are no identical elements in the vector or the observable behaviour of algorithm is independent of ties. Independence is a difficult property to achieve and thus one often uses conversion that guarantee uniqueness of vector elements. We give one such conversion in Section 4 and for now state that constructions based on oblivious shuffle do not leak information even in the case of equal elements.

Because many SMC implementations have highly efficient vector operations, vectorized naive protocols may sometimes be more efficient than protocols with a lower computational complexity and a lower degree of vectorization. In this paper, we propose a naive sorting protocol based on shuffle and vectorized comparisons called NaiveCompSort (Algorithm 1). In this algorithm, we first shuffle the input array and then compare every element with every other element in the array in one big vector operation. Finally, we rearrange the elements according to the declassified comparison results. This algorithm always works in the worst case time of $\mathcal{O}(n^2)$ and its runtime is, therefore, data-independent.

### 3.2  Constructions Based on Sorting Networks

A sorting network is a structure that consists of several stages of compare-and-exchange (CompEx) functions. A CompEx function takes two inputs, compares them according to a given condition and exchanges them, if the comparison result is true. An example CompEx function for sorting two values in ascending order is defined as

$$\mathsf{CompEx}(x, y) = (\mathsf{Min}(x, y), \mathsf{Max}(x, y)). \tag{1}$$

When all CompEx functions in the stages of the sorting network are applied on the input data array, the output data array will be sorted according to the desired condition. For a more detailed explanation of sorting networks, see [18].

---

**Algorithm 2.** Basic algorithm for sorting with a sorting network.

---

**Data**: Input array $x \in \mathbb{Z}_{2^k}^n$ and a sorting network $\mathcal{N} = (\mathcal{L}_1, \ldots, \mathcal{L}_m)$.
**Result**: Sorted output array $x \in \mathbb{Z}_{2^k}^n$.

1  **foreach** $\mathcal{L}_i \in \mathcal{N}$ **do**
2  $\quad$ **foreach** $(l, r) \in \mathcal{L}_i$ **do**
3  $\quad\quad$ $(x_l, x_r) \leftarrow \mathsf{CompEx}(x_l, x_r)$
4  $\quad$ **end**
5  **end**

---

The inputs of each $\mathsf{CompEx}$ function can be encoded with their indices in the input data array. Therefore, we will represent an $m$-stage sorting network as a tuple of tuples $\mathcal{N} = (\mathcal{L}_1, \ldots, \mathcal{L}_m)$, consisting of stages in the form $\mathcal{L}_i \in (\mathbb{N} \times \mathbb{N})^{\ell_i}$. Each stage $\mathcal{L}_i$ contains $\ell_i$ $\mathsf{CompEx}$ functions denoted by pair of indices $(l, r)$. The output of an individual $\mathsf{CompEx}$ function swaps elements $x_l$ and $x_r$ if necessary as per Equation 1. For efficiency, we prefer sorting networks where no index appears more than once in each individual stage as this lets us vectorize the implementation.

Algorithm 2 presents a basic algorithm for evaluating a sorting network in this representation. We can use the same array $x$ for storing the results of the compare-exchange operation because, according to our assumption, a single stage does not use the same array index twice.

As the structure of the sorting network is the same for all inputs, Algorithm 2 is trivially data-independent, given a data-independent implementation of the $\mathsf{CompEx}$ function. Such implementations are also easy to construct, following the minimum-maximum blueprint shown in Equation (1).

### 3.3 Constructions Specific for Bitwise Secret Sharing Schemes

If data is secret-shared using a bitwise secret-sharing scheme, access to individual bits is cheap. This allows us to design a very efficient count/radix sorting algorithm. Counting sort [7,10] is a sorting algorithm that can sort an array of integers in a small range by first constructing a frequency table and then rearranging items in the array according to this table.

Radix sort [16] sorts an array of integers by rearranging them based on counting sort results on digits in the same positions. It sorts data one digit position at a time, starting with the least significant digit. This works as the underlying counting sort is a stable sorting algorithm. Algorithm 3 shows the protocol of oblivious radix sort that uses binary counting sort as a subroutine. The underlying counting sort is made data-independent by obliviously updating counters $[\![c_0]\!]$, $[\![c_1]\!]$ and the order vector $[\![ord]\!]$. Such a data-independent counting sort is sufficient to make our radix sort data-independent as well. However, the data-independent counting sort protocol also uses addition and multiplication operations which are expensive protocols on bitwise shared data. Therefore, after creating a vector with bits on a given position, we convert it to additively shared data and work in this domain. Algorithm's output remains in a bitwise form.

---

**Algorithm 3.** Data-independent radix sort.

**Data:** Bitwise shared input array $[\![x]\!] \in \mathbb{Z}_{2^k}^n$.
**Result:** Bitwise shared sorted array $[\![x]\!] \in \mathbb{Z}_{2^k}^n$.
// Iterate over all digits starting with the least significant
digit:

1   **foreach** $m \in \{1, \ldots, k\}$ **do**
2     Let $[\![d]\!] = ([\![d_1]\!], \ldots, [\![d_n]\!])$ contain $m$-th bits of $[\![x]\!] = ([\![x_1]\!], \ldots, [\![x_n]\!])$.
3     Convert elements of $d$ from $\mathbb{Z}_2$ to additively shared $\mathbb{Z}_{2^k}$.
4     $[\![n_0]\!] \leftarrow n - sum([\![d]\!])$; // Count number of zeros.
5     $[\![c_0]\!] \leftarrow 0$; $[\![c_1]\!] \leftarrow 0$; // Keep counters for processed zeros and ones.
6     $[\![ord]\!]$; // Keep $n$-element shared order vector.
     // Put each element in the right position:
7     **foreach** $i \in 1 \ldots n$ **do**
8       $[\![c_0]\!] = [\![c_0]\!] + 1 - [\![d_i]\!]$
9       $[\![c_1]\!] = [\![c_1]\!] + [\![d_i]\!]$
       // Obliviously update order vector:
10      $[\![ord_i]\!] = (1 - [\![d_i]\!]) * [\![c_0]\!] + [\![d_i]\!] * ([\![n_0]\!] + [\![c_1]\!])$
11     **end**
12     $([\![x]\!], [\![ord]\!]) \leftarrow \mathsf{Shuffle}([\![x]\!], [\![ord]\!])$; // Shuffle two column database.
13     $ord \leftarrow \mathsf{Declassify}([\![ord]\!])$
14     Rearrange elements in $[\![x]\!]$ according to $ord$.
15 **end**
16 **return** $[\![x]\!]$

---

## 4   Optimization Methods

**Vectorization.** Data parallelization (SIMD operations) allows us to reduce the number of communication rounds and optimize the running time of algorithms for SMC. We designed the NaiveCompSort especially with vectorization in mind. Also, the quicksort design of [15] is vectorized by performing all comparisons at each depth of the quicksort algorithm at once.

Sorting network evaluation in Algorithm 2 can be vectorized by evaluating all CompEx functions of a given stage together. As mentioned previously, this is possible because of the assumption on the uniqueness of indices we made while describing the structure of the sorting network.

Similarly, we vectorize all secure operations in our counting sort algorithm design. We could apply counting sort on chunks of 2 or more bits and reduce the number of rounds for radix sort. However, this requires substituting the cheap oblivious choice subprotocol for a more expensive comparison protocol.

**Changing the Share Representation.** Both comparison-based sorting algorithms and sorting networks rely on the comparison operation. Comparison is a bit-level operation and works faster on bitwise shared data. Therefore, we can convert additively shared inputs into bitwise shared form and run the intended algorithm on the converted shares. The results can be converted back to additively shared form at the end of the algorithm.

Converting additive shares to bitwise shares requires a bit extraction protocol. However, for algorithms that perform many comparisons after one another, the benefits of many fast comparisons outweigh one costly conversion.

**Optimizations Specific to Sorting Networks.** Generating sorting networks takes a significant amount of time. As the sorting network structure is data-independent, we can store the sorting network after generation to re-use it later.

If we shuffle the inputs before sorting, we can optimize the CompFx function implementations by declassifying comparison results and performing the exchanges non-obliviously.

**Assuring Uniqueness.** As comparison-based sorting protocols like quicksort and NaiveCompSort declassify comparison results, they may leak the number of equal elements in the sortable vector. One possible solution is to convert the original data vector to a new vector by appending each element with enough bits to make it unique as described in [15]. Similarly, we can combine each element in data vector $[\![x]\!]$ with its secret shared index obtaining a vector of pairs $([\![x_i]\!], [\![i]\!])$. Obliviously shuffling this vector gives a random unknown permutation $\pi$:

$$([\![x_{\pi(1)}]\!], [\![\pi(1)]\!]), \ldots, ([\![x_{\pi(n)}]\!], [\![\pi(n)]\!]).$$

Additionally, we have to redefine a secure computation comparison operation that works on these pairs:

$$(x_1, y_1) > (x_2, y_2) \Leftrightarrow x_1 > x_2 \vee (x_1 = x_2 \wedge y_1 < y_2).$$

Note that both uniqueness transformations also make the shuffling and comparison-based sorting algorithms stable. This, for example, lets us sort matrices by two or more columns in sequence.

# 5 Sorting Secret-Shared Matrices

All described algorithms can be easily modified to support matrix sorting. Assume that our input data is in the form of a matrix $\mathcal{D}_{i,j}$ where $i = 1 \ldots n$ and $j = 1 \ldots m$. Let us also fix a column $k$ by which we want to sort the rows.

First, we obliviously shuffle the rows in the whole matrix[1]. Next, we extract the $k$-th column from the matrix and pass it to the sorting algorithm of our choice together with an $n$-element index vector with known values $(1, 2, \ldots, n)$.

The sorting protocol now swaps elements in the data vector and the index vector together. After sorting these two vectors, we declassify the output index vector and use it as a permutation to rearrange rows in the matrix. Declassifying the index vector shows how the elements were rearranged. However, as the input matrix was obliviously shuffled, this leaks no information on the data values or the original placement of rows in the initial matrix.

---

[1] Note that shuffling is already a part of comparison-based sorting protocols like quicksort and NaiveCompSort. However, this extra step has to be added for radix sort and sorting networks.

# 6   Experimental Evaluation of Oblivious Sorting Algorithms

## 6.1   Overview of Algorithm Implementations

Table 1 gives an overview of sorting algorithms implemented for this paper. We implemented all algorithms in the SECREC programming language [2] to run on the SHAREMIND secure multi-party computation system [1].

**Table 1.** An overview of oblivious sorting algorithms implemented for this paper

| Algorithm | Data-independence and leakage | References |
|---|---|---|
| Quicksort | Comparison results are declassified. Running time is data-dependent. May leak the number of equal elements. | [15] |
| Naive comparison sort (Algorithm 1) | Comparison results are declassified. Running time is data-independent. Leaks the number of equal elements. | this paper |
| Sorting network sort (Algorithm 2) | Fully data-independent | [25,17] |
| Radix sort (Algorithm 3) | Reordering decisions are declassified. Running time is data-independent. Does not leak the number of equal elements | this paper |

Our quicksort implementation is based on the work in [15] and personal communication with its authors. We implemented the algorithm as similarly as possible to achieve a fair comparison. The naive comparison sort and radix sort algorithms are implemented straightforwardly from Algorithms 1 and 3. In all cases the oblivious shuffling protocol is implemented as described in [19].

The sorting network implementation consists of two parts. We implemented sorting network generation using Florian Forster's `libsortnetwork` library[2]. SHAREMIND generates and caches sorting networks and encodes them for delivery to SECREC programs. The evaluation of the sorting network is implemented in SECREC. Our implementation generates Batcher's bitonic mergesort networks, as they were the fastest to generate and also have the smallest round count.

All algorithms are vectorized to optimize the running time using techniques described in Section 4. While this may lead to extensive memory usage, it allows us to demonstrate the performance of the algorithms.

We implemented vector sorting and matrix sorting for all algorithms, following the techniques described in Section 5. The performance results for matrix sorting are given in Appendix A.

---

[2] Available from `http://verplant.org/libsortnetwork/` in May, 2014.

## 6.2   Experimental Setup

The experiments were conducted using a SHAREMIND installation consisting of three servers connected by a 1 Gbps local area network. Each server was equipped with 48 GB of memory and a 12-core 3 GHz Intel processor.

We measured the running time and network usage using the profiling mechanism built into SHAREMIND. We marked code sections and SHAREMIND measured and logged the running time and network usage of each section invocation. We sampled the memory use reported for the SHAREMIND server process every one second and aligned this data with the running time data to find the peak memory usage for each experiment.

We ran each algorithm with bitwise-shared 64-bit unsigned integer data. We used worst-case data (all equal values) for each algorithm and additionally, used random data for the quicksort algorithm similarly to the experiments of [15]. We did not use data transformation described in Section 4 to guarantee uniqueness of elements.

## 6.3   Results and Analysis

**Theoretical complexities.** Before presenting the benchmark results, we give the secure computation complexities of all the implemented functions. We express the complexities in the number of subprotocol invocations. For example, $m\mathsf{Protocol}(n)$ means that the SMC protocol $\mathsf{Protocol}$ is invoked $m$ times with $n$ parallel elements for each invocation. Where necessary, oblivious addition operations are done on additively shared values. Hence, they do not require any network communication and are omitted from Table 2.

**Table 2.** Secure operation complexity of oblivious sorting algorithms. $n$ is the number of elements to sort and $k$ is number of digits, where applicable. For sorting networks, $m$ is the number of stages in the network and $\ell_i$ is the number of CompEx operations on the $i$-th stage.

| Algorithm | Secure operation complexity |
|---|---|
| Quicksort (average) | $\mathsf{Shuffle}(n) + \mathcal{O}(\log n)\mathsf{Comp}(\mathcal{O}(n)) + \mathcal{O}(\log n)\mathsf{Declassify}(\mathcal{O}(n))$ |
| Naive comparison sort | $\mathsf{Shuffle}(n) + \mathsf{Comp}(n(n-1)/2) + \mathsf{Declassify}(n(n-1)/2)$ |
| Sorting network | $\sum_{i=1}^{m} \mathsf{Comp}(\ell_i) + \mathsf{Mult}(4\ell_i)$ |
| Radix sort | $k \cdot (\mathsf{ShareConv}(n) + \mathsf{Mult}(n) + \mathsf{Shuffle}(n,2) + \mathsf{Declassify}(n))$ |

**Timing Profiles of Individual Sorting Algorithms.** Figure 1 shows the breakdown of the running times of oblivious sorting algorithms. We see that most of the time in naive sorting and quicksort is spent on comparisons. The time taken for sorting network evaluation begins with mostly comparisons and oblivious choice, but their importance is reduced as the time needed for generating the network increases. This is a strong motivator for the precomputing and caching of sorting networks. Radix sort has the most interesting profile, as it does not use comparisons. Instead, its most expensive part is oblivious choice.

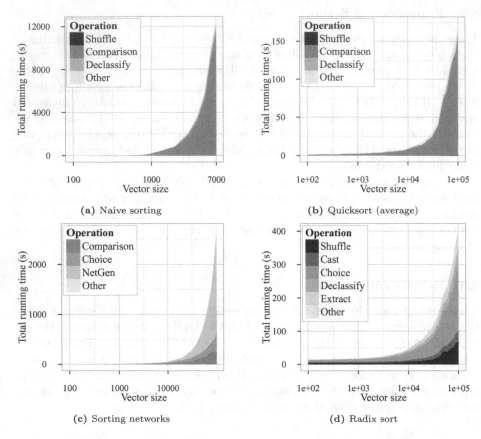

(a) Naive sorting

(b) Quicksort (average)

(c) Sorting networks

(d) Radix sort

**Fig. 1.** Running time breakdown for implemented sorting algorithms

**Comparison of different Sorting Algorithms.** We now present comparisons of all the algorithms. Note that the axes of the comparison figures are on a logarithmic scale. Figure 2 shows the comparison of the running time. Naive comparison sort is very fast on small inputs, but its high complexity makes it infeasible for larger inputs. Quicksort is the fastest of all algorithms, but only on its average case complexity where it achieves the same performance as reported in [15]. The worst-case complexity is significantly slower (depicted separately on the graph).

Radix sorting is not the most efficient on small inputs, but its use of cheap secure operations ensures that its running time does not grow as quickly as that of the other algorithms. The fact that our benchmarks show weaker results than those presented in [14] can be explained by two factors. First, we used 64-bit values instead of 32-bit ones and besides adding more network traffic this directly translates to twice as much communication rounds for radix sort. Secondly, our sorting algorithms were implemented in a high-level SECREC programming language that adds a level of indirection, whereas implementations in [14] use C++.

Sorting networks are efficient early, but the time needed to generate the network starts to grow significantly as the data size grows. If the sorting network structure is cached, sorting network evaluation is almost as fast as radix sorting. Moreover, from the described algorithms, sorting network is the only stable sorting algorithm (without making the elements longer) as it does not depend on oblivious shuffling routine.

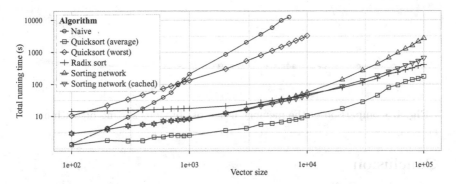

**Fig. 2.** Comparison of the running time of oblivious sorting algorithms

We see the network usage measurements in Figure 3. Naive sorting and quicksort on worst-case data require a lot of network communication. The other algorithms form a more efficient group, with quicksort on random data requiring the least communication and radix sort taking the second place.

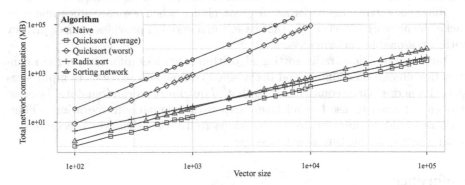

**Fig. 3.** Comparison of the network usage of oblivious sorting algorithms

Finally, Figure 4 shows the memory usage. The memory usage of the naive implementation grows squared in the size of data, making it infeasible for large inputs. The sorting network algorithm uses significant amounts of memory during the generation of the sorting network and reduced amounts after that. The memory requirements of oblivious radix and quicksort are low in comparison.

Memory usage of nearly all the algorithms can be reduced by breaking large vector operations to smaller pieces.

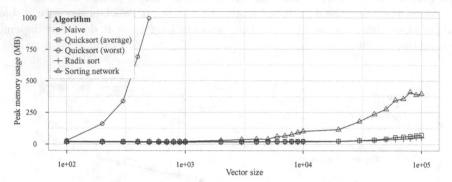

**Fig. 4.** Comparison of the memory usage of oblivious sorting algorithms

## 7    Conclusion

We describe four designs for oblivious versions of known sorting algorithms – naive comparison-based sort, quicksort, radix sort and sorting network based sort. The first three perform some declassifications to improve efficiency while the use of sorting networks results in a fully data-independent algorithm.

Our performance analysis shows that even though naive comparison-based sorting is fast on small inputs, its $\mathcal{O}(n^2)$ complexity makes it slow for practical use. While the oblivious version of quicksort is very efficient on distinct data, it requires preprocessing and more resources in the case of non-unique elements.

Oblivious sorting networks are a great choice when we can precompute or cache the network structure. In that case, the algorithm provides perfect privacy with a reasonable performance.

Our novel oblivious radix sorting algorithm leaks less information than constructions based on shuffling and declassified comparison results. As input sizes grow, its performance comes closer to that of quicksort on random data, because it does not need to use the relatively expensive comparison operations. Thus, authors would recommend to use oblivious radix sort whenever precomputing sorting network structure is not possible.

## References

1. Bogdanov, D.: Sharemind: programmable secure computations with practical applications. PhD thesis, University of Tartu (2013)
2. Bogdanov, D., Laud, P., Randmets, J.: Domain-Polymorphic Programming of Privacy-Preserving Applications. In: Proc. of PETShop 2013. ACM Digital Library, pp. 23–26. ACM (2013)
3. Bogdanov, D., Laur, S., Talviste, R.: Oblivious Sorting of Secret-Shared Data. Technical Report T-4-19, Cybernetica (2013), http://research.cyber.ee/

4. Bogdanov, D., Niitsoo, M., Toft, T., Willemson, J.: High-performance secure multi-party computation for data mining applications. International Journal of Information Security 11(6), 403–418 (2012)
5. Burkhart, M., Strasser, M., Many, D., Dimitropoulos, X.: SEPIA: privacy-preserving aggregation of multi-domain network events and statistics. In: Proc. of USENIX Conference on Security. USENIX Association (2010)
6. Canetti, R.: Universally composable security: A new paradigm for cryptographic protocols. In: Proc. of FOCS 2001, pp. 136–145. IEEE Computer Society (2001)
7. Cormen, T.H., Leiserson, C.E., Rivest, R.L., Stein, C.: Counting Sort. In: Introduction to Algorithms, ch. 8.2, 2nd edn., pp. 168–170. MIT Press, McGraw-Hill (2001)
8. Damgård, I., Pastro, V., Smart, N., Zakarias, S.: Multiparty computation from somewhat homomorphic encryption. In: Safavi-Naini, R., Canetti, R. (eds.) CRYPTO 2012. LNCS, vol. 7417, pp. 643–662. Springer, Heidelberg (2012)
9. Dwork, C.: Differential privacy. In: Bugliesi, M., Preneel, B., Sassone, V., Wegener, I. (eds.) ICALP 2006. LNCS, vol. 4052, pp. 1–12. Springer, Heidelberg (2006)
10. Edmonds, J.: Counting Sort (a Stable Sort). In: How to Think about Algorithms, ch. 5.2, pp. 72–75. Cambridge University Press (2008)
11. Evfimievski, A.V., Srikant, R., Agrawal, R., Gehrke, J.: Privacy preserving mining of association rules. In: Proc. of KDD 2002, pp. 217–228 (2002)
12. Gentry, C.: Fully homomorphic encryption using ideal lattices. In: Proc. of STOC 2009, pp. 169–178. ACM (2009)
13. Goethals, B., Laur, S., Lipmaa, H., Mielikäinen, T.: On private scalar product computation for privacy-preserving data mining. In: Park, C., Chee, S. (eds.) ICISC 2004. LNCS, vol. 3506, pp. 104–120. Springer, Heidelberg (2005)
14. Hamada, K., Ikarashi, D., Chida, K., Takahashi, K.: Oblivious radix sort: An efficient sorting algorithm for practical secure multi-party computation. Cryptology ePrint Archive, Report 2014/121 (2014), http://eprint.iacr.org/
15. Hamada, K., Kikuchi, R., Ikarashi, D., Chida, K., Takahashi, K.: Practically Efficient Multi-party Sorting Protocols from Comparison Sort Algorithms. In: Kwon, T., Lee, M.-K., Kwon, D. (eds.) ICISC 2012. LNCS, vol. 7839, pp. 202–216. Springer, Heidelberg (2013)
16. Hollerith, H.: US395781 (A) - ART OF COMPILING STATISTICS. European Patent Office (1889), http://worldwide.espacenet.com/publicationDetails/biblio?CC=US&NR=395781
17. Jónsson, K.V., Kreitz, G., Uddin, M.: Secure Multi-Party Sorting and Applications. Cryptology ePrint Archive, Report 2011/122 (2011), http://eprint.iacr.org/
18. Knuth, D.E.: The art of computer programming, 2nd edn. Sorting and searching, vol. 3. Addison Wesley Longman Publishing Co., Inc., USA (1998)
19. Laur, S., Willemson, J., Zhang, B.: Round-Efficient Oblivious Database Manipulation. In: Lai, X., Zhou, J., Li, H. (eds.) ISC 2011. LNCS, vol. 7001, pp. 262–277. Springer, Heidelberg (2011)
20. Machanavajjhala, A., Kifer, D., Gehrke, J., Venkitasubramaniam, M.: L-diversity: Privacy beyond k-anonymity. ACM Trans. Knowl. Discov. Data 1(1), 3 (2007)
21. Narayanan, A., Shmatikov, V.: Robust de-anonymization of large sparse datasets. In: Proc. of IEEE S&P 2008, pp. 111–125 (2008)
22. Paillier, P.: Public-key cryptosystems based on composite degree residuosity classes. In: Stern, J. (ed.) EUROCRYPT 1999. LNCS, vol. 1592, pp. 223–238. Springer, Heidelberg (1999)
23. Shamir, A.: How to share a secret. Comm. of the ACM 22, 612–613 (1979)

24. Sweeney, L.: k-anonymity: a model for protecting privacy. Int. J. Uncertain. Fuzziness Knowl.-Based Syst. 10(5), 557–570 (2002)
25. Wang, G., Luo, T., Goodrich, M.T., Du, W., Zhu, Z.: Bureaucratic protocols for secure two-party sorting, selection, and permuting. In: Proc. of ASIACCS 2010, pp. 226–237. ACM (2010)
26. Zhang, B.: Generic Constant-Round Oblivious Sorting Algorithm for MPC. In: Boyen, X., Chen, X. (eds.) ProvSec 2011. LNCS, vol. 6980, pp. 240–256. Springer, Heidelberg (2011)

## A     Performance Analysis of Matrix Sorting

We benchmarked matrix sorting on $n \times 10$-element matrices by sorting them based on the first column. For sorting networks, we used an alternative version of CompEx descibed in Appendix B.

Figure 5 shows that even though there are ten times more data, the running time is not increased tenfold. This is explained by the vectorization of the matrix sorting implementations. There is one significant change, as sorting networks no longer benefit as heavily from caching the network structure, the oblivious exchanges for the full columns take up quite some time.

While sorting ten times as much data does not necessarily take that much time, it still takes more resources, as can be seen from Figures 6 and 7. Otherwise, the relations between different implementations remain the same.

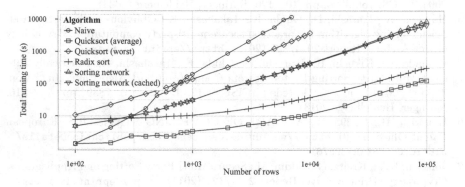

**Fig. 5.** Running time of oblivious sorting algorithms on matrices

For sorting networks, we also implemented sorting by two and three different columns. This involves more comparisons and logic operations to combine the comparison results. According to the results in Figure 8, the number of columns by which to sort does not make a significant difference in the running time.

## B     Compare-and-Exchange on Vectors

The general approach of using oblivious shuffle and permuting index vector for sorting matrices as described in Section 5 works for all mentioned algorithms.

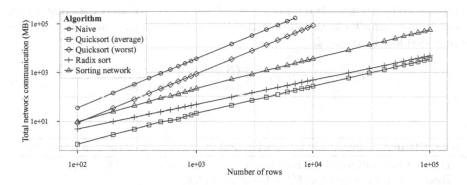

**Fig. 6.** Network usage of oblivious sorting algorithms on matrices

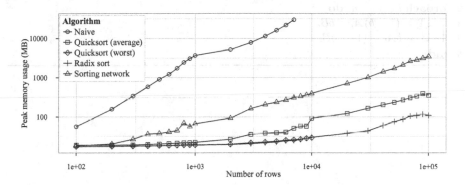

**Fig. 7.** Memory usage of oblivious sorting algorithms on matrices

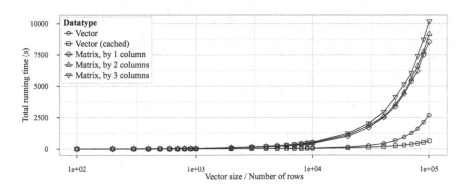

**Fig. 8.** Sorting networks running time on vector and matrix inputs. For matrix inputs, sorting is performed by one, two and three columns.

However, alternatively, for sorting networks we can redefine the CompEx operation to work on the rows of the matrix. We need a CompEx function that compares and exchanges two input arrays $\mathcal{A}$ and $\mathcal{B}$ according to the comparison result from column $k$ like the one described in Equation (2). A suitable algorithm is provided in Algorithm 4.

$$\mathsf{CompEx}(\mathcal{A}, \mathcal{B}, k) = \begin{cases} (\mathcal{B}, \mathcal{A}), & \text{if } \mathcal{A}_k > \mathcal{B}_k \\ (\mathcal{A}, \mathcal{B}), & \text{otherwise.} \end{cases} \tag{2}$$

---

**Algorithm 4.** Obliviously comparing and exchanging two rows in a matrix

---

**Data**: Two input arrays $\mathcal{A}, \mathcal{B}$ of length $m$, column index $k \in \{1 \ldots m\}$.
**Result**: Pair of arrays $(\mathcal{A}', \mathcal{B}') = \mathsf{CompEx}(\mathcal{A}, \mathcal{B}, k)$.

1 $b \leftarrow \begin{cases} 1, \text{ if } \mathcal{A}_k > \mathcal{B}_k \\ 0, \text{ otherwise.} \end{cases}$

2 **foreach** $i \in 1 \ldots m$ **do**

3 $\quad \mathcal{A}'_i = (1 - b)\mathcal{A}_i + b\mathcal{B}_i$

4 $\quad \mathcal{B}'_i = b\mathcal{A}_i + (1 - b)\mathcal{B}_i$

5 **end**

---

# Cloud, Big Data
# and Virtualization Security

# Security of OS-Level Virtualization Technologies

Elena Reshetova[1], Janne Karhunen[2], Thomas Nyman[3], and N. Asokan[4]

[1] Intel OTC, Finland
[2] Ericsson, Finland
[3] University of Helsinki, Finland
[4] Aalto University and University of Helsinki, Finland

**Abstract.** The need for flexible, low-overhead virtualization is evident on many fronts ranging from high-density cloud servers to mobile devices. During the past decade *OS-level virtualization* has emerged as a new, efficient approach for virtualization, with implementations in multiple different Unix-based systems. Despite its popularity, there has been no systematic study of OS-level virtualization from the point of view of security. In this paper, we conduct a comparative study of several OS-level virtualization systems, discuss their security and identify some gaps in current solutions.

## 1 Introduction

During the past couple of decades the use of different virtualization technologies has been on a steady rise. Since IBM CP-40 [19], the first virtual machine prototype in 1966, many different types of virtualization and their uses have been actively explored both by the research community and by the industry. A relatively recent approach, which is becoming increasingly popular due to its light-weight nature, is *Operating System-Level Virtualization*, where a number of distinct user space instances, often referred to as *containers*, are run on top of a shared operating system kernel. A fundamental difference between OS-level virtualization and more established competitors, such as Xen hypervisor [25], VMWare [49] and Linux *Kernel Virtual Machine* [30] (KVM), is that in OS-level virtualization, the virtualized artifacts are global kernel resources, as opposed to hardware. This allows multiple virtual environments to share a common host kernel and utilize underlying OS interfaces. As a result, OS-level virtualization incurs less CPU, memory and networking overhead, which is important not only for *High Performance Computing* (HPC), such as dense cloud configurations, but also for resource constrained environments such as mobile and embedded devices. The main disadvantage of OS-level virtualization is that each container can only contain a system of the same type as the host environment, e.g. Linux guests on a Linux host.

An important factor to take into account in the evaluation of the effectiveness of any virtualization technology is the level of *isolation* it provides. In the context of OS-level virtualization isolation can be defined as separation between containers, as well as the separation between containers and the host. In order

K. Bernsmed and S. Fischer-Hübner (Eds.): NordSec 2014, LNCS 8788, pp. 77–93, 2014.
DOI: 10.1007/978-3-319-11599-3_5, © Springer International Publishing Switzerland 2014

to systematically compare the level of isolation provided by different OS-level virtualization solutions, one first needs to establish a common system model.

The goal of this study is to propose a generic model for a typical OS-level virtualization setup, identify its security requirements, and compare a selection of OS-level virtualization solutions with respect to this model. While other technologies as HW supported secure storage, various encryption primitives and specific CPU/memory features can enhance the security of OS-level virtualization solutions, they are left out of the scope of this paper and present the potential future work. To the best of our knowledge this is the first study of this kind that focuses on the security aspects of OS-level virtualization technologies. We base our analysis on information collected from the documentation and/or wherever possible the source code of the respective systems. As a result of this comparison section 6 identifies a number of gaps in the current implementation of Linux OS-level virtualization solutions. The full version of this study can be found in the technical report [23].

## 2   System Model

In Figure 1(a) we present a system model for a typical container setup. There are a number of containers $C_1 \ldots C_n$ that run on a single physical host machine. The OS kernel is shared among all the containers, but the extent of shared host user space depends on a concrete setup (see Table 1):

**Full OS installation & management** corresponds to the most common case when the host user space layer comprises a complete OS installation with the container management layer on top. In this case some host resources may be shared between the host and one or more containers via bind-mounts [26] or overlay filesystems [20]. Each container can be one of two types:

- *Application containers* have a single application or service instance running inside. They are most commonly used as sandboxes to contain damage in case an application or a service misbehaves.
- *System containers* have an entire OS user space installation and are commonly used for server consolidation, where a set of distinct physical servers are substituted with a single physical server running a number of distinct virtual environments.

**Lightweight management** corresponds to the case where the host user space layer consists of merely a light-weight management layer used to initialize and run containers. This setup can be argued to be more secure, as it exhibits a reduced attack surface compared to a complete underlying host system. Again, each container can be one of two types:

- *Direct application/service setup* refers to the case when only a single application or service is installed in the container. It is more suitable for application isolation scenarios in which, for instance, a banking application is run in a separate container isolated from the rest of a less trusted OS running in another container.

– *Direct OS setup* refers to the case when a container runs an entire OS user space installation. It can provide an end-user the appearance of simultaneously running multiple OS instances, and is therefore well suited for the multi-OS experience that allows end-users the ability to use applications and services from different OS variants on the same device.

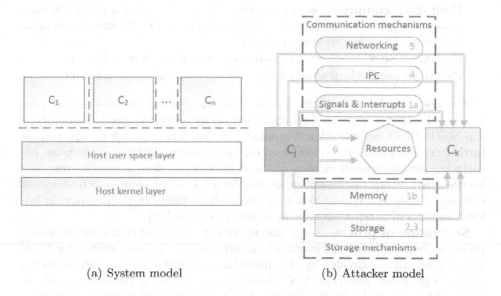

(a) System model                    (b) Attacker model

**Fig. 1.** OS-level virtualization

**Table 1.** Types of OS virtualization setups

| Host user space layer | Container | |
|---|---|---|
| | *Application/Service* | *Full OS installation* |
| *Full OS installation & management* | Application container | System container |
| *Lightweight management* | Direct Application/Service setup | Direct OS setup |

The system model described above intentionally omits cases where containers $C_1 \ldots C_n$ are not independent, but arranged in a hierarchical structure. While some systems, such as FreeBSD jails [29], allow such setups, they are rarely used in practice and are therefore left beyond the scope of this paper.

# 3  Attacker Model and Security Requirements

The attacker is assumed to have full control over a certain subset $\bar{C}$ of containers. The remaining set $C$ is assumed to be in the control of legitimate users. The goals of the attacker can be classified as follows:

- **Container compromise:** compromise $C_k \in C$ by means of illegitimate data access, *Man-in-the-Middle* (MitM) attacks or by affecting the control flow of instructions executed in $C_k \in C$.
- **Denial of Service:** disturb normal operation of the host or $C_k \in C$.
- **Privilege escalation:** obtain a privilege not originally granted to a $C_j \in \bar{C}$.

The above goals can be achieved via different types of attacks that can be roughly classified into distinct groups based on the interfaces available in a typical Single UNIX Specification compliant OS [46]. These attack groups can be further arranged into two classes based on the type of underlying mechanism: *attacks via communication mechanisms* and *attacks via storage mechanisms* (see Figure 1(b)). From this classification we derive a set of security requirements that each OS-level virtualization solution needs to fulfill. In the description below, numbers in parenthesis refer to arrows in Figure 1(b).

**Separation of processes** is a fundamental requirement that aims to isolate processes running in distinct containers to prevent $C_j \in \bar{C}$ from influencing $C_k \in C$ using interfaces provided by the operating system for process management, such as signals and interrupts (1a). In addition, it might be possible to directly access the memory of a process running in $C_k \in C$ by using special system calls, e.g. the *ptrace()* system call allows a debugger process to attach and monitor the memory of a debugged process (1b).

**Filesystem isolation** is required in order to prevent illegitimate access to filesystem objects belonging to $C_k \in C$ or the host (2).

**Device isolation** should protect device drivers shared between different containers and a host. Such drivers present another significant attack vector because they expose interfaces (3) to code running into the kernel space, which may be abused to gain illegitimate data access, escalate privileges or mount other attacks.

**IPC isolation** is needed in order to prevent $C_j \in \bar{C}$ from accessing or modifying data belonging to $C_k \in C$ being transmitted over different IPC channels (4). Such channels include traditional System V IPC primitives, such as semaphores, shared memory and message queues as well as POSIX message queues.

**Network isolation** aims to prevent attacks by $C_j \in \bar{C}$ via available network interfaces (5). In particular, an attacker can attempt to eavesdrop on or modify network traffic of the host or $C_j \in \bar{C}$, perform MitM attacks etc.

**Resource management** provides a way to limit the amount of resources available to each container depending on the system load. This is needed in order to prevent an attacker from exhausting physical resources available on a device, such as disk space or disk I/O limits, CPU cycles, network bandwidth and memory (6).

# 4    Comparison

We begin with a brief historical overview of the development OS-level virtualization solutions and then proceed to choose some state-of-the-art examples and compare them with respect to each of the security requirements described in the previous section.

## 4.1    Evolution of OS-Level Virtualization

The history of OS-level virtualization can be traced back to the usage of the *chroot()* system call in the Unix systems. While its primary goal has been to limit visibility of a filesystem root for a set of processes, *chroot()* has never been intended as a security mechanism. Nevertheless, it has often been used as a mechanism to limit filesystem access. Such usage is often referred to as *chroot() jails*. However since the *chroot()* environment is only limited to a filesystem and can be escaped by the privileged user [7], it cannot be used as it is in order to build a full OS-level virtualization solution.

The need for a more robust and complete jail implementation in order to have separate virtual compartments on a single host has motivated the emergence of the **FreeBSD Jails** project [29] in 2000. The same need in Linux led to the **Linux-VServer** project [9] with its first release in 2003. In Linux-VServer, separate virtual environments are referred to as Virtual Private Servers (VPSs). **Solaris Zones/Containers** project [36] was started in 2004 in order to provide a commercial OS-level virtualization solution. The **OpenVZ** project [12], another open source OS-level virtualization solution for Linux, began in 2005. OpenVZ uses the term Virtual Environments (VEs) [48] to refer to the containers. Both the Linux-VServer and OpenVZ projects provide their own set of kernel patches that in turn create additional usage difficulties. Notably, the OpenVZ project was the first one to implement the *Checkpoint and Restart* (CR) functionality for VEs [31]. CR allows processes to be moved between different physical or virtual environments. This can be useful for cluster load-balancing or in high-availability environments, as well as an utility for software development and testing on different UNIX platforms. The **Linux Containers (LxC)** project [10] is the only currently available OS-level virtualization solution for Linux that consists only of a set of user space tools. This is possible because LxC utilizes only those virtualization features already integrated into the upstream Linux kernel [1]. Another differentiating feature of LxC is the ability to use Linux Security Modules (LSMs) [42] to harden a container setup. Apparmor [1] and SELinux [39] profiles are officially supported, but in principle any LSM such as Smack [15] could be used. The **Cells** architecture [22] and the corresponding commercial Cellrox solution [2] are the only open source OS-level virtualization solutions developed specifically for smartphones. The primary design goal behind Cells is to support the *Bring Your Own Device* (BYOD) policy [38] on the Android platform.

---

[1] The term *upstream Linux kernel* refers to the Linux kernel source code tree maintained at *kernel.org*. This is the official Linux kernel source that contains all the released and upcoming features.

**Table 2.** Comparison of containerization approaches

|        | container structure | separate namespaces |
|--------|---------------------|---------------------|
| *pros* | simplicity, convenience | flexibility, incremental introduction of containerization |
| *cons* | possible information duplication, less flexibility | increased complexity |
| *used by* | FreeBSD, SolarisZones, Linux-VServer, OpenVZ | Linux-VServer, OpenVZ, LxC, Cells |

BYOD allows one physical device to be used simultaneously for personal and business needs resulting in a need of rigid separation between these two environments in order to guarantee user privacy while conforming to enterprise policies. Similar to LxC, Cells utilizes upstream kernel features to isolate virtual phones. However, since Android has some non-standard Linux extensions, the developers of Cells had to implement a number of additional isolation mechanisms.

Following [17], we define the notion of a *kernel namespace* as a set of identifiers representing a class of global kernel resources, such as process and user ids, IPC objects or filesystem mounts. The OS-level virtualization in the upstream Linux kernel is based on the usage of different kernel namespaces. The subsections below introduce the relevant namespaces and compare selected OS-level virtualization solutions, highlighted in bold in the previous paragraph, based on the security requirements listed in section 3.

## 4.2   Separation of Processes

The primary isolation mechanism required from any OS-level virtualization solution is that it is able to distinguish processes running in different containers from those running on the host, limit cross-container process visibility and to prevent memory and signaling-level attacks described in the section 3. The simplest solution to this problem is to embed a container identifier $C_i$ into the process data structure and to check the scope and the permissions of all syscall invocations.

FreeBSD Jails, Solaris Zones, OpenVZ and Linux-VServer implementations follow this approach by linking a structure describing the container to the process data structure. However, unlike FreeBSD and Solaris, the data structures describing OpenVZ and Linux-VServer containers are not used to achieve process separation. They only store related container data such as resource limits and capabilities. Instead, OpenVZ, Linux-VServer, LxC and Cells use *process id (pid) namespaces* that are part of the mainline Linux kernel. A pid namespace is a mechanism to group processes in order to control their ability to see (for example via *proc* pseudo-filesystem) and interact (for example by sending signals) with one another. The pid namespaces also provide pid virtualization: two processes in different pid namespaces may have the same pid.

Having a separate structure describing a container and storing a pointer to it in the process task structure is a convenient way to have all the relevant information concerning the container in one place. However, the upstream Linux kernel has followed a different approach of grouping different kernel resources into separate namespaces and using these namespaces to build containers. This approach incurs additional complexity, but adds the flexibility to choose a combination of namespaces that best fits the desired use case. It also allows gradual introduction of namespaces to an existing system, like the upstream Linux kernel, which also helps in testing and verification of the implementation [17]. Furthermore, it avoids information duplication when both the process and the container structures have similar information. The pros and cons of these two approaches are summarized in Table 2.

In addition to the ability to isolate and virtualize process ids, the upstream Linux kernel also allows virtualization and isolation of the user and group identifiers with the help of *user namespaces*. Typically the root user has all the privileges to perform various system administration tasks and is able to override all access control restrictions. However, it is not desired that a root user running inside a container would be given the privileges of the host root user. Therefore, the Linux user namespace implementation interprets a given Linux capability as authorizing an action within that namespace: for example, the *CAP_SYS_BOOT* capability inside a container grants the authority to reboot that container and not the host. Moreover, many capabilities such as *CAP_SYS_MODULE* cannot be safely granted for container in any meaningful manner. When a process attempts to perform an action guarded by such capability, the kernel always checks if the process possesses this capability in the host user namespace. All Linux OS-level virtualization solutions support the option of starting a new user namespace for each container, but all the related configuration such as mapping the user identifiers between the host and the container must be done manually.

### 4.3 Filesystem Isolation

The filesystem is one of the most important OS interfaces that allows processes to store and share data as well as to interact with one another. In order to prevent filesystem-based attacks described in section 3, it should be possible to isolate the filesystem between containers and to minimize the sharing of the data. The amount of sharing needed between the host and each container depends on the usage scenario. In the case of application isolation, it is not worthwhile to completely duplicate the OS setup inside a container and therefore some parts of the filesystem, such as common libraries, need to be securely shared with the host. On the other hand in the case of server consolidation, quite often it is best to completely separate the filesystems and create container filesystems from scratch.

All Linux-based OS virtualization solutions utilize a *mount namespace* that allows separation of mounts between the containers and the host. The design of upstream Linux mount namespaces[17] has been influenced by private namespaces [35] in Plan 9 from Bell Labs [34]. Namespaces in Plan 9 are file-orientated, and the principal purpose is to facilitate the customization of the environment visible to users and processes. Since all Linux based systems create each container within a new mount namespace, all the internal mount events are only effective inside the given container. However, it is important to underline that the mount namespace by itself is not a security measure. Running a container in a separate mount namespace does not give any additional guarantees concerning the data isolation between the containers since containers inherit the view of filesystem mounts from their parent and thus are able to access all parts of the filesystem similarly.

A typical approach for process filesystem access containment is by using the *chroot()* system call where process is bound within a subtree of the filesystem hierarchy. If desired, resources may be shared with the host by mounting them within the subtree visible inside the container. Since the *chroot()* system call [8] only affects pathname resolution, privileged processes (i.e. processes with the *CAP_SYS_CHROOT* privilege) can escape the chroot jail. This can be done for example by changing the root directory again via *chroot()* to a subdirectory relative to their current working directory. Of the virtualization solutions under comparison, only Cells relies on *chroot()* alone. Some systems, such as Linux-VServer utilize a *Secure chroot barrier* [9] to prevent processes in a VPS from escaping the modified environment.

Another approach, utilized by for instance LxC, is to not only modify the root directory for processes in a container, but modify the *root filesystem* as well. This can be achieved with the Linux specific *pivot_root()* system call [8], which is typically used during boot to change from a temporary root filesystem (e.g. an initrd) to the actual root filesystem. As its name suggests, the *pivot_root()* system call moves the mountpoint of the old root filesystem to a directory under the new root filesystem, and puts the new root filesystem at its place. When done inside a mount namespace, the old root filesystem can be unmounted, thus rendering the host root filesystem inaccessible for processes inside the container, without affecting processes belonging to the root mount namespace on the host system. At the time of writing, the implementation of *pivot_root()* also changes the root directory and current working directory of the process to the mountpoint of the new root filesystem if they point to the old root directory. OpenVZ relies on this behavior and uses the *pivot_root()* system call alone. However, as the behavior with regards to the current root directory and the current working directory remains unspecified, proper usage dictates that the caller of *pivot_root()* must ensure that processes with root directory or current working directory at the old root operate correctly regardless of the behavior of *pivot_root()*. To ensure this, LxC changes the root directory and current working directory to the mountpoint of the new root before invoking *pivot_root()*.

FreeBSD and Solaris also provide a sandbox-like environment for each jail/zone using similar *chroot()*-like calls that are claimed to avoid above mentioned security vulnerabilities [29], [36]. Mounting and unmounting of filesystems is prohibited by default for a process running inside a jail unless different *allow.mount.** options are specified.

A separate user namespace per container can further strengthen the filesystem isolation by mapping the user and group ids to a less privileged range of host uids and groups. Together with a mount namespace and a *pivot_root* environment it strengthens protection against filesystem-based attacks described in 3.

## 4.4  Device Isolation

In Unix, device nodes are special files that provide an interface to the host device drivers. In classical Unix configurations, the device nodes are separated from the rest of the filesystem and their inodes are placed in the */dev* directory. In the case of Linux, this task is usually performed by the udevd daemon process issuing the *mknod* system call upon receiving the event from the kernel. Device nodes are security-sensitive since an improperly exposed or shared device inside a container can lead to a number of easy attacks (see section 3). In the simplest example, if a container has an access to */dev/kmem* and */dev/mem* nodes, it is able to read and write all the memory of the host. Thus, in order to isolate containers from one another it is important to prevent containers from creating new device nodes and to make sure that containers are only allowed to access a "safe" set of devices listed below:

1. **Purely virtual devices**, such as pseudo-terminals and virtual network interfaces. The security guarantee comes from the fact that these devices are explicitly created for each container and not shared.
2. **Stateless devices**, such as *random*, *null* and others. Sharing these devices among all containers and the host is safe because they are stateless.
3. **User namespace-aware devices**. If a device supports verifying process capabilities in the corresponding user namespace, then it is safe to expose such device to a container, because the specified limitations will be enforced. The current 3.14-rc2 upstream kernel does not have any physical devices supporting this feature, but they are expected to appear in the future.

All compared systems allow the system administrator to define a unique set of device nodes for each container and by default create only a small set of stateless and virtual devices. In Linux, creation of new device nodes within containers can be controlled by limiting access to the *CAP_SYS_MKNOD* Linux capability and by ensuring that all mountpoints inside containers have the *nodev* flag set.

The biggest difference of the Cells implementation is the addition of a "*device namespace*" that attempts to make the Linux input/output devices namespace-aware. Cells assumes the host to have a single set of input/output devices and multiplexes access to the physical host device via virtual devices created in each container. One virtual device at a time is allowed to access physical devices, based on whether an application from a given container is "on the foreground" (ie. visible on the screen) or not. Security-wise such an exclusive-access solution is comparable to the "purely virtual" devices category mentioned above and can be considered safe.

As mentioned above, Linux device drivers controlling physical devices are currently not namespace-aware and thus cannot be securely used inside containers. Quite commonly these devices assume only one controlling master host and require privileges that are hard to grant for a unprivileged container securely (unless the device is used exclusively by a single container). In other words, namespace support inside the device drivers would require extensive modifications to the existing driver code base.

## 4.5  IPC Isolation

In order to achieve IPC isolation between containers, processes must be restricted to communicate via certain IPC primitives only within their own container. If the filesystem isolation is done correctly (see section 4.3), then filesystem-based IPC mechanisms (such as UNIX domain sockets and named pipes) are automatically isolated because the processes are not able to access filesystem paths outside of their own container. However, the isolation of the rest of the IPC objects (such as System V IPC objects and POSIX message queues) requires additional mechanisms. In Linux these IPC objects are isolated with the help of the *IPC namespaces* that allow the creation of a completely disjoint set of IPC objects. Linux-VServer, OpenVZ, LxC and Cells all spawn a new IPC namespace for each container in order to achieve the required isolation.

In addition to using IPC namespaces, Cells also has to implement namespace support for the Binder system since it is the primary IPC mechanism on the Android OS. The solution [11] includes having a separate Context Manager for each IPC namespace that is able to resolve Binder addresses only in that namespace and therefore provide isolation of Binder addresses between different containers.

Solaris Zones follow a different approach to isolate IPC objects that are not filesystem path-based. A zone ID is attached to each object based on the zone ID of the process that creates it, and processes are not able to access objects from other zones. An exception is made only for an administrator in the global zone that can access and manage all the objects. FreeBSD simply blocks SysV IPC object-related system calls if such calls are issued from within a jail. The *allow.sysvipc* option allows SysV IPC mechanisms for jailed processes but lacks any isolation between jails.

## 4.6  Network Isolation

The main goal of network isolation is to prevent network-based attacks described in section 3. Moreover, in order to be able to support applications that might contend for the same type of network resource (such as binding to the same network port), it also needs to provide a virtualized view of the network stack.

Network isolation methods differ in terms of the OSI layer of the TCP/IP stack where the isolation is implemented (see Table 3 for a comparison between these implementations). FreeBSD and Linux-VServer implement network isolation on Layer 3 with the help of bind filtering. They restrict a *bind()* call made from within a container to a set of specified IP addresses and therefore processes are only allowed to send and receive packets to/from these addresses. The benefit of such an approach is the small amount of code that needs to be modified in

**Table 3.** Comparison of network isolation

|  | Layer 3 bind filtering | Layer 3 VNI | Layer 2 VNI |
|---|---|---|---|
| *traffic shaping and policing* | no | yes | yes |
| *separate routing and filtering tables* | no | no | yes |
| *used by* | FreeBSD Jails, Linux-VServer | Solaris Zones, OpenVZ | Solaris Zones, OpenVZ, LxC, Cells |

the network implementation and a minimal performance overhead. However, the downside is that a lot of the standard networking functionality is not accessible for a process inside a container such as obtaining an address from the Dynamic Host configuration Protocol (DHCP), acting as a DHCP server or the usage of routing tables.

Another approach, supported by Solaris Zones and OpenVZ, provides a Layer 3 virtualized network interface (VNI) for each container. Compared to bind filtering this implementation is more flexible since it allows the configuration of different traffic control settings, such as traffic shaping and policing, from within the container. The Layer 3 implementation provided by OpenVZ is called *venet*, while Solaris uses the term *shared-IP zone*.

The third approach includes providing a Layer 2 virtualized network interface for each container with a valid Link layer address. This gives containers the ability to use many features that are not supported by the previous two solutions, such as DHCP autoconfiguration, separate routing information and filtering rules. This approach can also support a broader set of network configurations. However, the primary downsides include a performance penalty and the inability to control the container networking setup from the host. The latter can be important for the server consolidation case if the host administrator needs to be in the control of the overall network configuration. OpenVZ, Solaris, LxC and Cells all support the creation of the Layer 2 virtualized interfaces. On Linux platforms this feature is called virtual Ethernet (*veth*). On Solaris a similar configuration is named *exclusive-IP zone*.

The Linux Layer 2 network isolation is based on the concept of a *network namespace* that allows the creation of a number of networking stacks that appear to be completely independent. The simplest networking configuration for a container running in a separate network namespace includes a pair of virtually linked Ethernet (*veth*) interfaces and assigning one of them to the target namespace while keeping the other one in the host namespace. After the virtual link is established, interfaces can be configured and brought up [6].

Linux provides multiple ways for connecting containers to physical networks. One option is connecting the *veth* interface and the host physical interface by using a virtual network bridge device. Another option is to utilize routing tables to forward the traffic between virtual and physical interfaces. When a virtual

Table 4. Comparison of Linux resource management mechanisms

|  | rlimits | cgroups |
|---|---|---|
| scope | per process, inheritable | per process group, inheritable |
| managed resources | memory(limited), CPU(limited), filesystem, number of threads | memory, CPU, block I/O, devices, traffic controller |
| action when limit is reached | resource request denial and process termination | resource request denial, possibility to have a custom action |
| used by | Linux-VServer, Cells | OpenVZ, LxC, Linux-VServer, Cells |

bridge device is used, all container and host interfaces are attached to the same link layer bridge and thus receive all link layer traffic on the bridge. However, in the case of route configuration, containers are not able to communicate with each other unless a network route is explicitly provided. Also in the latter case, container addresses are not visible to outsiders like in bridged mode. Another way of providing network connectivity for containers is to use the MACVLAN interface [10] that allows each container to have its own separate link layer address. MACVLAN can be set to operate in a number of modes. In a private mode containers cannot communicate with each other or the host making it the strictest isolation setup. The bridge mode allows containers to communicate with one another, but not with the host. The Virtual Ethernet Port Aggregator (VEPA) mode by default isolates containers from one another, but leaves the possibility to have an upstream switch that can be configured to forward packets back to the corresponding interface. Currently LxC is the only solution that can support all the MACVLAN modes.

### 4.7 Resource Limiting

A good virtualization solution needs to provide support for limiting the amount of primary physical resources allocated to each container in order to prevent containers from carrying out denial of service attacks described in section 3.

Since the 9.0 release FreeBSD utilizes Hierarchical Resource Limits (RCTL) to provide resource limitation for users, processes or jails [13]. RCTL supports defining an action in case a specified limit is reached: deny new resource allocation, log a warning, send a signal (for example SIGHUP or SIGKILL) to a process that exceeded the limit or to send a notification to the device state change daemon.

Solaris implements resource management for zones using a number of techniques that can be either applied to a whole zone or to a specific process inside a zone. Resource partitioning, called resource pools, allows defining a set of resources, such as a physical processor set, to be exclusively used by a zone. A dynamic resource pool allows to adjusting the pool allocations based on the system load. Resource capping is able to limit the amount of the physical memory used by a zone.

The traditional way of managing resources on BSD-derived systems is the *rlimits* mechanism that allows specifying soft and hard limits for system resources for each process. Cells and Linux-VServer utilize *rlimits* to do resource management for containers. However, the main problem of rlimits is that it does not allow specifying limits for a set of processes or to define an action when a limit is reached. Also the CPU and memory controls are very limited and do not allow specifying the relative share of CPU time, number of virtual pages resident in RAM or physical CPU or memory bank allocations.

In an attempt to address some of these limitations, OpenVZ and Linux-VServer have implemented custom resource management extensions, such as new limits for the maximum size of shared and anonymous memory or new CPU scheduler mechanisms. In addition both virtualization solutions added the possibility to specify resource limits per container.

*Linux Control Groups (cgroups)* [3] is a relatively new mechanism that aims to address the downsides of *rlimits*. It allows arranging a set of processes into hierarchical groups and performs resource management for the whole group. The CPU and memory controls provided by *cgroups* are rich, and in addition it is possible to implement a complex recovery management in case processes exceed their assigned limits. LxC, Linux-VServer, OpenVZ and Cells provide a way to use cgroups as a container resource management mechanism.

Table 4 presents a comparison of different aspects between *rlimits* and *cgroups*. A combined use of these mechanisms allows protecting the container from a set of DoS attacks directed towards the CPU, memory, disk I/O and filesystem (*rlimits* combined with *filesystem quotas*). However, the future direction is to aggregate all resource management to *cgroups*, and allow *rlimits* to be changed by a privileged user inside a container[2].

# 5   Related Work

A number of previous studies have compared different aspects of the OS-level virtualization to other virtualization solutions. Padala et al. [33] analyze the performance of Xen vs. OpenVZ in the context of server consolidation. Chaudhary et al. [27], Regola et al. [37] and Xavier et al. [43] perform comparisons of different virtualization technologies for HPC. Yang et al. [44] study the impact of different virtualization technologies for the performance of the Hadoop framework [47].

The Capsicum sandboxing framework [40] introduced in FreeBSD 9 isolates processes from global kernel resources by disabling system calls which address resources via global namespaces. Instead, resources are accessed via capabilities which extend Unix file descriptors. Linux has a similar mechanism, called *seccomp* [18], that allows a process to restrict a set of systems calls that it can execute. Both Capsicum and *seccomp* require modifications to existing applications.

---

[2] Documentation in source code of `http://lxr.linux.no/#linux+v3.13.5/kernel/`
`sys.c#L1368`

**Table 5.** Summary of OS-level virtualization in upstream Linux kernel

| | separation of processes | file-system isolation | IPC isolation | device isolation | network isolation | resource limiting |
|---|---|---|---|---|---|---|
| *achieved by* | pid ns | mount ns, pivot_root | | | network ns, veth, MACVLAN | rlimits, cgroups |
| | user ns | | ipc ns | cgroups device controller, exclusive device usage | | |
| *open problems* | security ns | | IPC extensions | device ns, (pseudo)random devices, hotplug support | n/a | incomplete cgroups |

While there are OS-level virtualization solutions such as ICore [4] and Sandboxie [14] in existence for Microsoft Windows as add-on solutions, we have left them out this paper's scope due to their closed nature. Authors are not aware of any OS-level virtualization solutions for Mac OS X or iOS.

In addition to the OS-level virtualization solutions under comparison in this study, researchers have developed a number of other technologies. An attempt by Banga et al. [24] to do fine-grained resource management led to the creation of a new facility for resource management in server systems called *Resource Containers*. Zap [32] allows the grouping of processes into *Process Domains* (PODs) that provide a virtualized view of the system and support for CR. An OS-level virtual machine architecture for Windows is proposed by Yu et al. [45]. A partial OS-level virtualization is provided by the PDS environment by Alpern et al. [21]. Wessel et al. [41] propose a solution for isolating user space instances on Android similar to the Cells/Cellrox. The solution by Wessel et al. has a special focus on security extensions, such as remote management, integrity protection and storage encryption.

# 6    Discussion and Conclusions

All compared systems implement core container separation features in terms of the memory, storage, network and process isolation. However, while the initial innovation around containers happened on FreeBSD and Solaris, the mainline Linux has caught up in terms of features and the flexibility of the implementation. Linux is likely to have a complete user space process environment virtualization in course of time. Given the scale of deployment of Linux and the maturity of its OS-level virtualization features, we focus on Linux in the rest of this section.

Table 5 summaries the state of the OS-level virtualization supported by the current upstream Linux kernel. The first row shows how each type of isolation discussed in section 4 can be achieved using the currently available techniques. The second row presents a number of gaps that are briefly described below.

**Security Namespaces.** In order to reduce security exposure and adhere to the *principle of least privilege*, many OSs provide an integrated mandatory access control (MAC) mechanism. MACs can be used to strengthen the isolation between different containers and the host, as well as to enforce MAC policies for processes inside containers. The latter is especially important when the container has a full OS installation, because it usually comes with pre-configured MAC policies. Therefore, OS-level virtualization solutions should support the ability to use the common MAC mechanisms in the underlying host kernel to enforce independently defined (container-specific) MAC policies. However, currently none of the compared solutions fulfills this requirement. Linux kernel developers plan to address this limitation in the future by introducing a *security namespace* that would make LSMs container-aware.

**IPC Extensions.** While IPC namespaces and filesystem isolation techniques cover most of the inter-process communication methods available on Linux, exceptions exist. For example *Transparent Inter-process Communication* (TIPC) [16] is not currently covered. TIPC is a network protocol that is designed for an inter-cluster communication. Usage of such methods would break the IPC isolation borders between containers and if the given features are not needed, they should be disabled from the kernel configuration.

**Device Namespaces.** As discussed in section 4.4, secure access to device drivers from within a container remains an open problem. One way to approach it would be to create a new namespace class (a *device namespace*) and group all devices to belong in their own device namespaces in hierarchical manner, following the generic namespace design pattern. Given this, only processes within the same device namespace would be allowed to access devices belonging in it. However, since the core of such functionality would resemble more access/resource control than a fully featured namespace, it was initially decided to implement the functionality as a separate *cgroups* device controller. The discussions defining the full notion of the device namespace and its functionality continue in the kernel community [5].

**(Pseudo)random Number Generator Devices.** In section 4.4 we stated that using stateless devices such as */dev/random* or */dev/urandom* are secure within containers due to their stateless nature. This means that even if two containers share the same device, they cannot predict or influence the output from another device node within another container. However, it is important to note that exposing blocking devices, such as */dev/random*, poses a Denial-of-Service possibility. A malicious container can exhaust all available entropy and block the */dev/random* from being used in all other containers and the host, making it impossible to perform cryptographic operations requiring random input. Even if only non-blocking */dev/urandom* is exposed, there is a theoretical possibility that a malicious container can predict the random output for another container or a host. For example in [28] Dodis et al. give an assessment of both */dev/random* and */dev/urandom* showing that these devices do not accumulate entropy properly. A complete solution would be to implement a separate random device per namespace or even introduce a namespace for (pseudo)random number generators.

**Hotplug Support.** Desktop Linux relies heavily on the dynamic nature of device nodes. Once new devices are plugged in to the system, the kernel generates an *uevent* structure notifying the user space of the new hardware. As briefly explained in section 4.4, *Uevent* is typically handled by the *udevd* daemon which configures the device for system use. Traditionally it has also created the corresponding device node after device setup. As far as containers are concerned, this setup is risky and complicated - containers should not be allowed to configure hardware and/or have permissions for creating the new device nodes. As a result, safe device hotplug for containers remains an open problem.

**Incomplete Implementation of *cgroups*.** As was mentioned in the section 4.7, the current goal of the upstream Linux is to integrate all features supported by *rlimits* into the *cgroups* resource management. However this has not been done yet and currently remains as work in progress.

# References

1. AppArmor project wiki, http://wiki.apparmor.net/index.php/Main_Page
2. Cellrox project, http://www.cellrox.com/
3. Cgroups, https://www.kernel.org/doc/Documentation/cgroups/cgroups.txt
4. iCore project page, http://icoresoftware.com/
5. Linux Containers mailing list, http://lists.linuxfoundation.org/pipermail/containers/2013-September/033466.html
6. Linux Network Namespaces, http://www.opencloudblog.com/?p=42
7. Linux Programmer's Manual page on chroot(2) from 20.9.2010 (release 3.35)
8. Linux Programmer's Manual pages (release 3.35)
9. Linux-VServer project, http://linux-vserver.org
10. LxC project, http://linuxcontainers.org/
11. Namespace support for Android binder, http://lwn.net/Articles/577957/
12. OpenVZ project, http://openvz.org
13. RCTL, https://wiki.freebsd.org/Hierarchical_Resource_Limits
14. Sandboxie project page, http://www.sandboxie.com/
15. Smack project, http://schaufler-ca.com/home
16. TIPC project, http://tipc.sourceforge.net/
17. Biederman: Multiple Instances of the Global Linux Namespaces. In: Linux Symposium, pp. 101–112 (2006)
18. Corbet: Seccomp and sandboxing, http://lwn.net/Articles/332974/
19. Creasy: The origin of the VM/370 time-sharing system. IBM Journal of Research and Development, 483–490 (1981)
20. Edge: Another union filesystem approach, https://lwn.net/Articles/403012/
21. Alpern, et al.: PDS: a virtual execution environment for software deployment. In: VEE, pp. 175–185 (2005)
22. Andrus, et al.: Cells: a virtual mobile smartphone architecture. In: ACM SOSP, pp. 173–187 (2011)
23. Asokan, et al.: Security of OS-level virtualization technologies: Technical report, http://arxiv.org/abs/1407.4245

24. Banga, et al.: Resource containers: A new facility for resource management in server systems. In: OSDI, pp. 45–58 (1999)
25. Barham, et al.: Xen and the art of virtualization. In: ACM SIGOPS OSR, pp. 164–177 (2003)
26. Bhattiprolu, et al.: Virtual servers and checkpoint/restart in mainstream Linux. In: ACM SIGOPS OSR, pp. 104–113 (2008)
27. Chaudhary, et al.: A comparison of virtualization technologies for HPC. In: AINA, pp. 861–868 (2008)
28. Dodis, et al.: Security analysis of pseudo-random number generators with input:/dev/random is not robust. In: 2013 ACM SIGSAC, pp. 647–658 (2013)
29. Kamp, et al.: Jails: Confining the omnipotent root. In: SANE, p. 116 (2000)
30. Kivity, et al.: KVM: the Linux virtual machine monitor. In: Linux Symposium, vol. 1, pp. 225–230 (2007)
31. Mirkin, et al.: Containers checkpointing and live migration. In: Linux Symposium, pp. 85–92 (2008)
32. Osman, et al.: The design and implementation of Zap: A system for migrating computing environments. In: ACM SIGOPS OSR, pp. 361–376 (2002)
33. Padala, et al.: Performance evaluation of virtualization technologies for server consolidation. HP Labs Tec. Report (2007)
34. Pike, et al.: Plan 9 from Bell Labs. In: UKUUG, pp. 1–9 (1990)
35. Pike, et al.: The Use of Name Spaces in Plan 9. In: 5th Workshop on ACM SIGOPS European Workshop, pp. 1–5 (1992)
36. Price, et al.: Solaris Zones: Operating System Support for Consolidating Commercial Workloads. In: LISA, pp. 241–254 (2004)
37. Regola, et al.: Recommendations for virtualization technologies in high performance computing. In: IEEE CloudCom, pp. 409–416 (2010)
38. Shim, et al.: Bring Your Own Device (BYOD): Current Status, Issues, and Future Directions (2013)
39. Smalley, et al.: Implementing SELinux as a Linux security module. NAI Labs Report 1, 43 (2001)
40. Watson, et al.: Capsicum: Practical Capabilities for UNIX. In: USENIX, pp. 29–46 (2010)
41. Wessel, S., Stumpf, F., Herdt, I., Eckert, C.: Improving Mobile Device Security with Operating System-Level Virtualization. In: Janczewski, L.J., Wolfe, H.B., Shenoi, S. (eds.) SEC 2013. IFIP AICT, vol. 405, pp. 148–161. Springer, Heidelberg (2013)
42. Wright, et al.: Linux security module framework. In: Linux Symposium, pp. 604–617 (2002)
43. Xavier, et al.: Performance evaluation of container-based virtualization for high performance computing environments. In: PDP, pp. 233–240 (2013)
44. Yang, et al.: Impacts of Virtualization Technologies on Hadoop. In: ISDEA, pp. 846–849 (2013)
45. Yu, et al.: A feather-weight virtual machine for windows applications. In: VEE, pp. 24–34 (2006)
46. The Open Group. The Single UNIX® Specification: Authorized Guide to Version 4 (2010), http://www.unix.org/version4/theguide.html
47. Kizza: Virtualization Infrastructure and Related Security Issues. In: Guide to Computer Network Security, pp. 447–464 (2013)
48. Kolyshkin: Virtualization in Linux. White paper, OpenVZ (2006)
49. Rosenblum: VMware's Virtual Platform. In: Hot Chips, pp. 185–196 (1999)

# Processing Private Queries over an Obfuscated Database Using Hidden Vector Encryption

Alberto Trombetta[1], Giuseppe Persiano[2], and Stefano Braghin[3]

[1] University of Insubria, DiSTA, Varese, Italy
alberto.trombetta@uninsubria.it
[2] Università di Salerno, DI, Salerno, Italy
giuper@gmail.com
[3] IBM Research – Ireland, Smarter Cities Technology Centre, Dublin, Ireland
stefanob@ie.ibm.com

**Abstract.** Outsourcing data in the cloud has become nowadays very common. Since – generally speaking – cloud data storage and management providers cannot be fully trusted, mechanisms providing the confidentiality of the stored data are necessary. A possible solution is to encrypt all the data, but – of course – this poses serious problems about the effective usefulness of the stored data. In this work, we propose to apply a well-known attribute-based cryptographic scheme to cope with the problem of querying encrypted data. We have implemented the proposed scheme with a real-world, off-the-shelf RDBMS and we provide several experimental results showing the feasibility of our approach.

## 1 Introduction

The widespread and ever-growing deployment of cloud computing allow users to access a wide array of services, such as online data storage. The advantages in adopting such a solution are mitigated by the fact that outsourced data is not under the direct control of the legitimate owner, who has uploaded it to the storage service and one has to fully trust the service provider. As a typical solution, the data owner encrypts its data with a classical symmetric scheme before uploading it to the storage provider. This is not optimal in case the storage manager – or some third party other than the data owner – has to perform some kind of computation over the encrypted data. For example, it is impossible to search for a given content over encrypted data, or, more specifically, in the case of encrypted structured data (such as relational data), it is not possible to perform expressive, SQL-like queries. Several solutions have been proposed that solve the problem of searching over encrypted data. However, most of such solutions are not well-tailored for performing searches over structured data, such as relational tables. We refer to Section 2 for a discussion.

*Our motivating scenario.* Consider a data owner $U$ that collects data coming from an information source (say, a sensor network) and stores them in a cloud-based database, managed by a (possibly untrusted) third party. We assume that

K. Bernsmed and S. Fischer-Hübner (Eds.): NordSec 2014, LNCS 8788, pp. 94–109, 2014.
DOI: 10.1007/978-3-319-11599-3_6, © Springer International Publishing Switzerland 2014

the outsourced database is formed by a single table $T$. In the following, we describe the security requirements related to the collection and querying of such data. The information collected in the table $T$ is sensitive and should not be unconditionally disclosed. Hence, in this scenario the solutions typically adopted for ensuring the confidentiality (and then enforcing proper access policies to the data) do not apply. In fact, the DBMS is typically demanded to enforce the access control to the data stored in it, but – since in our case the DBMS could be untrusted – this solution is not viable. The first few rows of an instance of the table $T$ are as follows:

| ServiceId | TypeId | Availability | Certificate | Position | Description | Timestamp |
|---|---|---|---|---|---|---|
| 10 | 3 | yes | $cert_1$ | District2 | infrared camera | 2010-09-07 12:45:33 |
| 23 | 3 | yes | $cert_2$ | District3 | temperature | 2012-12-03 11:52:34 |
| 41 | 1 | yes | $cert_3$ | District3 | camera | 2012-06-12 07:22:45 |
| 12 | 2 | no | $cert_4$ | District1 | camera | 2012-04-07 14:33:28 |
| ... | ... | ... | ... | ... | ... | ... |

Furthermore, the data should be accessed by the legitimate users that can pose standard, select-from-where SQL queries like:

$Q1$                      $Q2$

```
select *                          select ServiceId, TypeId
from T                            from T
where TypeId = 3                 where Position = "District1"
and Position = "District1";       and Availability = "yes";
```

**Fig. 1.** Two conjunctive SFW queries

As an additional layer of security, the queries themselves are considered sensitive by the data owner $U$.

In this work, we propose an application-level database encryption technique, based on an attribute-based cryptographic scheme, for processing obfuscated selection-projection queries over an encrypted version of the table $T$, such that:

(i) data owner $U$ stores an encrypted version of the table $T$ on a non-private (possibly untrusted) RDBMS.

(ii) Each user $V$ entitled for running a query $Q$ over $T$ receives a corresponding decryption key $K_q$ encoding the query. That is, only users satisfying a given access policy may access data satisfying a corresponding query, and *only* such data.

(iii) The data owner issues the decryption keys in an initial setup phase.

(iv) The processing of the query is done by a trusted, separate query processor. Depending on architectural choices, such query processor may be under the control of end users, or managed by a trusted third party, detached from the rdbms server.

(v) Data stored in the encrypted table may be modified by the owner $U$ without the need of re-encrypting the entire table, nor recomputing existing decryption keys.

Note that in the proposed approach, access control is performed by the data owner by safely distributing to each user entitled to perform a query a corresponding decryption key. The encryption procedure is completely oblivious of the access control policy and this is a good feature since data can be encrypted even before potential readers with still-to-be defined access rights enroll into the system. Specifically, the addition of novel queries (or users) does not force the data owner to modify the encryption of the current data. Given that $U$ wants the encrypted data to be searched by queries like query $Q1$ and $Q2$ stated above, $U$ performs the following operations: it encrypts the tuples of table $T$ using an attribute-based encryption scheme that takes as additional input a vector $X$ containing (an encoding of) the values contained in the tuples. That is, there is a different vector $x$ for every different row; this has to be repeated as many times as there are attributes to be projected. In order to do this, we add a special attribute whose domain ranges over the indices encoding the positions of attributes; Afterwards, $U$ computes the corresponding secret decryption keys, that depend on the values to be searched, encoded in a vector $Y$. Since the attribute-based cryptographic scheme obfuscates the search values contained in the vector $Y$, it is referred to as *hidden vector encryption* (or *HVE*) scheme [1]. The decryption keys are then distributed by $U$ (or some other trusted authority) to the users satisfying the corresponding access policy. This is the last time in which users interact. After the decryption keys' distribution, the data owner can go offline. Note that in the aforemetioned scenario, the query is entirely defined by the data owner $U$, that fixes – among other things – the values to be searched in the table $T$. However, in real-world database-backed applications, it is the case that the end user $V$ may specify the values to be searched filling empty place-holders in an a-priori defined query. We show that a very simple modification of the proposed scheme allows the data owner $U$ to issue a "parametric" token $\overline{K}$ corresponding to a query with unspecified search values, that are to be provided by the user receiving such token. Note that the encryption depends on the data contained in the tuples and decryption keys only depend on the query. Note also that it is possible to adjoin or delete tuples from the database without the need to re-encrypt its entire content, but only the modified content has to be re-enciphered. We remark also that a single encryption of the database is sufficient for answering different obfuscated queries. The experimental results show that – quite expectedly – the space overhead for storing the encrypted data grows linearly with the number of columns of the cleartext database. This linear overhead holds for the execution time of an encrypted query, as well.

*Our contributions.* The technical core of our contribution is a novel encryption scheme for HVE [1] that is based on the dual pairing vector space framework of [2] (which supports very large alphabets having size, see Section 7 for precise estimates). Using such encryption scheme, we propose efficient, amortized way of storing the encrypted rows of a table in such a way that selection-projection queries can be directly performed on encrypted data. We as well propose a reference architecture that clarifies the roles of the different actors. The paper is structured as follows: in Section 2 are discussed the most relevant related works; in Section 3, a simplified version of the attribute-based encryption scheme of Okamoto and Takashima[2] suitable for our context is presented; in Section 4 we show how to use the above mentioned scheme for executing obfuscated SQL queries over an encrypted database, along with the important variant of parametric queries in Section 5; in Section 6 the main functional components of an architecture implementing our approach are presented; in Section 7 the results of the experiments with our implementation are shown; finally, in Section 8 the conclusions are drawn, along with a description of future extensions we are already working on.

## 2   Related Works

tHE ever-growing adoption of cloud-based data storage and management service has prompted several research efforts aiming at assuring a high security level of the stored data using cryptographic mechanisms that do not assume the service to be trusted. The problem of how to provide an adequate security level to the stored data by deploying cryptographic techniques has been addressed by the database research community as well as the cryptographic research community, each of them focusing on different aspects that are relevant for the respective community. See, for example, the scenarios described in [3].

There are several works in the database literature that deal with encrypted databases. Seminal works like [4] and [5] have underlined the need to devise novel mechanisms that complement the usual access control approaches in order to achieve a greater level of security, by storing an encrypted version of the data, as well as the need to devise efficient indexing techniques that allow reasonable query performance over encrypted data. The advent of fast networks and cheap online storage have made possible the management of encrypted data at application-level. One of the first works to present the paradigm *database as-a-service* is [6]. In [7] a database architecture based on a trusted hardware cryptographic module is presented. In [8], the authors propose a full-fledged system, named CryptDB, for performing SQL queries over encrypted data. While CryptDB may require multiple, different encryptions (or "onions", following the terminology of [8]) for the same data, depending on what queries are to be executed, our approach does not require them and a single version of the encrypted data is used for every possible query (with respect to the schema of the database). Another – related – point is that one can decide which queries to execute *after* the data encryption has been perfomed, without having to modify it.

All the major commercial RDBMS releases provide functionalities to encrypt the data they store, see for example [9]. All commercial solutions are based on database-level encryption, thus limiting the functionalities over encrypted data, that have to be deciphered at server side in order to processing queries over them. Apart from encryption techniques to deal with large quantities of data that are to be managed and searched over, issues like key management and indexes over encrypted data have been addressed. In [10], [11] are presented two short surveys of the major challenges that are relevant to the design of encrypted database as well as useful reference architectures. In the cryptographic (and more broadly, security) research community, the problem of how to query an an encrypted database has been viewed as a (very relevant) example of the broader problem of computing over encrypted data. As it is well known, the first general, fully homomorphic encryption scheme has been defined in [12]. However, it is too impractical to be applied to real-world scenarios. Therefore, more specialized techniques have been proposed in order to solve the (less general) problem of searching over encrypted data. One of the first works addressing the problem is [13], in which the authors define a public key scheme that – given a search keyword – allows for the creation of a corresponding decryption key that tests whether such keyword is contained in the ciphertext. A subsequent work[14] has introduced the notion of HVE, in which it is possible to pose conjunctive and range queries over encrypted data in suh a way that the query is itself obfuscated. Among the many works based on homomorphic encryption, we mention [15], that uses a "limited" (yet more efficient) version of homomorphic encryption to query an encrypted repository. We point out though that homomorphic encyrption is at the moment very inefficient and thus the approaches based on it cannot be considered practical. An approach using attribute-based encryption is described in [16], where the authors propose both key-policy and ciphertext-policy schemes for keyword searching over unstructured textual data, along with a mechanism for proving the truthfulness of the search results. However, our approach is different since data is accessed depending whether it satisfies a query (encoded as a secret decryption key) and not upon satisfaction of the user posing the query of an associated access policy (we do not address the problem of enforcing such access control, which can be done by a plethora of well-known mechanisms [17]).

An extensive amount of work has been done concerning how to access data without disclosing sensitive information using anonymous credentials see for example [18] and [19]. Finally, a related area is *private information retrieval* in which the goal is to preserve the privacy of queries. That is retrieve information from a database (typically represented as an unstructured sequence of bits) without letting the database know anything about the query [20]. While it is a very interesting approach from a theoretical point of view, its practical applicability is rather scarce and it only allows very simple queries (like retrieving a cell in a table) and does not enforce any control on what is accessed.

The approach presented in this work takes inspiration from attribute-based encryption schemes as defined, for example, in [21] or [14]. However, such schemes are optimized for a binary alphabet and thus they are not very efficient over large alphabets, such as those found in practice.

## 3    The Cryptographic Scheme Constructions

Due to space limitations, we present a succint description of the dual pairing vector space framework, that can be found in more extended version in [2]. We assume familiarity with the hidden vector encryption approach, as presented in [14]. We have an additive group $(\mathbb{G}, 0)$ and a multiplicative group $(\mathbb{G}_T, 1_T)$ of the same prime size $q$ and a bilinear map $\mathbf{e} : \mathbb{G} \times \mathbb{G} \to \mathbb{G}_T$. That is, for

$a, b, c \in \mathbb{G}$, we have $\mathbf{e}(a + b, c) = \mathbf{e}(a, c) \cdot \mathbf{e}(b, c)$ and $\mathbf{e}(a, b + c) = \mathbf{e}(a, b) \cdot \mathbf{e}(a, c)$ and $\mathbf{e}(0, a) = 1_T$ and $\mathbf{e}(a, 0) = 1_T$. The above imply that for all $s, t \in \mathbb{G}_T$ we have $\mathbf{e}(s \cdot a, t \cdot b) = \mathbf{e}(a, b)^{st}$. The bilinear map is extended to vectors over $\mathbb{G}$ as follows. For two vectors $X = (x_1, \ldots, x_n)$ and $Y = (y_1, \ldots, y_n)$ over $\mathbb{G}$, define

$$\mathbf{e}(X, Y) = \prod_{i=1}^{n} \mathbf{e}(x_i, y_i).$$

Note the abuse of notation by which we use $\mathbf{e}$ to denote the bilinear map defined over $\mathbb{G}$ and over the vector space over $\mathbb{G}$. Also, we observe that the extended bilinear map $\mathbf{e}$ is still bilinear in the sense that

$$\mathbf{e}(X + Y, Z) = \mathbf{e}(X, Z) \cdot \mathbf{e}(Y, Z) \quad \text{and} \quad \mathbf{e}(X, Z + Y) = \mathbf{e}(X, Z) \cdot \mathbf{e}(X, Y)$$

for all vectors $X, Y, Z$. For a fixed $g \in \mathbb{G}$, we define the *canonical base* $A_1, \ldots, A_n$ with respect to $g$ where, for $i = 1, \ldots, n$,

$$A_i = (\underbrace{0, \ldots, 0}_{i-1}, g, \underbrace{0, \ldots, 0}_{n-i}).$$

Notice that $\mathbf{e}(A_i, A_i) = \mathbf{e}(g, g)$ and $i \neq j$ implies $\mathbf{e}(A_i, A_j) = 1_T$. Let $B$ and $B^\star$ be two $n \times n$ matrices with columns $B = (B_1, \ldots, B_n)$ and $B^\star = (B_1^\star, \ldots, B_n^\star)$ and let $\psi \in \mathbb{F}_q$, where $\mathbb{F}_q$ denotes a finite field with cardinality $q$. We say that $(B, B^\star)$ is a pair of *$\psi$-orthogonal matrices* if, for all $1 \leq i < j \leq n$, $\mathbf{e}(B_i, B_i^\star) = \mathbf{e}(g, g)^\psi$ and $\mathbf{e}(B_i, B_j^\star) = 1_T$, where we set $g_T = \mathbf{e}(g, g)$. A pair of $\psi$-orthogonal matrices can be constructed as follows. Let $X = (x_{i,j}), X^\star = (x_{i,j}^\star) \subset \mathbb{F}_q^{n \times n}$ be matrices such that

$$X^T \cdot X^\star = \psi \cdot I.$$

for $i = 1, \ldots, n$, vectors $B_i$ and $B_i^\star$ are defined as follows

$$B_i = \sum_{j=1}^{n} x_{i,j} A_j \quad \text{and} \quad B_i^\star = \sum_{j=1}^{n} x_{i,j}^\star A_j.$$

For a vector $(x_1, \ldots, x_n) \in \mathbb{F}_q^{\,n}$ and a matrix $B = (B_1, \ldots, B_n)$, we define the vector $(x_1, \ldots, x_n)_B = \sum_{i=1}^{n} x_i B_i$.

## 3.1 HVE in the DPVS Framework

We first briefly recap what are the functionalities an HVE scheme and then give an implementation using the DPVS framework. The HVE function over $\mathbb{F}_q^\ell$ is defined as follows: for $X = (x_1, \ldots, x_\ell) \in \mathbb{F}_q^\ell$ and $Y = (y_1, \ldots, y_\ell) \in (\mathbb{F}_q \cup \{\star\})^\ell$, we define $\mathsf{HVE}(X, Y) = 1$ iff $\forall i \; y_i \neq \star \Rightarrow x_i = y_i$.

**Definition 1.** *An HVE encryption scheme is a quadruple of algorithms* HVE $=$ (*Setup, Encrypt, KeyGen, Decrypt*) *with the following syntax:*

1. *The* Setup *algorithm takes integers $q$ and $\ell$ and returns a master public key* MPK *and a master secret key* MSK.
2. *The* Encrypt *algorithm takes a plaintext $m$, an attribute vector $X = (x_1, \ldots, x_\ell) \in \mathbb{F}_q^\ell$ and a master public key* MPK *and returns a ciphertext* Ct.
3. *The* KeyGen *algorithm takes an attribute vector $Y = (y_1, \ldots, y_\ell) \in (\mathbb{F}_q \cup \{\star\})^\ell$ and master key* MSK *returns a key $K$ for $Y$.*
4. *The* Decrypt *algorithm takes a ciphertext* Ct *for plaintext $m$ and attribute vector $X$ computed using master public key* MPK *and a key $K$ for attribute vector $Y$ computed using master secret key* MSK *and returns the value $m$ iff* $\mathsf{HVE}(X, Y) = 1$.

We are now ready to describe our implementation of an HVE encryption scheme. We assume that a DPVS framework $(\mathbb{G}, \mathbb{G}_T, \mathbf{e}, q)$ is given.

1. Setup($\ell$). Randomly choose $\psi \in \mathbb{F}_q$ and $g \in \mathbb{G}$ and set $g_T = \mathbf{e}(g, g)^\psi$. For $i = 0, \ldots, \ell$ generate a pair $(B^i, C^i)$ of $\psi$-orthogonal $3 \times 3$ matrices. Return $\mathsf{MPK} = (B^0, \ldots, B^\ell, g_T)$ and $\mathsf{MSK} = (C^0, \ldots, C^\ell)$.
2. Encrypt($m, X, \mathsf{MPK}$). We assume $m \in \mathbb{G}_T$ and $X = (x_1, \ldots, x_\ell) \in \mathbb{F}_q^\ell$. Randomly choose $z, w_0, \ldots, w_\ell \in \mathbb{F}_q$, set $c = g_T^z \cdot m$ and $c_0 = (w_0, z, 0)_{B^0}$ and, for $t = 1, \ldots, \ell$, set $c_t = (w_t, w_t \cdot x_t, w_0)_{B^t}$. Return $\mathsf{Ct} = (c, c_0, c_1, \ldots, c_\ell)$.
3. KeyGen($Y, \mathsf{MSK}$). Assume $Y = (y_1, \ldots, y_\ell) \in (\mathbb{F}_q \cup \{\star\})^\ell$ and let $S$ be the set of $1 \leq t \leq \ell$ such that $y_t \neq \star$.
   Pick random $\eta \in \mathbb{F}_q$ and, for $t \in S$, pick random $d_t, s_t \in \mathbb{F}_q$ and set $s_0 = -\sum_{t \in S} s_t$. Set $k_0 = (s_0, 1, \eta)_{C^0}$ and $k_t = (d_t \cdot y_t, -d_t, s_t)_{C^t}$. Return $K = (k_0, (k_t)_{t \in S})$.
4. Decrypt($K, \mathsf{Ct}$). Write $K$ as $K = (k_0, (k_t)_{t \in S})$ and Ct as $\mathsf{Ct} = (c, c_0, \ldots, c_\ell)$. Return
$$\frac{c}{\mathbf{e}(k_0, c_0) \cdot \prod_{i \in S} \mathbf{e}(k_i, c_i)}.$$

Let us now show that our scheme is correct. Suppose that $\mathsf{HVE}(X, Y) = 1$. Then by the $\psi$-orthogonality of $B^0$ and $C^0$ we have
$$\mathbf{e}(k_0, c_0) = g_T^{s_0 \cdot w_0 + z}.$$

Moreover, the $\psi$-orthogonality of $B^i$ and $C^i$ gives
$$\mathbf{e}(k_t, c_t) = g_T^{d_t \cdot w_t \cdot (x_t - y_t) + w_0 \cdot s_t}.$$

Therefore if $x_t = y_t$ for $t \in S$ we have
$$\prod_{t \in S} \mathbf{e}(k_t, c_t) = g_T^{w_0 \cdot \sum_{t \in S} s_t} = g_T^{-s_0 \cdot w_0}$$

which implies that the Decrypt algorithm returns $m$. On the other hand if $x_t \neq y_t$ for some $t \in S$ the Decrypt algorithm returns a random value in $\mathbb{G}_T$.

Regarding the proof of security properties, we do not include them due to space limits [1]. Here, we observe that a ciphertext for plaintext $m$ with attribute vector $X$ does not reveal any information on $m$ and on attribute vector $X$. On the other hand, no security guarantee is made for a key $K$.

---

[1] See the extended version of this work at http://arxiv.org/abs/1403.2514

### 3.2 An Amortized Scheme

In our construction of secure database queries we will often have to encrypt $n$ messages $m^1, \ldots, m^n \in \mathbb{G}_T$ with closely related attributes. More specifically, message $m^j$ is encrypted with attributes $(x_1, \ldots, x_\ell, x^j_{\ell+1}) \in \mathbb{F}^{\ell+1}_q$; that is, the attributes of two messages coincide except for the $(\ell+1)$-st. If we use the HVE implementation of the previous section, the sum of the sizes of the ciphertexts of all messages is $\Theta(\ell \cdot n)$. In this section we describe a scheme that reduces the size to $\Theta(\ell + n)$.

1. $\mathsf{Setup^{am}}$. Same as Setup.
2. $\mathsf{Encr^{am}}(m^1, \ldots, m^n \in \mathbb{G}_T, x_1, \ldots, x_\ell, x^1_{\ell+1}, \ldots, x^n_{\ell+1}, \mathsf{MPK})$.
   Randomly choose $z, w_0, \ldots, w_\ell \in \mathbb{F}_q$ and set
   $c_0 = (w_0, z, 0)_{B^0}$ and $c_t = (w_t, w_t \cdot x_t, w_0)_{B^t}$ for $t = 1, \ldots, \ell$.
   The encryption of the $j$-th message $m^j$ is computed as follows: Pick random $z^j, w^j, w^j_0 \in \mathbb{F}_q$ and set

   $$c^j = g_T^{z+z^j} \cdot m^j$$

   and

   $$c^j_0 = (w^j_0, z^j, 0)_{B^{0,\star}} \quad \text{and} \quad c^j_{\ell+1} = (w^j, w^j \cdot x^j_{\ell+1}, w^j_0)_{B^{\ell+1}}.$$

   The cumulative ciphertext consists of

   $$\mathsf{Ct} = (c_0, c_1, \ldots, c_\ell, (c^1, c^1_0, c^1_{\ell+1}), \ldots, (c^n, c^n_0, c^n_{\ell+1})).$$

   The ciphertext corresponding to $m^j$ is

   $$\mathsf{Ct}^j = (c_0, c_1, \ldots, c_\ell, (c^j, c^j_0, c^j_{\ell+1})).$$

3. $\mathsf{KeyGen^{am}}(Y, \mathsf{MSK})$.
   Write $Y$ as $Y = (y_1, \ldots, y_\ell, y_{\ell+1})$ and let $S$ be the set of $1 \le t \le \ell$ such that $y_t \ne \star$. We assume that $y_{\ell+1} \ne \star$ and we stress that $\ell+1 \notin S$.
   Randomly choose $\eta \in \mathbb{F}_q$ and, for $t \in S$, randomly choose $d_t, s_t \in \mathbb{F}_q$ and set $s_0 = -\sum_{t \in S} s_t$. Set

   $$k_0 = (s_0, 1, \eta)_{C^0} \quad \text{and} \quad k_t = (d_t \cdot y_t, -d_t, s_t)_{C^t}.$$

   Randomly choose $s^\star_0, \eta^\star, d_{\ell+1} \in \mathbb{F}_q$ and output

   $$k^\star_0 = (s^\star_0, 1, \eta^\star)_{C^{0,\star}} \quad \text{and} \quad k_{\ell+1} = (d_{\ell+1} \cdot y_{\ell+1}, -d_{\ell+1}, -s^\star_0)_{C^{\ell+1}}.$$

   Return key $K = (k_0, (k_t)_{t \in S}, k^\star_0, k_{\ell+1})$.
4. $\mathsf{Decrypt^{am}}(K, \mathsf{Ct})$. Write $K = (k_0, (k_t)_{t \in S}, k^\star_0, k_{\ell+1})$ and $\mathsf{Ct} = (c_0, c_1, \ldots, c_\ell, (c^j, c^j_0, c^j_{\ell+1})^n_{j=1})$. Compute $m^j$ as

   $$\frac{c^j}{\mathbf{e}(c^j_0, k^\star_0) \cdot \mathbf{e}(c^j_{\ell+1}, k_{\ell+1}) \cdot \mathbf{e}(c_0, k_0) \cdot \prod_{t \in S} \mathbf{e}(c_t, k_t)}.$$

For correctness, suppose $\mathsf{HVE}(X, Y) = 1$. By the $\psi$-orthogonality we have

$$\mathbf{e}(c_0, k_0) = g_T^{s_0 \cdot w_0 + z}.$$

and, for $t \in S$

$$\mathbf{e}(c_t, k_t) = g_T^{s_t \cdot w_0}.$$

Therefore,

$$\prod_{t \in S} \mathbf{e}(c_t, k_t) = g_T^{\sum_{t \in S} s_t \cdot w_0} = g_T^{-s_0 \cdot w_0}.$$

and thus

$$\mathbf{e}(c_0, k_0) \cdot \prod_{t \in S} \mathbf{e}(c_t, k_t) = g_T^z.$$

Moreover, we have $\mathbf{e}(c_0^j, k_0^\star) = g_T^{s_0^\star \cdot w_0^j + z^j}$ and $\mathbf{e}(c_{\ell+1}^j, k_{\ell+1}) = g_T^{-s_0^\star \cdot w_0^j}$ and thus $\mathbf{e}(c_0^j, k_0^\star) \cdot \mathbf{e}(c_{\ell+1}^j, k_{\ell+1}) = g_T^{z^j}$.

# 4  Private Queries

In this section we describe how a table is encrypted using the HVE scheme presented in Section 3 and how to process a select-from-where query – encoded as a secret decryption key – over such encrypted data. Let us start by fixing our notation.

We assume that data owner $U$ holds table $T$, composed of $l$ columns $A_1, \ldots, A_l$ and of $u$ rows $R^1, \ldots, R^u$ and we write the $i$-th row $R^i$ as $R^i = \langle v_i^1, \ldots, v_i^l \rangle$.

*Encrypting a table.* We assume that the data owner $U$ has selected a DPVS framework with groups of size $q$ and an authenticated private-key block cipher $\mathsf{ABC} = (E, D)$ with key length $k < q$.

1. Generating the system parameters.
   $U$ runs algorithm $\mathsf{Setup}^{\mathsf{am}}(q, l)$ and obtains a pair of master public and secret key $(\mathsf{MPK}, \mathsf{MSK})$.
2. Encrypting row $R = \langle v_1, \ldots, v_l \rangle$.
   $U$ picks $l$ random keys $k_1, \ldots, k_l$ for $\mathsf{ABC}$ and use them to encrypt $R$. Specifically, compute $\tilde{R} = \langle \tilde{v}_1, \ldots, \tilde{v}_l \rangle$, where $\tilde{v}_i = E(k_i, v_i)$ for $i = 1, \ldots, l$.
   Then $U$ encrypts keys $k_i$ using the HVE scheme. Specifically, for $i = 1, \ldots, l$, $U$ computes $\tilde{k}$ by setting

$$\tilde{k} = \mathsf{Encrypt}^{\mathsf{am}}(k_1, \ldots, k_l, v_1, \ldots, v_l, 1, \ldots, l, \mathsf{MPK}).$$

That is, key $k_i$ is encrypted with attribute vector $(v_1, \ldots, v_l, i)$.

The encryption of row $R$ consists of the pair $(\tilde{R}, \tilde{k})$ and the encrypted table is simply the sequence $\tilde{T} = \langle (\tilde{R}^1, \tilde{k}^1), \ldots, (\tilde{R}^u, \tilde{k}^u) \rangle$ of the encrypted rows.

*Generating a key for a selection-projection query.* A typical selection-projection query (like $Q2$ in Figure 1 "**select** ServiceId, TypeId **from** T **where** Position = 'District1' **and** Availability = 'yes' ") is described by specifying the search values, along with "don't care" entries $\star$, and the columns that are to be projected in the corresponding attribute vectors (one for every column to be projected). More specifically, consider a query that specifies value $a_i$ for $i = 1, \ldots, l$ (it is possible that $a_i = \star$ for some values $i$ corresponding to don't care entries in the query) and column $c$ to be projected. We assume without loss of generality that only one columns is to be projected; in general one computes a different key for each column to be projected. For example, a selection-only query, like query $Q_1$: "**select** * **from** T **where** TypeId = 3 **and** Position = 'District 1' ", is a special case of selection-projection query in which *all* the columns of the table are to be projected. The key for such a query is obtained by running the procedure described as follows with $c = 1, \ldots, l$; the data owner $U$ releases key $K$ for the query $Q1$ by running KeyGen$^{am}(Y, MSK)$ for attribute vector $Y = (a_1, \ldots, a_l, c)$ and using master secret key MSK computed as part of the generation of the system parameter generation. The key $K$ is then sent to a user $V$ entitled to execute the query. We point out that in the description above we have implicitly assumed that values $a_i$ are elements of the field $\mathbb{F}_q$ or $\star$. This does not hold in general as in most applications values $a_i$ are strings over an alphabet; thus we derive values $a_i$ by applying an hash function that for each string returns an element of $\mathbb{F}_q$.

*Executing a selection-projection query.* Upon receiving key $K$, the user $V$ applies $K$ to the encrypted table as follows. For $i = 1, \ldots, u$, row $i$ $(\tilde{R}^i, \tilde{k}^i)$ of the encrypted table is used to compute $\hat{k}_c^i$ by selecting the $c$-th output of the Decrypt$^{am}$ algorithm on input $K$ and $\tilde{k}^i$. Key $\hat{k}_c^i$ is then used to run the decryption algorithm $D$ for ABC to decrypt $\hat{v}_c^i$. If the decryption algorithm succeeds then it returns $v_c^i$. Otherwise the row is not selected.

Indeed, if the key attribute vector of $K$ matches the attribute vector used to obtain $\tilde{k}^i$ then this means that row $i$ is to be selected and thus $\hat{k}_c^i = k_c^i$ and the decryption algorithm Decrypt$^{am}$ does not fail. If instead the key attribute vector of the key $K$ does not match the attribute vector of the row (that is, the row is not to be selected) then $\hat{k}_c^i$ is a random element of $\mathbb{G}_T$ and thus with very high probability the decryption algorithm fails.

## 5 Parametric Queries

In the previous sections, we have assumed that the data owner, in constructing the key $K$, completely determines the query that can be run over the encrypted database. That is, the values that are to be searched (and their corresponding columns) and the columns that are to be returned. However, in real-world, database-backed applications what usually happens is that the user asking for the query execution has the ability to fix by itself the values to be searched. Specifically, the data owner might want to be able to generate a key that allows to search a specified column (or set of columns) for values to be specified later. We remark that the way tokens are computed by the KeyGen procedure easily allows for a two-step computation of a token encoding a given query: namely, the first step is performed by the data owner which computes an intermediate, *"parametric"* decryption key; the second step then consists in specifying the parameters into the parametric decryption key thus obtaining a complete decryption key. More precisely, we observe that the computation of decryption key components $k_t$, for $1 \leq t \leq l$ (the ones that depend on the values to be searched (see Section 3) can be performed by the following modified version of the KeyGen$^{am}$ procedure:

The decryption key is computed by a two-step process: (i) for every decryption key $K$, for $t \in S$, pick random $s_t, d_t$ from $\mathbb{F}_q$ and set $\overline{k_t} = (d_t, -d_t, s_t)_{C^t}$ ($k_0$ is defined as in KeyGen$^{am}$); (ii) multiply element-wise the vector $\overline{k_t}$ (which is composed by three elements) with the vector $(y_t, 1, 1)$, obtaining the component $k_t$ of the decryption key $K$.

We note that Steps (i) and (ii) may be performed by different entities. In fact, with respect to Query $Q2$, following Step 1 user $U$ computes the parametric decryption keys $\overline{K_1}, \overline{K_2}$ that correspond to the parametric query "select columns *ServiceId* and *TypeId* of all the rows of the table $T$ such that columns *Availability* and *Position* contain values *'value1'* and *'value2'* respectively". A (possibly different) user $V$ then after having received $\overline{K_1}, \overline{K_2}$ from $U$, computes the decryption keys $K_1, K_2$ by specifying values $y_1, y_2$ corresponding to search values *'yes'*, *'District3'*. In other words the data owner $U$ can delegate restricted search capabilities to user $V$.

For the security we observe that the parametric key does not allow to generate keys other than the ones that can be obtained by specifying the values of the parameters.

# 6   Architectural Overview

The high-level overview of the architecture (as shown in Figure 2(a)) assumes that there are users $V$, $V'$,..., a data owner $U$, and a server split in two components: a *proxy* query processor $P$ hosted on a trusted, separate application server, and a (possibly untrusted) DBMS server $S$. The encryption and decryption operations are thus delegated outside the DBMS server (compare, for example, with the application-level architecture in the taxonomy presented in [11]). For sake of simplicity, we assume that the data owner $U$ generates the public parameters, as well as the key material deployed in the execution of the cryptographic schemes described in the previous sections[2]. Also, we assume that the proxy query processor $P$ (whose task is to decrypt the (parts of the) rows having matching values with the encryption attribute vector) communicates with the other components via secure and authenticated channels. Confidentiality of both data and queries

---

[2] As a more realistic setting, we may assume that the tokens are generated by users having proper credentials or by other trusted third parties that check such credentials.

hold as long as the proxy $P$ and the server $S$ do not collude. We now illustrate the workflow occurring among the data owner, the trusted proxy query processor, the untrusted server and users who wish to pose queries to the encrypted database. We consider the non-amortized case, being the amortized one rather similar in the sequence of actions to be performed.

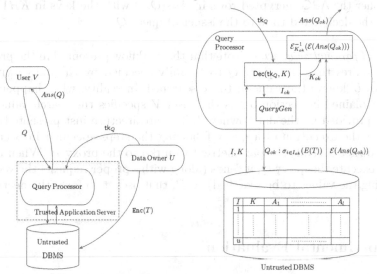

(a) The high-level architecture      (b) The query processor structure

**Fig. 2.** The architecture of our system

The *data owner* $U$ runs the Setup procedure (see Section 3), producing the secret master key $C^0, \ldots, C^l$ and the public key $g_T = \mathbf{e}(g,g)^\psi, B^0, \ldots, B^l$. $U$ randomly generates the secret ABC keys $k_1, \ldots, k_u$, as well . $U$ then encrypts the table in two steps: (i) rows are encrypted with symmetric scheme ABC and (ii) the corresponding secret keys are encrypted with the public keys using the HVE-based Encrypt procedure. The encrypted database $E(T)$ (composed of the ABC-encrypted rows and the HVE-encrypted ABC keys and an additional column that stores a row counter) is uploaded in the untrusted DBMS server. Afterwards, given a query $Q$, $U$ proceeds in computing the corresponding token $\mathrm{tk}_Q$, using the secret master key and the the vector containing the values specified in the query $Q$). Finally, the decryption key $K_Q$ is sent to the query processor. At this point, the data owner $u$ may go offline. Upon receiving a request from user $V$ for executing query $Q$, the proxy query processor $P$ performs the following steps (see Figure 2(b)):

(i) retrieve with a table scan from the encrypted database (stored in the server $S$) the columns containing the row counter and the HVE-encrypted ABC keys (which we denote $I$ and $KHVE$, respectively) from the encrypted database;

(ii) execute the procedure Decrypt with $K_Q$ on each HVE-encrypted ABC key in $KHVE$; for every successfully decrypted ABC key, put the corresponding value of the row counter into $I_{ok}$; put the deciphered ABC keys in $KHVE_{ok}$;

(iii) execute the following SQL query over the encrypted database:

$$Q_{ok} = \textbf{select} * \textbf{from } E(T) \textbf{ where } I \textbf{ in } I_{ok}$$

(iv) retrieve the answer $Ans(Q_{ok})$;
 (v) decipher the ABC-encrypted rows in $Ans(Q_{ok})$ with the keys in $KHVE_{ok}$;
(vi) send the deciphered rows to the issuer of query $Q$

*The case of parametric queries.* Note that the workflow presented in the previous section requires that the query $Q$ to be fully specified by the data owner. In particular, $U$ knows the value(s) to be searched. In reality, what happens – as already explained in Section 5 – is that user $V$ specifies the search values in a query $Q$, provided by the data owner $U$. The architecture just presented allows as well for the execution of a query following the steps specified in Section 5: the data owner $U$ sends the parametric token $\overline{tk_Q}$ to the proxy $P$. When user $V$ wants to execute the query $Q$, it sends (along with s proper request) the vector $Y$ (containing the values to be searched) to $P$, that uses it to form the decryption key $K_Q$.

## 7   Experimental Evaluation

We now describe the experimental results of the application of the schema presented in Section 3 and 4. We implemented the schemes presented in Section 3 in Python, using the Charm library[3] and the relational database SQLite[4]. Charm is a Python-based library that offers support for the rapid prototyping and experimentation of cryptographic schemes. In particular, we rely on the support offered by Charm for dealing with pairings, which is in turn based on the well-known C library PBC[5]. The implementation has been tested on a machine with two Intel Xeon E7-8850 cpus at 2.00GHz, with 16GB ram, running Ubuntu 12.04.

*Asymptotic complexity.* Tables 1 and 2 show the complexities of the procedures presented respectively in Section 3.1 and Section 3.2. The operations we take into account in measuring time complexity are: pairings (denoted as $P$), exponentiations in $G_T$ (denoted as $EG_T$) and row products (denoted as $RW$). As for space complexity, we denote with $|g|$ and $|g_T|$ the bit-size of elements in $G$ and $G_T$[6]. Given a SFW query to be privately executed over an encrypted version of table $T$, we remind that $c$, $t$ anc $l$ respectively denote the number of projected columns in the **select** clause, the number of columns in the table $T$, specified in the **from** clause and the number of search predicates in the **where** clause.

---

[3] http://www.charm-crypto.com/Main.html
[4] http://www.sqlite.org
[5] http://crypto.stanford.edu/pbc/
[6] We remark that the order of $G_T$ is the size of the alphabet from which values $y_i$ are drawn.

**Table 1.** Asymptotic complexity of non-amortized scheme

|        | number of operations | output size |
|--------|:---:|:---:|
| Setup  | $1 \cdot P$ | $\|g_T\| + 18l \cdot \|g\|$ |
| Enc    | $EG_T + (l+1) \cdot RW$ | $\|g_T\| + 10l \cdot \|g\|$ |
| KeyGen | $(t+1) \cdot RW$ | $3(t+1) \cdot \|g\|$ |
| Dec    | $3(t+1) \cdot P$ | |

**Table 2.** Asymptotic complexity of amortized scheme

|        | number of operations | output size |
|--------|:---:|:---:|
| Setup  | $1 \cdot P$ | $\|g_T\| + 18l \cdot \|g\|$ |
| Enc    | $l \cdot EG_T + (l^2 + l) \cdot RW$ | $\|g_T\| + 13l \cdot \|g\|$ |
| KeyGen | $c(t+1) \cdot RW$ | $3(t+3) \cdot \|g\|$ |
| Dec    | $3c(t+1) \cdot P$ | |

*Executions with real data.* We have executed several tests on datasets of growing sizes, deploying different curve parameters. More precisely, we have generated several synthetic relational tables of varying sizes; we have encrypted them at row level with AES and subsequently we have encrypted the corresponding 256-bit AES keys with HVE using as curves parameters MNT159 ($G_1$, $G_2$[7], $G_T$ elements' bitsizes are respectively 159, 477, 954), SS512 ($G_1$, $G_2$, $G_T$ elements' bitsizes are respectively 512, 512, 1024) and MNT224 (with $G_1$, $G_2$, $G_T$ elements' bitsizes of 224, 672, 1344) MNT159 parameters have a security level equivalent to 954-bit DLOG, while SS512 and MNT have security levels equivalent respectively to 1024 and 1344-bit DLOG. In Figure 3(a), are shown the execution times of encrypted queries corresponding, respectively, to the SQL queries with **where** clauses of increasing length, having up to eight search predicates. As it is expected, for a given row in the cleartext table, the encryption execution time linearly depends on the number of table columns and the major time cost is due to the computation of pairings. The queries have been performed on the largest database. We remind that an encrypted query execution is composed of the following steps (see Section 6): (i) retrieve from the encrypted database the rows index and the the HVE-encrypted AES keys, (ii) for every retrieved encrypted key, run the decryption procedure with the attribute vector encoding the query and, for each key that has a successful match, store the corresponding row index in the index result set $I_{ok}$, (iii) retrieve from the encrypted database the AES-encrypted rows whose row indexes are contained in $I_{ok}$, (iv) finally, decipher the rows with the corresponding aes keys that have been successfully decrypted in Step (iii). In Figure 3(b), the space occupied by the plaintext database and by the corresponding encrypted versions are shown. Again as expected, the expansion factor linearly depends on the number of columns employed by the HVE encryption procedure. With respect to the datasets used in the experiments, the expansion factor of the HVE encryption is roughly 5.5. Such factor is directly

---

[7] In this case, the pairing is asymmetric.

proportional on the number of columns in the cleartext database schema – as already pointed out in Table 2 – and directly proportional to the size of the cleartext database as well. This is due, of course, to the fact that values in the cleartext database (which can be of arbitrary size) are mapped to $\mathbb{F}_q$ elements (which are of fixed size). As a rule of thumb for decreasing the size of the encrypted database, one should limit the columns on which the encryption depends only on the ones that are actually involved in the search predicates.

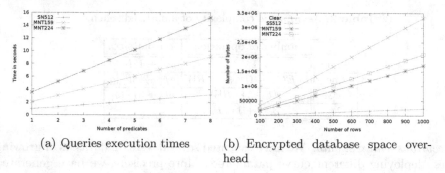

(a) Queries execution times     (b) Encrypted database space overhead

**Fig. 3.** Time and space performances

## 8 Conclusions

In this work we have presented an attribute-based encryption scheme based on the DPVS framework and we have used it to define a system for privately query with standard SQL conjunctive queries an encrypted, off-the-shelf, non-private relational database without the need to decipher the stored data during the execution of the intermediate query processing steps. We have implemented our scheme using an off-the-shelf RDBMS, and we provided experimental results that show the feasibility of our approach, both in terms of query execution times and database size expansion. Regarding the extensions of the present work, we are currently working on privately executing (i) join queries and (ii) aggregate queries on encrypted tables. We are investigating ways for deploying indexes in order to avoid full table scans. Finally, we plan to add mechanisms for verifying whether the query processor has faithfully executed the query.

## References

1. Katz, J., Sahai, A., Waters, B.: Predicate encryption supporting disjunctions, polynomial equations, and inner products. J. Cryptology 26(2), 191–224 (2013)
2. Okamoto, T., Takashima, K.: Adaptively attribute-hiding (hierarchical) inner product encryption. In: Pointcheval, D., Johansson, T. (eds.) EUROCRYPT 2012. LNCS, vol. 7237, pp. 591–608. Springer, Heidelberg (2012)
3. Samarati, P., de Capitani di Vimercati, S.: Data protection in outsourcing scenarios: issues and directions. In: Proceedings of the 5th ACM Symposium on Information, Computer and Communications Security (ASIACCS), Beijing, China, pp. 1–14 (2010)

4. Davida, G.I., Wells, D.L., Kam, J.B.: A database encryption system with subkeys. ACM Trans. Database Syst. 6(2), 312–328 (1981)

5. Bayer, R., Metzger, J.K.: On the encipherment of search trees and random access files. ACM Trans. Database Syst. 1(1), 37–52 (1976)

6. Hacigümüs, H., Iyer, B.R., Li, C., Mehrotra, S.: Executing sql over encrypted data in the database-service-provider model. In: Proceedings of the ACM SIGMOD Conference on Management of Data, pp. 216–227 (2002)

7. Bajaj, S., Sion, R.: Trusteddb: A trusted hardware based outsourced database engine. PVLDB 4(12), 1359–1362 (2011)

8. Popa, R.A., Redfield, C.M.S., Zeldovich, N., Balakrishnan, H.: Cryptdb: protecting confidentiality with encrypted query processing. In: Proceedings of the 23rd ACM Symposium on Operating Systems Principles (SOSP), pp. 85–100 (2011)

9. Corp. Oracle: Oracle advences security transparent data encryption best practices. White paper (2012)

10. Shmueli, E., Vaisenberg, R., Elovici, Y., Glezer, C.: Database encryption: an overview of contemporary challenges and design considerations. SIGMOD Record 38(3), 29–34 (2009)

11. Bouganim, L., Guo, Y.: Database encryption. In: Encyclopedia of Cryptography and Security, 2nd edn., pp. 307–312 (2011)

12. Gentry, C.: Fully homomorphic encryption using ideal lattices. In: Proceedings of the 41st Annual ACM Symposium on Theory of Computing, STOC 2009, Bethesda, MD, USA, pp. 169–178 (2009)

13. Boneh, D., Di Crescenzo, G., Ostrovsky, R., Persiano, G.: Public key encryption with keyword search. In: Cachin, C., Camenisch, J.L. (eds.) EUROCRYPT 2004. LNCS, vol. 3027, pp. 506–522. Springer, Heidelberg (2004)

14. Boneh, D., Waters, B.: Conjunctive, subset, and range queries on encrypted data. In: Vadhan, S.P. (ed.) TCC 2007. LNCS, vol. 4392, pp. 535–554. Springer, Heidelberg (2007)

15. Boneh, D., Gentry, C., Halevi, S., Wang, F., Wu, D.J.: Private database queries using somewhat homomorphic encryption. In: Jacobson, M., Locasto, M., Mohassel, P., Safavi-Naini, R. (eds.) ACNS 2013. LNCS, vol. 7954, pp. 102–118. Springer, Heidelberg (2013)

16. Zheng, Q., Xu, S., Ateniese, G.: Vabks: Verifiable attribute-based keyword search over outsourced encrypted data. IACR Cryptology ePrint Archive 2013 (2013)

17. Samarati, P., de Capitani di Vimercati, S.: Access control: Policies, models, and mechanisms. In: Focardi, R., Gorrieri, R. (eds.) FOSAD 2000. LNCS, vol. 2171, pp. 137–196. Springer, Heidelberg (2001)

18. Bangerter, E., Camenisch, J., Lysyanskaya, A.: A cryptographic framework for the controlled release of certified data. In: Christianson, B., Crispo, B., Malcolm, J.A., Roe, M. (eds.) Security Protocols 2004. LNCS, vol. 3957, pp. 20–42. Springer, Heidelberg (2006)

19. Camenisch, J., Dubovitskaya, M., Lehmann, A., Neven, G., Paquin, C., Preiss, F.-S.: Concepts and languages for privacy-preserving attribute-based authentication. In: Fischer-Hübner, S., de Leeuw, E., Mitchell, C. (eds.) IDMAN 2013. IFIP AICT, vol. 396, pp. 34–52. Springer, Heidelberg (2013)

20. Gasarch, W.I.: A survey on private information retrieval (column: Computational complexity). Bulletin of the EATCS 82, 72–107 (2004)

21. Iovino, V., Persiano, G.: Hidden-vector encryption with groups of prime order. In: Galbraith, S.D., Paterson, K.G. (eds.) Pairing 2008. LNCS, vol. 5209, pp. 75–88. Springer, Heidelberg (2008)

# π-Cipher:
# Authenticated Encryption for Big Data

Danilo Gligoroski[1], Hristina Mihajloska[2], Simona Samardjiska[1,2,4],
Håkon Jacobsen[1,4], Rune Erlend Jensen[3], and Mohamed El-Hadedy[1]

[1] ITEM, NTNU, Trondheim, Norway
{danilog,simonas,hakoja}@item.ntnu.no, hadedy@alumni.ntnu.no
[2] FCSE, "Ss Cyril and Methodius" University, Skopje, Republic of Macedonia
hristina.mihajloska@finki.ukim.mk
[3] IDI, NTNU, Trondheim, Norway
runeerle@stud.ntnu.no
[4] Supported by the COINS Research
School of Computer and Information Security

**Abstract.** In today's world of big data and rapidly increasing telecommunications, using secure cryptographic primitives that are parallelizable and incremental is becoming ever more important design goal. π-Cipher is parallel, incremental, nonce based authenticated encryption cipher with associated data. It is designed with the special purpose of providing confidentiality and integrity for big data in transit or at rest. It has, as an option, a secret part of the nonce which provides nonce-misuse resistance. The design involves operations of several solid cryptographic concepts such as the Encrypt-then-MAC principle, the XOR MAC scheme and the two-pass sponge construction. It contains parameters that can provide the functionality of tweakable block ciphers for authenticated encryption of data at rest. The security of the cipher relies on the core permutation function based on ARX (Addition, Rotation and XOR) operations. π-Cipher offers several security levels ranging from 96 to 256 bits.

**Keywords:** Authenticated encryption, AEAD, parallelizability, incrementality, nonce-misuse resistance, sponge construction.

## 1  Introduction

The possibility to have both encryption and authentication in one mode of operation of a block cipher, was first mentioned in Jutla's paper "Encryption Modes with Almost Free Message Integrity" [14] submitted to NIST [21] for their call for proposals for new modes of operation for AES. Soon after that, Jutla proposed a highly parallelizable authenticated encryption mode in [15]. Then, a whole series of proposals appeared in the open literature such as OCB [22], CCM [6], EAX [17] and GCM [18].

The interest for authenticated encryption with associated data was recently intensified with the announced new competition "CAESAR" for authenticated

K. Bernsmed and S. Fischer-Hübner (Eds.): NordSec 2014, LNCS 8788, pp. 110–128, 2014.
DOI: 10.1007/978-3-319-11599-3_7, © Springer International Publishing Switzerland 2014

ciphers [2]. The scope of this competition is not just to seek for authenticated modes of operations for AES, but also for proposals of new ciphers that offer advantages over AES-GCM and are suitable for widespread adoption.

$\pi$-Cipher is a proposal for an authenticated cipher with associated data for the ongoing "CAESAR" crypto competition. The recent developments with the introduction of AES-NI instructions in latest Intel CPUs [12] made AES-GCM mode really efficient. Thus, in order to design a cipher that will offer advantages over AES-GCM we anticipated the following trends:

1. The exponential increase of the data in rest continues. Our modern civilization has entered the era where the total size of the digital universe has surpassed the zettabyte size and is entering the zettabyte communication era with a fast pace. For example "The EMC Digital Universe study - with research and analysis by IDC" [7] reports that in 2013 the size of our digital universe was 4.4 zettabytes, and it projects that *"by 2020 the digital universe - the data we create and copy annually - will reach 44 zettabytes, or 44 trillion gigabytes."*
2. The trend of the exponential drop (in US\$/MB) of the cost of computer memory and storage continues (for example see [8]).
3. The exponential increase of the global telecommunication traffic continues. In the report prepared by Cisco, the Cisco Visual Networking Index [5] predicts that *"Annual global IP traffic will pass the zettabyte threshold by the end of 2015, and will reach 1.4 zettabytes per year by 2017."*
4. The trend of increasing the number of cores in modern CPUs continues. From dual-core or quad-core processors nowadays we have processors with tens or even hundreds of cores.
5. The trend of increasing the SIMD (Single Instriction Multiple Data) computing power continues (from SSE registers with 128 bits, up to 256 bits in AVX2, and even 512 bits in the next AVX-512).

Taking everything previously mentioned in consideration, we designed $\pi$-Cipher with the following characteristics:

− The parallelism in $\pi$-Cipher is simpler than in AES-GCM.
− It is more suitable than AES-GCM for encrypting data in rest with tunable parameters that fit the sizes of modern disk sectors.
− Achieving incrementality with $\pi$-Cipher will be much simpler than achieving it with AES-GCM.
− It has, as an option, a secret part of the nonce which provides much more robust nonce-misuse resistance than AES-GCM.
− By tuning the parameters in $\pi$-Cipher, a certain level of tag preimage resistance can be achieved that is non-existing in AES-GCM.

**Organization of the Paper.** The rest of the paper is organized as follows. In Section 2 we provide a general description of the $\pi$-Cipher. The details of how it is designed are given in the following design rationale section. Section 4 presents some of the security goals and analysis of the $\pi$-Cipher, and Section 5 is dedicated to the software performances of it. Finally we conclude our paper in Section 6.

## 2  π-Cipher: General Description

π-Cipher is parallel, incremental, nonce based authenticated encryption cipher with associated data. Its design involves several solid cryptographic concepts such as:

1. Encrypt-then-MAC principle.
2. Its parallel and incremental design is similar to the design of the randomized XOR MAC scheme of Bellare et al. [1], but there are also some intrinsic differences.

   First of all, both schemes rely on the randomize-then-combine paradigm, by processing the message blocks using a keyed pseudo-random function, and then combining the results via a group operation. However, the π-cipher, in order to achieve light tag-second-preimage, when the key is known, instead of the XOR operation for the intermediate tag components (as in XOR MAC), uses componentwise addition of two $d$-dimensional vectors of $\omega$-bit words in $(\mathbb{Z}_{2^\omega})^d$.

   In both cases, the independent processing of the message blocks provides straightforward parallelism and incrementality, and in both cases, two important mechanisms protect against forgeries, the inclusion of the ordinal number of the message blocks, and a publicly known nonce. The first protects against forgeries using rearrangements of the message blocks. The second protects against forgeries obtained by combining valid tags, and further ensures that we always get a different tag even when encrypting the same message. But, there is also an important difference. In XOR MAC the publicly known nonce is processed independently of the message, but this approach is not desirable in an AEAD scheme, since we want the different nonce to influence all of the processed blocks. Thus, the nonce in π-cipher is included in the internal state and is an input to each of the calls of the internal permutation. Furthermore, the π-cipher also provides an option of using a secret nonce in addition to the public one.
3. In [4, Sec. 3.3] the authors mention that it is possible to construct an authenticated encryption using single pass sponge construction [3] that is proven to be secure as long as the underlying sponge permutation has no structural distinguishers. In the same paper [4] the duplex sponge construction is introduced. Although these constructions have the property to be tag second-preimage resistant, neither of them is incremental and parallel. An incremental and parallel two pass scheme is proposed in [19]. However, the design goal for that scheme was not to be nonce-misuse resistance. Combining all these ideas, in our design we use a two pass counter based sponge component that we call *triplex component*. Our design is fully parallelizable, incremental and lightly tag second-preimage resistant. The used π permutation is based on ARX (Addition, Rotation and XOR) operations.

## 2.1    Authenticated Encryption

The encryption/authentication procedure of $\pi$-Cipher accepts key $K$ with fixed-length of $klen$ bytes, message $M$ with $mlen$ bytes and associated data $AD$ with $adlen$ bytes. The cipher uses a fixed-length public message number $PMN$ and secret message number $SMN$. The output of the encryption/authentication procedure is a ciphertext $C$ with $clen$ bytes and a tag $T$ with fixed-length of $tlen$ bytes. The length $clen$ of the ciphertext $C$ is a sum of the byte length of the message, the authentication tag and the encrypted secret message number. The decryption/verification procedure accepts key $K$, associated data $AD$, ciphertext $C$, public message number $PMN$, secret message number $SMN$ and tag $T$, and returns the decrypted message $M$ if the tag has been verified or $\perp$ otherwise.

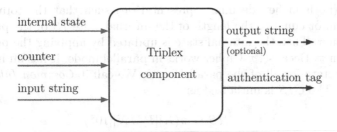

**Fig. 1.** A general scheme of the triplex component

The main building element in the operations of encryption/authentication and decryption/verification is our new construction related to the duplex sponge, called triplex component. It uses the permutation function $\pi$ twice, it injects a counter into the internal state and digests an input string. The triplex component always outputs a tag. Optionally after the first call of the permutation function it can output a string (that can be a ciphertext block or a message block). The general scheme of the triplex component is presented in Figure 1.

Because of the differences in the encryption/authentication and decryption/verification procedures, there are two different variants of the triplex component. We call them *e-triplex* (for the phase of encryption) and *d-triplex* (for the phase of decryption). The only difference in these two components is how the input string is treated after the first call of the permutation function. In the first one, the input string (plaintext) is XORed with the current internal state and the result proceeds to the second invocation of the permutation function $\pi$. In the d-triplex component, the input string (ciphertext) is directly injected as part of the internal state before the second invocation of the permutation function $\pi$. The graphical representation of the e-triplex and d-triplex components is given in Figure 2.

The encryption/authentication operation of $\pi$-Cipher can be described in four phases:

1. **Initialization.** In this phase we first initialize the internal state to $K||PMN||10^*$, where $10^*$ denotes a single "1", and the smallest number

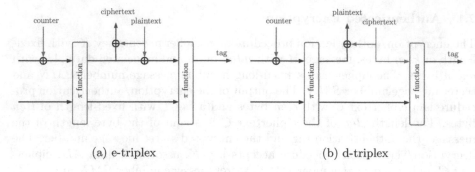

(a) e-triplex                           (b) d-triplex

**Fig. 2.** The Triplex component

of 0's (both in hexadecimal representation) such that the total length is less than or equal to the length of the internal state $IS$ of the permutation function $\pi$. Then the internal state is updated by applying the permutation function $\pi$. Because, $\pi$-Cipher works in parallel mode, it has an initial value for the state for all of the parallel parts. We call it *Common Internal State (CIS)*. The $CIS$ is initialized as:

$$CIS \leftarrow \pi(K||PMN||10^*).$$

The next part of this phase is initializing the counter $ctr$.
Since $CIS = CIS_{bitrate}||||CIS_{capacity}$ we initialize the $ctr$ as the first 64 bits (little endian representation) of the $CIS_{capacity}$. $||||$ is an operator of interleaved concatenation in order to correctly denote a concatenation of the *bitrate* and *capaity* parts that restore the internal state. In this case, $CIS_{bitrate} = I_1||I_3||\ldots||I_{N-1}$ and $CIS_{capacity} = I_2||I_4||\ldots||I_N$, where $I_i$ is a chunk of the internal state, and $N$ is the number of chunks. The Initialization phase is depicted in Figure 3.

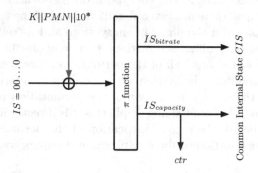

**Fig. 3.** Initialization step

2. **Processing the Associated Data**
   The associated data $AD = AD_1||\ldots||AD_i||\ldots||AD_a$ is processed block by block in parallel using e–triplex components. The padding rule for the last block is the following:

$$AD_a \leftarrow \begin{cases} AD_a & \text{if } |AD_a| = bitrate, \\ AD_a||10^* & \text{if } |AD_a| < bitrate. \end{cases}$$

To every block $AD_i$ we associate a unique counter calculated as a sum of the initial counter $ctr$ and the ordinal number of the processed block $i$. The input to every e–triplex component is $CIS$, $ctr + i$ and $AD_i$, and the output is a block tag $t'_i$. The tag $T'$ for the associated data is computed as

$$T' = \boxplus_d{}_{i=1}^{a} t'_i = t'_1 \boxplus_d t'_2 \boxplus_d \ldots \boxplus_d t'_a$$

where $\boxplus_d$ denotes component-wise addition, $t'_i = (t'_{i1}, t'_{i2}, \ldots, t'_{id}) \in (\mathbb{Z}_{2^\omega})^d$, and $d$ is the number of $\omega$-bit words in the $bitrate$.
The final part of this phase is to update the value of the *Common Internal State CIS* as

$$CIS \leftarrow \pi(CIS_{bitrate} \oplus T' \quad |||| \quad CIS_{capacity})$$

This step is described graphically in Figure 4.

3. **Processing the Secret Message Number.** This phase is omitted if the length of the secret message number $SMN$ is 0 (it is the empty string). If $SMN$ is not the empty string, then the first step in this phase is a call to the e–triplex component. The input is the following triplet: $(CIS, ctr + a + 1, SMN)$, and the output is the following pair: $(C_0, t_0)$. The second step of this phase is updating the $CIS$ (for free) which becomes the value of the current internal state after the processing of $SMN$. Formally, the updating can be described by the following two expressions:

$$IS \leftarrow \pi(CIS_{bitrate} \oplus (ctr + a + 1) \quad |||| \quad CIS_{capacity}),$$
$$CIS \leftarrow \pi(IS_{bitrate} \oplus SMN \quad |||| \quad IS_{capacity})$$

The tag produced from this phase is $T'' = T' \boxplus_d t_0$. This phase is depicted in Figure 5.

4. **Processing the Message.** The message $M = M_1||\ldots||M_j||\ldots||M_m$ is processed block by block in parallel by e–triplex components. The padding rule for the last block is the following:

$$M_m \leftarrow \begin{cases} M_m & \text{if } |M_m| = bitrate, \\ M_m||10^* & \text{if } |M_m| < bitrate. \end{cases}$$

To every block $M_j$ we associate a unique block counter as:

$$ctr \leftarrow \begin{cases} ctr + a + j & \text{if } |SMN| = 0, \\ ctr + a + 1 + j & \text{if } |SMN| = bitrate, \end{cases}$$

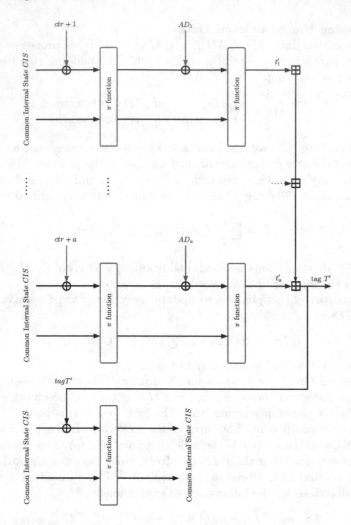

**Fig. 4.** Processing the associated data $AD$ with $a$ blocks in parallel

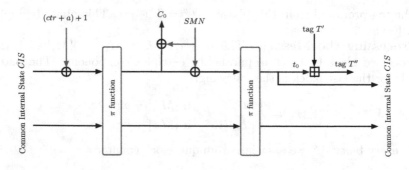

**Fig. 5.** Processing the secret message number $SMN$

where $j$ is the ordinal number of the processed block in the message, and $0 < j \leqslant m$. The input to every e–triplex component is the $CIS$, block $ctr$ and $M_j$, and the output is a pair $(C_j, t_j)$. By definition we put that the length of the final ciphertext block $C_m$ is the same as the length of the un-padded last plaintext block $M_m$ i.e., $|C_m| = |M_m|$. The final tag $T$ is obtained as:

$$T = T'' \boxplus_d t_1 \boxplus_d \ldots \boxplus_d t_j \boxplus_d \ldots \boxplus_d t_m,$$

where $t_j = (t_{j1}, t_{j2}, \ldots, t_{jd})$ is a $d$-dimensional vector of $\omega$-bit words. This phase is described graphically in Figure 6.

The output of the encryption/authentication procedure is the ciphertext

$$C = C_0 || C_1 || \ldots || C_m || T.$$

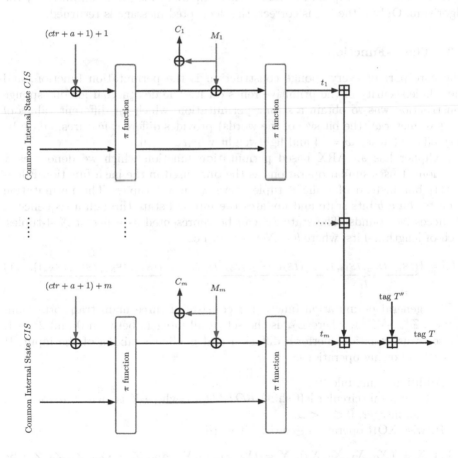

**Fig. 6.** Processing the message $M$ with $m$ blocks in parallel

## 2.2   Decryption and Verification

The decryption/verification procedure is defined correspondingly. There are four phases and the only difference is in the last two (so the Initialization phase and Processing the associated data phase are completely the same as in the encryption/authentication procedure).

The decryption of the $SMN$ is performed in the phase of Processing the secret message number. Thus, instead of using an e-triplex component, we use a d-triplex component. The input parameters are: $CIS$, incremented counter $ctr + a + 1$ and the ciphertext block $C_0$. The output is a pair $(SMN, t_0)$. The tag is processed in the same way as in the encryption/authentication procedure.

For the decryption of the rest of the ciphertext we continue to use a d-triplex component (instead of e-triplex). The output is now a decrypted message block and a tag value.

At the end, the supplied tag value $T$ is compared to the one computed by the algorithm. Only if the tag is correct, the decrypted message is returned.

## 2.3   The $\pi$-Function

The core part of every sponge construction is the permutation function, and the whole security of the primitive relies on it. The design goal for our sponge construction was to obtain a strong permutation, which for different values of the parameter $\omega$ (the bit size of the words) provides different features, i.e. to be very efficient when $\omega = 64$ and lightweight when $\omega = 16$.

$\pi$-Cipher has an ARX based permutation function which we denote as $\pi$ function. It uses similar operations as the ones used in the hash function Edon-R [11] but instead of using 8–tuples here we use 4–tuples. The permutation operates on a $b$ bits state and updates the internal state through a sequence of $R$ successive rounds. The state $IS$ can be represented as a list of $N$ 4-tuples, each of length $\omega$-bits, where $b = N \times 4 \times \omega$, i.e.,

$$IS = (\underbrace{(IS_{11}, IS_{12}, IS_{13}, IS_{14})}_{I_1}, \underbrace{(IS_{21}, IS_{22}, IS_{23}, IS_{24})}_{I_2}, \ldots, \underbrace{(IS_{N1}, IS_{N2}, IS_{N3}, IS_{N4})}_{I_N}). \quad (1)$$

The general permutation function $\pi$ consists of three main transformations $\mu, \nu, \sigma : \mathbb{Z}_{2^\omega}^4 \to \mathbb{Z}_{2^\omega}^4$, where $\mathbb{Z}_{2^\omega}$ is the set of all integers between 0 and $2^\omega - 1$. These transformations perform diffusion and nonlinear mixing of the input. It uses the following operations:

- Addition + modulo $2^\omega$;
- Left rotation (circular left shift) $ROTL^r(X)$, where $X$ is an $\omega$–bit word and $r$ is an integer, $0 \leqslant r < \omega$;
- Bitwise XOR operation $\oplus$ on $\omega$–bit words.

Let $\mathbf{X} = (X_0, X_1, X_2, X_3)$, $\mathbf{Y} = (Y_0, Y_1, Y_2, Y_3)$ and $\mathbf{Z} = (Z_0, Z_1, Z_2, Z_3)$ be three 4-tuples of $\omega$–bit words. Further, denote by $*$ the following operation:

$$\mathbf{Z} = \mathbf{X} * \mathbf{Y} \equiv \sigma(\mu(\mathbf{X}) \boxplus_4 \nu(\mathbf{Y})) \quad (2)$$

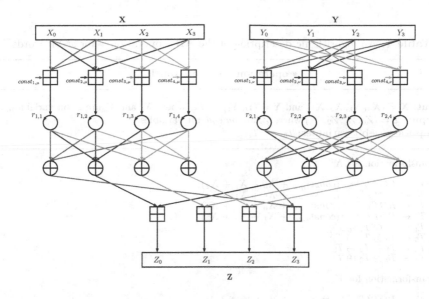

**Fig. 7.** Graphical representation of the ARX operation $*$

where $\boxplus_4$ is the component-wise addition of two 4-dimensional vectors in $\left(\mathbb{Z}_{2^\omega}\right)^4$.

An algorithmic definition of the $*$ operation over two 4–dimensional vectors **X** and **Y** for $\omega$-bit words is given in Table 1. The values of the rotation vectors $r_{1,\omega}$ and $r_{2,\omega}$ and of the constants $const_{i,\mu\omega}$, $const_{i,\nu\omega}$, $i = 1, 2, 3, 4$ used in the $\mu$ and $\nu$ transformations are given in the official documentation of the $\pi$-Cipher [10]. A graphical representation of the $*$ operation is given in Figure 7.

Let us recall equation (1) where the internal state is presented as $IS = (I_1, I_2, \ldots, I_N)$. One round of the $\pi$ function consists of two consecutive transformations $E_1$ and $E_2$ defined as follows.

**Definition 1.** *The function* $E_1 : (\mathbb{Z}_{2^\omega}^4)^{N+1} \to (\mathbb{Z}_{2^\omega}^4)^N$ *used in the* $\pi$ *function is defined as:*

$$E_1(C, I_1, \ldots, I_N) = (J_1, \ldots, J_N),$$

*where* $J_1 = C * I_1, J_i = J_{i-1} * I_i$, $i = 2, \ldots, N$ *and* $C$ *is a 4-tuple of* $\omega$-*bit constant values.*

**Definition 2.** *The function* $E_2 : (\mathbb{Z}_{2^\omega}^4)^{N+1} \to (\mathbb{Z}_{2^\omega}^4)^N$ *used in the* $\pi$ *function is defined as:*

$$E_2(C, I_1, \ldots, I_N) = (J_1, \ldots, J_N),$$

*where* $J_N = I_N * C, J_{N-i} = I_{N-i} * J_{N-i+1}$, $i = 1, \ldots, N-1$ *and* $C$ *is a 4-tuple of* $\omega$-*bit constant values.*

Finally, one round of the $\pi$ function is defined as:

$$\pi(I_1, \ldots, I_N) = E_2(C2, E_1(C1, I_1, \ldots, I_N)) \tag{3}$$

**Table 1.** An algorithmic description of the ARX operation $*$ for $\omega$–bit words

| $*$ operation for $\omega$–bit words |
| --- |
| **Input:** $\mathbf{X} = (X_0, X_1, X_2, X_3)$ and $\mathbf{Y} = (Y_0, Y_1, Y_2, Y_3)$ where $X_i$ and $Y_i$ are $\omega$–bit variables. **Output:** $\mathbf{Z} = (Z_0, Z_1, Z_2, Z_3)$ where $Z_i$ are $omega$–bit variables. **Temporary $\omega$–bit variables:** $T_0, \ldots, T_{11}$. |

$\mu$–transformation for $X$:

$$1. \quad \begin{aligned} T_0 &\leftarrow ROTL^{r_1,\omega,1}(const_{1,\mu\omega} + X_0 + X_1 + X_2); \\ T_1 &\leftarrow ROTL^{r_1,\omega,2}(const_{2,\mu\omega} + X_0 + X_1 + X_3); \\ T_2 &\leftarrow ROTL^{r_1,\omega,3}(const_{3,\mu\omega} + X_0 + X_2 + X_3); \\ T_3 &\leftarrow ROTL^{r_1,\omega,4}(const_{4,\mu\omega} + X_1 + X_2 + X_3); \end{aligned}$$

$$2. \quad \begin{aligned} T_4 &\leftarrow T_0 \oplus T_1 \oplus T_3; \\ T_5 &\leftarrow T_0 \oplus T_1 \oplus T_2; \\ T_6 &\leftarrow T_1 \oplus T_2 \oplus T_3; \\ T_7 &\leftarrow T_0 \oplus T_2 \oplus T_3; \end{aligned}$$

$\nu$–transformation for $Y$:

$$1. \quad \begin{aligned} T_0 &\leftarrow ROTL^{r_2,\omega,1}(const_{1,\nu\omega} + Y_0 + Y_2 + Y_3); \\ T_1 &\leftarrow ROTL^{r_2,\omega,2}(const_{2,\nu\omega} + Y_1 + Y_2 + Y_3); \\ T_2 &\leftarrow ROTL^{r_2,\omega,3}(const_{3,\nu\omega} + Y_0 + Y_1 + Y_2); \\ T_3 &\leftarrow ROTL^{r_2,\omega,4}(const_{4,\nu\omega} + Y_0 + Y_1 + Y_3); \end{aligned}$$

$$2. \quad \begin{aligned} T_8 &\leftarrow T_1 \oplus T_2 \oplus T_3; \\ T_9 &\leftarrow T_0 \oplus T_2 \oplus T_3; \\ T_{10} &\leftarrow T_0 \oplus T_1 \oplus T_3; \\ T_{11} &\leftarrow T_0 \oplus T_1 \oplus T_2; \end{aligned}$$

$\sigma$–transformation for both $\mu(X)$ and $\nu(Y)$:

$$1. \quad \begin{aligned} Z_3 &\leftarrow T_4 + T_8; \\ Z_0 &\leftarrow T_5 + T_9; \\ Z_1 &\leftarrow T_6 + T_{10}; \\ Z_2 &\leftarrow T_7 + T_{11}; \end{aligned}$$

One round of the cipher is graphically described in Figure 8. In the figure, the diagonal arrows can be interpreted as $*$ operations between the source and destination, and the vertical or horizontal arrows as equality signs " $=$ ".

The number of rounds $R$ is a tweakable parameter. We recommend $R = 4$. The complete formula for the $\pi$ function with $R = 4$ is the following:

$$\pi(I_1, \ldots, I_N) = E_2(C8, E_1(C7, E_2(C6, E_1(C5, E_2(C4, E_1(C3, E_2(C2, E_1(C1, I_1, \ldots, I_N)))))))))$$

The constants $C1, C2, \ldots, C8$ are generated in the same way as the constants of the $*$ operation and their values are given in the official documentation of the $\pi$-Cipher [10].

# 3  Design Rationale

$\pi$-Cipher is designed to be tweakable for different word sizes, different block sizes and different security levels. The recommended variants are presented in Table 2.

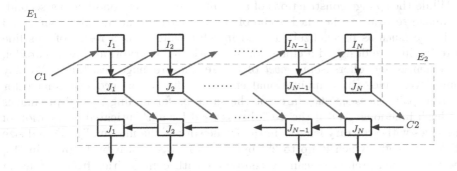

**Fig. 8.** One round of $\pi$-Cipher

The goal of $\pi$-Cipher is to achieve both high performance and strong security. To achieve the goal of having high performance we designed $\pi$-Cipher to be trivially parallel and to have a tweakable parameter that will enable it to work with wide sizes of the blocks (thus to be suitable to process multiple disk sectors in the same time). For example, the computer industry is moving to a 4096 (4K) byte sector size for hard disk drives called Advanced Format [13]. The new AF HDD storage devices read data from or write data to 4K-byte (4,096 bytes) physical sectors on the HDD media. However, using the encryption algorithm that can encrypt one sector as one block of message will also be an advantage. We can very efficiently use $\pi$64-Cipher128 or $\pi$64-Cipher256 with N=32 (instead of the recommended value N=4) for encrypting the whole disk, where every sector will be processed independently and in parallel.

**Table 2.** Basic characteristics of all variants of the $\pi$-Cipher

| | Word size $\omega$ (in bits) | klen (in bits) | PMN (in bits) | SMN (in bits) | b (in bits) | N | bitrate (in bits) | Tag t (in bits) | R |
|---|---|---|---|---|---|---|---|---|---|
| $\pi$16-Cipher096 | 16 | 96 | 32 | 0 or 128 | 256 | 4 | 128 | 128 | 4 |
| $\pi$16-Cipher128 | 16 | 128 | 32 | 0 or 128 | 256 | 4 | 128 | 128 | 4 |
| $\pi$32-Cipher128 | 32 | 128 | 128 | 0 or 256 | 512 | 4 | 256 | 256 | 4 |
| $\pi$32-Cipher256 | 32 | 256 | 128 | 0 or 256 | 512 | 4 | 256 | 256 | 4 |
| $\pi$64-Cipher128 | 64 | 128 | 128 | 0 or 512 | 1024 | 4 | 512 | 512 | 4 |
| $\pi$64-Cipher256 | 64 | 256 | 128 | 0 or 512 | 1024 | 4 | 512 | 512 | 4 |

Another design rationale about $\pi$-Cipher is its feature of being tag second-preimage resistant. While AES-GCM can be parallelized and can be used to perform incremental updates of the ciphertext and the tag, it is not tag second-preimage resistant. Still, since *Robustness* is a major goal for an AEAD cipher, we believe tag second-preimage resistance should be one of the features that it should posses. In other words, MACs should retain some hash properties when the key is known. There exist realistic scenarios (for ex. "Secure audit logs" and Multi-cast authentication) when the lack of tag second-preimage resistance in authenticated encryption can be exploited [9].

While the sponge constructions of authenticated encryption offer tag second-preimage resistance, they lack some of the properties that are also useful and desirable (such as parallelizability and incrementality). As a result of this line of reasoning, we designed a cipher for authenticated encryption that is parallel, incremental and offers *some level* of tag second-preimage resistance. We say some level, since the computational efforts for finding a second-preimage for a given pair *(message, tag)* are not the same as for finding second-preimages for hash functions. And if the $\pi$-Cipher is used for authenticated encryption of messages with arbitrary length (in the framework of the maximally allowed size of the messages which is up to $2^{64}$ bytes), as it was shown by Leurent in [16] the tag second-preimages can be computed with complexities from $2^{22}$ using messages that are long $2^{11}$ blocks up to complexity $2^{45}$ using messages that are long $2^{22}$ blocks. Laurent's analysis was based on Wagner's generalized birthday attack [23] which complexity can be described as follows. The complexity of finding a preimage message $M = M_1 || M_2 || \dots || M_m$ where $m$ is a power of 2 and $m \leq N_{max}$ (the largest number of blocks in any message that we plan to authenticate) is:

$$\min_{m \leq N_{max}} O(m \cdot 2^{\frac{tlen}{1+\lg\lceil m \rceil}}). \tag{4}$$

If the length of the messages is not restricted, then the minimum in equation (4) is achieved for messages of $m = 2^{\sqrt{tlen}-1}$ blocks.

However, there are situations when we need to encrypt relatively short messages. For example, if we use the $\pi$-Cipher in IPSec or TLS where the most common IP packet size is 1500 bytes, then for $\pi$64-Cipher128 or $\pi$64-Cipher256 the encrypted and authenticated message (each IP packet of a communication session) will have just 24 blocks ($m = 24$). In this case the Wagners generalized birthday attack in order to find a second-preimage for a given tag of one IP packet will need $2^{106.4}$ e-triplex invocations and a space of $2^{113}$ bytes.

We point out another property of the $\pi$-Cipher to address the issue of producing second-preimage resistant tags: the whole IP packet can be processed as a one block, by choosing the parameter $N = 48$ (instead of the recommended value $N = 4$). In this case, the tag second-preimage resistance is $2^{512}$ because of the fact that $m = 1$.

## 4    Security of $\pi$-Cipher

The following requirements should be satisfied in order to use $\pi$-Cipher securely:

1. The key should be secret and generated uniformly at random;
2. A nonce in the $\pi$-Cipher can be only PMN, or (PMN, SMN) pair;
   If the legitimate key holder uses the same nonce to encrypt two different pairs of (plaintext, associated data) $(M_1, AD)$ and $(M_2, AD)$ with the same secret key $K$ then the confidentiality and the integrity of the plaintexts are not preserved in $\pi$–Cipher. This can be achieved under the assumption that $PMN$ is always different for any two pairs of messages with the same key.

Additionally, $\pi$-Cipher offers an intermediate level of robustness when a legitimate key holder uses the same secret key $K$, the same associated data $AD$, the same public message number $PMN$ but different secret message numbers $SMN_1$ and $SMN_2$ for encrypting two different plaintexts $M_1$ and $M_2$. In that case confidentiality and integrity of the plaintexts are preserved. However, in that case the confidentiality of $SMN_1$ and $SMN_2$ is not preserved.

3. If verification fails, the decrypted message and the wrong tag should not be given as an output;

*Cipher-structure (Encrypt than MAC).* First we want to point out that it is relatively straightforward to show that the $\pi$-Cipher is an Encrypt-then-MAC authenticated cipher. Let us recall the definition for the Encrypt-then-MAC authenticated cipher: We say that the authenticated cipher is Encrypt-then-MAC if a message $M$ is encrypted under a secret key $K_1$ and then the tag $T$ is calculated with another secret key $K_2$ as $MAC(K_2, C)$. The pair $(C, T)$ is the output of the authenticated encryption procedure.

If we describe the e-triplex component used in $\pi$-Cipher in a mathematical form we have the following. First the message $M$ is encrypted producing the ciphertext $C$ as

$$IS \leftarrow \pi(CIS_{bitrate} \oplus counter \;\|\|\| \; CIS_{capacity}),$$

$$C \leftarrow M \oplus IS_{bitrate}.$$

Then, the tag $T$ is calculated as

$$t \leftarrow \pi(C \;\|\|\| \; IS_{capacity})_{bitrate}.$$

Here, the value of $CIS_{bitrate} \oplus counter \;\|\|\| \; CIS_{capacity}$ has the role of $K_1$ in the definition of Encrypt-then-MAC, and the value of $C \;\|\|\| \; IS_{capacity}$ has the role of the pair $(K_2, C)$ in the $MAC(K_2, C)$ part of the definition of Encrypt-then-MAC.

*Associated Data and NONCE reuse.* If we encrypt two different plaintexts $M_1$ and $M_2$ with the same secret key $K$, associated data $AD$ and nonce $NONCE = (PMN, SMN)$, then neither the confidentiality nor the integrity of the plaintexts are preserved in the $\pi$–Cipher. However, as one measure to reduce the risks of a complete reuse of the $NONCE$ we have adopted the strategy of a composite $NONCE = (PMN, SMN)$. If either $PMN$ or $SMN$ are different, then both the confidentiality and integrity of plaintexts are preserved.

*Plaintext corruption, associated-data corruption, message-number corruption, ciphertext corruption.* We posit that the $\pi$-Cipher can straightforwardly be proven INT-CTXT secure under the assumption that the permutation $\pi$ is an ideal random permutation without any structural distinguishers, by adapting the proof of the XOR-MAC scheme [1]. This is due to the close resemblance of the tag-generation part of the $\pi$-Cipher with the XOR-MAC.

*Ciphertext prediction.* The best distinguishing attack that we know for the $\pi$-Cipher is for the versions $\pi16$-Cipher096 and $\pi16$-Cipher128 with just one round and is described in [10]. The complexity of the attack is $2^{65}$ computations of the operation $*$, and the space is $2^{65} \times 16 = 2^{69}$ bytes.

*Replay and reordering.* For the $\pi$-Cipher, the standard defense against both replay and reordering is for the sender to use strictly increasing public message numbers $PMN$s, and for the receiver to refuse any message whose message number is no larger than the largest number of any verified message. This requires both the sender and receiver to keep state.

*Sabotage.* The $\pi$-Cipher puts the encryption of the $SMN$ value as the first block of the ciphertext $C$. Thus, in protocols that use the $\pi$-Cipher, the receiver can make an early reject of invalid messages by decrypting the first block (containing the SMN) and comparing it to its expected value. Only if this check passes the receiver continues with the rest of the decryption and tag computation. Note however, that this requires the protocol to not return error messages to the sender, in order to avoid timing attacks. AES-GCM does not have this property.

*Plaintext espionage.* Since the attacker's goal here is to figure out the user's secret message, the only feasible attack can happen when the size of the secret message is small by building a table of encrypted secret messages. To defend against this attack the $\pi$-Cipher requires the nonce pair $NONCE = (PMN, SMN)$ to have a unique value for every encryption.

*Message-number espionage.* In the $\pi$-Cipher there is a dedicated phase for encrypting the secret message number $SMN$, and figuring out the value of $SMN$ is equivalent to breaking the whole cipher which is infeasible under the assumptions that the permutation $\pi()$ is random.

*General input scheduling.* The $\pi$-Cipher can offer two ways for reducing the latency: **(1)** If the key $K$ and the public message number $PMN$ are known in advance and used repeatedly, then it is possible to precompute phase 1. and store the resulting Common Internal State (CIS) for subsequent applications of the cipher. **(2)** If the key $K$, the public message number $PMN$ and the associated data $AD$ are known in advance and used repeatedly, then it is possible to precompute both phase 1. *and* phase 2. for subsequent uses. In both cases, in order to preserve the confidentiality and the integrity of the plaintext, for every encryption the secret message numbers $SMN$'s must be unique.

## 4.1  Security Analysis

We give a bit diffusion analysis for one round of the $\pi$ function of $\pi16$-Cipher, $\pi32$-Cipher and $\pi64$-Cipher.

In our analysis, we examine the propagation of a one bit difference in a 1000 randomly generated Internal states $IS$ for one round of the $\pi$ function.

We performed several experiments for different word sizes ($\omega = 16, 32, 64$). We measure the Hamming distance between the outputs ($\pi(IS)$ and $\pi(IS')$), where one bit is changed in the $IS$ ($HammingDistance(IS, IS') = 1$). The results for $\omega = 16, 32, 64$ are shown in Figure 9, Figure 10 and Figure 11.

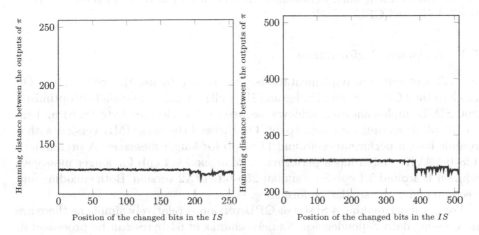

**Fig. 9.** Avalanche effect of one round of the $\pi$ function where $\omega = 16$ ($Min = 120.732$, **Avg = 127.255**, $Max = 128.731$)

**Fig. 10.** Avalanche effect of one round of the $\pi$ function where $\omega = 32$ ($Min = 226.063$, **Avg = 256.765**, $Max = 251.472$)

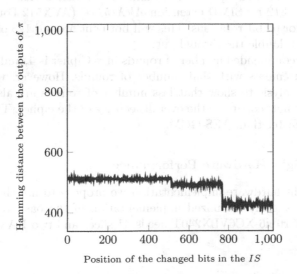

**Fig. 11.** Avalanche effect of one round of the $\pi$ function where $\omega = 64$ ($Min = 400.88$, **Avg = 485.646**, $Max = 515.76$)

# 5    Performances

Measurement bias has been shown to be commonplace and significant in real applications [20]. In order to minimize bias we have disabled any frequency scaling, disabled Address Space Layout Randomization and verified that there are no environment bias. Performance has been obtained on an Intel® Core™ i7-4771 Haswell CPU.

## 5.1    Software Performance

For efficient software implementations, we propose to use the $\pi$64-Cipher. On modern Intel CPUs (Sandy Bridge and Haswell) the initial and slightly optimized non-SIMD implementation achieves between 6.5 cycles per byte (cpb) and up to 12 cpb depending on round count. On Haswell the non-SIMD version with 4 rounds have a performance around 11.8 cpb for longer messages. A preliminary 128-bit AVX version has a performance of around 9.4 cpb for longer messages, while it is around 5.1 cpb for a similar 256-bit AVX2 version. Both encoding and decoding have the similar performance.

For $\pi$-Cipher making a SIMD or GPU version is relatively simple as there are no crossing data dependencies. Namely, chunks of 64 bytes can be processed in parallel, and only a single SIMD wide horizontal addition is required at the very end, independent of how many chunks have been processed.

The main reason the performance scaling is not linear for the AVX version is that Haswell has more scalar pipelines than AVX and the lack of a AVX rotate instruction. Rotate must therefore be emulated with two shifts and one *or* instructions. For SSE up to 2 additional move instructions are needed as well. Intel's new 512-bit SIMD extention *AVX-512F* (AVX512 Foundation) has direct support for 64 bit rotations. This will both cut around 1/3 of the required instructions and double the throughput.

The initial recommended number of rounds in $\pi$-Cipher is 4, and we presented here the measurements with that number of rounds. However, we expect the ongoing cryptanalysis to show that less number of rounds are also sufficiently secure and does not jeopardize the overall security of the cipher. That will make $\pi$-Cipher even faster than AES-GCM.

## 5.2    Lightweight Hardware Performance

For a lightweight hardware implementation we propose to use the $\pi$16-Cipher. Our initial and slightly optimized implementation of the basic operation * on FPGA Xilinx Virtex6-XC6VLX240T needs 41 slices and two RAM blocks.

# 6 Conclusion

We have presented the design of π-Cipher. It is parallel, incremental, nonce based authenticated encryption cipher with associated data. It is designed with the special purpose of providing confidentiality and integrity for big data in transit or at rest and it offers many advantages compared with AES-GCM. Additionally, it has as an option, a secret part of the nonce which provides nonce-misuse resistance.

The design is based on several solid cryptographic concepts such as the Encrypt-then-MAC principle, the XOR MAC scheme and the two-pass sponge construction. It contains parameters that can provide the functionality of tweakable block ciphers for authenticated encryption of data at rest.

The security of the cipher relies on the core permutation function based on ARX (Addition, Rotation and XOR) operations. π-Cipher offers several security levels ranging from 96 to 256 bits.

# References

1. Bellare, M., Guérin, R., Rogaway, P.: XOR MACs: New methods for message authentication using finite pseudorandom functions. In: Coppersmith, D. (ed.) CRYPTO 1995. LNCS, vol. 963, pp. 15–28. Springer, Heidelberg (1995)
2. Bernstein, D.J.: Caesar: Competition for authenticated encryption: Security, applicability, and robustness. CAESAR web page (2013), http://competitions.cr.yp.to/index.html
3. Bertoni, G., Daemen, J., Peeters, M., Van Assche, G.: On the indifferentiability of the sponge construction. In: Smart, N.P. (ed.) EUROCRYPT 2008. LNCS, vol. 4965, pp. 181–197. Springer, Heidelberg (2008)
4. Bertoni, G., Daemen, J., Peeters, M., Van Assche, G.: Duplexing the sponge: Single-pass authenticated encryption and other applications. In: Miri, A., Vaudenay, S. (eds.) SAC 2011. LNCS, vol. 7118, pp. 320–337. Springer, Heidelberg (2012)
5. Cisco. Cisco visual networking index: Forecast and methodology, 2012-2017. White Paper (May 2013), http://www.cisco.com/c/en/us/solutions/collateral/service-provider/visual-networking-index-vni/VNI_Hyperconnectivity_WP.pdf
6. Ferguson, N., Whiting, D., Housley, R.: Counter with cbc-mac (ccm). IETF Request for Comments: 3610 (September 2003), http://tools.ietf.org/html/rfc3610
7. EMC: The emc digital universe study – with research and analysis by idc. Open Report (April 2014), http://www.emc.com/leadership/digital-universe/index.htm?pid=home-dig-uni-090414
8. Electronics Freedom and Tech. Historical cost of computer memory and storage. hblok.net (February 2013), http://hblok.net/blog/storage/
9. Gligoroski, D., Mihajloska, H., Jacobsen, H.: Should MAC's retain hash properties when the key is known in the next AEAD? Presentation at DIAC 2013 (2013), http://2013.diac.cr.yp.to/slides/gligoroski.pdf
10. Gligoroski, D., Mihajloska, H., Samardjiska, S., Jacobsen, H., El-Hadedy, M., Jensen, R.E.: π-cipher v1. Cryptographic competitions: CAESAR (2014), http://competitions.cr.yp.to/caesar-submissions.htmls

11. Gligoroski, D., Ødegård, R.S., Mihova, M., Knapskog, S.J., Kocarev, L., Drápal, A., Klima, V.: Cryptographic hash function EDON-$\mathcal{R}'$. In: 1st International Workshop on Security and Communication Networks, Trondheim, Norway, pp. 85–95. IEEE (May 2009)
12. Gueron, S.: Intel's new AES instructions for enhanced performance and security. In: Dunkelman, O. (ed.) FSE 2009. LNCS, vol. 5665, pp. 51–66. Springer, Heidelberg (2009)
13. IDEMA. The advent of advanced format. idema.org (2013), http://www.idema.org/?page_id=2369
14. Jutla, C.S.: Encryption modes with almost free message integrity. Cryptology ePrint Archive, Report 2000/039 (2000), http://eprint.iacr.org/
15. Jutla, C.S.: Encryption modes with almost free message integrity. In: Pfitzmann, B. (ed.) EUROCRYPT 2001. LNCS, vol. 2045, pp. 529–544. Springer, Heidelberg (2001)
16. Leurent, G.: Tag Second-preimage Attack against $\pi$-cipher (March 2014)
17. Wagner, D., Bellare, M., Rogaway, P.: A conventional authenticated-encryption mode. NIST Modes Operation Symmetric Key Block Ciphers (2003), http://csrc.nist.gov/groups/ST/toolkit/BCM/documents/proposedmodes/eax/eax-spec.pdf
18. McGrew, D.A., Viega, J.: The galois/counter mode of operation (gcm). NIST Modes Operation Symmetric Key Block Ciphers (2005), http://www.csrc.nist.gov/CryptoToolkit/modes/proposedmodes/gcm/gcmrevised-spec.pdf
19. Morawiecki, P., Pieprzyk, J.: Parallel authenticated encryption with the duplex construction. Cryptology ePrint Archive, Report 2013/658 (2013), http://eprint.iacr.org/
20. Mytkowicz, T., Diwan, A., Hauswirth, M., Sweeney, P.F.: Producing wrong data without doing anything obviously wrong! In: Proceedings of the 14th International Conference on Architectural Support for Programming Languages and Operating Systems, ASPLOS XIV, pp. 265–276. ACM, New York (2009)
21. National Institute of Standards and Technology (NIST). Modes development. Computer Security Resource Center (2000), http://csrc.nist.gov/groups/ST/toolkit/BCM/modes_development.html
22. Rogaway, P., Bellare, M., Black, J., Krovetz, T.: Ocb: a block-cipher mode of operation for efficient authenticated encryption. In: Reiter, M.K., Samarati, P. (eds.) ACM Conference on Computer and Communications Security, pp. 196–205. ACM (2001)
23. Wagner, D.: A generalized birthday problem. In: Yung, M. (ed.) CRYPTO 2002. LNCS, vol. 2442, pp. 288–303. Springer, Heidelberg (2002)

# What Would It Take for You to Tell Your Secrets to a Cloud?

## Studying Decision Factors When Disclosing Information to Cloud Services

Julio Angulo[1], Erik Wästlund[2], and Johan Högberg[3]

[1] Dep. of Information Management, Karlstad University, Sweden
julio.angulo@kau.se
[2] Dep. of Psychology, Karlstad University, Sweden
erik.wastlund@kau.se
[3] Dep. of IT Management, Swedish Consumer Agency, Sweden
johan.hogberg@konsumentverket.se

**Abstract.** We investigate the end users' behaviours and attitudes with regards to the control they place in the personal information that they disclose to cloud storage services. Three controlled experiments were carried out to study the influence in users' decisions to retain or surrender control over their personal information depending on different factors. The results of these experiments reveal, among other things, the users' willingness to surrender control over personal information that is perceived as non-sensitive in exchange for valuable rewards, and that users would value the possibility of knowing and controlling the parties who are granted access to their data in the cloud. Based on the results from the experiments we provide implications for the design of end-user tools that can promote transparency and accountability in cloud computing environments.

**Keywords:** Cloud computing, mental models, HCI, UX, privacy, security, accountability, transparency, psychology, information control.

## 1 Introduction

A survey commissioned by Citrix in the Autumn of 2012 [1] revealed that 51% of American respondents believed that the weather can affect cloud computing and 31% indicated that privacy concerns is one of the main disincentives for adopting cloud computing. Similar statements were found in [2]. These results show that individuals who are not technically oriented or computer savvy can have strong misconceptions regarding what cloud computing really is and how it is being used in their daily lives. This in turn implies that people lack knowledge about appropriate approaches to protect and retain control over their personal information in cloud computing environments.

K. Bernsmed and S. Fischer-Hübner (Eds.): NordSec 2014, LNCS 8788, pp. 129–145, 2014.
DOI: 10.1007/978-3-319-11599-3_8, © Springer International Publishing Switzerland 2014

There is a need to further understand users' perceptions and reactions to cloud computing in order to design appropriate ex ante transparency tools[1] that will help these users make informed decisions about the type of personal data that they disclose in their daily interactions with cloud services. Furthermore, accountable cloud service providers could benefit from knowledge about some of the factors that can induce users' trust at the moment of registering to these services, and the types of information that people are willing to disseminate to these services.

We designed and carried out three controlled experiments with the purpose of investigating some of the factors that influence the users' willingness to control their data disclosures to online cloud services. This paper reports on the results of these experiments and the implications for the design of technological solutions and transparency enhancing tools (TETs) that have the goal of promoting the trustworthiness of cloud computing services by allowing cloud service providers across entire cloud service value chains to become accountable for the privacy and confidentiality of the information they hold and process in a cloud ecosystem.

In this paper, we first present some related work in Section 2 on the users' perception of the control of their personal data and studies on their willingness to disseminate information to online services. Then, Section 3 formulates two hypotheses and a research question regarding users' decisions to retain or surrender control over their data, and the possible features to protect these data. The approaches for the three experiments are then described in Section 4 along with the corresponding results. Section 5 presents some implications and discussions surrounding the design of transparency tools in cloud services and also the limitations of the study. Concluding remarks are presented in Section 7.

## 2    Related Work

Previous studies have investigated the relationship between privacy concerns and the perceived control people have over their personal information on the Internet. For instance, Xu [3] describes how the introduction of privacy-enhancing technologies (PETs), government legislations and industry self-regulations are factors that increase users' perceived control over their information, and thus mitigate privacy concerns. Similarly, Hoadley et al. [4] investigated the privacy concerns of Online Social Network users when an illusory loss of privacy control was introduced to a social network platform, suggesting that users' who believe their information is more accessible to others will present higher privacy concerns and show more willingness to adjust their privacy settings. Additionally, studies by Brandimarte et al. [5] revealed effects on privacy concerns where increased perceived control over the release of personal information also increases the willingness of people to keep releasing sensitive information.

These studies suggest paradoxical and irrational behaviours by people when it comes to the value they place on their privacy when acting online. In particular, people who have an illusionary sense of control over their data are less likely

---

[1] We refer to *ex ante transparency* to the act of clearly describing data handling practices *before* disclosing information.

to protect their privacy in reality [6]. However, people seldom have an accurate perception on the actual amount of control they have over their information. Other similar studies have corroborated that people's stated privacy concerns are not necessarily strong predictors for actual privacy related behaviours [7–9]. Recently, a study by Adjerid et al. [10] argued that attempts to simplify privacy policies in order to make the data handling practices more transparent to users have lesser impact on users' disclosure decisions than what is commonly thought by policy makers and privacy advocates.

Regarding privacy in cloud services, Ion et al. [11] have shown that individual end users of cloud services have strong privacy concerns, trust local storage devices more than cloud storage when dealing with sensitive data, but are not fully aware of the risks posed by cloud storage services. Their study shows that end users have a strong belief that the Internet is intrinsically insecure and present a cultural comparisons in users' attitudes towards cloud computing. Similarly, other studies have shown that people are concerned and express negative feelings about the fact that services spread their information to third parties (even when they inadvertently consented to it) [12].

Marshall & Tang [13], identify five common use cases among individual end users of these kind of services, including using the cloud as a repository to exchange files between own devices, using the cloud as a shared repository to collaboratively edit content in the cloud, backing up and editing content of own files offline, editing content of files reflected in others' devices, and synchronization of files. Based on their empirical work, the authors suggest some design implications on how cloud storage providers could improve the user experience, including designing for transparency of the syncing processes.

Complementing the research done by the studies mentioned above, we set out to investigate the extent to which people are willing to retain or give away control over their personal information in exchange for perceived valuables (such as saving time, less cognitive burdens, more cloud storage space or additional transparency features), as well as the way in which service providers can influence people's control decisions based on the way these providers frame their service offerings. The results can be beneficial for cloud providers who want to be seen as trustworthy and accountable for their data handling practices. There is also a lack of research on the possible privacy- and transparency features that cloud consumers would appreciate and find useful at the moment of protecting and controlling their data stored and handled by cloud service providers.

## 3    Research Hypotheses and Questions

Motivated by the findings of previous research, we formulated a series of hypotheses with the intention of getting a better understanding of what users value, what they think is important, and some of the factors that will motivate them to take the decision to either retain or surrender control over their personal data that they disclose to cloud service providers.

Based on studies that suggest that people are willing to receive small monetary value in exchange of their personal data [14–16], the first hypothesis ($H_1$) for

**Table 1.** Descriptions of the four experiments

| Hypotheses / question | Experiment | $n$ |
|---|---|---|
| $H_1$:End users are more willing to give away control of their personal data to a cloud service in exchange for observable valuables (such as free cloud storage) | Section 4.1: Users' willingness to surrender control over personal data based on value gained | 120 |
| $H_2$:End users willingness to release personal data depends on how the cloud service expresses benefits in terms of cognitive effort or time spent at the moment of releasing data | Section 4.2: Users' willingness to disclose data depending on how a cloud service frames the effort required to disclose these data | 117 |
| $Q_1$:End users have preferences over certain features for managing their data released to a cloud service | Section 4.3: Desired features of cloud storage services | 179 |

this study states that *people are more willing to give up control of their data if they are offered an observable valuable by the cloud provider*, such as extra cloud storage space.

The second hypothesis ($H_2$) is based on decision and choice theories suggesting that a decision problem described in different ways will render different results [17]. Therefore $H_2$ states that *people are more willing to give away control of their personal information when the option for giving away control is framed by the cloud provider as demanding less time or cognitive effort.*

Lastly, we investigate a research question ($Q_1$) stating *what are people's preferences for privacy and transparency features if they were to be offered by a cloud service provider?*

Table 1 shows a summary description of the two hypotheses and the research question, along with the corresponding experiments to address them and the number of people ($n$) who participated in each experiment.

## 4    Experimental Approach

To capture people's decision process regarding the perceived control they have over their personal data, we created a registration page for a fictitious cloud storage service provider, which we named *SheepCloud*, shown in Figure 1. We considered the ecological validity of the study by simulating a real-world situation as close as possible [18, pp.471], while trying to respect the privacy of the participants. Therefore, participants of the experiments were deceived into believing that SheepCloud was a real, newly started cloud service that allowed them to meet new people with their same interests based on the content that they stored and shared in this cloud storage service. They were told that the service needed to be populated with new users in order to test and improve the algorithm for matching people with similar interests.

To register into SheepCloud test participants needed to provide some personal attributes (as defined by the EU Directive 95/46/EC) and they needed to answer a set of ten questions[2] with possible answers being "Yes", "No", or "No comment". Requesting these data was done to elicit the belief that participants

---

[2] The ten questions were initially inspired by previous studies on the paradox of control [5], and were later refined to fit the purposes of our study. The two groups of ten questions used can be found in [19].

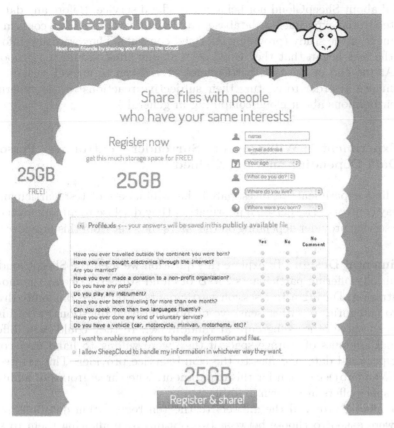

**Fig. 1.** SheepCloud, a fictitious cloud storage service used in the experiments

were not anonymous and could be directly identified. In fact, their personal data was actually not collected or stored at this point, neither were the specific answers to the ten questions (only the total sum of "Yes", "No", or "No comment" responses). All the necessary steps were taken to adhere to the Swedish Research Councils' principles of ethical research [20].

Participants were made to believe that their answers to these questions would be stored in a public file accessible by everyone on their newly created storage space. In order to test people's willingness to retain or give away control over their data, participants of the first experiment (Section 4.1) and the third experiment (Section 4.3) were randomly allocated into two groups, in which the control group was shown ten questions that were considered of a non-sensitive nature, and the experimental group was shown ten questions that were considered privacy sensitive. A Mann–Whitney U Test for independence samples [21] confirmed that these two sets of questions were actually experienced differently between the two groups of participants (in Experiment 1 $U(97) = 656.50, Z = -4.831, \rho < 0.001$; and in Experiment 3 $U(151) = 1957.00, Z = -3.498, \rho < 0.001$).

Once participants clicked on the "Register & share" button and thought they had submitted their information and answers to the ten questions, they were debriefed about SheepCloud not being a real cloud service. Before any data was submitted to the experiments' database, participants were asked to confirm their involvement in the study (providing informed consent). They were also informed before the test began that they could stop at any time, would they choose to do so. At the end of the test, participants were asked to answer a short post-questionnaire in order to capture their subjective reactions to the experiment and their opinions about cloud computing in general.

## 4.1 Experiment 1: Willingness to Surrender Control over Personal Data Depending on Value Gained

In this first experiment we investigated the willingness of test participants to give away control of the personal information they disclose to an unknown cloud storage service provider depending on the offers they get from this provider ($H_1$).

**Experimental Design.** To explore this question we used the SheepCloud scenario initially offering participants $25GB$ of cloud storage space at the moment of registration. During a test session participants, who were randomly divided into two categories of either sensitive or non-sensitive questions, were further assigned to three other subgroups at random, where they could earn different additional amounts of storage space if they were willing to hand over control of their personal data and files to the cloud service provider. This created a 2 x 3 between subject design for this experiment. The three groups of additional storage space offers are shown in Table 2.

After having provided the answers to the ten registration questions participants were asked to choose between two options, one allowing them to select privacy and control features and the other one stating that they were willing to allow SheepCloud to control their information. Choosing the second option would reward them with extra storage space (except in the case of the control group). We made sure that the offered storage space was always visible to participants. These two options were carefully phrased as follows:

- *"I want to choose how SheepCloud handles my information and files."*
- *"I allow SheepCloud to handle my information in whichever way they want."*

**Table 2.** Conditions of storage space offers for Experiment 1

| Condition | Description |
|-----------|-------------|
| 0 GB baseline | No additional extra storage offered |
| +25 GB | Double the initial storage offered |
| +100 GB | Large amount of storage offered |

**Fig. 2.** Participants were rewarded with extra GB of storage space if they were willing to give away control of their data

Figure 2 shows an example of group three, where a participant can increase the initial offer of $25GB$ to $125GB$ if she chooses to give away control of her information to SheepCloud at the moment of registration.

**Participants.** For this experiment a total of 140 participants submitted a response. Approximately 25 of these participants were recruited face-to-face, and the rest of participants were recruited through an international crowdsourcing service[3]. These participants were rewarded with about 0.20¢ if they completed the test satisfactorily. The data were analyzed to detect and exclude those remote participants who did not take the test seriously, leaving a total of 120 participants considered for the experiment. From these, 66 were between 18-23 years old, 45 were between 24-30, 18 were between 31-40, and 5 were older than 41 years old.

**Results.** A logistic regression analysis showed no statistical significant influence on the willingness to control personal data by neither the level of the sensitivity of the questions, $\rho > 0.58$, or by the amount of cloud storage space offered, $\rho > 0.06$.

However, considering only the participants who were assigned to the non-sensitive data group as the baseline, it can be observed in Table 3 that for this group there is a difference on the willingness to control data depending on the amount of storage offered. The chi-square statistic, $\chi^2(2, n = 54) = 10.19, \rho < 0.01$, indicates that the level of storage space offered is a predictor on the users' choice of control over their data in this case. This implies that hypothesis $H_1$ is confirmed for this group, meaning that participants were actually willing to give away control of their data in exchange of free storage space as long as these data were seen as non-sensitive. Nevertheless, this is not the case when looking only at the participants assigned to the sensitive data group, $\chi^2(2, n = 66) = 1.84, \rho > 0.39$.

The answers to the post-questionnaire reveal that a 70% of participants who stated that they have never heard the term "cloud computing" did in fact use at least one cloud service, suggesting that people do not comprehend the actual

---

[3] Microworkers http://www.microworkers.org

meaning of their data being stored in the "cloud" and its consequences. Also, 41% of participants indicated that they would appreciate it a lot if a service provider made it easier to understand their legal rights with regards to the use of their data.

**Table 3.** Crosstabulation of the willingness to control data depending on the sensitivity of the data and the amount of storage offered

|  |  | Choice of control | | Total |
|---|---|---|---|---|
|  |  | User control | Cloud control |  |
| Sensitive | 0 GB | 6 | 2 | 8 |
|  | + 25 GB | 15 | 16 | 31 |
|  | + 100 GB | 15 | 12 | 27 |
| Non-sensitive | 0 GB | 13 | 3 | 16 |
|  | + 25 GB | 11 | 11 | 22 |
|  | + 100 GB | 4 | 12 | 16 |
|  | Total | 64 | 56 | 120 |

## 4.2  Experiment 2: Framing of Required Effort

The objective of this experiment was to investigate if test participants are willing to give up their privacy in order to save time or spend less cognitive effort when registering to a cloud service. This was achieved by varying the way in which choice of control over personal data was framed to participants at the moment of registration and then measuring these users' privacy behaviours in terms of retaining or giving up control of their personal data ($H_2$).

**Experimental Design.** In this experiment, after giving away their initial registration information and answering ten non-sensitive personal questions, participants were given the choice of completing SheepCloud's registration process either by filling their profile information manually (i.e., having more control over the data their were releasing) or by fetching information automatically from a third party identity provider (i.e., lesser control). A sample screenshot is shown in Figure 3.

The experiment had a 1 x 3 between subjects design, where participants were assigned to experimental groups randomly until all conditions reached about 40 responses. In this case, the independent variable *framing* could take the values of "no framing", "full control" and "save time". Three conditions were tested based on these values, as summarized in Table 4.

**Participants.** For this experiment the responses of 121 individuals were considered. Among them 54 were within the age range of 19-23 years old, 45 within 24-30, 11 within 31-40, 9 within 41-50 and 2 within 51-60. For this experiment, all participants were recruited face-to-face, the majority at the University campus. About 65% percent of the approached persons agreed to participate in the study.

**Table 4.** Three framing conditions for testing required effort

| Condition | Description |
|---|---|
| **No framing** baseline | *"You can choose automatic or manual registration"* |
| **Full control framing** | *"You can control exactly what information you want to give us by choosing manual registration"* |
| **Save time framing** | *"You can save five minutes by choosing automatic registration"* |

**Results.** A Pearson chi-square test for independence was conducted showing that the independent variable caused a significant change, $\chi^2(2, n = 121) = 13.20, \rho < 0.001$, on the acceptance to give away control, with a medium effect size ($Cramer's\ V = 0.33$) according to Cohen's conventions for Cramer's V [22]. Comparing the individual framing conditions post hoc two Pearson chi-square tests (with Yates continuity correction) were conducted. Using Bonferroni adjusted alpha levels of 0.025 (0.05/2) there was a significant increase in the acceptance of giving away control $\chi^2(2, n = 84) = 7.00, \rho < 0.008$ (with a medium effect size $Cramer's\ V = 0.31$) when the saving time condition was presented compared to the no framing condition. This effect was not seen when the framing for full control was used $\chi^2(1, n = 80) = 0.039, \rho < 0.842$ compared to the no framing condition. Descriptive statistics of the results of this experiment are laid out in Table 5.

The results of this experiment showed that users accept loss of control when disclosing their own data to a greater extent when the low control alternative (i.e., automatic registration) is framed as saving time (thus, demanding less effort). This supports $H_2$ stated earlier. However, the opposite was not the case, in other words when the manual registration was framed as getting full control.

**Fig. 3.** Framing the choice of automatic registration as a way to save five minutes in the save time framing condition

**Table 5.** Percentage of chosen level of control for the no frame, the save time and the full control frame condition

| Chosen control level | Full control (n = 37) | Save time (n = 41) | No frame (n = 43) |
|---|---|---|---|
| High (Manual registration) | 81.10% | 46.30% | 76.70% |
| Low (Automatic registration) | 18.90% | 53.70% | 23.30% |

### 4.3    Experiment 3: Desired Features of Cloud Storage Services

The purpose for this last experiment was to determine possible privacy and transparency-enhancing features that an accountable cloud provider could offer its users which would be most valued and prioritized by these users ($Q_1$).

The possible features presented to participants in this experiment were selected from previous elicitation activities that took place within the [Anonymized] project. Through a series of earlier stakeholder workshops and focus groups, described in [23] and [19], a set of six important features for endowing users with control of their data and transparency of data practices were identified. These features included the possibilities for *data portability*, specifying levels of *visibility/accessibility* of data, *labelling* data into different categories, defining the levels of *security* for one or many data items, and deciding on the *locations* of the storage of the data which dictate the regulations that apply in these locations.

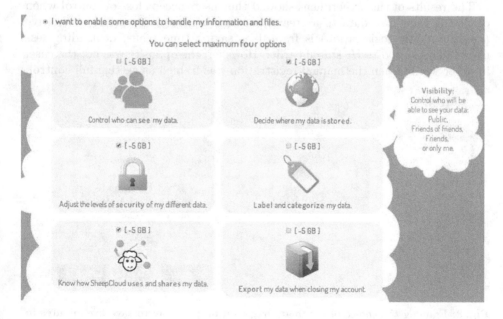

**Fig. 4.** Six privacy and transparency features offered by SheepCloud

In this experiment, for each of these features a brief description was shown to the participants inside a small "cloud tool-tip" that would appear on the side when the participant hovered the mouse over the corresponding feature.

**Experimental Design.** As in Experiment 1 (Section 4.1), participants were randomly selected into two groups, one group was asked a series of questions that were perceived as sensitive, whereas the other group was asked non-sensitive questions.

In order to force participants to select a set of preferred features out of the six offered, participants who decided to be in control of their own data were then given the option to select only four of the control features. All participants in this experiment were given an initial offer of $25GB$ of free storage space when they first accessed the SheepCloud registration page, but, in order to further encourage participants to make a careful choice of control features that they care about, for every control feature chosen the amount of free storage was reduced by $5GB$. The order in which the six features were shown was randomized. Figure 4 demonstrates the look-and-feel of the feature selection using the SheepCloud scenario. In this figure, three of the features have been selected, and thus $15GB$ have been deducted from the initial offering of $25GB$, hence leaving the user with $10GB$.

**Participants.** For this experiment, 24 participants were recruited in person and 162 participants were recruited through the same crowdsourcing service as in the first experiment, and data entries were screened for possible unmotivated or dishonest participants. At the end, the entries from 179 participants were considered for this experiment. From these, 60 were between 18-23 years old, 57 were 24-30, 39 were 31-40, and 24 were 41 or older. Respondents were located in many different parts of the world, including 102 of them in various countries of Europe and 39 of Asia.

**Results.** Out of the 179 people that completed the test, there were 101 participants who were shown questions considered sensitive and the remaining 78 participants were presented with non-sensitive questions. Only 68 (38%) enabled the options for controlling their own information and files. The remaining 111 (62%) indicated that they would let SheepCloud handle their information and files in whichever way this service provider wanted.

As with the first experiment, a Person chi-square test for independence revealed that there is no significant difference between the number of participants that wanted to have control over their own data and the ones giving away their control, when the sensitivity of the data was manipulated, $\chi^2(1, n = 179) = 0.181, \rho > 0.67$. In other words, 62% of participants chose to delegate control over their data and information to an unfamiliar cloud service provider, regardless of whether their data were sensitive or not.

This strengthens the earlier findings of Experiment 2 that show many people are not willing to spend too much cognitive effort at controlling certain aspects of

**Table 6.** Popularity of control features

| Feature | Description | Freq. | Percent |
|---|---|---|---|
| Visibility | Control who will be able to see your data (Public, friends of friends, friends or only me) | 36 | 52.90% |
| Usage | Determine the way SheepCloud uses and shares your data with other companies | 26 | 38.20% |
| Security | Control the levels of encryption of individual data items or groups of data | 22 | 32.40% |
| Location | Control where your data is stored and the laws that apply | 16 | 23.50% |
| Portability | Be able to download all your data locally in a standard format | 16 | 23.50% |
| Labelling | Tag your data with different labels, like "work", "family holidays", "high school", etc. | 9 | 13.20% |

their data. One possible reason for this is that lay users might find it confusing, burdensome or time consuming to select controls that help them protect their data and preserve their privacy (i.e. the same story of privacy getting in the way of the users' ultimate goal [24]). Another explanation is that they might not be well aware about the practical consequences of releasing personal information to a cloud service, and thus they lack the motivation to spend cognitive efforts at setting these controls.

Table 6 summarizes the preferred features as selected by the 68 participants who wanted control over their own data. Results show that participants would value most the possibility to decide who will have access to their data (i.e. 52.90% would like to have the "Visibility/Accessibility" feature), followed by the option to decide how the cloud service provider will use and share their data with third parties (38.20% value the "Usage" feature), as well as the opportunity to select the levels of security that apply to different data items (32.40% would like the "Security" feature).

## 5    Implications and Discussions

In general, the results from the experiments described in this article show that there are certain subtle influencing factors that can mold users' behaviours with regards to the decision they take about exercising control over their personal information. Based on our findings we present some implications for the design of solutions that can promote accountability and transparency in cloud services.

**Nudging Users into 'Sensitivity Mode'.** The results from Experiment 1 suggest that users might be willing to give away control of the data that are not seen as sensitive in exchange for something that they might perceived as valuable (in the case of this experiment, large amounts of free cloud storage space).

Based on this finding, it is advisable for accountable cloud service providers and designers of ex ante transparency solutions to nudge their users into realizing that data, which might not be initially perceived as sensitive, might become sensitive under other contexts. Illustrative examples of the consequences of distributing sensitive data can also be made available to users. By doing this, many users can be discouraged from giving away control over their data when they are nudged into perceiving these data as sensitive.

**Influencing Users to Make the Right Choice.** Results from Experiment 2 suggests that participants could be influenced in their decision of surrendering control over their data if the cloud service provider phrases its advantages as requiring less time or cognitive effort. At the same time, the responses from Experiment 3 hint that too much choices can lead participants to become confused or overwhelmed. This implies that an accountable cloud provider should simplify users' decision regarding control choices and perhaps eliminate alternative options that can lead users to become careless about the amount of control they have over their personal data. Instead, reasonable and adaptive default values should be in place. Clearly stating some of the possible consequences of giving away control over one's data is also crucial for motivating users in making the right choice and become more careful. Using the influence of framing to motivate users to select those choices that are more likely to protect their information can be good approach towards delivering accountable services.

**Avoid Overwhelming Users with Choices.** In Experiment 3 the majority of users chose to delegate the control over their data and files to an unfamiliar cloud service provider, regardless of whether these data were sensitive or not. The latter finding suggests that many people are not willing to spend too much time or cognitive effort at choosing controls to control their data. This finding is backed up by the results of Experiment 2, which showed that people accept giving away control of their data to an unknown cloud service if they are told they can save time. Furthermore, the surprising proportion of participants who chose to give away control to the cloud provider in Experiment 3 (62.01%) when compared to Experiment 1 (46.67%), can also suggest that the possibility to choose among alternatives to protect one's data can actually be overwhelming for the user.

It is recommended to endow the user interfaces of transparency tools with tooltips and concise help texts to clarify consequences of the users' actions at the moment when those actions are taking place. Also, displaying ex ante visualizations of possible data flows across chains of service providers (i.e. providing visual descriptions) could make users aware of the distribution, usage and access of their data while at the same time demanding less cognitive effort than reading long textual explanations.

**Choosing Transparency Features.** Experiment 3, which was motivated by the results of preliminary research activities shown in [19], showed that people would appreciate knowing who has access to their data and being informed of how these data are used. Cloud services that want to promote accountability and transparency could prioritize the implementation of these features on their graphical interfaces and APIs. However, a fine balance has to be found in which users are notified of certain aspects of the handling practices of their data without these notifications becoming tedious, ignored or perceived as spam. Displaying the possible parties involved in accessing users' data in an intuitive, informative and interesting manner is still an open design challenge.

# 6   Limitations

While we placed a lot of effort in trying to obtain the best results through the proper design of the experiments, the collection of data and the analysis, we are aware of some of the limitations of our study.

For instance, some criticism has been given to the recruitment of participants through crowdsourcing platforms, where higher financial incentives can increase the number of participants but not the quality of their responses [25]. In our studies, our crowd recruits were thanked with very small amounts of money, making the assumption that people who registered for the test were more interested in acquiring the cloud service than to receive monetary rewards (worth less than the prices given to the participants recruited in person). Besides, we took steps to filter responses that seemed irrelevant, not serious, or hurried.

Unfortunately, by recruiting people remotely, it was also hard for us to capture the number of participants who actually refused to register to the fictitious cloud storage service, SheepCloud, due to privacy concerns that arouse from the sensitive questions asked and the fact that SheepCloud was unknown to them as a cloud service. In the face-to-face recruitment processes some participants actually decided to abrupt the registration process (and thus opted out of the experiment) before clicking on the "Register & share!" button, since they did not want to release their information to this unknown service. Information about the proportion of people who decided not to release their data to SheepCloud would have been valuable, and this could be part of future studies.

Results from Experiment 1 and Experiment 3 did not show a strong relationship between the sensitivity of the data and the willingness to control it. The significance of the results from the third experiment could have been improved by examining only participants in the group with non-sensitive questions (since a statistically significant difference was shown in this group for Experiment 1). However, from the 68 participants in Experiment 3 who chose to control their own data only 31 got non-sensitive questions, which was not a large enough sample.

# 7   Concluding Remarks

This paper presented our attempt to understand users attitudes and behaviours with regards to their choice of retaining or giving control away of their personal data when disclosing these data to cloud service providers. To this end, we carried out a series of experiments making participants believe that they were about to disclose data to a new cloud service provider called SheepCloud. Besides understanding the users' willingness to control their data in the cloud, the results from these experiments provide some insights on the possible relevant factors that should be considered when designing ex ante transparency enhancing technologies (TETs) that can support users' informed decisions and their right to exercise control over the use of their own data in cloud environments.

Results have shown that there are indeed some factors that could induce people to tell their 'secrets' to a cloud and to grant control over these secrets. The following points summarize the relevant conclusions reached in the study:

*Experiment 1:*

- Perceived sensitivity of data can influence users' behaviour with regards to exercising control over these data.
- Users are willing to give away control of their non-sensitive data in exchange for a reward that they perceive as very valuable.
- Users are unaware or not well informed about the way certain types of online services handle their data and the consequences to their personal privacy.

*Experiment 2:*

- The way cloud services frame their offerings in terms of required effort can have an influence on the users' decision to surrender control over their released data.

*Experiment 3:*

- Users are unmotivated to spend cognitive effort or time at setting preference to protect their data in the cloud.
- Users can become sceptical towards unknown services that make exaggerated promises regarding their protection of their data.
- Users value most the possibility of knowing who is able to see their data (i.e. who has access to their data), as well as the having the ability to determine the way their data is being used and shared.

**Acknowledgments.** This work is partly funded by the European FP7 Project A4Cloud[4]. We would like to acknowledge the efforts of Hampus Sandstöm for his work within the project, as well as John-Sören Pettersson and Robin Larsson for the help with the data collection. Also, our thanks go to Simone Fischer-Hübner and to the other anonymous reviewers for their useful comments and advise.

# References

1. Wakefield Research: Partly cloudy – about cloud computing. Survey: Many believe 'the cloud' requires a rain coat. Technical report, Citrix (August 2012)
2. Barber, C.J., Oswalt, B., Smith, L.A.: Head in a cloud? A preliminary study of what business students know about cloud computing. Association of Business Information Systems, 63 (2013)

---

[4] A4Cloud - Accountability for the cloud and other future Internet services, http://www.a4cloud.eu

3. Xu, H.: The effects of self-construal and perceived control on privacy concerns. In: Twenty Eighth International Conference on Information Systems (ICIS), Montreal, Canada, p. 125. Citeseer (2007)
4. Hoadley, C.M., Xu, H., Lee, J.J., Rosson, M.B.: Privacy as information access and illusory control: The case of the facebook news feed privacy outcry. Electronic Commerce Research and Applications 9(1), 50–60 (2010)
5. Brandimarte, L., Acquisti, A., Loewenstein, G.: Misplaced confidences privacy and the control paradox. Social Psychological and Personality Science 4(3), 340–347 (2013)
6. Gross, R., Acquisti, A.: Information revelation and privacy in online social networks. In: Proceedings of the 2005 ACM Workshop on Privacy in the Electronic Society, WPES 2005, pp. 71–80. ACM, New York (2005)
7. Barnes, S.B.: A privacy paradox: Social networking in the united states. First Monday 11(9) (2006)
8. Spiekermann, S., Grossklags, J., Berendt, B.: E-privacy in 2nd generation e-commerce: privacy preferences versus actual behavior. In: Proceedings of the 3rd ACM Conference on Electronic Commerce, EC 2001, pp. 38–47. ACM, New York (2001)
9. Tufekci, Z.: Can you see me now? audience and disclosure regulation in online social network sites. Bulletin of Science, Technology & Society 28(1), 20–36 (2008)
10. Adjerid, I., Acquisti, A., Brandimarte, L., Loewenstein, G.: Sleights of privacy: framing, disclosures, and the limits of transparency. In: Proceedings of the Ninth Symposium on Usable Privacy and Security (SOUPS), Newcastle, UK, p. 9. ACM (July 2013)
11. Ion, I., Sachdeva, N., Kumaraguru, P., Čapkun, S.: Home is safer than the cloud!: privacy concerns for consumer cloud storage. In: Proceedings of the Seventh Symposium on Usable Privacy and Security, SOUPS 2011, pp. 13:1–13:20. ACM, New York (2011)
12. King, J., Lampinen, A., Smolen, A.: Privacy: Is there an app for that? In: Proceedings of the Seventh Symposium on Usable Privacy and Security, p. 12. ACM (2011)
13. Marshall, C., Tang, J.C.: That syncing feeling: Early user experiences with the cloud. In: Proceedings of the Designing Interactive Systems Conference, pp. 544–553. ACM (2012)
14. Danezis, G., Lewis, S., Anderson, R.J.: How much is location privacy worth? In: Proceedings of Fourth Workshop on Economics of Information Security (WEIS), Harvard, UK, vol. 5. Kennedy School of Government (2005)
15. Grossklags, J., Acquisti, A.: When 25 cents is too much: An experiment on willingness-to-sell and willingness-to-protect personal information. In: Proceedings of Sixth Workshop on the Economics of Information Security (WEIS 2007), Pittsburgh, PA, USA (June 2007)
16. Hann, I.H., Hui, K.L., Lee, S.Y.T., Png, I.P.: Online information privacy: Measuring the cost-benefit trade-off. In: International Conference on Information Systems (ICIS), Barcelona, Spain, p. 1 (December 2002)
17. Tversky, A., Kahneman, D.: The framing of decisions and the psychology of choice. Science 211(4481), 453–458 (1981)
18. Rogers, Y., Sharp, H., Preece, J.: Interaction Design: Beyond Human–Computer Interaction. In: Interaction Design: Beyond Human-computer Interaction. John Wiley & Sons (2011)

19. Angulo, J., Fischer-Hübner, S., Pettersson, J.S., Wästlund, E., Martucci, L.: D:C-7.1 General HCI principles and guidelines for accountability and transparency in the cloud. Project deliverable D:C-7.1, A4Cloud Project (September 2013)
20. Vetenskapsrådet:    Forskningsetiska    principer-inom    humanistisk-samhällsvetenskaplig forskning (2002)
21. Sawilowsky, S.S.: Nonparametric tests of interaction in experimental design. Review of Educational Research 60(1), 91–126 (1990)
22. Cohen, J.: Statistical power analysis for the behavioral sciences. Psychology Press (1988)
23. Brede Moe, N., Gilje Jaatun, M., Haugset, B., Niezen, M., Felizi, M.: D:b-2.4 stakeholder workshop 1 results (initial requirements). Technical report, A4Cloud Project (2013)
24. Whitten, A., Tygar, J.D.: Why Johnny Can't Encrypt: A Usability Evaluation of PGP 5.0. In: Proceedings of the 8th USENIX Security Symposium (1999)
25. Mason, W., Watts, D.J.: Financial incentives and the performance of crowds. ACM SigKDD Explorations Newsletter 11(2), 100–108 (2010)

# Network Security and Logging

# Efficient Record-Level Keyless Signatures for Audit Logs

Ahto Buldas[1], Ahto Truu[1], Risto Laanoja[1], and Rainer Gerhards[2]

[1] Guardtime AS, Tallinn, Estonia
{ahto.buldas,ahto.truu,risto.laanoja}@guardtime.com
[2] Adiscon GmbH, Großrinderfeld, Germany
rgerhards@adiscon.com

**Abstract.** We propose a log signing scheme that enables (a) verification of the integrity of the whole log, and (b) presentation of any record, along with a compact proof that the record has not been altered since the log was signed, without leaking any information about the contents of other records in the log. We give a formal security proof of the scheme, discuss practical considerations, and provide an implementation case study.

**Keywords:** applied security, secure logging, keyless signatures, cryptographic time-stamps, syslog, rsyslog.

## 1 Introduction

Increasingly, logs from various information systems are used as evidence and also the requirements on maintenance and presentation of the log data are growing. Availability is clearly the most important property. If the logs are not available when needed, any other qualities of the log data don't really matter. However, ensuring availability is outside of the scope of the current discussion.

Integrity and authenticity—confidence that the log has not been tampered with or replaced with another—are also quite obvious requirements, especially if the log is to be admitted as evidence in legal proceedings. Signing and time-stamping are standard solutions for proving authenticity and integrity of data.

As information systems usually log all their activities sequentially, often the details of the relevant transactions are interspersed with other information in a log. To protect the confidentiality of the unrelated events, it is desirable to be able to extract records from the signed log and still prove their integrity.

An example of such a case is a dispute between a bank and a customer. On one hand, the bank can't just present the whole log, as the log contains also information about transactions of other customers. On the other hand, the customer involved in the dispute should have a chance to verify the integrity of the relevant records. This feature has been asked for by several European financial institutions. Similar concerns arise in the context of multi-tenant cloud environments. Hence, an ideal log signing scheme should have the following properties:

- The integrity of the whole log can be verified by the owner of the log: no records can be added, removed or altered undetectably.

K. Bernsmed and S. Fischer-Hübner (Eds.): NordSec 2014, LNCS 8788, pp. 149–164, 2014.
DOI: 10.1007/978-3-319-11599-3_9, © Springer International Publishing Switzerland 2014

- The integrity of any record can be proven to a third party without leaking any information about the contents of any other records in the log.
- The signing process is efficient in both time and space. (Ideally, there is a small constant per-record processing overhead and a small constant per-log storage overhead.)
- The extraction process is efficient in both time and space. (Ideally, a small constant-sized proof of integrity can be extracted for any record in time sub-linear in the size of the log.)
- The verification process is efficient in time. (Ideally, it should be running in time linear in the size of the data to be verified—whether verifying the whole log or a single record.)

### 1.1    Related Work

Schneier and Kelsey [14] proposed a log protection scheme that encrypts the records using one-time keys and links them using cryptographic hash functions. The scheme allows both for verification of the integrity of the whole log and for selective disclosure of the one-time encryption keys. However, it needs a third party trusted by both the logger and the verifier and requires active participation of this trusted party in both phases of the protocol.

Holt [8] replaced the symmetric cryptographic primitives used in [14] and enabled verification without the trusted party. However, Holt's scheme requires public-key signatures on individual records, which adds high computational and storage overhead to the logging process. Also, the size of the information required to prove the integrity of one record is at least proportional to the square root of the distance of the record from the beginning of the log. Other proposed amendments [15,1] to the protocol from [14] have similar weaknesses.

Kelsey *et al* [11] proposed a log signing scheme where records are signed in blocks, by first computing a hash value of each record in a block and then signing the sequence of hash values. This enables efficient verification of the integrity of the whole block, significantly reduces the overhead compared to having a signature per record, and also removes the need to ship the whole log block when a single record is needed as evidence. But still the size of the proof of a record is linear in the size of the block. Also, other records in the same block are not protected from the informed brute-force attack discussed in Sec. 2.1.

Ma and Tsudik [12] utilised the authentication technique they called *FSSA* (*Forward-Secure Sequential Aggregate*) to construct a logging protocol which provides *forward-secure stream integrity*, retaining the provable security of the underlying primitives. They also proposed a possibility to store individual signatures to gain better granularity, at the expense of storage efficiency.

### 1.2    Our Contribution

We propose a log signing scheme based on Merkle tree aggregation [13]. While using Merkle trees to aggregate data before signing is not new, we are not aware of previous applications in logging context. Aside from application case study, our main scientific contribution is the method for generating multiple blinding masks from a single random value to achieve blinding that is provably as good as using independently generated random masks.

Compared to previous log signing schemes with selective disclosure, our method offers improvements as follows: unlike [14], or scheme does not require a trusted third party; the proof of integrity of a record is $O(\log N)$ in our scheme, compared to $O(\sqrt{N})$ in [8] and $O(N)$ in [11]; while the asymptotic complexities are not directly comparable, based on the performance comparison table provided in [12], where the best-case signer computation cost is 5.55 ms per log record (albeit on slightly weaker hardware than in our experiment), we can estimate that our scheme is two to three orders of magnitude faster.

An extended version of the paper with more technical details is available from the Cryptology ePrint Archive [5].

## 2    Data Model

We now present the design of a signing scheme that will allow us to achieve almost all of the goals (there will be some trade-offs on the efficiency goals, but no compromises on the security goals).

A computational process producing a log may, in principle, run indefinitely and thus the log as an abstract entity may not have a well-defined beginning and end. In the following, we model the log as an ordered sequence of blocks, where each block in turn is an ordered sequence of a finite number of records. Many practical logging systems work this way, for example in the case of `syslog` output being sent to a log file that is periodically rotated.

Signing each record individually would, of course, have very high overhead in both processing and storage, as signing is quite expensive operation and the size of a signature may easily exceed the size of a typical log record. More importantly, it would also fail to fully ensure the integrity of the log as a whole—deletion of a record along with its signature would not be detected. Signing each log block as a unit would satisfy all the requirements related to processing of the whole block, but would make it impossible to prove the integrity of individual records without exposing everything else in the block.

An improvement over both of the above naive strategies would be to compute a hash value of each record in a log block and then sign the sequence of hash values instead of the records themselves (as proposed by Kelsey et al in [11]). This would ensure the integrity of the whole log block, significantly reduce the overhead compared to signing each record separately and also remove the need to ship the whole log block when a single record is needed as evidence. But still the size of the proof of a record would be linear in the size of the block (and the latter could easily run into multiple millions of records for a busy system).

### 2.1    Merkle Trees with Blinding Masks

To further reduce the size of the evidence for a single record, the records can instead be aggregated using a data structure known as Merkle tree—a binary

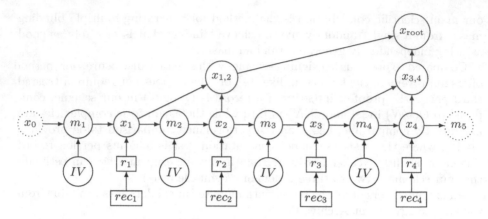

**Fig. 1.** Log signing using a Merkle tree with interlinks and blinding masks: $rec_i$ are the log records; $r_i$ are the hash values of the records; $IV$ is the random seed; $m_i$ are the blinding masks; $x_i$ are leaves and $x_{a,b}$ are internal nodes of the Merkle tree; $x_{\text{root}}$ is the value to be signed

tree whose leaves are the hash values of the records and each non-leaf node is the hash value of the concatenation its child nodes. The hash value in the root node of the tree can then be signed and for each leaf node a compact (logarithmic in the number of leaves) proof extracted showing that the hash value in the leaf participated in the computation that led to the signed root hash value. [13]

There are two complications left to be dealt with. The first one is that the security of such an aggregation scheme against retroactive fabrication of hash chains can in general be proven only if some restrictions are placed on the hash chains allowed as participation proofs. Fortunately, just appending the height of the sub-tree to the concatenated hash values from the child nodes before hashing is sufficient. This limits the length of the hash chains accepted during verification and allows for the security of the scheme to be formally proven. [4]

The second complication is that the hash chain extracted from the Merkle tree for one node contains the values of other nodes. A strong hash function can't be directly reversed to learn the input value from which a hash value in the chain was created. However, a typical log record may contain insufficient entropy to make that argument—an attacker who knows the pattern of the input could exhaustively test all possible variants to find the one that yields the hash value actually in the chain and thus learn the contents of the record. To prevent this kind of informed brute-force attack, a blinding mask with sufficient entropy can be added to each record before aggregating the hash values.

Generating cryptographically secure random values is expensive. Also, when an independent random mask would be used for each record, all these values would have to be stored for later verification. It is therefore much more efficient to derive all the blinding masks from a single random seed, as in the data structure shown on Fig. 1, where each node with incoming arrows contains the hash value of the concatenation of the contents of the respective source nodes.

# 3  Security Proof

We now show that the integrity proof for any record does not leak any information about the contents of any other records. The security of the scheme against modification of the log data has already been shown in [4].

We give the proof under the PRF assumption. Informally, the PRF assumption means that a 2-to-1 hash function $h : \{0,1\}^{2n} \to \{0,1\}^n$ can be assumed to behave like a random function $\Omega : \{0,1\}^n \to \{0,1\}^n$ when the first half of the input is a randomly chosen secret value $r \leftarrow \{0,1\}^n$.

**Definition 1 (PRF, Pseudo-Random Function Family).** *By an S-secure pseudo-random function family we mean an efficiently computable two-argument function h, such that if the first argument r is randomly chosen then the one-argument function $h(r, \cdot)$ (given to the distinguisher as a black box without direct access to r) is S-indistinguishable from the true random oracle $\Omega$ of the same type, i.e. for any t-time distinguisher D:*

$$\mathsf{Adv}(D) = \left| \Pr\left[1 \leftarrow D^{h(r, \cdot)}\right] - \Pr\left[1 \leftarrow D^{\Omega(\cdot)}\right] \right| \leq \frac{t}{S} ,$$

*where $r \leftarrow \{0,1\}^n$, $h : \{0,1\}^n \times \{0,1\}^p \to \{0,1\}^m$ and $\Omega : \{0,1\}^p \to \{0,1\}^m$.*

Note that the PRF assumption is very natural when $h$ is a 2-to-1 hash function, considering the design principles of hash functions, especially of those constructed from block ciphers.

**Definition 2 (IND-CPA, Indistinguishability under Chosen-Plaintext Attack).** *The log signing scheme is said to be S-secure IND-CPA content concealing, if any t-time adversary $A = (A_1, A_2)$ has success probability $\delta \leq \frac{t}{S}$ in the following attack scenario (Fig. 2, left):*

1. *The first stage $A_1$ of the adversary chooses the position $i$ and a list of records $rec_1, \ldots, rec_{i-1}, rec_{i+1}, \ldots, rec_\ell$, as well as two test records $rec_i^0, rec_i^1$ and an advice string $a$.*
2. *The environment picks randomly $x_0 \leftarrow 0^n$, $IV \leftarrow \{0,1\}^n$ and $b \leftarrow \{0,1\}$, assigns $rec_i \leftarrow rec_i^b$ and for every $j \in \{1, \ldots, \ell\}$ computes: $m_j \leftarrow h(IV, x_{j-1})$, $r_j \leftarrow \mathsf{H}(rec_j)$, and $x_j \leftarrow h(m_j, r_j)$.*
3. *The second stage $A_2$ of the adversary, given as input the advice string $a$ and the lists of hash values $x_1, \ldots, x_\ell$, and $m_1, \ldots, m_{i-1}, m_{i+1}, \ldots, m_\ell$, tries to guess the value of $b$ by outputting the guessed value $\hat{b}$.*

*The advantage of A is defined as $\delta = 2 \left| \Pr\left[\hat{b} = b\right] - \frac{1}{2} \right|$.*

**Theorem 1.** *If $h(IV, \cdot)$ is an S-secure pseudorandom function family, then the log signing scheme is $\frac{S}{4}$-secure IND-CPA content concealing.*

Game$_0$ or the original attack game:

1. $i, rec_1, \ldots, rec_{i-1}, rec_{i+1}, \ldots, rec_\ell,$
   $rec_i^0, rec_i^1, a \leftarrow A_1$
2. $x_0 \leftarrow 0^n,\ IV \leftarrow \{0,1\}^n,\ b \leftarrow \{0,1\}$
3. $rec_i \leftarrow rec_i^b$
4. **for each** $j \in \{1, \ldots, \ell\}$:
   (a) $m_j \leftarrow h(IV, x_{j-1})$
   (b) $r_j \leftarrow H(rec_j)$
   (c) $x_j \leftarrow h(m_j, r_j)$
5. $\hat{b} \leftarrow A_2(a, x_1, \ldots, x_\ell,$
   $m_1, \ldots, m_{i-1}, m_{i+1}, \ldots, m_\ell)$
6. **if** $\hat{b} = b$ **then** output 1
   **else** output 0

Game$_2$ or the Simulator $\mathcal{S}$:

1. $i, rec_1, \ldots, rec_{i-1}, rec_{i+1}, \ldots, rec_\ell,$
   $rec_i^0, rec_i^1, a \leftarrow A_1$
2. $x_0 \leftarrow 0^n,\ b \leftarrow \{0,1\}$
3. $rec_i \leftarrow rec_i^b$
4. **for each** $j \in \{1, \ldots, \ell\}$:
   (a) **if** $\exists k < j : x_{j-1} = x_{k-1}$
      **then** $m_j \leftarrow m_k$
      **else** $m_j \leftarrow \{0,1\}^n$
   (b) $r_j \leftarrow H(rec_j)$
   (c) **if** $j = i$
      **then** $x_j \leftarrow \{0,1\}^n$
      **else** $x_j \leftarrow h(m_j, r_j)$
5. $\hat{b} \leftarrow A_2(a, x_1, \ldots, x_\ell,$
   $m_1, \ldots, m_{i-1}, m_{i+1}, \ldots, m_\ell)$
6. **if** $\hat{b} = b$ **then** output 1
   **else** output 0

**Fig. 2.** The original attack game and the simulator

*Proof.* Let $A$ be a $t$-time adversary with success $\delta$. We define three games Game$_0$, Game$_1$, and Game$_2$, where Game$_0$ is the original attack game, Game$_2$ is a simulator in which the input of $A_2$ does not depend on $b$ and hence $\Pr\left[\hat{b} = b\right] = \frac{1}{2}$ in this game (Fig. 2), and Game$_1$ is an intermediate game, where $A$ tries to break the scheme with independent random masks (Fig. 3), i.e. the mask generation steps $m_j \leftarrow h(IV, x_{j-1})$ are replaced with independent uniform random choices $m_j \leftarrow \{0,1\}^n$. However, as $m_j$ is a function of $x_{j-1}$, we will use the same value for $m_j$ and $m_k$ in case $x_{j-1} = x_{k-1}$. This allows us to view the numbers $m_j$ as outputs of a random oracle $\Omega$ and perfect simulation is possible.

Game$_1$ or the intermediate game:

1. $i, rec_1, \ldots, rec_{i-1}, rec_{i+1}, \ldots, rec_\ell, rec_i^0, rec_i^1, a \leftarrow A_1$
2. $x_0 \leftarrow 0^n,\ b \leftarrow \{0,1\}$
3. $rec_i \leftarrow rec_i^b$
4. **for each** $j \in \{1, \ldots, \ell\}$:
   (a) **if** $\exists k < j : x_{j-1} = x_{k-1}$
      **then** $m_j \leftarrow m_k$
      **else** $m_j \leftarrow \{0,1\}^n$
   (b) $r_j \leftarrow H(rec_j)$
   (c) $x_j \leftarrow h(m_j, r_j)$
5. $\hat{b} \leftarrow A_2(a, x_1, \ldots, x_\ell, m_1, \ldots, m_{i-1}, m_{i+1}, \ldots, m_\ell)$
6. **if** $\hat{b} = b$ **then** output 1 **else** output 0

**Fig. 3.** The intermediate game for the security proof

| Distinguisher $D_{01}^{\Phi}$: | Distinguisher $D_{12}^{\Phi}$: |
|---|---|
| 1. $i, rec_1, \ldots, rec_{i-1}, rec_{i+1}, \ldots, rec_\ell,$<br>$\quad rec_i^0, rec_i^1, a \leftarrow A_1$<br>2. $x_0 \leftarrow 0^n, b \leftarrow \{0,1\}$<br>3. $rec_i \leftarrow rec_i^b$<br>4. **for each** $j \in \{1, \ldots, \ell\}$:<br>$\quad$ (a) $m_j \leftarrow \Phi(x_{j-1})$<br>$\quad$ (b) $r_j \leftarrow \mathsf{H}(rec_j)$<br>$\quad$ (c) $x_j \leftarrow h(m_j, r_j)$<br>5. $\hat{b} \leftarrow A_2(a, x_1, \ldots, x_\ell,$<br>$\quad m_1, \ldots, m_{i-1}, m_{i+1}, \ldots, m_\ell)$<br>6. **if** $\hat{b} = b$ **then** output 1<br>$\quad$ **else** output 0 | 1. $i, rec_1, \ldots, rec_{i-1}, rec_{i+1}, \ldots, rec_\ell,$<br>$\quad rec_i^0, rec_i^1, a \leftarrow A_1$<br>2. $x_0 \leftarrow 0^n, b \leftarrow \{0,1\}$<br>3. $rec_i \leftarrow rec_i^b$<br>4. **for each** $j \in \{1, \ldots, \ell\}$:<br>$\quad$ (a) **if** $\exists k < j : x_{j-1} = x_{k-1}$<br>$\quad\quad$ **then** $m_j \leftarrow m_k$<br>$\quad\quad$ **else** $m_j \leftarrow \{0,1\}^n$<br>$\quad$ (b) $r_j \leftarrow \mathsf{H}(rec_j)$<br>$\quad$ (c) **if** $j = i$<br>$\quad\quad$ **then** $x_j \leftarrow \Phi(r_i)$<br>$\quad\quad$ **else** $x_j \leftarrow h(m_j, r_j)$<br>5. $\hat{b} \leftarrow A_2(a, x_1, \ldots, x_\ell,$<br>$\quad m_1, \ldots, m_{i-1}, m_{i+1}, \ldots, m_\ell)$<br>6. **if** $\hat{b} = b$ **then** output 1<br>$\quad$ **else** output 0 |

**Fig. 4.** The distinguishers

Let $\delta_i$ $(i = 0, 1, 2)$ denote the probability that the adversary correctly guessed the value of $b$ (i.e. $\hat{b} = b$) in the game $\mathsf{Game}_i$. Hence, $\delta_2 = \frac{1}{2}$ and $\delta = 2|\delta_0 - \delta_2|$. We will now show that the games are negligibly close in terms of the adversary's advantage, and hence the adversary's success cannot be considerably higher in the original attacking game $\mathsf{Game}_0$ compared to the simulator $\mathcal{S}$. To show that $\mathsf{Game}_0$ is close to $\mathsf{Game}_1$, we define a distinguisher $D_{01}^{\Phi}$ (with running time $t_1 \approx t$) between $\Phi = \Omega$ and $\Phi = h(r, \cdot)$ with success at least $|\delta_0 - \delta_1|$. Similarly, to show that $\mathsf{Game}_1$ is close to $\mathsf{Game}_2$, we define a distinguisher $D_{12}^{\Phi}$ (with running time $t_2 \approx t$) between $\Phi = \Omega$ and $\Phi = h(r, \cdot)$ with success at least $|\delta_1 - \delta_2|$.

The distinguisher $D_{01}^{\Phi}$ is constructed (Fig. 4, left) so that in case of the oracle $h(IV, \cdot)$ it perfectly simulates $\mathsf{Game}_0$ (the original attacking game), and in case of the random oracle $\Omega(\cdot)$ it perfectly simulates $\mathsf{Game}_1$ (where random masks are used). Hence, $\mathsf{Adv}(D_{01}^{\Phi}) = |\delta_0 - \delta_1|$.

The other distinguisher $D_{12}^{\Phi}$ is constructed (Fig. 4, right) so that in case of the oracle $h(IV, \cdot)$ it perfectly simulates $\mathsf{Game}_1$, whereas in case of the random oracle $\Omega$ it simulates $\mathsf{Game}_2$ (the simulator $\mathcal{S}$). Hence, $\mathsf{Adv}(D_{12}^{\Phi}) = |\delta_1 - \delta_2|$, and

$$\delta = 2|\delta_0 - \delta_2| \leq 2(|\delta_0 - \delta_1| + |\delta_1 - \delta_2|) = 2\left(\mathsf{Adv}(D_{01}^{\Phi}) + \mathsf{Adv}(D_{12}^{\Phi})\right)$$
$$\leq 2\left(\frac{t_1}{S} + \frac{t_2}{S}\right) = 4\frac{t}{S} ,$$

and hence the log signing scheme is $\frac{S}{4}$-secure IND-CPA content concealing. $\quad\square$

# 4   Reference Algorithms

We now present reference algorithms for aggregating a log block, extracting an integrity proof for an individual record, and verifying a record based on such proof. We also discuss some potential trade-offs where additional security benefits or runtime reductions could be gained at the cost of increased storage overhead.

## 4.1   Canonical Binary Trees

So far we have not specified the shape of the Merkle tree. If the number of leaves is an even power of two, building a perfect binary tree seems natural, but in other cases the appropriate shape is not necessarily obvious.

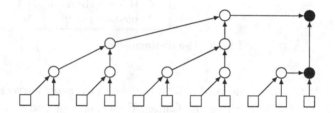

**Fig. 5.** A canonical binary tree: 11 leaves (squares) grouped into three perfect trees (white circles) and merged into a single tree with minimal height (black circles)

Of course, it is crucial to build the tree in a deterministic manner so that the verifier would be able to construct the exact same tree as the signer did. Another consideration is that to achieve the logarithmic size of the integrity proofs of the individual records, the tree should not be overly unbalanced. Thus, we define the *canonical binary tree* with $n$ leaf nodes (shown for $n = 11$ on Fig. 5) to be built as follows:

1. The leaf nodes are laid out *from left to right* (square nodes on the figure).
2. The leaf nodes are collected into perfect binary trees *from left to right*, making each tree as big as possible using the leaves still available (adding the white circles on the figure).
3. The perfect trees are merged into a single tree *from right to left* which means joining the two smallest trees on each step (adding the black circles on the figure).

A useful property of canonical trees is that they can be built on-line, as the leaf nodes arrive, without knowing in advance the eventual size of the tree, and keeping in memory only logarithmic number of nodes (the root nodes of the complete binary trees constructed so far).

## 4.2   Aggregation of Log Records

Algorithm AGGR (Fig. 6) aggregates a block of records into a canonical Merkle tree for signing or verification. The input description numbers the records $1 \ldots N$, but the value of $N$ is not used and the algorithm can easily be implemented for processing the records on-line.

The algorithm also enforces the hash chain length limiting as mentioned in Sec. 2.1. The level of a leaf node is defined to be 1 and the level of a non-leaf node to be 1 more than the maximum of the levels of its child nodes.

An amortized constant number of hashing operations is needed per record and the worst-case actual processing time per record is logarithmic in the number of records in the block, as is the size of the auxiliary working memory needed.
To sign a log block, AGGR could be used in the following manner:

1. A fresh random value is generated for $IV$.
2. The $IV$, the last leaf hash value from the previous block, and the log records of the current block are fed into AGGR.
3. The resulting root hash value is signed and the last leaf hash value from this block passed on to aggregation of the next block.
4. At the very least the $IV$ and the signature on the root hash value must be saved for later verification.

Given the above, the way to verify a signed log block is quite obvious:

1. The $IV$ saved during signing, the last leaf hash value from the previous block, and the log records are fed into AGGR.
2. The re-computed root hash value is verified against the saved signature.

A placeholder value filled with zeros is used for the last leaf hash value of the previous block in the very first block of the log (when there is no previous block) or when there has been a discontinuity in the log (for example, when the logging service has been down).

Although not strictly required in theory, in practice the last leaf hash value of the previous log block should also be saved along with the $IV$ and the signature. Otherwise the verification of the current block would need to re-hash the previous block to obtain the required input, which in turn would need to re-hash the next previous block, etc. While this would obviously be inefficient, an even more dangerous consequence would be that any damage to any log block would make it impossible to verify any following log blocks, as one of the required inputs for verification would no longer be available.

Considering the negative scenarios in more detail, the only conclusion that can be derived from a failed verification in the minimal case above would be that something has been changed in either the log block or the authentication data. If it is desirable to be able to detect the changes more precisely, either the record hash values $r_i$ or the leaf hash values $x_i$ computed by AGGR could be saved along with the other authentication data. Then the sequence of hash values could be authenticated against the signature and each record checked against its hash value, at the expense of small per-record storage overhead.

**Algorithm AGGR:**

Aggregates a block of records for signing or verification.

inputs
   $rec_{1...N}$: input records
   $IV$: initial value for the blinding masks
   $x_0$: last leaf hash of previous block (zero for first block)

do
   {Initialize block:}
   {create empty roots list}
   $R :=$ empty list
   {Process records:}
   {add to Merkle forest in order}
   for $i := 1$ to $N$ do
      $r_i :=$ hash($rec_i$)
      $m_i :=$ hash($x_{i-1}, IV$)
      $x_i :=$ hash($m_i, r_i, 1$)
      {Add $x_i$ to the forest as new leaf}
      {and update roots list}
      $t := x_i$
      for $j := 1$ to length($R$) do
         if $R_j =$ none then
            $R_j := t$; $t :=$ none
         else if $t \neq$ none then
            $t :=$ hash($R_j, t, j+1$)
            $R_j :=$ none
      if $t \neq$ none then
         $R := R \parallel t$; $t :=$ none
   {Finalize block:}
   {merge forest into a single tree}
   $root :=$ none
   for $j := 1$ to length($R$) do
      if $root =$ none then
         $root := R_j$; $R_j :=$ none
      else if $R_j \neq$ none then
         $root :=$ hash($R_j, root, j+1$)
         $R_j :=$ none

outputs
   $root$: root hash of this block (to be signed or verified)
   $x_N$: last leaf hash of this block (for linking next block)

**Algorithm EXTR:**

Extracts the hash chain for proving or verifying an individual record.

inputs
   $rec_{1...N}$: input records
   $pos$: position of the object record within the block $(1 \ldots N)$
   $IV$: initial value for the blinding masks
   $x_0$: last leaf hash of previous block (zero for first block)

do
   {Initialize block}
   $R :=$ empty list; $C :=$ empty list
   {object record not in any level yet}
   $\ell :=$ none
   {Process records,}
   {keeping track of the object}
   for $i := 1$ to $N$ do
      $r_i :=$ hash($rec_i$)
      $m_i :=$ hash($x_{i-1}, IV$)
      $x_i :=$ hash($m_i, r_i, 1$)
      if $i = pos$ then
         $C := C \parallel$ (**right**, $m_i, 0$) {compute $x_i$}

         {add $x_i$ as a right leaf}
         $\ell := 1$; $d :=$ **right**
      {Add $x_i$ to the forest as new leaf}
      $t := x_i$
      for $j := 1$ to length($R$) do
         if $R_j =$ none then
            if $j = \ell$ then $d :=$ **left**
            $R_j := t$; $t :=$ none
         else if $t \neq$ none then
            if $j = \ell$ then
               if $d =$ **right** then
                  $S := R_j$
               else
                  $S := t$
               $C := C \parallel (d, S, 0)$
               $\ell := j+1$; $d :=$ **right**
            $t :=$ hash($R_j, t, j+1$)
            $R_j :=$ none
      if $t \neq$ none then
         if length($R$) $< \ell$ then $d :=$ **left**
         $R := R \parallel t$; $t :=$ none
   {Finalize block}
   $root :=$ none
   for $j := 1$ to length($R$) do
      if $root =$ none then
         if $j = \ell$ then $d :=$ **right**
         $root := R_j$; $R_j :=$ none
      else if $R_j \neq$ none then
         if $j \geq \ell$ then
            if $d =$ **right** then
               $S := R_j$
            else
               $S := root$
            $C := C \parallel (d, S, j - \ell)$
            $\ell := j+1$; $d :=$ **right**
         $root :=$ hash($R_j, root, j+1$)
         $R_j :=$ none

outputs
   $C$: hash chain from the object to the root of the block

**Fig. 6.** Algorithms AGGR and EXTR

It should also be noted that when the record hashes are saved, they should be kept with the same confidentiality as the log data itself, to prevent the informed brute-force attack discussed in Sec. 2.1.

## 4.3   Extraction of Hash Chains

Algorithm EXTR (Fig. 6) extracts the hash chain needed to prove or verify the integrity of an individual record. The core is similar to AGGR, with additional tracking of the hash values that depend on the object record and collecting a hash chain based on that tracking.

The output value is a sequence of (*direction, sibling hash, level correction*) triples. The direction means the order of concatenation of the incoming hash value and the sibling hash value. The level correction value is needed to account for cases when two sub-trees of unequal height are merged and the node level value increases by more than 1 on the step from the root of the lower sub-tree to the root of the merged tree. (The step from the lower black node to the higher one on Fig. 5 is an example.)

Because EXTR is closely based on AGGR, its performance is also similar and thus it falls somewhat short of our ideal of sub-linear runtime for hash chain extraction. We do not expect this to be a real issue in practice, as locating the records to be presented as evidence is typically already a linear-time task and thus reducing the proof extraction time would not bring a significant improvement in the total time. Also note that the need to access the full log file in this algorithm is not a compromise of our confidentiality goals, as the extraction process is executed by the owner of the log file and only the relevant log records and the hash chains computed for them by EXTR are shipped to outside parties.

```
Algorithm Comp:
Re-computes the root hash of a block for verifying a
record
    inputs
        rec: input record
        C: hash chain from the record to the root of block
    do
        root := hash(rec); ℓ := 0
        for i := 1 to length(C) do
            {direction, sibling, level correction}
            (d, S, L) := C_i
            ℓ := ℓ + L + 1
            if d = left then
                root := hash(root, S, ℓ)
            else
                root := hash(S, root, ℓ)
    outputs
        root: root hash of the block (for verification)
```

**Fig. 7.** Algorithm COMP re-computes the root hash of a block for verifying a record

However, it would be possible to trade space for time and extra confidentiality, if desired. At the cost of storing two extra hash values per record, logarithmic runtime could be achieved and the need to look at any actual records during the hash chain extraction could be removed. Indeed, if the hash values from all the Merkle tree nodes ($x_i$ on Fig. 1) were kept, the whole hash chain could be extracted without any new hash computations. If the values (all of the same fixed size) would be stored in the order in which they are computed as $x_i$ and $R_j$ in AGGR, each of them could be seeked to in constant time.

### 4.4   Computation of Hash Chains

Algorithm COMP (Fig. 7) computes the root hash value of the Merkle tree from which the input hash chain was extracted. The hash chain produced by EXTR and the corresponding log record should be fed into COMP, and the output hash value verified against the signature to prove the integrity of the record.

## 5   Implementation

In this section we outline some practical concerns regarding the implementation of the proposed scheme for signing `syslog` messages. Out of the many possible deployment scenarios we concentrate on signing the output directed to a text file on a log collector device. (See [7], Sec. 4.1 for more details.)

### 5.1   General Technical Considerations

**Log File Rotation, Block Size.** In Sec. 2 we modeled the log as an ordered sequence of blocks, where each block in turn is an ordered sequence of a finite number of records, and noted that the case of `syslog` output being sent to a periodically rotated log file could be viewed as an instantiation of this model.

We now refine the model to distinguish the logical blocks (implied by signing) from the physical blocks (the rotated files), because it is often desirable to sign the records in a finer granularity than the frequency of file rotation. A log file could contain several signed blocks, but for file management reasons, a signed block should be confined to a single file. This means that when log files are rotated, the current signature block should always be closed and a new one started from the beginning of the new file. The hash links from the last record of previous block to the first record of the next block should span the file boundaries, though, to enable verification of the integrity of the whole log, however the files may have been rotated.

Implementations could support limiting the block sizes both by number of records and time duration. When a limit on the number of records is set and a block reaches that many records, it should be signed and a new block started. Likewise, when a duration limit is set and the oldest record in a block reaches the given age, the block should be signed and a new one started. When both limits are set, reaching either one should cause the block to be closed and also reset both counters. Applying both limits could then be useful for systems with uneven activity. In this case the size limit would prevent the blocks growing too big during busy times and the time limit would prevent the earlier records in a block staying unsigned for too long during quiet times. When neither limit is given, each block would cover a whole log file, as rotating the output files should close the current block and start a new one in any case.

**Record Canonicalization.** When log records are individually hashed for signing before they are saved to the output file, it is critical that the file could be unambiguously split back into records for verification. End-of-line markers are used as separators in text-based `syslog` files and then multi-line records could not be recovered correctly unless the line breaks within the records are escaped.

**Signature Technologies.** Once the log blocks are aggregated, the root hash values have to be protected from future modifications. While it could seem natural to sign them using a standard public-key signature such as an OpenPGP [6] or PKCS#7 [10,9] one, these off-line signing technologies do not provide good forward security in case the logging server is compromised or privileged insiders abuse their access. An attacker could modify the logs and then re-hash and re-sign all the blocks starting from the earliest modified one, as the signing keys would be available on the log collector host.

A cryptographic time-stamping service [2] could be used as a mitigation. Note that a time-stamp generally only provides evidence of the time and integrity of the time-stamped datum, but not the identity of the requesting party, so a time-stamp alone would not be sufficient to prevent a log file from another system being submitted instead of the original one. Therefore, time-stamps should be used in addition to, not in place of, signatures.

An alternative would be to use the OpenKSI keyless signatures [3] that combine the hash value of the signed datum, the identity of the requesting system, and the signing time into one independently verifiable cryptographic token. As verification of keyless signatures does not rely on secrecy of keys and does not need trusted third parties, they are well-suited when logs are signed for evidence.

## 5.2   Case Study: rsyslog Integration

The proposed log signing scheme has been implemented in `rsyslog`, a popular logging server implementing the `syslog` protocol and included as a standard component in several major Linux distributions.

**Architecture and Configuration.** The `rsyslog` server has a modular architecture, with a number of input and output modules available to receive log messages from various sources and store logs using different formats and storage engines. Log signing has been implemented as a new optional functionality in the `omfile` output module that stores log data in plain text files. When signing is enabled, the signatures and related helper data items are stored in a binary file next to the log file. As the data is a sequence of non-human-readable binary tokens (hash values and signatures), there would be no benefit in keeping it in a text format. Both files are needed for verification of log integrity. It is the responsibility of the log maintenance processes to ensure that the files do not get separated when the log files are archived or otherwise managed. The `rsyslog` configuration is specified as a number of sets of rules applied to incoming messages. The following minimal example configures the server to listen for incoming messages on TCP port 514 and apply the `perftest` rules to all of them:

```
module(load="imtcp")
input(type="imtcp" port="514" ruleset="perftest")
ruleset(name="perftest"){
  action(type="omfile" file="/var/log/signed.log" sig.provider="gt")
}
```

The rules in turn just write all the records to the specified text file with no filtering or transformations.

**Performance.** We tested the performance of the implementation on a quad-core Intel Xeon E5606 CPU. We used 64-bit CentOS 6.4 operating system and installed `rsyslog` version 7.3.15-2 from the Adiscon package repository. There was excess of memory and I/O resources, in all tests the performance was CPU-bound. Load was generated using the `loggen` utility which is part of the `syslog-ng 3.5.0 alpha0` package, another `syslog` server implementation. We used TCP socket for logging in order to avoid potential message loss and mimic a real-life scenario with central logging server. We note that UDP and kernel device interface gave comparable results. The `rsyslog` configuration was as shown above: the simplest possible, without any message processing.

Without signing we achieved sustained logging rate of $\approx$400,000 messages per second. At this point the `rsyslog` input thread saturated one CPU core. Multiple input threads and multiple main queue worker threads allowed us to achieve slightly better performance. Here and below the average message size was 256 bytes, and the default SHA2-256 hash was used when signing was enabled.

Signed logging rate was constantly higher than 100,000 messages per second. The limiting factor was the main queue worker thread which saturated one CPU core. For one signed output file the building of the hash tree can't be parallelized in an efficient way, because the order of the log messages must be preserved. Although possible to configure, multiple parallel worker queues would spend most of their time waiting for synchronization and total signing performance would be inferior. Storage of the record hash values and intermediate Merkle tree hash values did not affect the signing performance significantly. Also, using different hash algorithms did not have a significant impact.

Aggregating a log message incurs approximately three hash algorithm invocations. Considering that one CPU core can perform roughly one million hash calculations on small inputs, the log signing performance achieved is reasonably close to optimal. It should also be noted that the four-fold decrease of throughput from 400,000 messages per second to 100,000 messages per second is extreme, as in the baseline scenario no CPU power was spent on filtering the records.

Storage overhead depends on whether the record and tree hashes are stored, hash algorithm output size, and signature block size. In case of 256-byte log records and 32-byte hash values, the storage overhead is about 12% for keeping the record hashes and about 25% for keeping the tree hashes. The storage overhead caused by signatures themselves is negligible in practical scenarios.

**Table 1.** Storage, runtime and verification feature trade-offs ($N$ is log block size)

| Characteristic | No hashes kept | Record hashes | Tree hashes |
|---|---|---|---|
| | Signing | | |
| Per-record storage | none | 1 hash value | 2 hash values |
| Per-record computation | 3 hashings | 3 hashings | 3 hashings |
| Per-block storage | 1 signature value | 1 signature value | 1 signature value |
| Per-block computation | 1 signing | 1 signing | 1 signing |
| Memory | $O(\log N)$ | $O(\log N)$ | $O(\log N)$ |
| | Whole log verification | | |
| Report granularity | block | record | record |
| Time | $O(N)$ | $O(N)$ | $O(N)$ |
| Memory | $O(\log N)$ | $O(\log N)$ | $O(\log N)$ |
| | Record proof extraction | | |
| Per-record storage | $O(\log N)^*$ | $O(\log N)^*$ | $O(\log N)^*$ |
| Time | $O(N)$ | $O(N)$ | $O(\log N)$ |
| Memory | $O(\log N)$ | $O(\log N)$ | $O(1)$ |
| | Record proof verification | | |
| Report granularity | record | record | record |
| Time | $O(\log N)$ | $O(\log N)$ | $O(\log N)$ |
| Memory | $O(1)$ | $O(1)$ | $O(1)$ |

$^*$ Asymptotically it's $O(\log N)$, but in practice, the $O(1)$ signature size dominates over the $O(\log N)$ hash chain size. For example, for 3600-byte signatures and 32-byte hash values used in our case study, the signature size exceeds the hash chain size for all $N < 2^{100}$.

# 6   Conclusions

We have proposed a log signing scheme with good security properties and low overhead in both computational and storage resources. The integrity of either the whole log or any record can be verified, and in the latter case also a compact proof produced without leaking any information about the contents of other records. The scheme also allows for some flexibility in providing additional verification features and proof extraction performance gains at the cost of increased storage overhead, as listed in Table 1.

An interesting direction for future development would be to extend the scheme for use in configurations where the log is signed at a source device, transported over one or more relay devices and then stored at a collector device. The current scheme would be usable only if the relay devices do not perform any filtering of the records, which is rarely the case in practice.

# References

1. Accorsi, R.: BBox: A distributed secure log architecture. In: Camenisch, J., Lambrinoudakis, C. (eds.) EuroPKI 2010. LNCS, vol. 6711, pp. 109–124. Springer, Heidelberg (2011)
2. Adams, C., Cain, P., Pinkas, D., Zuccherato, R.: Internet X.509 public key infrastructure time-stamp protocol (TSP). IETF RFC 3161 (2001)
3. Buldas, A., Kroonmaa, A., Park, A.: OpenKSI digital signature format (2012)
4. Buldas, A., Saarepera, M.: On provably secure time-stamping schemes. In: Lee, P.J. (ed.) ASIACRYPT 2004. LNCS, vol. 3329, pp. 500–514. Springer, Heidelberg (2004)
5. Buldas, A., Truu, A., Laanoja, R., Gerhards, R.: Efficient record-level keyless signatures for audit logs. Cryptology ePrint Archive, Report 2014/552 (2014)
6. Callas, J., Donnerhacke, L., Finney, H., Thayer, R.: OpenPGP message format. IETF RFC 4880 (2007)
7. Gerhards, R.: The syslog protocol. IETF RFC 5424 (2009)
8. Holt, J.E.: Logcrypt: Forward security and public verification for secure audit logs. In: Buyya, R., Ma, T., Safavi-Naini, R., Steketee, C., Susilo, W. (eds.) AISW 2006, pp. 203–211. Australian Computer Society (2006)
9. Housley, R.: Cryptographic message syntax (CMS). IETF RFC 5652 (2009)
10. Kaliski, B.: PKCS#7: Cryptographic message syntax v 1.5. IETF RFC 2315 (1998)
11. Kelsey, J., Callas, J., Clemm, A.: Signed syslog messages. IETF RFC 5848 (2010)
12. Ma, D., Tsudik, G.: A new approach to secure logging. ACM Transactions on Storage 5(1), 2:1–2:21 (2009)
13. Merkle, R.C.: Protocols for public key cryptosystems. In: IEEE Symposium on Security and Privacy, pp. 122–134. IEEE Computer Society (1980)
14. Schneier, B., Kelsey, J.: Secure audit logs to support computer forensics. ACM Transactions on Information Systems Security 2(2), 159–176 (1999)
15. Stathopoulos, V., Kotzanikolaou, P., Magkos, E.: A framework for secure and verifiable logging in public communication networks. In: López, J. (ed.) CRITIS 2006. LNCS, vol. 4347, pp. 273–284. Springer, Heidelberg (2006)

# Static Semantics of Secret Channel Abstractions

Marco Giunti

CRACS/INESC-TEC
Universidade do Porto

**Abstract.** The secret $\pi$-calculus extends the $\pi$-calculus by adding an *hide* operator that permits to declare channels as secret. The main aim is confidentiality, which is gained by restricting the access of the object of the communication. Communication channels protected by *hide* are more secure since they have static scope and do not allow the context's interaction, and can be implemented as dedicated channels. In this paper, we present static semantics of secret channel abstractions by introducing a type system that considers two type modalities for channels (scope): static and dynamic. We show that secret $\pi$-calculus channels protected by *hide* can be represented in the $\pi$-calculus by prescribing a static type modality. We illustrate the feasibility of our approach by introducing a security *API* for message-passing communication which works for a standard ($\pi$-calculus) middleware while featuring secret channels. Interestingly, we just require the programmer to declare which channels are meant to be secret, leaving the burden of managing the security type abstractions to the API compiler.

## 1 Introduction

The proliferation of interacting computer devices and the growing complexity of the software components continuously cause security issues; see [20] for the list of vulnerabilities discovered at Google in the last years, which includes the recent Heartbeat OpenSSL bug. Secrecy and confidentiality are major concerns in most systems of communicating agents. Either because some of the agents are untrusted, or because the communication uses insecure channels, there may be the risk of sensitive information being leaked to potentially malicious entities. The price to pay for such security breaches may also be very high. It is not surprising, therefore, that secrecy and confidentiality have become central issues in the formal specification and verification of communicating systems. Formal methods have been indeed advocated as an effective tool to analyze and deploy secure communicating programs and protocols [13]. Process calculi, in particular, allow to study prototypal security analysis techniques that could be embedded into next-generation compilers for distributed languages, and to investigate high-level security abstractions that can be effectively deployed into lower-level languages, thus providing for *APIs* for secure process interaction (e.g. [9]).

The $\pi$-calculus and especially its variants enriched with mechanisms to express cryptographic operations, the spi calculus [5] and the applied $\pi$-calculus [4], have

K. Bernsmed and S. Fischer-Hübner (Eds.): NordSec 2014, LNCS 8788, pp. 165–180, 2014.
DOI: 10.1007/978-3-319-11599-3_10, © Springer International Publishing Switzerland 2014

become popular formalisms for security applications. They all feature the operator new (restriction) and make crucial use of it in the definition of security protocols. The prominent aspects of new are the capability of creating a new channel name, whose use is restricted within a certain scope, and the possibility of enlarging its scope by communicating it to other processes. The latter property is central to the most interesting feature of the $\pi$-calculus: the *mobility* of the communication structure. Although in principle the restriction aspect of new should guarantee that the channel is used for communication within a secure environment only, the capability of extruding the scope leads to security problems. In particular, it makes it unnatural to implement the communication using dedicated channels, and non-dedicated channels are not secure by default. The spi calculus and the applied $\pi$-calculus do not assume, indeed, any security guarantee on the channel, and implement security by using cryptographic encryption.

By way of motivation, consider the $\pi$-calculus process below, which describes a protocol to exchange a confidential information.

$$P = (\mathsf{new}\, c)((\mathsf{new}\, s)(\overline{c}\langle s\rangle.\overline{s}\langle \text{ATMpwd}\rangle) \mid c(x).x(y).\overline{p}\langle x\rangle) \tag{1}$$

This protocol is composed by two threads communicating over a restricted channel $c$ to exchange a password to access the ATM: the thread on the left generates a (secure) channel $s$ and sends it over $c$, and later sends the password over $s$; the thread on the right waits to receive from $c$ a channel (that will instantiate) $x$, waits on $x$ to receive a value, and subsequently releases $x$ over a public channel $p$ to allow further use of the channel. Still, implementing this solution in untrusted environments is difficult, since we cannot rely on dedicated channels for communication on names created by the new operator. One natural approach to cope with this problem is to map the private communication within the scope of the new into open communications protected by cryptography.

For instance, we may resort to the spi calculus and map the command $(\mathsf{new}\, s)$ into the generation of two cryptographic keys, noted $(\mathsf{new}\, s^+, s^-)$, to be sent over the network through the crypto-packet $\{s^+, s^-\}_{c^+}$. The packet is encrypted with the public key $c^+$ and can be only open by a process that knows the decryption key $c^-$, that is the (spi calculus representation of the) receiver on the right:

$$net(z).\mathsf{decrypt}\ z\ \mathsf{as}\ \{x^+, x^-\}_{c^-}\ \mathsf{in}\ net(w).\mathsf{decrypt}\ w\ \mathsf{as}\ \{y\}_{x^-}\ \mathsf{in}\ \overline{p}\langle x^+, x^-\rangle$$

The aim is to protect the exchange of the confidential information by encrypting the password with the cryptographic key $s^+$, noted $\{\text{ATMpwd}\}_{s^+}$. Unfortunately, the naive protocol above suffers from a number of problems, among which the most serious is the lack of forward secrecy [1]: the content of the crypto-packet encrypted with $s^+$ can be retrieved by a spi calculus context that first buffers the encrypted message and later receives the decryption key $s^-$.

Stated differently, the spi calculus protocol above does not preserve the semantics of $P$, which can be formalized by means of the behavioural equivalence in (2), where we assume $p$ free in $P$:

$$P \cong (\mathsf{new}\, s)(\overline{p}\langle s\rangle) \tag{2}$$

This equation establishes a well-known fact, that is that in the $\pi$-calculus communication on restricted channels is invisible: in contrast, the naive spi calculus protocol above allows the context to retrieve the content of the secret exchange. While a solution to recover the behavioral theory of $\pi$-calculus is available [9], the price to pay is a complex cryptographic protocol that relies on a set of trusted authorities acting as proxies.

Based on these considerations, in [18] we argue that the restriction operator of $\pi$-calculus does not adequately ensure confidentiality, and we introduce an operator to program explicitly secret communications, called hide. The operator is static: that is, we assume that the scope of hidden channels can not be extruded. The motivation is that all processes using a private channel shall be included in the scope of its hide declaration; processes outside the scope represent another location, and must not interfere with the protocol. Since the hide cannot extrude the scope of secret channels, we can use it to directly build specifications that preserves forward secrecy. In contrast, we regard the restriction operator of the $\pi$-calculus, new, as useful to create a new channel for message passing with scope extrusion, and which does not provide secrecy guarantees. Still, this approach assumes specialized semantics for communicating processes, that is: to enforce static scope for secret channels, we rely on a special-purpose middleware that checks the content of each exchange and only allows interactions that do not cause a security break.

In this paper, we show that the static scope mechanism can be enforced in a $\pi$-calculus enjoying standard semantics (cf. [24]) by using strong static typing. The hide security operator is accessible as a macro of an idealized *API* for secure programming: programs using secret channels are transformed into typed $\pi$-calculus processes and checked: when type-checking succeeds, the scope of channels protected by hide cannot be enlarged during the computation. The API language inherits the the syntax of [18] and allows to patch the protocol $P$ in (1) by re-programming the secure channel with hide: note that the scope delimited by the square parentheses crucially includes the receiver, otherwise the protocol would be rejected.

$$H = (\text{new}\,c)([\text{hide}\,s][H'])  \qquad  H' = \overline{c}\langle s\rangle.\overline{s}\langle\text{ATMpwd}\rangle \mid c(x).x(y).\overline{p}\langle x\rangle \qquad (3)$$

User programs are mapped into a typed $\pi$-calculus where channel types are *decorated* with modality qualifiers: d for dynamic channels and s for static (secret) channels. The hide declaration in (3) is compiled into a restriction decorated with a static type, where we guess the channel type of $s$ (cf. [27]), which is $\text{chan}\langle\top\rangle$:

$$[\![[\text{hide}\,s][H']]\!] = (\text{new}\,s: \text{s}\,\text{chan}\langle\top\rangle)(H')$$

The encoding of $H$ is obtained similarly below by guessing the channel type of $c$, which is $\text{chan}\langle\text{chan}\langle\top\rangle\rangle$. Note that the compilation assigns a dynamic type to the payload of $c$: the type system allows to send $s$ having a static type over $c$ by upcasting the type of the payload from dynamic to static.

$$[\![H]\!] = (\text{new}\,c: \text{d}\,\text{chan}\langle\text{d}\,\text{chan}\langle\top\rangle\rangle)[\![[\text{hide}\,s][H']]\!] \qquad (4)$$

*Types and Processes*

| $T ::=$ | Types: | $P ::=$ | Processes: |
|---|---|---|---|
| $m\,\mathsf{chan}\langle T\rangle_i$ | channel | $x(y \div B).P$ | input |
| $\top$ | top | $\overline{x}\langle v\rangle.P$ | output |
| $m ::=$ | Modalities | $(\mathsf{new}\,x : T)(P)$ | restriction |
| $\mathsf{s}$ | static | $P \mid Q$ | composition |
| $\mathsf{d}$ | dynamic | $\mathbf{0}$ | inaction |
| $i ::=$ | Identifiers | $!P$ | replication |
| $\forall$ | universal | $B ::=$ | Blocked entries: |
| $n$ | unique number | $\emptyset$ | empty |
| | | $B \cup \{T\}$ | type |

**Fig. 1.** $\pi$-calculus: syntax

*Contribution*

- We introduce a type system to enforce a static scope for $\pi$-calculus channels by decorating channel types with *static* and *dynamic* type modalities
- We show that a fragment of the secret $\pi$-calculus [18] can be encoded into the typed calculus while preserving an operational correspondence. The compilation requires the type of the payload of channels to be guessed (when possible), while type modalities are inferred automatically. An upcast mechanism allows to send static channels over channels exchanging dynamic variables.
- We discuss possible applications of the proposed technique, which we interpret as an abstract API for secure message-passing.

*Structure of the paper.* Section 2 introduces the syntax and the static and dynamic semantics of the typed $\pi$-calculus. Section 3 reviews the secret $\pi$-calculus, and presents a semantics-preserving compilation of the secret $\pi$-calculus into the typed $\pi$-calculus. In Section 4 we discuss some applications of our technique. We conclude in Section 5 by envisioning future work and by discussing a few related papers.

## 2    Typed $\pi$-calculus

In this section we introduce the syntax of the typed $\pi$-calculus, and its static and dynamic semantics. We use $x, y, v$ to range over variables, and $n$ to range over unique numbers (identifiers). The syntax of types in Figure 1 include *channel* types decorated with static (s) and dynamic (d) type modalities, and the *top* type, noted $\top$. The type modalities, ranged by $m$, are the core of the security mechanism of the typed $\pi$-calculus and allow to enforce constraints on the mobility of channels. Type identifiers, ranged by $i$, are used to identify static types and to disallow their disclosure by means of structural rearrangement of processes. Variables of type top can be passed around but cannot be used in input/output. We assume that input processes are decorated with a set of *blocked types* and that this set is managed automatically through structural congruence, leaving the details of the mechanism to implementations. For the purpose of the presentation, we make type identifiers explicit and assume two forms for identifiers: *universal*, noted $\forall$, and unique numbers $n$ produced by a clash-free generator, noted gen(); in implementations, type identification would be managed transparently by the compiler.

The syntax of processes is standard, but for input. The input process $x(y \div B).P$ includes a set of (blocked) types $B$ in its definition. When $B$ is the empty set, the input process is the standard one of the $\pi$-calculus, otherwise, $B$ contains types $T$ that cannot be received by the input process, for any type assignment of $x$. Notably, this has impact only on the static semantics, while the dynamic semantics of the language is unaffected. Process $(\text{new } y \colon T)(P)$ is the restriction process, and introduces a new variable $y$ of type $T$ with scope in $P$.

The binders of processes appear in parenthesis: $(\text{new } y \colon T)(P)$ and $x(y \div B).P$ bind the free occurrences of $y$ in $P$. Considering the usual notions of free and bound variables, $\alpha$-conversion, as well as of substitution, cf. [24], we use $\text{fv}(P)$ and $\text{bv}(P)$ to indicate respectively the set of free and bound variables of $P$, which we assume disjoint by following Barendregt's variable convention [6]. We will often avoid trailing nils and write $\overline{x}\langle v \rangle$ and $x(y)$ to indicate respectively processes $\overline{x}\langle v \rangle.0$ and $x(y).0$, and write $x(y).P$ to indicate the input process $x(y \div \emptyset).P$. Structural congruence is the smallest relation on processes including the rules in Figure 2. We embed the type block mechanism in the rules for structural congruence through the block binary function, noted $\uplus$, defined in the same figure. *Blocked types could indeed be introduced both statically and dynamically*, i.e. when structural congruence is performed during the computation. We leave the time when the system blocks explicitly the type in components as an implementation detail. The axioms of structural congruence are below in Figure 2. Most rules are standard but the axiom in the second line, which deal with restriction of a variable having a static type. The scope of $x$ having type $T$ is enlarged to $Q \uplus T$: all inputs in $Q$ are forbidden to receive values of type $T$ by means of the block function defined above, which instructs the typing system. Note that, due to variable convention, $x$ bound in $(\text{new } x \colon T)(P)$, cannot be free in $Q$, and that an input of the form $x(y \div m \text{ chan}\langle T \rangle_i).P$ can receive values of type $m \text{ chan}\langle T \rangle_j$ whenever $i \neq j$. The reduction is the binary relation on processes defined by the rules in Figure 2. The [R-COM] rule communicates variable $v$ from an output prefixed process $\overline{x}\langle v \rangle.P$ to an input prefix $x(y \div B).Q$; the result is the parallel composition of the continuation processes, where, in the input process, the bound variable $y$ is replaced by $v$. The presence of the blocked types $B$ in the input, as introduced, allows to instruct the type checker and has no impact on communication. The rules in the last line allow reduction to happen underneath scope restriction and parallel composition, and incorporate structural congruence into reduction.

$\boxed{P \uplus T = P}$ *Type blocking*

$$(x(y \div B).P) \uplus T \overset{\text{def}}{=} x(y \div B \cup \{T\}).(P \uplus T)$$

$$((\text{new}\,x : T)(P)) \uplus T' \overset{\text{def}}{=} (\text{new}\,x : T)(P \uplus T')$$

$$(\overline{x}\langle v \rangle.P) \uplus T \overset{\text{def}}{=} \overline{x}\langle v \rangle.(P \uplus T) \qquad (P \mid Q) \uplus T \overset{\text{def}}{=} P \uplus T \mid Q \uplus T$$

$$(!P) \uplus T \overset{\text{def}}{=} !(P \uplus T) \qquad \mathbf{0} \uplus T \overset{\text{def}}{=} \mathbf{0}$$

$\boxed{P \equiv P}$ *Rules for structural congruence*

$$P \mid Q \equiv Q \mid P \qquad (P \mid Q) \mid J \equiv P \mid (Q \mid J) \qquad !P \equiv P \mid !P \qquad P \equiv P \mid \mathbf{0}$$

$$(\text{new}\,x : \mathsf{s}\,\mathsf{chan}\langle T \rangle_n)(P) \mid Q \equiv (\text{new}\,x : \mathsf{s}\,\mathsf{chan}\langle T \rangle_n)(P \mid Q \uplus \mathsf{s}\,\mathsf{chan}\langle T \rangle_n)$$

$$(\text{new}\,x : T)(P) \mid Q \equiv (\text{new}\,x : T)(P \mid Q) \qquad T \ne \mathsf{s}\,\mathsf{chan}\langle T' \rangle_n$$

$$(\text{new}\,x : T)(\mathbf{0}) \equiv \mathbf{0} \qquad (\text{new}\,x : T_1)(\text{new}\,y : T_2)(P) \equiv (\text{new}\,y : T_2)(\text{new}\,x : T_1)(P)$$

$\boxed{P \to P}$ *Rules for reduction*

$$\overline{x}\langle v \rangle.P \mid x(y \div B).Q \to P \mid Q\{v/y\} \qquad\qquad\qquad \text{[R-Com]}$$

$$\frac{P \to Q}{(\text{new}\,x : T)(P) \to (\text{new}\,x : T)(Q)} \qquad \frac{P \to P'}{P \mid Q \to P' \mid Q} \qquad \frac{P \equiv P' \quad P' \to Q' \quad Q' \equiv Q}{P \to Q}$$

$$\text{[R-Res] [R-Par] [R-Struct]}$$

**Fig. 2.** $\pi$-calculus: type-based blocking and reduction semantics

*Static semantics* We consider typing judgments for processes of the form $\Gamma \vdash P \rhd \Delta$ with $\text{fv}(P) \subseteq \text{dom}(\Gamma)$ and $\text{dom}(\Delta) = \text{dom}(\Gamma)$. *Type environments* or contexts $\Gamma$ are a map from variables to types $T$; *return type environments* or return contexts $\Delta$ are map from variables to *return types* $U$, which include types $T$ in Figure 1 and the *void* type, noted $\bullet$.

$$U ::= T \mid \bullet$$

The void type is managed transparently by the type system and is not used to decorate restricted channels. Return contexts are used to convey the actual use of channels, which can differ from the one described by the type environment. In particular, channels having a void return type cannot be accessed by processes running in parallel, while (dynamic) channels that are not used by the process can be promoted to type $\top$. In order to specify the typing system, in Figure 3 we introduce auxiliary operations on types, type environments and return type environments. The *upcast* partial operation, noted $\uparrow$, is used to upcast the payload of a channel type from dynamic to static. The *downcast* operation, noted $\downarrow_i^\bullet$, transforms dynamic types exchanging a static channel identified by $i$ into the void type, disallowing further interaction of the context. This is enforced in the rule to type a parallel composition by means of a *composition* partial binary

$\boxed{T\!\uparrow = T}$ *Type upcast*

$$\mathsf{d\,chan}\langle T\rangle_\forall\uparrow = \mathsf{s\,chan}\langle T\rangle_n \qquad n = \mathsf{gen}()$$

$\boxed{\Delta\!\downarrow^\bullet_i = \Delta}$ *Return context downcast*

$$U\!\downarrow^\bullet_i = \begin{cases} \bullet & U = \mathsf{d\,chan}\langle\mathsf{s\,chan}\langle T\rangle_n\rangle_\forall \text{ and } i = n \\ U & \text{else} \end{cases}$$

$$\emptyset\!\downarrow^\bullet_i = \emptyset \qquad \frac{\Delta\!\downarrow^\bullet_i = \Delta_1}{(\Delta, x : U)\!\downarrow^\bullet_i = \Delta_1, x : U\!\downarrow^\bullet_i}$$

$\boxed{\Delta \otimes \Delta = \Delta}$ *Return context composition*

$$U \otimes \top = U \qquad \top \otimes U = U \qquad \top \otimes \top = \top$$

$$\emptyset \otimes \emptyset = \emptyset \qquad \frac{\Delta_1 = \Delta_3, x : U_1 \qquad \Delta_2 = \Delta_4, x : U_2}{\Delta_1 \otimes \Delta_2 = \Delta_3 \otimes \Delta_4, x : U_1 \otimes U_2}$$

**Fig. 3.** Type system: auxiliary operations

operation over return contexts, noted $\otimes$, which only allows to compose void types with top types.

The typing system in Figure 4 introduces typing rules for values and processes. We illustrate the most interesting rules. Rule [T-PAR] allows to type a parallel composition $P_1 \mid P_2$ by composing the return contexts $\Delta_1$ and $\Delta_2$ produced respectively by typing $P_1$ and $P_2$, when the $\otimes$ operation is defined. In rule [T-REPL] we accept replicated processes that do not send static channels over dynamic channels, to disallow instances of $P$ to enlarge the scope of a static channel. Rule [T-RES-S] allows to type a restricted variable having a static type identified by a unique number $n$. To this aim, the continuation must be typed by adding to the context the new entry for the variable and return a context $\Delta$ that does not change the type of the restricted variable. The top-level return context is built by pruning the restricted variable and by downcasting $\Delta$. We have two rules for input, [T-IN] and [T-IN-UP], and to rules for output, [T-OUT] and [T-OUT-UP], which correspond respectively to input, upcast in input, output, and upcast in output. We allow to upcast the payload of channels from dynamic to static in input (a) and output (b), given that: a) the upcasted type is not blocked; b) the type of the channel's object is equal to the upcasted type. Note that in rules [T-IN-UP],[T-OUT-UP] the return type of the channel is different from the type in the type environment.

Rule [T-IN] allows to type an input process $x(y \div B).P$ with a channel of the form $m\,\mathsf{chan}\langle T'\rangle_i$, given that $T' \notin B$ and that the continuation can be typed by adding the entry $y : T'$ to the context. The return type of the bound variable $y$ must not change in the continuation: to upcast the type of a variable bound by an input, one has to use rule [T-IN-UP]. The top-level call returns the

$\boxed{\Gamma \vdash v : T}$ *Typing rule for variables*

$$\Gamma, v : T \vdash v : T \qquad\qquad\qquad\qquad \text{[T-VAR]}$$

$\boxed{\Gamma \vdash P \triangleright \Delta}$ *Typing rules for processes*

$$\frac{\Gamma \vdash P_1 \triangleright \Delta_1 \qquad \Gamma \vdash P_2 \triangleright \Delta_2}{\Gamma \vdash P_1 \mid P_2 \triangleright \Delta_1 \otimes \Delta_2} \qquad \frac{\Gamma \vdash P \triangleright \Delta \qquad \bullet \notin \mathrm{range}(\Delta)}{\Gamma \vdash\, !P \triangleright \Delta} \qquad \text{[T-PAR] [T-REPL]}$$

$$\frac{\Gamma, y : T \vdash P \triangleright \Delta, y : U}{\Gamma \vdash (\mathsf{new}\, y : T)(P) \triangleright \Delta} \qquad \frac{\Gamma, y : T \vdash P \triangleright \Delta, y : T}{\Gamma \vdash (\mathsf{new}\, y : \mathsf{s}\,\mathsf{chan}\langle T\rangle_n)(P) \triangleright \Delta\!\downarrow_n^\bullet} \qquad \text{[T-RES],[T-RES-S]}$$

$$\frac{\begin{array}{c} T = m\,\mathsf{chan}\langle T'\rangle_i \qquad T' = m'\,\mathsf{chan}\langle T''\rangle_j \qquad T' \notin B \\ \Gamma, x : T, y : T' \vdash P \triangleright \Delta, x : T, y : T' \end{array}}{\Gamma, x : T \vdash x(y \div B).P \triangleright (\Delta\!\downarrow_j^\bullet), x : T} \qquad \text{[T-IN]}$$

$$\frac{\begin{array}{c} T{\uparrow} = \mathsf{s}\,\mathsf{chan}\langle T'\rangle_n \qquad T{\uparrow} \notin B \\ \Gamma, x : m\,\mathsf{chan}\langle T{\uparrow}\rangle_i, y : T{\uparrow} \vdash P \triangleright \Delta, x : m\,\mathsf{chan}\langle T{\uparrow}\rangle_i, y : T{\uparrow} \end{array}}{\Gamma, x : m\,\mathsf{chan}\langle T\rangle_i \vdash x(y \div B).P \triangleright (\Delta\!\downarrow_n^\bullet), x : m\,\mathsf{chan}\langle T{\uparrow}\rangle_i} \qquad \text{[T-IN-UP]}$$

$$\frac{T = m\,\mathsf{chan}\langle T'\rangle_i \qquad \Gamma \vdash v : T' \qquad \Gamma, x : T \vdash P \triangleright \Delta, x : T \qquad \Delta \vdash v : T'}{\Gamma, x : T \vdash \overline{x}\langle v\rangle.P \triangleright \Delta, x : T} \qquad \text{[T-OUT]}$$

$$\frac{\begin{array}{c} T{\uparrow} = \mathsf{s}\,\mathsf{chan}\langle T'\rangle_n \qquad \Gamma \vdash y : T{\uparrow} \\ \Gamma, x : m\,\mathsf{chan}\langle T{\uparrow}\rangle_i \vdash P \triangleright \Delta, x : m\,\mathsf{chan}\langle T{\uparrow}\rangle_i \qquad \Delta \vdash y : T{\uparrow} \end{array}}{\Gamma, x : m\,\mathsf{chan}\langle T\rangle_i \vdash \overline{x}\langle y\rangle.P \triangleright \Delta, x : m\,\mathsf{chan}\langle T{\uparrow}\rangle_i} \qquad \text{[T-OUT-UP]}$$

$$\emptyset \vdash \mathbf{0} \triangleright \emptyset \qquad \frac{U = T \text{ or } (T = \mathsf{d}\,\mathsf{chan}\langle T'\rangle_i \text{ and } U = \top) \qquad \Gamma \vdash \mathbf{0} \triangleright \Delta}{\Gamma, x : T \vdash \mathbf{0} \triangleright \Delta, x : U}$$
$$\text{[T-INACT-E],[T-INACT]}$$

**Fig. 4.** $\pi$-calculus: type checking

environment $\Delta\!\downarrow_j^\bullet, x : T$, where $\Delta$ is obtained by the call for the continuation, and $j$ is the identifier of the payload type $T'$: this disallows attempts to declassify secret channels by means of forwarding (cf. Section 4). Rule [T-IN-UP] allows to type an input process $x(y \div B).P$ with a type of the form of the form $m\,\mathsf{chan}\langle T\rangle_i$, given that $T{\uparrow}$ is defined and that $T{\uparrow} \notin B$, and that the continuation can be typed by both changing the type of $x$ to $m\,\mathsf{chan}\langle T{\uparrow}\rangle_i$, and by adding the entry $y : T{\uparrow}$. Note that the return type of $x$ cannot change, and that the return context $\Delta$ is downcasted: this operation changes the type of channels that are exchanging $y$ to void, thus disallowing further interaction of the context. Rule [T-OUT] allows to type an output process and is standard: to enforce a consistent use of the variable in the context, the return type of the sent variable must not change. Rule [T-OUT-UP] is specular to [T-IN-UP], while there is no need to downcast the return type environment since the object of the output has already a static type: as in [T-OUT], we enforce that the return type of the object does not change. We have two rules for inaction, [T-INACT-E] and [T-INACT], corresponding to empty and non-empty contexts. In rule [T-INACT], we allow to promote each return type of the form d chan$\langle T \rangle_\forall$ to type $\top$: this permits compositions with processes that are not using i/o channel capabilities (cf. [19]).

The subject reduction theorem ensures that the static semantics of the $\pi$-calculus agrees with its dynamic semantics. As usual, the proof relies on two auxiliaries results: type preservation under structural congruence, and a substitution lemma. See [17] for all details.

**Theorem 1 (Subject reduction).** *If* $\Gamma \vdash P \triangleright \Delta$ *and* $P \to Q$ *then there is* $\Delta'$ *such that one of the following hold:*

1. $\Gamma \vdash Q \triangleright \Delta'$;
2. $\Gamma = \Gamma_1, x \colon m\,\mathsf{chan}\langle T \rangle_i$ *and* $\Gamma_1, x \colon m\,\mathsf{chan}\langle T{\uparrow} \rangle_i \vdash Q \triangleright \Delta'$, *for some* $x \in \mathrm{dom}(\Gamma)$.

The last result of this section establishes the soundness of the typed analysis namely: well-typed processes do not try to enlarge the scope of a channel decorated as static. The theorem below formalizes this intuition.

**Theorem 2 (Soundness).** *If* $\Gamma \vdash P \triangleright \Delta$ *and* $P$ *reduces in zero or more steps to* $(\mathsf{new}\,x_1 : T_1) \cdots (\mathsf{new}\,x_m : T_m)(Q \mid R)$ *then none of the following cases happen:*

1. $Q = (\mathsf{new}\,y \colon \mathsf{s}\,\mathsf{chan}\langle T \rangle_n)(\overline{x}\langle y \rangle.Q_1 \mid Q_2) \mid x(z \div B).Q_3$
2. $Q = (\mathsf{new}\,y \colon \mathsf{s}\,\mathsf{chan}\langle T \rangle_n)(\overline{x}\langle y \rangle.Q_1 \mid Q_2 \mid x(z \div B \cup \mathsf{s}\,\mathsf{chan}\langle T \rangle_n).Q_3)$

## 3    An API for Secure Programming

Rather than ask to programmers to use the security type abstractions presented in the previous section, we want to provide an high-level language featuring secret channels and transparently compile it in the typed $\pi$-calculus. In the remainder of the section we present the language, which is inspired by the secret $\pi$-calculus [18], and its compilation in the typed $\pi$-calculus of Section 2. We conclude by proving that the static and dynamic semantics of the translated programs agree with the dynamic semantics of the secret $\pi$-calculus, thus showing that our approach is sound. This provides an abstract *API* for secure programming: the programmer writes the security protocol in the high-level language, the protocol is compiled into the typed $\pi$-calculus, type-checking is performed before execution. When the protocol is well-typed, our main result is that direct information flows on secure channels are not allowed (while attacks based on indirect flows are still possible, cf. [26]).

*Programmer Language.* The syntax[1] in Figure 5 is inspired by the secret $\pi$-calculus [18]. To depict channel-based communication we consider an infinite set $\mathcal{N}$ of channels or *variables* ranged over by $x, y, z$ and $v$. We use $\mathcal{A}, \mathcal{B}, \mathcal{C}$ to denote subsets of $\mathcal{N}$. The programmer syntax includes, in addition to the standard operators of the $\pi$-calculus [24], a *secret channel* process [hide $x$][$H$], which is a process

---

[1] The original formulation of the secret $\pi$-calculus is untyped and also features a form of trusted input, which is outside the scope of the paper.

*Programmer syntax*

| $H ::=$ | | Programs: | $!H$ | replication |
| | $\overline{x}\langle v\rangle.H$ | output | $H \mid K$ | composition |
| | $x(y).H$ | input | $\mathbf{0}$ | inaction |
| | $[\text{hide } x][H]$ | secret channel | $(\text{new } x)(H)$ | channel |

*Extended syntax*

| $A ::=$ | | Types | $[\text{hide } x : A][M]$ | secret channel |
| | $\text{chan}\langle A\rangle$ | channel | $(\text{new } x : A)(M)$ | channel |
| | $\top$ | top | $!M$ | replication |
| $M ::=$ | | Processes: | $M \mid N$ | composition |
| | $\overline{x}\langle v\rangle.M$ | output | $\mathbf{0}$ | inaction |
| | $x(y \div \mathcal{B}).M$ | input | | |

**Fig. 5.** Secret $\pi$-calculus

that creates an invisible channel $x$ and continue as $H$. The programmer must be carefully include in the scope delimited by the square parentheses all processes that are meant to communicate over a secret channel: (compiled) processes that try to open the scope of a secret channel are rejected by the typed analysis. The extended syntax in the same figure introduces two modifications, which are transparent to the programmer: a set of blocked variables in input, noted $\mathcal{B}$, and channel type decorations in channel and secret channel creation. The binders of the extended language appear in parenthesis: $x(y \div \mathcal{B}).M$, $(\text{new } y)(M)$ and $[\text{hide } y][M]$ bind the free occurrences of $y$ in $M$. The set $\mathcal{B}$ allows to embed the block mechanism in the axioms of structural congruence, which is required by the secret $\pi$-calculus semantics. For space limitations, we illustrate this mechanism with an example, and refer to [18] for all the details. Consider the secret $\pi$-calculus process $M_1$ below, where we assume $x, z$ different from $y$ and $w$.

$$M_1 = [\text{hide } y : \top][\overline{x}\langle z\rangle.\overline{x}\langle y\rangle] \mid x(w \div \emptyset).\overline{x}\langle w\rangle \tag{5}$$

The reduction $M_1 \to [\text{hide } y : \top][\overline{x}\langle y\rangle \mid \overline{x}\langle z\rangle]$ is enforced in two steps: first, by the structural congruence axioms, we establish $M_1 \equiv [\text{hide } y : \top][\overline{x}\langle z\rangle.\overline{x}\langle y\rangle \mid x(w \div \{y\}).\overline{x}\langle w\rangle]$, then we allow the inner composition to interact since $z$ sent in output is different from $y$ blocked in input.

*Compilation* The compilation of programs $H$ into typed $\pi$-calculus processes $P$ is in two steps. User programs $H$ are transformed into secret $\pi$-calculus processes $M$ by means of a function $\langle\!\langle \cdot \rangle\!\rangle_I$ that guesses[2] the channel types of the restricted

---

[2] In practice, channel types would be inferred by using techniques based on constraint systems, e.g. [29,23].

*Assignment of type modalities*

$$[\![\mathsf{chan}\langle A\rangle]\!]_{\mathsf{d}} = \mathsf{d}\,\mathsf{chan}\langle [\![A]\!]_{\mathsf{d}}\rangle_{\forall} \qquad [\![\mathsf{chan}\langle A\rangle]\!]_{\mathsf{s}} = \mathsf{s}\,\mathsf{chan}\langle [\![A]\!]_{\mathsf{d}}\rangle_{\mathsf{gen}()}$$

$$[\![\top]\!]_m = \top \qquad m = \mathsf{s}, \mathsf{d}$$

*Encoding processes*

$$[\![(\mathsf{hide}\,x\colon A][M]]\!]_\Gamma = (\mathsf{new}\,x\colon [\![A]\!]_{\mathsf{s}})([\![M]\!]_{\Gamma, x\colon [\![A]\!]_{\mathsf{s}}})$$

$$[\![(\mathsf{new}\,x\colon A)(M)]\!]_\Gamma = (\mathsf{new}\,x\colon [\![A]\!]_{\mathsf{d}})([\![M]\!]_{\Gamma, x\colon [\![A]\!]_{\mathsf{d}}})$$

$$[\![\overline{x}\langle y\rangle.M]\!]_\Gamma = \overline{x}\langle y\rangle.[\![M]\!]_\Gamma$$

$$[\![x(y \div \mathcal{B}).M]\!]_\Gamma = x(y \div B).[\![M]\!]_\Gamma \qquad \mathcal{B} = \{x_1, \ldots, x_n\},\ B = \{\Gamma(x_1), \ldots, \Gamma(x_n)\}$$

$$[\![M \mid N]\!]_\Gamma = [\![M]\!]_\Gamma \mid [\![N]\!]_\Gamma$$

$$[\![!M]\!]_\Gamma = \,![\![M]\!]_\Gamma$$

$$[\![0]\!]_\Gamma = 0$$

**Fig. 6.** Compilation of secret $\pi$-calculus

channels of $H$ (when possible), where $I = A_1 \cdots A_n$ is a stack of types such that $A_1$ is on top of the stack. The encoding is below: the remaining cases are homomorphic.

$$\langle\!\langle x(y).H \rangle\!\rangle_I = x(y \div \emptyset).\langle\!\langle H \rangle\!\rangle_I \qquad \langle\!\langle (\mathsf{new}\,x)H \rangle\!\rangle_{A \cdot I} = (\mathsf{new}\,x\colon A)\langle\!\langle H \rangle\!\rangle_I$$

$$\langle\!\langle [\mathsf{hide}\,x]H \rangle\!\rangle_{A \cdot I} = [\mathsf{hide}\,x\colon A]\langle\!\langle H \rangle\!\rangle_I \qquad \langle\!\langle H \mid K \rangle\!\rangle_{I_1 \cdot I_2} = \langle\!\langle H \rangle\!\rangle_{I_1} \mid \langle\!\langle K \rangle\!\rangle_{I_2}$$

The encoding in Figure 6 from secret $\pi$-calculus processes $M$ to $\pi$-calculus processes $P$, noted $[\![\cdot]\!]_\Gamma$, is parametrized by a type environment $\Gamma$. We use $\Gamma$ to transform blocked variables of a secret $\pi$-calculus input process into blocked types of a typed $\pi$-calculus process, while constructing the type environment from the program code. Standard types $A$ are encoded into types $T$ of Figure 1 by means of the compilation $[\![\cdot]\!]_m$ defined in the same Figure. Note that the payload of types is qualified as dynamic since the typing system allows to upcast it to a static type, as introduced in Section 2. The encoding of restricted channels assigns a dynamic type modality to channels programmed with new, and a static type modality to channels programmed with hide, as expected.

The main result of this section is that compiled processes that type-check preserve the dynamic semantics of the secret $\pi$-calculus, in the following sense.

**Theorem 3.** *Let $M$ be a secret $\pi$-calculus process. If there are $\Gamma, \Gamma_1$ and $\Delta_1$ such that $\Gamma_1 \vdash [\![M]\!]_\Gamma \triangleright \Delta_1$, then the following hold.*

1. *If $M \to M'$ then $[\![M]\!]_\Gamma \to [\![M']\!]_\Gamma$*
2. *If $[\![M]\!]_\Gamma \to Q$ then there is $M'$ such that $M \to M'$ and $[\![M']\!]_\Gamma = Q$*

A simple counter-example is the secret $\pi$-calculus process $N = [\text{hide}\, y \colon \top][\overline{x}\langle y\rangle.N'] \mid x(z \div \emptyset).N''$: the compilation $[\![N]\!]_\Gamma$ does not type check, for any $\Gamma$, since the type system rejects the attempt of reading from a channel sending a secret variable. Other counter-examples are the secret $\pi$-calculus processes $\overline{x}\langle x\rangle$ and $\overline{x}\langle y\rangle \mid \overline{y}\langle x\rangle$, because we do not consider recursive types (for simplicity), as well as processes that are decorated with the wrong types.

# 4   Applications

To illustrate possible usages of the API, we start by drawing an example based on a process that potentially attempts to declassify a secret channel by means of forwarding it on a public channel $x$, where we assume $w, y, x, z$ all distinct.

$$M_2 = [\text{hide}\, y \colon \text{chan}\langle\top\rangle][\overline{w}\langle y\rangle \mid w(z \div \emptyset).\overline{x}\langle z\rangle] \tag{6}$$

The encoding of $M_2$ is process $P_2$ below, which type-checks: types $T_1, T_2$ describe the free channels of $P$, while type $T_4$ is a return type of $P$.

$$P_2 = (\text{new}\, y \colon T_3)(\overline{w}\langle y\rangle \mid w(z \div \emptyset).\overline{x}\langle z\rangle)$$
$$T_1 = \text{d chan}\langle T_2\rangle_\forall \qquad T_2 = \text{d chan}\langle\top\rangle_\forall$$
$$T_3 = \text{s chan}\langle\top\rangle_1 \qquad T_4 = \text{d chan}\langle T_3\rangle_\forall$$

Indeed this process, taken in isolation, is safe, while its interaction can entail a security break, as we discuss at end of the paragraph.

Take the type environment $\Gamma = w \colon T_1, x \colon T_1$. Informally, the type system allows to send the static channel $y$ over $w$ and $x$ by upcasting the type of the payload of $w$ and $x$, and by downcasting their return type. We first outline a derivation for the left thread of $P_2$: note that we change the return type of $x$ through (three applications of) [T-INACT], since $x$ is not used.

$$\frac{\dfrac{}{w \colon T_4, x \colon T_1, y \colon T_3 \vdash \mathbf{0} \triangleright w \colon T_4, x \colon \top, y \colon T_3}\ ([\text{T-Inact}])}{\Gamma, y \colon T_3 \vdash \overline{w}\langle y\rangle \triangleright w \colon T_4, x \colon \top, y \colon T_3}\ ([\text{T-Out-Up}])\ (*)$$

A derivation for the right thread is below; note that the return type of $x$ is set to void, since the secret variable $z$ is sent over $x$.

$$\frac{\dfrac{\dfrac{}{w \colon T_4, x \colon T_4, y \colon T_3, z \colon T_3 \vdash \mathbf{0} \triangleright w \colon T_4, x \colon T_4, y \colon T_3, z \colon T_3}\ ([\text{T-Inact}])}{w \colon T_4, x \colon T_1, y \colon T_3, z \colon T_3 \vdash \overline{x}\langle z\rangle \triangleright w \colon T_4, x \colon T_4, y \colon T_3, z \colon T_3}\ ([\text{T-Out-Up}])}{\Gamma, y \colon T_3 \vdash w(z).\overline{x}\langle z\rangle \triangleright w \colon T_4, x \colon \bullet, y \colon T_3}\ ([\text{T-In-Up}])\ (**)$$

We glue together the two derivations by using [T-PAR], and finish by applying [T-RES-S]: the final effect is to set the return type of $w$ to void.

$$\frac{\dfrac{(*) \qquad (**)}{\Gamma, y \colon T_3 \vdash \overline{w}\langle y\rangle \mid w(z).\overline{x}\langle z\rangle \triangleright w \colon T_4, x \colon \bullet, y \colon T_3}\ ([\text{T-Par}])}{\Gamma \vdash P_2 \triangleright w \colon \bullet, x \colon \bullet}\ ([\text{T-Res-S}])$$

$$\{\!| \; () \; |\!\}_z = \overline{z}\langle \bot, \bot, \bot \rangle$$

$$\{\!| \; (\langle a_0, b_0 \rangle, \ldots, \langle a_n, b_n \rangle) \; |\!\}_z = (\text{new } z')(\overline{z}\langle a_0, b_0, z' \rangle \mid \{\!| \; (\langle a_1, b_1 \rangle, \ldots, \langle a_n, b_n \rangle) \; |\!\}_{z'})$$

$$\text{ADD}(x, y, z) = z(h_1, h_2, z').((\text{new } z'')(\overline{z}\langle x, y, z'' \rangle \mid \overline{z''}\langle h_1, h_2, z' \rangle) \mid$$

$$\overline{\text{port818}}\langle h_1, h_2 \rangle) \qquad \%\% \text{ Suspicious}$$

**Fig. 7.** A malicious list handler

A void return type acts as a protection against contexts trying to leak secrets from the process. For instance, a composition of the form $P_2 \mid x(u).P'$ does not type check, i.e. $\Gamma \nvdash P_2 \mid x(u).P' \rhd \Delta$, for any $P'$. This holds because the composition $(w: \bullet, x: \bullet) \otimes (w: U_1, x: U_2)$ is undefined whenever $U_1 \neq \top, U_2 \neq \top$, and because if $\Gamma \vdash x(u).P' \rhd \Delta'$ then $\Delta'(x) \neq \top$. Similarly, $P_2 \mid Q$ is ill-typed if $w$ appears free as subject of an input or output in $Q$, for any $Q$.

*Safe programming with third-party libraries* The abstract security API can be useful to protect against malicious behaviour of third-party libraries. The malicious code that we consider in Figure 7 is an implementation of a linked list in a polyadic extension of the programmer language in Figure 5: the code is inspired by [10]. A list of paired names $(\langle a_0, b_0 \rangle, \ldots, \langle a_n, b_n \rangle)$ is programmed through the encoding $\{\!| \cdot |\!\}$ as a list of processes linked by pointers: process $\overline{z_i}\langle x_i, y_i, z_{i+1} \rangle$ represents the entry $\langle x_i, y_i \rangle$, where $z_i$ is the reference to the next pair. A pair $\langle x, y \rangle$ can be added to a list $z$ by means of the meta-process ADD, noted $\text{ADD}(x, y, z)$. The question we face is: how to detect if the library provides a backdoor by forwarding the content of the list on some port, as in the last line of process ADD? Rather than checking the code of the library, programmers may trust the list implementation and use it to store secure channels in a data structure that allows to customize operations, e.g. searches.

$$\text{STORESECCH}(H, y) = [\text{hide } x][H \mid (\text{new } z)(\{\!| \; () \; |\!\}_z \mid \text{ADD}(x, y, z))]$$

To ensure that the secure channel is not disclosed when composing $\text{STORESECCH}(H, y)$ with some $H'$, we may compile the composition and run the type-checker. If the result is positive, Theorem 3.2 ensures that the translation preserves the invariant prescribed by the dynamic semantics of the secret $\pi$-calculus, that is that process $H'$ will not receive channel $x$ during the computation. This allows to use the secret $\pi$-calculus as an abstract API language for secure protocols.

*Enforcing mandatory access control* We review an example discussed in [18]. D-Bus [25] is an IPC system for software applications that is used in many desktop environments. Applications of each user share a private bus for asynchronous message-passing communication; a system bus permits to broadcast messages among applications of different users. Versions smaller than 0.36 contain an erroneous access policy for channels which allows users to send and listen to messages on another user's channel if the address of the socket is known. The code for the attack is synthesized below.

```
[marco@localhost]# echo $DBUS_SESSION_BUS_ADDRESS > Public/address
[guest@localhost]# dbus-monitor --address /home/marco/Public/address
```

The correct policy, subsequently released by Fedora, restricts the access to the user's bus to applications with the same user-id. The policy is mandatory and cannot be changed by users, otherwise security is broken: this is enforced directly in the (untyped) Unix-like access control method. Our interpretation of this vulnerability is that the user's bus can be abstracted as an hidden channel, that is a channel that must not be disclosed by means of internal attacks or Trojan horses. To ensure this invariant, we can program the D-Bus protocol in the secret $\pi$-calculus, translate it in the $\pi$-calculus, and run the type-checker: this will ensure that, when type-checking succeeds, the mandatory policy is enforced, without the need of relying on explicit access control methods. We refer to [18] for a possible implementation of the D-Bus protocol in the secret $\pi$-calculus.

## 5  Discussion

We introduce a type system to enforce static scope for channels in the $\pi$-calculus, and defend that the static analysis can help in devise programs featuring secret channels by providing a semantics-preserving translation of a fragment of the secret $\pi$-calculus [18] into our typed $\pi$-calculus.

While we analyze some simple application of our technique, which we interpret as an abstract API for secure message passing, we leave for future work a precise comparison with calculi and frameworks for secret protocols (e.g. [5,4,2,14]) and $\pi$-calculus dialects featuring static channels (e.g. [15,30]), as well as a (typed) behavioural theory to establish secrecy equations (cf. [16,18]). Other extensions we are interested in consist in study the integration among static and dynamic type qualifiers and session types [19], develop type-inference techniques á la [29,23] to fully automatize the process compilation, and devise a type checking algorithm to resolve the sources of non-determinism in the typing system (cf. the rules for input and for inaction).

Many analysis and programming techniques for security have been developed for process calculi. Among these, we would mention the security analysis enforced by means of static and dynamic type-checking (e.g. [11,21,8]), the verification of secure implementations and protocols that are protected by cryptographic encryption (e.g. [7,3,9]), and programming models that consider a notion of location (e.g. [22,28,12,18]). The most related papers are [18,11]. The paper in [18] introduces the secret $\pi$-calculus, its behavioural theory, and a characterization based on bisimulation semantics. The presence of a *spy* context allows to break some of the standard observational equivalences for restriction, which can be recovered by using the secret channel operator. It would be interesting to investigate whether the untyped theory of [18] would match a typed behavioural theory based on static and dynamic type qualifiers. The work in [11] introduces a $\pi$-calculus featuring a group creation operator, and a typing system that disallows channels to be sent outside of the group. Programmers must declare which is the group type of the payload: the typing system rules out processes of the form $(\mathsf{new}\, p \colon U)(P \mid (\mathsf{new}\, G)(\mathsf{new}\, x \colon G[\,])(\overline{p}\langle x \rangle))$ since the type $U$ of the public channel $p$ cannot mention the secret type $G$, which is local. Differently, we accept processes of this form and do not require such effort to programmers: instead, we automatically infer the "group types" of processes declared with the hide macro, and allow secret channels to be sent over "untyped" channels: i.e. we type-check (the compilation of) process $(\mathsf{new}\, p)(p'(y) \mid [\mathsf{hide}\, x][\overline{p}\langle x \rangle])$ whenever $p' \neq p$, and reject it otherwise. Our main motivation is to shift the middleware support for secret channels (cf. [18]) to a software support in a transparent way: we show how this can be achieved, thus establishing an operational correspondence among untyped and typed semantics of secret channels. From the API language design point of view, we share some similarity with the ideas behind the boxed $\pi$-calculus [28]. A box in [28] acts as wrapper where we can confine untrusted processes; communication among the box and the context is subject to a fine-grained control that prevents the untrusted process to harm the protocol. Our hide macro is based on the symmetric principle, but requires stronger conditions, because we map the macro in a restriction process of the $\pi$-calculus: for a process to be (type-)checked, we require the context outside the scope of an hide to do not listen on channels exchanging secrets.

**Acknowledgements.** This work is supported by the North Portugal Regional Operational Programme under contract NORTE-07-0124-FEDER-000062, by the European Regional Development Fund through the COMPETE Programme under contract FCOMP-01-0124-FEDER-037281 (PEST), and by national funds through FCT - Fundação para a Ciência e a Tecnologia. I warmly thank PEST for travel support; I also thank the Center for Informatics and Information Technologies (CITI, citi.di.fct.unl.pt) for the support of facilities. The final version of this paper has been improved thanks to the detailed comments and useful criticism of the anonymous reviewers, to whom I am especially grateful.

# References

1. Abadi, M.: Protection in programming-language translations. In: Larsen, K.G., Skyum, S., Winskel, G. (eds.) ICALP 1998. LNCS, vol. 1443, pp. 868–883. Springer, Heidelberg (1998)
2. Abadi, M., Blanchet, B.: Analyzing security protocols with secrecy types and logic programs. J. ACM 52(1), 102–146 (2005)
3. Abadi, M., Blanchet, B., Fournet, C.: Just fast keying in the pi calculus. ACM Trans. Inf. Syst. Secur. 10(3) (2007)
4. Abadi, M., Fournet, C.: Mobile values, new names, and secure communication. In: POPL, pp. 104–115. ACM Press (2001)
5. Abadi, M., Gordon, A.D.: A calculus for cryptographic protocols: The spi calculus. Inf. Comput. 148(1), 1–70 (1999)
6. Barendregt, H.: The Lambda Calculus - Its Syntax and Semantics. North-Holland (1981 (1st edn.), revised 1984)
7. Boreale, M., De Nicola, R., Pugliese, R.: Proof techniques for cryptographic processes. SIAM J. Comput. 31(3), 947–986 (2001)

8. Bugliesi, M., Giunti, M.: Typed processes in untyped contexts. In: De Nicola, R., Sangiorgi, D. (eds.) TGC 2005. LNCS, vol. 3705, pp. 19–32. Springer, Heidelberg (2005)
9. Bugliesi, M., Giunti, M.: Secure implementations of typed channel abstractions. In: POPL, pp. 251–262. ACM (2007)
10. Cai, X., Fu, Y.: The λ-calculus in the π-calculus. Math. Struct. Comp. Sci. 21(5), 943–996 (2011)
11. Cardelli, L., Ghelli, G., Gordon, A.D.: Secrecy and group creation. Inf. Comput. 196(2), 127–155 (2005)
12. Castagna, G., Vitek, J., Nardelli, F.Z.: The seal calculus. Inf. Comput. 201(1), 1–54 (2005)
13. Cortier, V., Kremer, S. (eds.): Formal Models and Techniques for Analyzing Security Protocols, Cryptology and Information Security, vol. 5. IOS Press (2011)
14. Cortier, V., Rusinowitch, M., Zalinescu, E.: Relating two standard notions of secrecy. Logical Methods in Computer Science 3(3) (2007)
15. Fournet, C., Gonthier, G.: The reflexive cham and the join-calculus. In: POPL, pp. 372–385. ACM Press (1996)
16. Giunti, M.: Secure Implementations of Typed Channel Abstractions. PhD Thesis TD-2007-1, Department of Informatics, Ca' Foscari University of Venice (2007)
17. Giunti, M.: Static semantics of secret channel abstractions, technical report (2014), http://tinyurl.com/n14-report
18. Giunti, M., Palamidessi, C., Valencia, F.D.: Hide and New in the Pi-Calculus. In: EXPRESS/SOS. EPTCS, vol. 89, pp. 65–79 (2012)
19. Giunti, M., Vasconcelos, V.T.: Linearity, session types and the pi calculus. Math. Struct. Comp. Sci. (2013) (to appear), http://tinyurl.com/mscs2013
20. Google: Application security, http://google.com/about/appsecurity/research (accessed April 2014)
21. Hennessy, M.: The security pi-calculus and non-interference. J. Log. Algebr. Program. 63(1), 3–34 (2005)
22. Hennessy, M.: A Distributed Pi-calculus. Cambridge University Press (2007)
23. Lienhardt, M., Mezzina, C.A., Schmitt, A., Stefani, J.-B.: Typing component-based communication systems. In: Lee, D., Lopes, A., Poetzsch-Heffter, A. (eds.) FMOODS/FORTE 2009. LNCS, vol. 5522, pp. 167–181. Springer, Heidelberg (2009)
24. Milner, R.: Communicating and mobile systems - the Pi-calculus. Cambridge University Press (1999)
25. Pennington, H., Carlsson, A., Larsson, A., Herzberg, S., McVittie, S., Zeuthen, D.: D-Bus specification, http://dbus.freedesktop.org
26. Sabelfeld, A., Myers, A.C.: Language-based information-flow security. IEEE Journal on Selected Areas in Communications 21(1), 5–19 (2003)
27. Sangiorgi, D., Walker, D.: The pi-calculus, a theory of mobile processes. Cambridge University Press (2001)
28. Sewell, P., Vitek, J.: Secure composition of untrusted code: Box pi, wrappers, and causality. J. Comp. Sec. 11(2), 135–188 (2003)
29. Vasconcelos, V.T., Honda, K.: Principal typing schemes in a polyadic π-calculus. In: Best, E. (ed.) CONCUR 1993. LNCS, vol. 715, pp. 524–538. Springer, Heidelberg (1993)
30. Vivas, J.-L., Dam, M.: From higher-order π-calculus to π-calculus in the presence of static operators. In: Sangiorgi, D., de Simone, R. (eds.) CONCUR 1998. LNCS, vol. 1466, pp. 115–130. Springer, Heidelberg (1998)

# Browser Randomisation against Fingerprinting: A Quantitative Information Flow Approach

Frédéric Besson, Nataliia Bielova, and Thomas Jensen*

Inria, France

**Abstract.** Web tracking companies use device fingerprinting to distinguish the users of the websites by checking the numerous properties of their machines and web browsers. One way to protect the users' privacy is to make them switch between different machine and browser configurations. We propose a formalisation of this privacy enforcement mechanism. We use information-theoretic channels to model the knowledge of the tracker and the fingerprinting program, and show how to synthesise a randomisation mechanism that defines the distribution of configurations for each user. This mechanism provides a strong guarantee of *privacy* (the probability of identifying the user is bounded by a given threshold) while maximising *usability* (the user switches to other configurations rarely). To find an optimal solution, we express the enforcement problem of randomisation by a linear program. We investigate and compare several approaches to randomisation and find that more efficient privacy enforcement would often provide lower usability. Finally, we relax the requirement of knowing the fingerprinting program in advance, by proposing a randomisation mechanism that guarantees privacy for an arbitrary program.

## 1 Introduction

Web tracking companies are actively using device fingerprinting to identify the users of the websites by checking the numerous properties of their machines and web browsers. While this technique is of great value to trackers, it is a threat to users' privacy. The Panopticlick project [10] was the first to demonstrate the power of fingerprinting, while recent research shows that this technique is widely used by web tracking companies [1, 18]. Today, only few solutions exist for protecting the users from being fingerprinted. Acar *et al.* [1] have analysed these solutions and concluded that none of them can guarantee user privacy. For example, the Firegloves [5] browser extension returns randomised values when queried for certain browser attributes. However since the same attributes can be retrieved via different browser APIs, the users of Firegloves become more uniquely identifiable than users who do not install this extension. Nevertheless, the idea of such randomisation is a promising approach to counter fingerprinting

---

* This research was partially supported by the French ANR-10-LABX-07-01 Laboratoire d'excellence CominLabs.

K. Bernsmed and S. Fischer-Hübner (Eds.): NordSec 2014, LNCS 8788, pp. 181–196, 2014.
DOI: 10.1007/978-3-319-11599-3_11, © Springer International Publishing Switzerland 2014

but its foundations should be developed further. In this paper, we propose a theory of privacy enforcement by randomisation and show *what privacy guarantee can be achieved*. From this theory, we derive an enforcement mechanism for obtaining this guarantee.

*Example 1.* For a simple illustration, consider the distribution of the browser names and the potentially fingerprinting program P1 from Fig. 1. The distribution of browser names is known to the tracker and is called an *a priori distribution*, and a concrete program output transforms it into an *a posteriori distribution* that we show for o = B. Assuming there are 50 visitors to the website, only one will have an Opera browser, and hence will be uniquely identified by executing the program. Notice that other 49 visitors are indistinguishable since the execution of the program will yield an output o = B for all of them.

| name | $p(\text{name})$ |
|---------|------|
| Firefox | 0.49 |
| Chrome  | 0.49 |
| Opera   | 0.02 |

```
1 if (name = "Opera")
2 then o := A;
3 else o := B;
4 output o;
```

| name | $p(\text{name}|B)$ |
|---------|------|
| Firefox | 0.5 |
| Chrome  | 0.5 |
| Opera   | 0.0 |

**Fig. 1.** Pre-distribution, program P1, post-distribution after observing B

Inspired by Clarkson *et al.*'s work on belief revision [6], Mardziel *et al.* [16,17] propose a definition of *knowledge threshold security* stating that a program is secure if all the post-beliefs of all possible secrets are bounded by some threshold $t$. Espinoza and Smith [11] discuss this definition and name it *worst-case posterior vulnerability* underlining that it is very biased towards the worst output. In order to enforce *knowledge threshold security*, Mardziel *et al.* [16,17] suggest to: i) run the program if the threshold holds for all the values of the secret input; ii) not run the program in case there is at least one value for which the guarantee does not hold. This radical approach forbids all the safe users to run the program. Typically, the program of Fig. 1 would not run because the single Opera user would be identified whereas 98% of the users could run the program safely.

In this paper, we show how to enforce *knowledge threshold security* using a more flexible mechanism based on randomisation. For example, given 50 website visitors, program P will be evaluated to provide a worst-case probability of guessing the identity equal to 1 for Opera users and $\frac{1}{49}$ for Firefox and Chrome users. Then, for a threshold $t = \frac{1}{25}$, we will provide a mechanism that randomises the browser name for Opera users, and not influence the experience of other users.

## 1.1 Attacker Model and Assumptions

We consider terminating (deterministic or probabilistic) programs operating over a finite range of inputs. Upon termination, the program returns a single value. As we only consider terminating programs, the attacker will always observe a value. In our model, the attacker has arbitrary computing power, he provides the program and observes the output. The input of the program is secret and represents a browser configuration. However, the attacker has perfect knowledge over the distribution of the secret inputs. Our enforcement works by randomising the program inputs. We consider that the attacker has access to the precise description of the randomisation mechanism.

The main contributions can be summarised as:

- A model of the problem of privacy protection against fingerprinting programs, based on information-theoretic channels representing the statistics of browser properties and the program.
- A novel definition of privacy for such systems, that ensures that the probability of an attacker identifying a user is bounded by a given threshold. We show that the enforcement of privacy can be achieved by randomising the browser properties, and that this randomisation problem can be reduced to solving linear programs.
- Algorithms (a global, a greedy and a decentralised) for enforcing privacy against a particular fingerprinting program. All algorithms ensure the strong privacy guarantee, *i.e.*, that the probability of being identified is smaller than a given threshold. The algorithms optimise the solution with respect to additional "usability" constraints, which ensure that randomisation is used as little as possible.
- A general result about how user privacy can be guaranteed for any program that the user might run. This represents the worst case scenario, in which a program checks all the possible browser properties of the user. This result is important in the case where it is difficult or impossible to construct the information-theoretic channel that models the program (*e.g.*, due to the complexity of a language such as JavaScript).

The paper is organised as follows. In Section 2, we show how to model fingerprinting in information-theoretic terms. In particular, we define $t$-privacy which is our formal notion of privacy. We also formally introduce the problem of enforcing $t$-privacy. In Section 3, we show that the enforcement problem reduces to solving a Linear Program. In Section 4, we present several enforcement algorithms that trade optimality for efficiency. In Section 5, we propose an enforcement that ensures $t$-privacy for any program. Related works are discussed in Section 6 and Section 7 concludes. More details, in particular proofs of theorems, can be found in a companion report [3].

## 2    Threshold-Based Privacy and Usability for Fingerprinting

This section shows how to model fingerprinting in terms of information-theoretic channels [7]. The input to the fingerprinting script is the browser configuration that is the user's secret. A script $P$ can be modelled by an information-theoretic

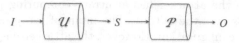

**Fig. 2.** Cascade of channels $\mathcal{U}$ and $\mathcal{P}$

channel $\mathcal{P} = (S, O, P)$ which produces an output $o \in O$ given a secret configuration $s \in S$. The input/output transformation is given by a matrix $P$ such that $P[s, o]$ is the conditional probability $p(s|o)$ of observing the output $o$ given the secret input $s$. For deterministic scripts, the corresponding channel can be extracted by running the script for all the possible inputs. These inputs are the possible browser configurations whose distribution is known to the attacker. For probabilistic scripts, probabilistic sampling would construct a reliable but approximate channel. Even better, we can construct an exact channel using symbolic computations over probability distributions. For each possible input, we can evaluate the script semantics expressed as a distribution transformer [6]. Symmetrically, we can run a weakest pre-expectation calculus [12] which extends weakest precondition calculus to probabilistic programs. The model acquisition problem is not in the scope of this paper, and henceforth we just assume that a channel matrix is given.

User identities are related to the browser configurations by browser statistics. We model this mapping by a deterministic channel $\mathcal{U} = (I, S, U)$, where $I$ is a finite set of user identities, $S$ is a finite set of possible browser configurations and $U$ is a channel matrix, where

$$U[i, s] = \begin{cases} 1 \text{ if user } i \text{ has configuration } s \\ 0 \text{ otherwise.} \end{cases}$$

By construction the matrix $U$ is deterministic, meaning that each row contains only one entry equal to 1, and the rest are 0s. In other words, $U[i, s]$ means that a user $i$ possesses only one configuration $s$. For a deterministic channel $\mathcal{C}$, we write $Im(C, i)$ for the unique $o$ such that $C[i, o] = 1$ and $Pre(C, o)$ for the set of inputs that can produce $o$: $Im(C, i) = o$ iff $C[i, o] = 1$ and $Pre(C, o) = \{i | C[i, o] = 1\}$.

Initially, all the users are equally indistinguishable and therefore the initial attacker knowledge of user identities is modelled by the uniform distribution. The worst-case probability of guessing a user identity by observing a run of the cascade of channels $\mathcal{U} \otimes \mathcal{P}$ (Fig. 2) is given by

$$\mathbb{P}(\mathcal{U} \otimes \mathcal{P}) = \max_{i \in I, o \in O} p(i|o) = \max_{i \in I, o \in O} \frac{\sum_{s \in S} U[i, s] \cdot P[s, o]}{\sum_{i'} \sum_{s \in S} U[i', s] \cdot P[s, o]}.$$

This result specialises the definition of worst-case a posteriori distribution for the a priori uniform distribution and a sequence of channels [3, Section 4.1]. Suppose that this quantity equals a threshold $t$ then for all user $i$ the probability of being identified by an attacker observing a run of the fingerprinting script is below $t$. Definition 1 formalises this notion of threshold-based privacy.

**Definition 1 (Threshold-based privacy).** *A channel $\mathcal{C}$ is $t$-private if the probability of guessing the channel's input is bounded by $t$: $\mathbb{P}(\mathcal{C}) \leq t$.*

Note that a fingerprinting script only runs once per session of a given user. Therefore an attacker cannot accumulate knowledge by observing several runs of several fingerprinting scripts. In other words, different runs of fingerprinting scripts cannot be correlated and the maximum fingerprinting capability of a script is adequately modelled by the quantity $\mathbb{P}(\mathcal{U} \otimes \mathcal{P})$.

| $U$ | Firefox | Opera |
|-----|---------|-------|
| $i_1$ | 1 | 0 |
| $i_2$ | 1 | 0 |
| $i_3$ | 1 | 0 |
| $i_4$ | 1 | 0 |
| $i_5$ | 0 | 1 |

| $P$ | A | B |
|-----|---|---|
| Firefox | 0 | 1 |
| Opera | 1 | 0 |

**Fig. 3.** User channel and channel for program P1

*Example 2.* Consider the program P1 from Example 1. Fig. 3 shows the matrix of a user channel $\mathcal{U}$ representing (simplified) browser statistics and the matrix of a channel $\mathcal{P}$ for program P1. When a user with identity $i_5$ runs the program P, a tracker observes an output A and knows that the user has the configuration Opera. The channel $\mathcal{U}$ then makes the user $i_5$ uniquely identifiable, therefore the a posteriori probability is $p(i_5|\text{A}) = \frac{U[i_5,\text{Opera}] \cdot P[\text{Opera,A}]}{U[i_5,\text{Opera}] \cdot P[\text{Opera,A}]} = 1$. When an attacker observes output B, he concludes that the user has a configuration different from Opera. The channel $\mathcal{U}$ makes the users different from $i_5$ indistinguishable for the attacker thanks to the program output B. Therefore for all these users $p(i|\text{B}) = \frac{1}{4}$ since output B can be obtained from Firefox configurations. We conclude that the worst-case probability of guessing the user identity is:

$$\mathbb{P}(\mathcal{U} \otimes \mathcal{P}) = \max_{i \in I}\{p(i|\text{A}); p(i|\text{B})\} = \max\{1; 1/4\} = 1.$$

In the following, we propose enforcement mechanisms which replace the channel $\mathcal{U}$ with a randomised channel $\mathcal{R}$ so that the cascade $\mathcal{R} \otimes \mathcal{P}$ is $t$-private for a given threshold $t$. The enforcement will also minimise the randomisation characterised by a quantity $\mathbb{U}(\mathcal{R}, \mathcal{U})$ (see Def. 3). However, not every threshold can be enforced by user channel randomisation. We state our enforceability theorem as follows.

**Definition 2 (Enforceable threshold).** *A threshold $t$ is enforceable for a user channel $\mathcal{U}$ and program channel $\mathcal{P}$ if there exists a randomised channel $\mathcal{R}$, such that $\mathcal{R} \otimes \mathcal{P}$ is $t$-private ($\mathbb{P}(\mathcal{R} \otimes \mathcal{P}) \leq t$).*

**Theorem 1 (Enforceability).** *A threshold $t$ is enforceable for a user channel $\mathcal{U} = (I, S, U)$ and any program channel $\mathcal{P}$ if and only if $\frac{1}{|I|} \leq t$.*

*Proof.* See companion report [3, Theorem 3]. □

Our enforcement mechanism does not pick an arbitrary randomised channel $\mathcal{R}$ but aims at maximising the informal usability requirement that "the users do not want to switch to other configurations too often since they prefer to use their original configurations as much as possible". Formally, this requirement is captured by the following definition.

**Definition 3 (Usability).** *Given a channel $\mathcal{U}$, the usability of a channel $\mathcal{R}$ is* $\mathbb{U}(\mathcal{R},\mathcal{U}) = \sum_i R[i, Im(U,i)]$.

Usability quantifies the amount of switching of configurations incurred by a given channel $\mathcal{R}$. We aim at maximising usability *i.e.*, minimising the probability that a user needs to switch between configurations. The maximum theoretical usability is obviously obtained when $\mathcal{R} = \mathcal{U}$ and $\mathbb{U}(\mathcal{U},\mathcal{U}) = |I|$.

For the program P1, we can graphically represent the space of possible randomisation channels $\mathcal{R}$ that enforce $t$-privacy, where all Firefox users would get a probability $x$ for Firefox and $1 - x$ for Opera, dually Opera users would get probability $y$ for using Opera and $1 - y$ for Firefox. The probability of guessing the user identity of a channel $\mathcal{R} \otimes \mathcal{P}$ is:

$$\max\left\{ \frac{x}{4x + 1 - y}, \frac{1 - x}{4 - 4x + y}, \frac{1 - y}{4x + 1 - y}, \frac{y}{4 - 4x + y} \right\}.$$

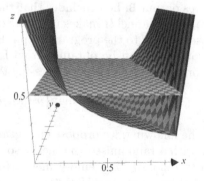

**Fig. 4.** The dark green surface represents the probability of guessing the user identity of a channel $\mathcal{R} \otimes \mathcal{P}$, while the yellow plane shows the probability of guessing the identity set to $\frac{1}{2}$. The blue points $x = 0.9, y = 0.4$ and $x = 0.8, y = 0.8$ are reaching the threshold $t$. The red point $x = 0.75$, $y = 0.3$ corresponds to the randomisation channel $\mathcal{R}_0$ of Fig. 5 and belongs to the surface below the threshold $t$.

while the usability of a channel $\mathcal{R}$ is $\mathbb{U}(\mathcal{R},\mathcal{U}) = 4x + y$. Therefore, the usability of the channel $\mathcal{R}_0$ (red point) is $\mathbb{U}(\mathcal{R}_0,\mathcal{U}) = 4 \cdot 0.75 + 0.3 = 3.3$, while the usability of randomisation channels presented by blue points is $4 \cdot 0.9 + 0.4 = 4$ and $4 \cdot 0.8 + 0.8 = 4$ respectively. In the next section we show that the usability of 4 is the maximum possible usability of a randomisation channel that enforces $\frac{1}{2}$-privacy given the user channel $\mathcal{U}$ and the program P1.

# 3   Reduction to Linear Programming

This section shows how to construct a randomised channel $\mathcal{R}$ that ensures $t$-privacy for the composed channel $\mathcal{R} \otimes \mathcal{P}$. We parametrised the matrix of the channel $\mathcal{R}$ using the variables $R[i, s] = x_{is}$, where $i \in I, s \in S$ and define a system of constraints that such a channel must satisfy. Finding the best possible channel can then be expressed as a Linear Program (LP).

**Channel Correctness.** The channel matrix $R$ represents conditional probabilities, therefore:

- $0 \leq x_{is} \leq 1$ for all $i \in I, s \in S$, meaning each parameter is a probability.
- $\sum_{s \in S} x_{is} = 1$ for all $i \in I$, meaning each matrix row is a distribution.

**$t$-privacy:** the channel $\mathcal{R}$ must guarantee $t$-privacy for the composed program channel $\mathcal{P}$ i.e., $\mathbb{P}(\mathcal{R} \otimes \mathcal{P}) \leq t$. Expanding this expression, we get:

$$\max_{i \in I, o \in O} \frac{\sum_{s \in S} x_{is} \cdot P[s, o]}{\sum_{j \in I} \sum_{s \in S} x_{js} \cdot P[s, o]} \leq t.$$

This can be rewritten as a system of linear inequalities for all $i \in I, o \in O$:

$$\sum_{s \in S} x_{is} \cdot P[s, o] - t \cdot \sum_{j \in I} \sum_{s \in S} x_{js} \cdot P[s, o] \leq 0.$$

The system of constraints presented by the channel correctness and $t$-privacy requirements have a number of solutions. One solution is a channel $\mathcal{R}$ where all the matrix elements are equal to $\frac{1}{|S|}$. To see this, observe that 1) the channel is correct : $\sum_{s \in S} \frac{1}{|S|} = 1$; 2) $t$-privacy is guaranteed for any $\mathcal{P}$ since $\mathbb{P}(\mathcal{R} \otimes \mathcal{P}) \leq \mathbb{P}(\mathcal{R})$ (see [3, Theorem 2]), and $\mathbb{P}(\mathcal{R}) = \frac{1/|S|}{\sum_{j \in I} 1/|S|} = \frac{1}{|I|} \leq t$ for any enforceable $t$ (Theorem 1). However, this solution might not guarantee the best usability: it forces each user to use other configurations as often as his original configuration.

This last observation motivates a third requirement:

**Usability.** Our usability requirement (see Definition 3) exactly describes the desire of users to switch to other configurations as rarely as possible. Therefore, the usability of a randomised channel $\mathcal{R}$ must be maximised. Remember that usability $\mathbb{U}(\mathcal{R}, \mathcal{U}) = \sum_{i \in I} R[i, Im(U, i)]$ represents a sum of all entries in $R$ where $U[i, s] = 1$. Therefore, we can rewrite it as a requirement to maximise the function $\sum_{(i \in I): U[i,s]=1} x_{is}$.

Combining the requirements presented in this section, we can state our problem as a *Linear Program*, where the usability must be maximised while the channel correctness and $t$-privacy constraints are satisfied:

$$max \ \sum_{(i \in I): U[i,s]=1} x_{is} \ \text{s.t.}$$

$$\begin{cases} 0 \leq x_{is} \leq 1 & \forall i \in I, s \in S \\ \sum_{s \in S} x_{is} = 1 & \forall i \in I \\ \sum_{s \in S} x_{is} \cdot P[s, o] - t \cdot \sum_{j \in I} \sum_{s \in S} x_{js} \cdot P[s, o] \leq 0 & \forall i \in I, o \in O \end{cases}$$

*Example 3.* Consider again the program P1 from Example 2. For a user channel $\mathcal{U} = (U, I, S)$, the randomised channel $\mathcal{R}$ has a matrix of $|I| \times |S|$ parameters denoted by $x_{is}$ (see Fig. 5). The usability of $\mathcal{R}$ is computed as follows:

$$\mathbb{U}(\mathcal{R}, \mathcal{U}) = \sum_{(i \in I):U[i,s]=1} x_{is} = x_{11} + x_{21} + x_{31} + x_{41} + x_{52}.$$

The constraints imposed by channel correctness are straightforward to write down. Here, we present the constraints provided by the $t$-privacy requirement, where the threshold $t = \frac{1}{2}$:

$$+\tfrac{1}{2}\,x_{11} - \tfrac{1}{2}\,x_{21} - \tfrac{1}{2}\,x_{31} - \tfrac{1}{2}\,x_{41} - \tfrac{1}{2}\,x_{51} \le 0$$

$$-\tfrac{1}{2}\,x_{11} + \tfrac{1}{2}\,x_{21} - \tfrac{1}{2}\,x_{31} - \tfrac{1}{2}\,x_{41} - \tfrac{1}{2}\,x_{51} \le 0$$

$$\ldots$$

$$-\tfrac{1}{2}\,x_{12} - \tfrac{1}{2}\,x_{22} - \tfrac{1}{2}\,x_{32} + \tfrac{1}{2}\,x_{42} - \tfrac{1}{2}\,x_{52} \le 0$$

$$-\tfrac{1}{2}\,x_{12} - \tfrac{1}{2}\,x_{22} - \tfrac{1}{2}\,x_{32} - \tfrac{1}{2}\,x_{42} + \tfrac{1}{2}\,x_{52} \le 0$$

This LP has several solutions. In Fig. 5 we have the optimal channel $\mathcal{R}_1$ with usability $\mathbb{U}(\mathcal{R}_1, \mathcal{U}) = 4$ and the non-optimal channel $\mathcal{R}_0$ of Fig 4.

| $R$ | Firefox | Opera |
|---|---|---|
| $i_1$ | $x_{11}$ | $x_{12}$ |
| $i_2$ | $x_{21}$ | $x_{22}$ |
| $i_3$ | $x_{31}$ | $x_{32}$ |
| $i_4$ | $x_{41}$ | $x_{42}$ |
| $i_5$ | $x_{51}$ | $x_{52}$ |

| $R_0$ | Firefox | Opera |
|---|---|---|
| $i_1$ | 0.75 | 0.25 |
| $i_2$ | 0.75 | 0.25 |
| $i_3$ | 0.75 | 0.25 |
| $i_4$ | 0.75 | 0.25 |
| $i_5$ | 0.7 | 0.3 |

| $R_1$ | Firefox | Opera |
|---|---|---|
| $i_1$ | 0.9 | 0.1 |
| $i_2$ | 0.8 | 0.2 |
| $i_3$ | 0.7 | 0.3 |
| $i_4$ | 0.6 | 0.4 |
| $i_5$ | 0 | 1 |

**Fig. 5.** Parametrised channel $\mathcal{R}$ and randomised channels $R_0$ and $R_1$

### 3.1   Feasibility

In practice, switching to a particular configuration might not be technically feasible. For instance, faithfully emulating a foreign OS might be considered too drastic a change. Other switchings of configurations could hinder an optimal user experience. For instance, switching to an arbitrary language could have undesirable side-effects. For personal reasons, certain users might also wish to keep their configuration unaltered. To model those feasibility constraints, we can introduce a relation $Imp \subseteq I \times S$ representing the configuration switches that are considered impossible. The fact that those switchings between configurations might be impossible can be encoded into the Linear Program in a straightforward way. Each pair $(i, s) \in Imp$ yields the constraint $x_{is} = 0$. These constraints can be used to pre-process the problem and substitute $x_{is}$ for 0, thus reducing the number of variables of the problem.

# 4   Enforcement Algorithms

Linear programs can be solved in polynomial time using interior points methods. Despite a worst-case exponential complexity, the Simplex algorithm is usually superior and, on average, only a linear number of pivot steps are needed. Furthermore, for probabilistic models, this average linear bound can be formally established [20]. Yet, the complexity is fairly high and solving the linear program directly might not be computationally feasible. In particular, the complexity is parametrised by the number of identities $|I|$ and does not exploit properties of the program channel. In the following, we show that it is possible to substantially reduce the number of parameters needed to construct an optimal channel $\mathcal{R}$.

*Indistinguishable identities.* A key insight is that two identities $i$ and $i'$ are indistinguishable for a script $\mathcal{P}$ as soon as they are mapped to the same secret configuration $s$ by the channel $\mathcal{U}$ ($U[i] = U[i']$). In the companion report [3, Theorem 4 of Section 6.2], we prove that there exists an optimal randomised channel $\mathcal{R}$ such that indistinguishable identities get the same enforcement ($R[i] = R[i']$). We exploit this property to simplify the LP formulation and reduce the number of variables from $|I| \cdot |S|$ to $|S| \cdot |S|$ and the number of constraints from $|I| \cdot |O| + |I| \cdot |S| + |I|$ to $|S| \cdot |O| + |S| \cdot |S| + |S|$. This transformation has a drastic impact on the size of the resulting linear program which becomes independent from the number of identities.

*Greedy algorithm.* We can exploit the structure of the program and reduce further the complexity at the cost of a potential non-optimal utility. In particular, we can detect identities $i$ whose probability of guessing is below the threshold with the original channel $\mathcal{U}$. Definition 4 captures this notion.

**Definition 4.** *Given channels $\mathcal{P}$ and $\mathcal{U}$, an identity $i$ is* locally safe *iff*

$$\frac{1}{|Eq_{\mathcal{U}\otimes\mathcal{P}}(i)|} \leq t \text{ where } Eq_C(i) = \{i' | \forall o, C[i,o] = C[i',o]\}.$$

In other words, the probability of guessing of *locally safe* identities is below the threshold $t$ whatever the mapping of other identities.

**Theorem 2.** *Let Safe be the locally safe identities for $P$ w.r.t. $\mathcal{U}$. Then there is a channel $\mathcal{R}$ such that $\mathbb{P}(\mathcal{R} \otimes \mathcal{P}) \leq t$ and $\forall i \in Safe : R[i, Im(U, i)] = 1$.*

*Proof.* Given an identity $i_0 \in Safe$, the channel $\mathcal{R}$ can be constructed as follows:

$$\forall i \in Safe, R[i,j] = \begin{cases} 1 \text{ if } j = Im(U, i) \\ 0 \text{ if } j \neq Im(U, i) \end{cases} \quad \forall i \notin Safe, R[i,j] = \begin{cases} 1 \text{ if } j = Im(U, i_0) \\ 0 \text{ if } j \neq Im(U, i_0) \end{cases}$$

All locally safe identities $i \in Safe$ are unmodified and therefore their probability of guessing is below the threshold $t$. All the other identities $i \notin Safe$ are modified so that they are undistinguishable from the safe identity $i_0$ and therefore their probability of guessing is also below the threshold $t$.

Using Theorem 2, we devise a greedy algorithm for solving the linear program. Identifying the locally safe identities can be done by performing the channel composition $\mathcal{U} \otimes \mathcal{P}$ and counting the number of identical lines. The remaining constraints can be solved using standard linear programming algorithms. The size of the LP has been further reduced: there are $|S| \cdot (|S| - |Safe|)$ variables and $(1 + |S|) \cdot (|S| - |Safe|) + |S| \cdot |O|$ constraints. This is a substantial gain: the number of variables is decreasing as a linear function of $|Safe|$. Moreover, even if the remaining constraints do not completely vanish, they are sparser.

This algorithm is maximising usability locally because *locally safe* identities are not modified. However, there is no guarantee that this strategy would provide the maximum usability.

*Example 4.* Consider a threshold $t = \frac{1}{2}$ and the enforcement of $\frac{1}{2}$-privacy for the channels $\mathcal{U}$ and program $\mathcal{P}$ given below:

```
1 if name="Firefox"
2 then o:=A
3 else{
4   if name="Opera"
5   then o:=B
6   else o:=C}
```

| $U$ | Firefox | Opera | Chrome |
|-----|---------|-------|--------|
| $i_1$ | 1 | 0 | 0 |
| $i_2$ | 1 | 0 | 0 |
| $i_3$ | 0 | 1 | 0 |
| $i_4$ | 0 | 0 | 1 |

| $P$ | A | B | C |
|-----|---|---|---|
| Firefox | 1 | 0 | 0 |
| Opera | 0 | 1 | 0 |
| Chrome | 0 | 0 | 1 |

Note that identities $i_1$ and $i_2$ are indistinguishable. As the threshold is $\frac{1}{2}$, $i_1$ and $i_2$ are locally safe

$$Equ_{\otimes \mathcal{P}}(i_1) = Equ_{\otimes \mathcal{P}}(i_2) = \{i_1, i_2\}.$$

Hence, the *greedy algorithm* is solving the following parametrised $\mathcal{R}$ channel:

| $R$ | Firefox | Opera | Chrome |
|-----|---------|-------|--------|
| $i_1$ | 1 | 0 | 0 |
| $i_2$ | 1 | 0 | 0 |
| $i_3$ | $x_{20}$ | $x_{21}$ | $x_{22}$ |
| $i_4$ | $x_{30}$ | $x_{31}$ | $x_{32}$ |

The best solution with $\mathbb{U}(\mathcal{R}, \mathcal{U}) = 3$ is obtained for

$$x_{20} = x_{30} = 0 \qquad x_{21} = x_{22} = x_{31} = x_{32} = \tfrac{1}{2}.$$

Here, the identities $i_1$ and $i_2$ keep their secrets while $i_3$ and $i_4$ are uniformly randomised over Opera and Chrome.

*Decentralised algorithm* The previous algorithm can be modified to work in a completely decentralised fashion where each row of the channel $R$ can be computed independently. If an identity $i$ is *locally safe*, we get

$$R[i, j] = \begin{cases} 1 & \text{if } j = Im(U, i) \\ 0 & \text{otherwise} \end{cases}.$$

Otherwise, if an identity $i'$ is not locally safe, it needs to switch configuration. This can be done by identifying an identity that is locally safe. If there is none, the identity $i$ maximising $|Equ_{\otimes \mathcal{P}}(i)|$ can be chosen and therefore the identities are all indistinguishable.

*Example 5.* Continuing with the channels of Example. 4, the decentralised algorithm also allows identities $i_1$ and $i_2$ to keep their secrets unchanged. However, $i_3$ and $i_4$ would switch to the safe identity $i_1$. Compared to the greedy algorithm, the decentralised algorithm obtains a smaller usability : $\mathbb{U}(\mathcal{R}, \mathcal{U}) = 2$.

For deterministic programs, a dynamic (or hybrid) information flow monitor [2] can evaluate if the knowledge contained in a program result is below the threshold. Using the decentralised algorithm, if the quantity of information is below the threshold, it is safe to output the result. If the identity is not proved locally safe by the dynamic monitor, the identity $i$ maximising $|Eq_{\mathcal{U} \otimes \mathcal{P}}(i)|$ can be obtained using the previous algorithm. This identity $i$ should be used instead of the original user identity. Returning a result $\bot$ distinct from existing outputs *i.e.,* an observable termination of the program does not achieve the same privacy guarantee. In practice, we can expect that there are many *locally* safe configurations that can be identified *e.g.,* by enumerating identities by decreasing popularity and running a hybrid monitor. Using this scheme, the usability might not be optimal but the computation is decentralised and the overhead small for identities for which local safety can be established by hybrid monitoring.

## 5    Enforcing *t*-privacy for any Program

Finally, we consider the case when the program channel $\mathcal{P}$ is unknown or cannot be computed. In this case, only the user channel $\mathcal{U} = (I, S, U)$ is given, and we need to ensure that for any program $\mathcal{P}$, the probability of identifying the user is bounded by $t$.

### 5.1    Randomisation of the Identity User Channel $\mathcal{U}_{Id}$

Before providing a generic solution for any user channel, we first consider the simpler case where the user channel denotes a 1-1 mapping between user identities and configurations. Without loss of generality, we have that $I = S$ and we denote this channel by $\mathcal{U}_{Id} = (I, I, U_{Id})$, where $U_{Id}$ is the identity matrix.

Like in previous sections, we find a randomised channel $\mathcal{R}_{Id} = (I, I, R_{Id})$ s.t. $t$-privacy is enforced while usability is maximised by solving a (simplified) linear program. Notice that the threshold $t$ must be enforceable for a channel $\mathcal{U}_{Id}$ in the sense of Theorem 1.

$$max \ \sum x_{ii} \ \text{s.t.}$$
$$\begin{cases} 0 \le x_{ij} \le 1 & \forall i, j \in I \\ \sum_{j \in I} x_{ij} = 1 & \forall i \in I \\ x_{ik} - t \cdot \sum_{j \in I} x_{jk} \le 0 & \forall i, k \in I \end{cases}$$

This problem has the following solution:

$$R_{Id}[i, j] = \begin{cases} t & \text{if } i = j \\ \frac{1-t}{|I|-1} & \text{otherwise} \end{cases}$$

with the probability of guessing: $\mathbb{P}(\mathcal{R}_{Id}) = t$ and the usability: $\mathbb{U}(\mathcal{R}_{Id}, \mathcal{U}_{Id}) = t \cdot |I|$. Interestingly, usability depends on the threshold: the higher the threshold $t$, the bigger is the probability that the user can be identified, hence his original configuration should change less, and therefore more usability would be provided.

## 5.2    Randomisation of an Arbitrary Channel $\mathcal{U}$

We now construct a randomised user channel $\mathcal{R}$ from a given user channel $\mathcal{U}$, that satisfies the $t$-privacy for any program channel $\mathcal{P}$: $\forall \mathcal{P} : \mathbb{P}(\mathcal{R} \otimes \mathcal{P}) \leq t$. Like before, a threshold $t$ must be enforceable in a sense of Theorem 1.

We build channel $\mathcal{R}$ by starting from a channel $\mathcal{R}_{Id}$ and merging the columns of the identities that share the same configuration in the user channel $\mathcal{U}$.

$$R[i, s] = \begin{cases} t + \frac{1-t}{|I|-1} \cdot (n_s - 1) & \text{if } i \in Pre(U, s) \\ \frac{1-t}{|I|-1} \cdot n_s & \text{otherwise} \end{cases} \tag{1}$$

where $n_s = |Pre(U, s)|$ (the set $Pre$ was defined in Section 2). We now prove the main properties of the constructed channel $\mathcal{R}$.

**Lemma 1 (Well-formedness).** *Given a user channel $\mathcal{U} = (I, S, U)$, a randomised channel $\mathcal{R} = (I, S, R)$, where $R$ is computed by equation (1) is well-formed, i.e.,*

- *$0 \leq R[i, s] \leq 1$ for all $i \in I$, $s \in S$, meaning each parameter is a probability*
- *$\sum_{s \in S} R[i, s] = 1$ for all $i \in I$, meaning each matrix row is a distribution*

**Lemma 2 ($t$-privacy).** *Given a user channel $\mathcal{U}$, the randomised channel $\mathcal{R}$, where $R$ is computed by equation (1) for an enforceable threshold $t$, is $t$-private:*

$$\mathbb{P}(\mathcal{R}) \leq t.$$

We can now prove the main theorem of this section: a constructed randomised user channel $\mathcal{R}$ can ensure $t$-privacy for any program channel $\mathcal{P}$.

**Theorem 3.** *For any user channel $\mathcal{U} = (I, S, U)$, the randomised user channel $\mathcal{R}$ ensures $t$-privacy for any program channel $\mathcal{P} = (S, O, P)$:*

$$\forall \mathcal{P} : \mathbb{P}(\mathcal{R} \otimes \mathcal{P}) \leq t$$

We do not prove that the randomised user channel $\mathcal{R}$ provides an optimal usability. The usability of the solution $\mathcal{R}$ given a user channel $\mathcal{U}$ is:

$$\mathbb{U}(\mathcal{R}, \mathcal{U}) = \sum_{s \in S} |Pre(U, s)| \cdot (t + \frac{1-t}{|I|-1} \cdot (|Pre(U, s)| - 1)).$$

We now state the lower and upper bounds of the usability that is defined by the characteristics of the channel $\mathcal{U}$:

$$t \cdot |I| \leq l \cdot |S| \cdot (t + \frac{1-t}{|I|-1} \cdot (l-1)) \leq \mathbb{U}(\mathcal{R}, \mathcal{U}) \leq h \cdot |S| \cdot (t + \frac{1-t}{|I|-1} \cdot (h-1)) \leq |I|$$

where $l = \min_{s \in S} Pre(U, s)$ and $h = \max_{s \in S} Pre(U, s)$.

In the general case, the randomised user channel $\mathcal{R}$ constructed in this section will provide a solution with reduced usability compared to the solutions provided by other approaches in previous sections. The reason for this is the fact that a program channel $\mathcal{P}$ may already make some of the configurations indistinguishable. For the users of such configurations, it is (in principle) possible to obtain a better usability.

# 6  Related Work

**Evaluation of Information Flow.** Mardziel et al. [16,17] define the notion of *knowledge threshold secure* program. This is a generalisation of $t$-privacy allowing to attach different thresholds to different secrets. In our context, as we wish to protect privacy (and not secrets), only a single threshold is needed. Mardziel et al. are using an abstract domain of probabilistic polyhedra for computing an over-approximation of the threshold security of a program. They exploit this information to implement a simple enforcement algorithm: If the program is *threshold secure*, it runs without modification; if it is not *threshold secure*, it does not run at all. Our enforcement offers a better usability at the price of randomising the program inputs. Yet, our enforcement algorithms can ensure a minimum randomisation that is thus affecting a minimal set of users. For example, a greedy algorithm ensures that locally safe users will always run the program without any changes.

Klebanov [13,14] has proposed efficient algorithms for exactly computing standard quantitative information flow measures of programs such as conditional (minimal) guessing entropy. The algorithms are either based on SAT-solving techniques [14] or on *extended Barvinok counting* [22]. These techniques are applied only to restricted classes of programs. SAT-based techniques require a propositional encoding of programs. Extended Barvinok counting consists in computing the number of integer points in a parametrised polyhedron and thus applies to programs that can be specified using linear integer arithmetic. In our theoretical setting, channels can model arbitrary terminating programs with a finite input/output relation but constructing explicitly the channel matrix could be costly. More efficient enforcement algorithms could certainly benefit from syntactic program restrictions. For deterministic programs, Klebanov's approaches can be adapted for deciding whether a program is $t$-private. Notice that Klebanov is only concerned with the problem of quantifying information flows and does not consider enforcement. However, this information can be directly exploited to implement the simple enforcement proposed by Mardziel et al..

Köpf and Rybalchenko [15] approximate the entropy of a program using a combination of static and dynamic analyses, where random sampling is enhanced by a symbolic backward analysis. The method ensures a rapid convergence rate but the guarantee is probabilistic. Because $t$-privacy is a property quantifying over all the program inputs, it cannot be established by random sampling. Moreover, the purpose of $t$-privacy is to protect all users (especially those whose configurations are rare).

**k-anonymity.** Sweeney [21] proposes *k-anonymity* that requires that every individual is anonymous within some set of at least size $k$. $k$-anonymity was not widely adopted as a privacy definition for two major reasons: 1) the values of sensitive attributes in the remaining set could be discovered due to their little diversity; 2) attackers with background knowledge of the distribution of the secret inputs can still infer some information about the secrets despite the fact that $k$-anonymity is enforced. The first problem related to $k$-anonymity is shown by an example when a program's output could have been caused by one of $k$ possible inputs, but one of those inputs is much more probable than the rest. After observing a $k$-anonymous answer of a query, the a posteriori distribution of the secrets represents this knowledge of the attacker. The probability of guessing the secret given this knowledge is bounded by $t$ thanks to $t$-privacy guarantee. The second problem is not applicable in our case since the attacker does not have any background knowledge: he collects all the data about the user through the execution of the program, and he has no history of interaction with the user because he cannot identify the user.

**Differential Privacy.** Dwork et al. [8] proposed a new privacy definition: a query to the database is $\epsilon$-*differentially private* if and only if its answer is very similar to this query answer over a database that differs in only one record. In other words, one record in a database does not significantly change the answer of a query. Differential privacy was designed to reason about databases, while our probability of guessing is defined over guessing the only one secret: the user identity. Mardziel *et al.*, [17] make the observation that threshold based privacy and differential privacy can by formally compared using the notion of $\epsilon$-*adversarial privacy* [19]. This notion was proven to be equivalent to differential privacy for a certain class of a priori distributions of input secrets (uniform distribution in our case). In our notations $\epsilon$-adversarial privacy can be defined as follows.

**Definition 5.** *A channel* $C = (C, I, O)$ *is* $\epsilon$-adversarially private *iff for all input secrets* $i \in I$ *and for all output* $o \in O$ *we have* $p(i|o) \leq e^\epsilon p(i)$.

As we consider only one a priori distribution of secrets, $\epsilon$-*adversarial privacy* definition coincides with our definition of $t$-*privacy* where $t = \frac{e^\epsilon}{|I|}$. Because differential privacy protects against a class of attackers the security guarantee is formally stronger. For this reason, algorithms for differential privacy [9] would therefore randomise scripts that are already $t$-private (but not $\epsilon$-*adversarial private*) thus reducing their usability. In our fingerprinting context, we exploit the attacker's a priori knowledge for synthesising a channel that is $t$-private with minimal randomisation.

# 7    Conclusions and Further Work

Web tracking uses browser fingerprinting to identify users via scripts that obtain information about the browser's configuration. To protect users from such tracking, we propose a privacy enforcement mechanism based on randomisation of the script input. Our security guarantee is that the probability of guessing an identity by observing a script output is below a threshold $t$. We have presented a series of algorithms for enforcing $t$-privacy, all based on a Linear Programming formulation of the problem. The algorithms provide various trade-off between efficiency and *usability* where usability means that as little randomisation as possible is used. The exact resolution of the LP provides optimal usability. We also provide an enforcement mechanism ensuring the $t$-privacy of arbitrary programs at the cost of a reduced usability.

In our model, the attacker and the enforcement mechanism have perfect knowledge of the channel $\mathcal{U}$ *i.e.*, the distribution of the configurations is known. In a fingerprinting context, there are databases providing detailed information about the statistics of browser configurations [10] but a perfect knowledge of the distribution of the browser configuration worldwide is not realistic. As future work, we will investigate how to extend our framework to model partial knowledge *e.g.*, the fact that the user channel $\mathcal{U}$ belongs to a set $\mathbf{U}$.

One extension could *e.g.*, consist in synthesising a channel $\mathcal{R}$ that would ensure $t$-privacy with respect to the set $\mathbf{U}$. If $\mathbf{U}$ is expressed as a parametrised distribution, the enforcement problem can be stated as a non-linear optimisation problem instead of a Linear Program. Another extension consists in considering that the attacker might have an imprecise pre-belief [6] ($\mathcal{U} \in \mathbf{U}$) and ensure, for instance, that the channel is $t$-private with high probability. We could also consider that the attacker does not know the precise $\mathcal{R}$ channel but only the properties it enforces. In that case, the enforcement could ensure $t$-privacy at a better usability.

A longer-term extension of our model consists in modelling the dynamics of browser configurations. This dynamics is an obstacle to fingerprinting as fingerprints need to resist to modification of configurations. In theory, this should allow to design enforcement mechanisms providing a better usability. One of the author has started a preliminary practical evaluation of the evolution of fingerprints [4]. However, more research is needed to incorporate this knowledge into a formal model.

# References

1. Acar, G., Juárez, M., Nikiforakis, N., Díaz, C., Gürses, S.F., Piessens, F., Preneel, B.: FPDetective: dusting the web for fingerprinters. In: CCS 2013, pp. 1129–1140. ACM (2013)
2. Besson, F., Bielova, N., Jensen, T.: Hybrid information flow monitoring against web tracking. In: CSF 2013, pp. 240–254. IEEE (2013)
3. Besson, F., Bielova, N., Jensen, T.: Enforcing browser anonymity with quantitative information flow. Technical Report 8532, Inria (2014)
4. Bielova, N., Palladino, P.: Stopfingerprinting (2013), https://stopfingerprinting.inria.fr/
5. Boda, K.: Firegloves, http://fingerprint.pet-portal.eu/?menu=6
6. Clarkson, M.R., Myers, A.C., Schneider, F.B.: Quantifying information flow with beliefs. Journal of Computer Security 17(5), 655–701 (2009)

7. Cover, T.M., Thomas, J.A.: Elements of Information Theory, 2nd edn. Wiley (2006)
8. Dwork, C.: Differential privacy. In: Bugliesi, M., Preneel, B., Sassone, V., Wegener, I. (eds.) ICALP 2006. LNCS, vol. 4052, pp. 1–12. Springer, Heidelberg (2006)
9. Dwork, C., McSherry, F., Nissim, K., Smith, A.: Calibrating noise to sensitivity in private data analysis. In: Halevi, S., Rabin, T. (eds.) TCC 2006. LNCS, vol. 3876, pp. 265–284. Springer, Heidelberg (2006)
10. Eckersley, P.: The Panopticlick project, https://panopticlick.eff.org
11. Espinoza, B., Smith, G.: Min-entropy as a resource. Inf. Comp. 226, 57–75 (2013)
12. Gretz, F., Katoen, J.-P., McIver, A.: Operational versus weakest precondition semantics for the probabilistic guarded command language. In: QEST, pp. 168–177. IEEE (2012)
13. Klebanov, V.: Precise quantitative information flow analysis - a symbolic approach. Theor. Comput. Sci. 538, 124–139 (2014)
14. Klebanov, V., Manthey, N., Muise, C.: SAT-based analysis and quantification of information flow in programs. In: Joshi, K., Siegle, M., Stoelinga, M., D'Argenio, P.R. (eds.) QEST 2013. LNCS, vol. 8054, pp. 177–192. Springer, Heidelberg (2013)
15. Köpf, B., Rybalchenko, A.: Approximation and randomization for quantitative information-flow analysis. In: CSF 2010, pp. 3–14. IEEE (2010)
16. Mardziel, P., Magill, S., Hicks, M., Srivatsa, M.: Dynamic Enforcement of Knowledge-based Security Policies. In: CSF 2011, pp. 114–128. IEEE (2011)
17. Mardziel, P., Magill, S., Hicks, M., Srivatsa, M.: Dynamic enforcement of knowledge-based security policies using probabilistic abstract interpretation. Journal of Computer Security 21(4), 463–532 (2013)
18. Nikiforakis, N., Kapravelos, A., Joosen, W., Kruegel, C., Piessens, F., Vigna, G.: Cookieless monster: Exploring the ecosystem of web-based device fingerprinting. In: IEEE Symposium on Security and Privacy, pp. 541–555 (2013)
19. Rastogi, V., Hay, M., Miklau, G., Suciu, D.: Relationship privacy: Output perturbation for queries with joins. In: PODS 2009, pp. 107–116. ACM (2009)
20. Schrijver, A.: Theory of Linear and Integer Programming. Wiley (1998)
21. Sweeney, L.: Achieving k-anonymity privacy protection using generalization and suppression. Int. J. Uncertain. Fuzziness Knowl.-Based Syst. 10(5), 571–588 (2002)
22. Verdoolaege, S., Seghir, R., Beyls, K., Loechner, V., Bruynooghe, M.: Counting integer points in parametric polytopes using barvinok's rational functions. Algorithmica 48(1), 37–66 (2007)

# Attacks and Defenses

# Attacker Profiling in Quantitative Security Assessment Based on Attack Trees

Aleksandr Lenin[1,2], Jan Willemson[1], and Dyan Permata Sari[2,*]

[1] Cybernetica AS, Mäealuse 2/1, Tallinn, Estonia
[2] Tallinn University of Technology, Ehitajate tee 5, Tallinn, Estonia

**Abstract.** Providing meaningful estimations for the quantitative annotations on the steps of complex multi-step attacks is hard, as they are jointly influenced by the infrastructure and attacker properties. The paper introduces *attacker profiling* as the concept of separation of the infrastructure properties from the properties of malicious agents undertaking strategic decisions in the considered environment. We show that attacker profiling may be integrated into existing quantitative security assessment tools without any significant performance penalty. As an example of such integration we introduce the new analysis tool named ApproxTree+ which is an extension of the existing ApproxTree tool, enhancing it by incorporating attacker profiling capabilities into it.

## 1 Introduction

Targeted malicious attacks are intentional by their nature and may be interpreted as sequences of actions (attack steps) performed by malicious agents undertaking informed strategic decisions in the target infrastructure. This way we can distinguish between the two landscapes – the one which we call the *threat landscape* and the *vulnerability landscape*. The threat landscape is formed by various kinds of malicious agents – they have different sets of properties, available resources, varying intentions, motivations, views, and expectations of the target infrastructure. These properties determine strategic preferences of the agents, and eventually their behavior. The vulnerability landscape is formed by the infrastructure of the organization, its employees, assets, policies, processes, etc. Both landscapes are dynamic by their nature and are constantly changing. The threat landscape may change due to the agent behavior (e.g. increase in resources available to the agent) as well as external events, while the vulnerability landscape may change due to the infrastructure updates (e.g. patching, component replacement, awareness training, deployment of defensive measures, etc.) as well as unintentional events.

* This research was supported by the European Regional Development Fund through Centre of Excellence in Computer Science (EXCS), the Estonian Research Council under Institutional Research Grant IUT27-1 and European Union Seventh Framework Programme (FP7/2007-2013) under grant agreement ICT-318003 (TREsPASS). This publication reflects only the authors' views and the Union is not liable for any use that may be made of the information contained herein.

K. Bernsmed and S. Fischer-Hübner (Eds.): NordSec 2014, LNCS 8788, pp. 199–212, 2014.
DOI: 10.1007/978-3-319-11599-3_12, © Springer International Publishing Switzerland 2014

We propose the separation between the infrastructure properties (the vulnerability landscape) and the adversarial properties (the threat landscape), represented by an *attacker profile*. This separation adds flexibility to the quantitative security analysis enabling the assessment of operational security risks using different combinations of attacker profiles and infrastructure properties providing much deeper insight on the surrounding risk landscape. Besides, attacker profiling increases the reliability of the analysis results as the separation of infrastructure properties and attacker properties allows to update these values in a timely manner independently from each other and reflect the ever changing risk landscape in a more reliable way.

The paper aims at introducing attacker profiling in the context of quantitative security analysis based on attack trees and demonstrates integration of attacker profiling into existing security assessment tools introducing the new tool named ApproxTree+. In the introduced ApproxTree+ model the considered infrastructure properties (cost, difficulty, minimal required attack time) are quantitative annotations on the attack tree leaves, while the adversarial properties (budget, skill, available time) are described by attacker profiles. Additionally we compare the performance of the profiling computations to the ApproxTree approach [1] and reassess if the genetic algorithm parameters, used by ApproxTree for fast approximations, are optimal for the profiling computations.

The outline of the paper is the following: Section 2 outlines the state of the art in quantitative security assessment, attack trees, and attacker profiling. Section 3 describes motivation for the attacker profiling in security risk assessment. Section 4 introduces the ApproxTree+ tool, while Section 5 outlines the tool performance analysis results. Section 6 briefly lists the achievements made so far and outlines areas for future research.

# 2  Related Work

## 2.1  Attack Trees

Attack trees as one of the ways of quantitative security assessment, evolved from fault trees [2] and were popularized by Schneier [3] who suggested to use them as a way to model security threats and to perform quantitative security assessment using this convenient hierarchical representation by means of bottom-up single parameter propagation. Quantitative security assessment has been studied by various researchers [4–8] and different variations of techniques and methodologies were suggested.

Buldas *et al.* [9] suggested to use multi-parameter approach instead of the historical single-parameter one and applied economic reasoning by propagating adversarial utility. This kind of analysis allowed to assess whether the analyzed system is secure against targeted rational profit-oriented attacks.

Jürgenson and Willemson improved the model of Buldas *et al.*, making their parallel [10] and serial [11] models consistent with Mauw and Oostijk foundations [12] and introducing genetic approach to speed up computations. The parallel model assumed that the attacker launches attack steps, required to fulfil the attack scenario, simultaneously, while the serial model assumed that an attacker launches the attack steps in a predefined order.

Later, Buldas and Stepanenko introduced the failure-free model [13] suggesting not to limit the adversary in any way and thus analyzing fully adaptive adversarial utility upper bounds. This approach was later improved by Buldas and Lenin [14]. Their model better conforms to the upper bounds ideology and is computationally less complex.

For a more thorough overview of the quantitative security analysis using attack trees we refer the reader to [15].

## 2.2 Attacker Profiling

Back in 1998, Philips et al. [16] outlined the importance of the attacker feature in attack graphs for network vulnerability analysis. Several research projects have focused on attacker profiling using honeypot in "Know Your Enemies" series [17–19] which outlined the range of techniques and tools that were used by attackers for reconnaissance and also motives of the blackhat community. Several researchers proposed the concept of attacker personas, which was related to goal, motivations, attitudes, and skills [20–23]. Faily et al. highlighted insider threat motivations and characteristics, as well as the use of attacker personas for threat identification.

Pardue et al. [24] mentioned the importance of attacker characteristics and also the complexity of the attacks assessing risks of an e-voting system. The authors argue that the likelihood of attacks can be referred to as *cost* of an attacker, which can be estimated on various scales and measured in various units, such as dollars, number of attackers, time invested into attacking, and effort. In addition, Sallhammar et al. [25] demonstrate the process of deriving the probability of the expected attacker behavior in assumption that the attacker has complete information about the vulnerabilities of the targeted systems. Tipton et al. [26] argue that risk aversion, degree of difficulty, discoverability, ease of access, effectiveness of controls, effort, incentive, interest, skill level, motivation, resources required, risk of detection, and special equipment needed are the factors that can be included in attacker profiling. There are some common parameters that are most often used in research projects to define an attacker profile – these values are more feasible for quantitative analysis and give clear understanding of attacker properties.

## 2.3 Parallel Model

The parallel model [10] by Jürgenson et al. allows to assess whether the analyzed system is secure against targeted rational profit-oriented attacks by assessing adversarial utility. In case the utility is positive, the system is considered to be insecure, as profitable attack vectors which may result in positive outcome for an attacker are likely to exist. Otherwise the analysis assumed that the system is reasonably secure to withstand emerging attacks.

An attack scenario, represented by an attack tree, is treated as a monotone Boolean function, each variable of which corresponds to a leaf node in the attack tree, and logic operators correspond to the refined nodes in the attack tree. The successful outcome of an elementary attack is modelled by assigning value 1 to the corresponding variable in the Boolean function. If the Boolean function is satisfied, the attacker has succeeded in the security scenario. More complex multi-step attacks are modelled as *attack suites*.

The computational method maximizes the adversarial utility over the entire set of satisfying attack suites. The complexity of the approach arises from the need to process the entire set of $2^n$ attack suites, which introduces unnecessary overhead. Even with the optimizations proposed [10] this approach was able to analyze attack trees of at most 20 leaves in reasonable time which has made this method inapplicable for the practical case analysis.

To overcome limitations of the parallel model [10], a set of further optimizations was proposed by Jürgenson *et al.* [1] and implemented in the tool later called ApproxTree.

More significant contribution of the paper is the development of genetic algorithm for fast approximations, which increased performance compared to [10]. The implementation of the approach described in the paper reached 89% confidence[1] level within 2 seconds of computation for the tree having up to 29 leaves. As the genetic algorithm is very scalable it has potential to be used for the analysis of practical attack trees containing more than 100 leaves. The computational complexity of the suggested approximation algorithm in the worst case was estimated to be $\mathcal{O}(n^4)$. The authors have performed benchmarking tests and experimentally derived the optimal set of values for genetic algorithm parameters.

## 3    Motivation for the Attacker Profiling

An attack tree is a hierarchical description of possible attacks against the target infrastructure. Constructing an attack tree, analysts include all possible attack scenarios in the tree. Some of them are more realistic, some are less, considering the environment in which such a system is deployed. This way, attack tree analysis assumes an overpowered attacker who is capable of launching every possible attack, included in the attack tree, against the system. However, real life attacks are, as a rule, not so powerful and thus analysis assuming the almighty adversary concept does not provide deep insight on the security risks taking into account the surrounding risk landscape. Applying attacker profile to the attack tree invalidates certain nodes and eventually entire subtrees in the initial attack tree, thus enabling the independent analysis of the derived attack scenarios, containing attacks feasible for the considered class of malicious agents. Depending on the severity of adversarial limitations used in the profile, the derived attack scenario may be much smaller and thus much easier to analyze.

---

[1] By confidence authors mean the ratio of the trees actually computed correctly by the suggested approximation technique, compared to the precise outcome.

Quantitative security analysis relies on quantitative annotations (e.g. likelihood of success in an attack step, time required to launch an attack step, etc.) assigned to single attack steps in complex multi-step attacks. We believe that the quantitative metrics of these annotations is jointly influenced by various sets of underlying components in threat- as well as vulnerability landscapes. Thus it is rather difficult to provide a trustworthy and reliable quantitative estimation for such parameters as it is practically impossible to estimate the cumulative effect of several underlying factors altogether. Such kind of joint estimations are, as a rule, imprecise and contain reasonable degree of uncertainty.

For example, it is almost impossible to provide a meaningful estimation for the time parameter, as the time, required for an attack step, depends on the attacker skills, capabilities, available resources, previous experience, etc. (agent properties), as well as on the difficulty of the attack step itself (infrastructure property). Similarly, the likelihood of success depends on attacker skill, difficulty of the attack step, and time invested into attacking. The more skilful and experienced the attacker is, the more likely he is to succeed in an attack step. The more resources are available to the attacker, the more likely will he be successful in an attack step. Similar reasoning may be applied to the skill parameter – the more experienced the attacker is, the less difficult is the process for him, the less time it will take to succeed in an attack step. Less skilled attacker, given sufficient time, may be as efficient (in terms of likelihood of success) as a more skilled attacker who has less time for attacking. Similar logic may be applied to other parameters as well.

Despite that, the analysis has to deal somehow with the ever changing nature of each of the landscapes mentioned above and update (or re-assess) the estimations of the corresponding quantitative annotations in a timely manner. It is unclear how to update such joint estimations in case some of its components change while the others remain unchanged, or, on the contrary, when all its components change.

In order to tackle the difficulties outlined above we propose attacker profiling as a step forward in dealing with the challenges of security metrics.

# 4   The ApproxTree+ Model

We introduce the ApproxTree+ model – the new model for quantitative assessment of operational security risks. The computational method is built on the logic of the parallel attack tree model [10] and fast approximations of ApproxTree [1], improved by adding attacker profiling considerations into the method.

## 4.1   Definitions

We will use the same notation as in [10]. Let us have a set of all possible elementary attacks $\mathcal{X} = \{\mathcal{X}_1, \mathcal{X}_2, \ldots, \mathcal{X}_n\}$, and a Boolean function $\mathcal{F}$ corresponding to the attack tree.

**Definition 1 (Attack Suite).** *Attack suite $\sigma \subseteq X$ is a set of elementary attacks which have been chosen by the attacker to be launched and used to try to achieve the attacker goal.*

**Definition 2 (Satisfying attack suite).** *A satisfying attack suite $\sigma$ evaluates $\mathcal{F}$ to true when all the elementary attacks from the attack suite $\sigma$ have been evaluated to true.*

**Definition 3 (Attacker profile).** *An attacker profile is a pair $(t, \mathcal{P}_t)$ where $t$ is an n-tuple of attacker properties $(p_1, p_2, \ldots, p_n)$ and a function $\mathcal{P}_t(\sigma)$ defined by $t$ which takes an attack suite $\sigma$ as input and returns true, iff the attacker with the considered properties $t$ is capable of launching all the attacks in $\sigma$, and false otherwise.*

Each of the elements $p_k$ in $t$ belongs to a certain domain $P_k$ which provides quantitative metrics to the parameter. Some of the domains may represent continuous values, e.g. money, so we can take $P_k = \mathbb{R}$. Others parameters may be measured on an ordinal scale to reflect the magnitude and measured in levels e.g. High, Medium, and Low, in which case $P_k = \{H, M, L\}$.

In our research we use the following attacker properties:

1. *Budget* $t_b \in \mathbb{R}$ – the monetary resource of the attacker, measured in currency units.
2. *Skill* $t_s \in \{L, M, H\}$ – the skill level of the attacker, measured on an ordinal scale (Low/Medium/High).
3. *Time* $t_a \in \{S, MT, HR, D\}$ – the available time resource of the attacker, measured on an ordinal scale (Seconds/Minutes/Hours/Days).

The attacker properties outlined above define function $\mathcal{P}_f(\sigma)$, which returns *true* iff:

1. $t_b \geqslant \sum_{i=1}^{n} \text{Cost}(X_i)$,
2. $\forall X_i \in \sigma : t_s \geqslant \text{Difficulty}(X_i)$, and
3. $\forall X_i \in \sigma : t_a \geqslant \text{Time}(X_i)$.

**Definition 4 (Profile satisfying attack suite).** *A profile satisfying attack suite $\sigma$ is a satisfying attack suite which satisfies all the constraints of the chosen attacker profile $(t, \mathcal{P}_t)$.*

## 4.2 Description of the Approach

The analysis method can be described by the following rules [10]:

1. The attacker constructs the attack tree and evaluates the parameters of each of the elementary attacks following these considerations:
   - The attacker has to spend $Cost_i$ resources to prepare and launch an attack $X_i$.

- The attack $\mathcal{X}_i$ succeeds with probability $p_i$ and fails with probability $1 - p_i$.
- Depending on the detective security measures, the attacker sometimes has to carry additional costs after failing or succeeding with the attack. The sum of preparation and additional costs is denoted as $Expenses_i$ parameter.
- Additionally, there is global parameter $Profit$ for the whole attack scenario, which describes the benefit of the attacker, in case the root node is achieved.

2. The attacker considers all potential attack suites – subsets $\sigma \subseteq \mathcal{X}$, where $\mathcal{X} = \{\mathcal{X}_1, \ldots, \mathcal{X}_n\}$ is the set of all elementary attacks considered in the attack scenario. Some of the attack suites satisfy the Boolean function $\mathcal{F}$, some do not. For the satisfying attack suites the attacker computes the outcome value $Outcome_\sigma$.

3. Finally, the attacker chooses the most profitable attack suite and launches the corresponding elementary attacks simultaneously.

The computational method presented in [10] aims at maximizing the expression

$$Outcome_\sigma = p_\sigma \cdot Profit - \sum_{\mathcal{X}_i \in \sigma} Expenses_i$$

over all the assignments $\sigma \subseteq \mathcal{X}$ that turn the monotone Boolean function $\mathcal{F}$ to true. The success probability of the primary threat $p_\sigma$ can be computed in time linear in the size of elementary attacks $n$:

$$p_\sigma = \sum_{\substack{\mathcal{R} \subseteq \sigma \\ \mathcal{F}(\mathcal{R}:=true)=true}} \prod_{\mathcal{X}_i \in \mathcal{R}} p_i \prod_{\mathcal{X}_j \in \sigma \setminus \mathcal{R}} (1 - p_j) \ . \tag{1}$$

In order to tackle the potential exponential amount of computations in (1), a genetic algorithm was proposed and benchmarked by Jürgenson *et al.* [1].

## 4.3   Approximation

The ApproxTree+ method uses the genetic algorithm to facilitate the usage of the computational method for large attack trees:

1. Create the first generation of $n$ individuals (profile satisfying attack suites, not all of them are necessarily distinct).
2. All the individuals in the initial population are crossed with everybody else producing $\binom{n}{2}$ new individuals.
3. Each individual is mutated with probability $p$.
4. The mutated population is joined with the initial population.
5. Finally, $n$ fittest profile satisfying individuals out of the $\binom{n}{2} + n$ individuals are selected and form the next generation.

The reproduction phase terminates when $k$ last generations do not increase outcome. The complexity of the suggested approach was measured to be approximately $\mathcal{O}(0.85^n)$ using exponential regression.

# 5   Performance Analysis

In order to assess the performance of the introduced computational method we have randomly generated a set of attack trees. The attack tree generation procedure was a two-step process. First, the random Boolean function with the predefined number of variables (leaves in the attack tree) was generated. It contained from 2 to 5 operands per operator – the values of operands in each case were chosen randomly. The next step was to provide quantitative annotations on the leaves of the attack tree. These values were chosen randomly from the predefined intervals: the *cost* parameter was estimated in the interval $[100, 1000]$, the *success probability* parameter was estimated in the interval $(0, 1)$. The value for the *difficulty* parameter was chosen from uniformly distributed values *low*, *medium*, *high*, and *very high*. The value for the *time* parameter was chosen from uniformly distributed values *seconds*, *minutes*, *hours*, and *days*[2].

One of the questions that needs to be answered is if attacker profiling adds extra computational overhead. It can be seen on the cumulative time distribution diagram (see Fig. 1) that attacker profiling does not add any significant computational overhead (in the case of a single attacker profile being analyzed) compared to the ApproxTree approach (see Fig. 2). In both methods the initial population generation phase is almost immediate, as well as the mutation phase. The main workload is performed by the crossover phase and consumes approximately 85-99% of the cumulative time distribution among all the phases. The last phase, the best individuals selection phase, does not introduce any significant workload and consumes approximately 1 - 15%. The crossover phase is the most time consuming as each individual is crossed with every other individual in the population producing $\mathcal{N} \times \mathcal{N}$ cross operations, where $\mathcal{N}$ is the amount of individuals in the initial population. Fig. 3 shows that the execution time of the ApproxTree+ approach is proportional to the ApproxTree approach. The increased execution time arises from the fact that, as a rule, one doesn't assess risks using just a single adversarial profile, as it is reasonable to assess risks using the entire set of possible adversarial profiles so that the results would produce meaningful insight on the risk landscape – thus the overall execution time is proportional to the number of the attacker profiles under consideration.

The analysis of the speed of convergence shows that the convergence speed of ApproxTree does not exceed the convergence speed of ApproxTree+. Additionally, it does not depend on the size of the attack tree – independently of the size of the tree, the convergence speed stays approximately at the same level.

Additionally, we have analyzed the effect of the genetic algorithm parameters such as mutation rate and initial population size on the convergence speed to assess whether the parameters of the genetic algorithm used by ApproxTree [1] are optimal for the ApproxTree+ approach.

The convergence speed decreases with the increase in the percentage of mutations from approximately 2 generations in the case when the mutation rate is 10% up to 6 generations in the case when mutation rate is 90% (see Fig. 5).

---

[2] Assuming uniform distribution of the PRNG output.

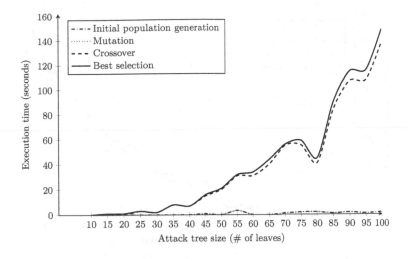

**Fig. 1.** Cumulative time distribution of ApptoxTree+ phases

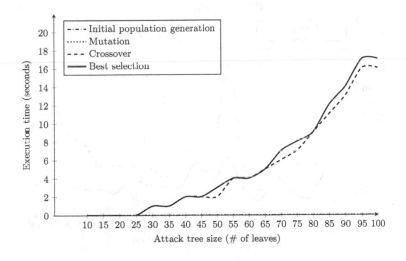

**Fig. 2.** Cumulative time distribution of ApproxTree phases

Independently of the mutation rate, the speed of convergence of ApproxTree+ does not exceed the speed of convergence of ApproxTree.

Benchmarking results have shown that the mutation step has no significant effect on the convergence speed at all. We were unable to find any case where the method would get stuck in the local optimum. Even when the mutation step was excluded entirely (as a phase of the genetic algorithm) – the global optimum was always reached. This may happen because of "good" initial population genera-tion – if the size of the initial population is rather big compared to the number of satisfying solutions, it is highly likely that the initial population will contain

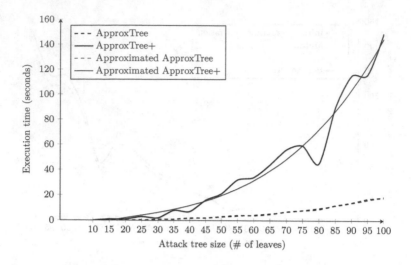

**Fig. 3.** Execution time

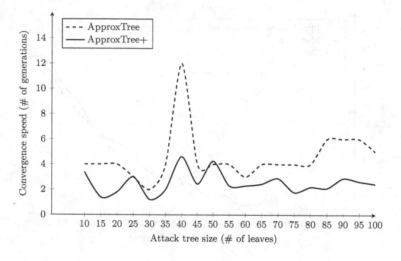

**Fig. 4.** Convergence speed

all the solutions (profile satisfying attack suites). In this case the convergence is immediate, which was observed in some cases during benchmarking. If the initial population does not contain all the solutions, still it may be "good enough" so that the crossover step produces the entire domain of solutions.

With the increase in the initial population size (see Fig. 6) the convergence speed increases, stabilising at a value of approximately 1.6 generations for the initial population size greater than $4n$ ($n$ being the number of leaves in the attack tree) in the case of the ApproxTree approach. In the case of ApproxTree+ we can see slight, but firm decrease in the convergence speed. In some cases when

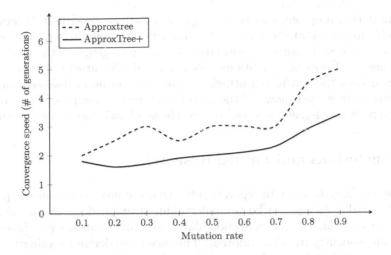

**Fig. 5.** Convergence speed as a function of the mutation rate

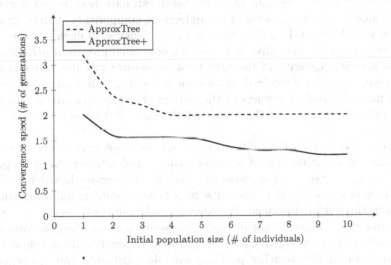

**Fig. 6.** Convergence speed as a function the size of the initial population

initial population size was less than $n$ the computational method was unable to reach global optimum, which may happen when rather small initial population limits the amount of possible solutions that may be reached and the mutation rate is small enough and does not improve the situation.

The precision assessment shows that in ApproxTree+, as well as in Approx-Tree, either the result converges to the global optimum (most profitable attack suite) or the computational method fails to generate the initial population of individuals. In case of profiling, the attacker profile may contain so strict constraints that not a single profile satisfying attack suite may exist. The more strict constraints are used in the considered attacker profiles the higher is the probability that no profile satisfying assignments will be generated. However we are unable to state that the profile satisfying solutions definitely do not exist in this case, as the state when ApproxTree+ is unable to generate the initial population means 2 possible conditions – either no profile satisfying attack suites exist (and thus the considered attack scenario has no profitable solutions), or such attack suites exist, however the attack suite generation procedure failed to generate profile satisfying solutions due to the stochastic nature of the process.

# 6    Conclusions and Future Research

Attacker profiling is a way to separate infrastructure properties and the properties of the malicious agents who are undertaking strategic decisions in the target infrastructure. This kind of separation allows to estimate and assess these properties independently from one another. This allows to derive meaningful values for the quantitative annotations on the attack steps in complex multi-step attacks from the underlying properties instead of providing joint estimations to these values directly. One can more precisely estimate how would a complex value change in case when some of its underlying components change. In example, how would the likelihood of success in an attack step change if instead of profit-oriented malicious individuals we face organized groups of attackers or a national security agency and the target infrastructure was patched meanwhile and the employees have received an awareness training? Thus, attacker profiling enables more detailed assessment of the impact of the fluctuations in threat and vulnerability landscapes on the values of the quantitative annotations on the attack steps.

Additionally, it adds flexibility to the analysis in general, enabling analysis using different combinations of attacker profiles and infrastructure properties, making comprehensive risk assessment possible. It provides broader and more detailed overview of the risk landscape in a timely manner, following constant changes in the risk environment. It allows to make informed decisions in assessing the cost-effectiveness of the defensive measures and enabling the prediction, prioritization and prevention of emerging attacks in nearly semi-automated way.

We introduced the attacker profiling and demonstrated the application of profiling in the framework of attack tree analysis by introducing the new analysis tool named ApproxTree+ and demonstrating that integrating attacker profiling into an existing analysis method does not introduce any significant performance penalty.

The constraint based approach, outlined in the paper, is only one possible interpretation of attacker profiling. Another possibility is to apply Item Response Theory to represent the relation between various underlying components in the threat and vulnerability landscapes. Such a relation may be represented, in example, in the form of a logistic function in its simplest form indicating that the likelihood of success will be assigned value 0.5 when the skill ($\beta$) and difficulty ($\gamma$) are equal: $p = \left(e^{\beta-\delta}\right)/(1 + e^{\beta-\delta})$. In more complex scenarios the function may be extended to take 3 arguments, as the likelihood of success depends on

the invested time parameter as well, and in this case it will take the form of:
$p = f(\beta, \delta, \gamma)$ where $\gamma$ is the time invested into attacking.

We see the way forward in implementing the above mentioned interpretation of profiling, integrating ApproxTree+ in the existing risk assessment frameworks and tools, and validating the approach in real-case risk analysis.

# References

1. Jürgenson, A., Willemson, J.: On Fast and Approximate Attack Tree Computations. In: Kwak, J., Deng, R.H., Won, Y., Wang, G. (eds.) ISPEC 2010. LNCS, vol. 6047, pp. 56–66. Springer, Heidelberg (2010)
2. Vesely, W.E., Goldberg, F.F., Roberts, N.H., Haasl, D.F.: Fault Tree Handbook. U.S. Nuclear Regulatory Commission, Washington, DC (1981)
3. Schneier, B.: Attack trees. Dr. Dobb's Journal of Software Tools 24(12), 21–22, 24, 26, 28–29 (1999)
4. Schumacher, M.: Security Engineering with Patterns. LNCS, vol. 2754. Springer, Heidelberg (2003)
5. Miede, A., Nedyalkov, N., Gottron, C., König, A., Repp, N., Steinmetz, R.: A Generic Metamodel for IT Security. In: ARES, pp. 430–437. IEEE Computer Society (2010)
6. Trivedi, K.S., Kim, D.S., Roy, A., Medhi, D.: Dependability and Security Models. In: Proceedings of the 7th IEEE International Workshop on the Design of Reliable Communication Networks (DRCN), Washington, DC, pp. 11–20 (October 2009)
7. Schneier, B.: Secrets & Lies: Digital Security in a Networked World, 1st edn. John Wiley & Sons, Inc., New York (2000)
8. Kordy, B., Mauw, S., Radomirović, S., Schweitzer, P.: Attack–Defense Trees. Journal of Logic and Computation 24(1), 55–87 (2014)
9. Buldas, A., Laud, P., Priisalu, J., Saarepera, M., Willemson, J.: Rational Choice of Security Measures Via Multi-parameter Attack Trees. In: López, J. (ed.) CRITIS 2006. LNCS, vol. 4347, pp. 235–248. Springer, Heidelberg (2006)
10. Jürgenson, A., Willemson, J.: Computing Exact Outcomes of Multi-parameter Attack Trees. In: Meersman, R., Tari, Z. (eds.) OTM 2008, Part II. LNCS, vol. 5332, pp. 1036–1051. Springer, Heidelberg (2008)
11. Jürgenson, A., Willemson, J.: Serial Model for Attack Tree Computations. In: Lee, D., Hong, S. (eds.) ICISC 2009. LNCS, vol. 5984, pp. 118–128. Springer, Heidelberg (2010)
12. Mauw, S., Oostdijk, M.: Foundations of Attack Trees. In: Won, D., Kim, S. (eds.) ICISC 2005. LNCS, vol. 3935, pp. 186–198. Springer, Heidelberg (2006)
13. Buldas, A., Stepanenko, R.: Upper Bounds for Adversaries' Utility in Attack Trees. In: Grossklags, J., Walrand, J. (eds.) GameSec 2012. LNCS, vol. 7638, pp. 98–117. Springer, Heidelberg (2012)
14. Buldas, A., Lenin, A.: New Efficient Utility Upper Bounds for the Fully Adaptive Model of Attack Trees. In: Das, S.K., Nita-Rotaru, C., Kantarcioglu, M. (eds.) GameSec 2013. LNCS, vol. 8252, pp. 192–205. Springer, Heidelberg (2013)
15. Kordy, B., Pietre-Cambacedes, L., Schweitzer, P.: DAG-Based Attack and Defense Modeling: Don't Miss the Forest for the Attack Trees. CoRR abs/1303.7397 (2013)
16. Phillips, C., Swiler, L.P.: A Graph-based System for Network-vulnerability Analysis. In: Proceedings of the 1998 Workshop on New Security Paradigms, NSPW 1998, pp. 71–79. ACM, New York (1998)

17. "Know Your Enemies" series: Honeynet Project. Know Your Enemy The Tools and Methodologies of the Script Kiddie (July 2000), http://project.honeynet.org
18. "Know Your Enemies" series: Honeynet Project. Know Your Enemy II: Tracking the blackhat's moves (June 2001), http://project.honeynet.org
19. "Know Your Enemies" series: Honeynet Project. Know Your Enemy III: They Gain Root (March 2000), http://project.honeynet.org
20. Blomquist, A., Arvola, M.: Personas in action: Ethnography in an interaction design team. In: Proceedings of the Second Nordic Conference on Human-computer Interaction, NordiCHI 2002, pp. 197–200. ACM, New York (2002)
21. Castro, J.W., Acuña, S.T., Juzgado, N.J.: Integrating the Personas Technique into the Requirements Analysis Activity. In: Gelbukh, A.F., Adiba, M.E. (eds.) ENC, pp. 104–112. IEEE Computer Society (2008)
22. Faily, S., Flechais, I.: Barry is not the weakest link: eliciting secure system requirements with personas. In: McEwan, T., McKinnon, L. (eds.) BCS HCI, pp. 124–132. ACM (2010)
23. Faily, S., Flechais, I.: Persona cases: A technique for grounding personas. In: Tan, D.S., Amershi, S., Begole, B., Kellogg, W.A., Tungare, M. (eds.) CHI, pp. 2267–2270. ACM (2011)
24. Pardue, H., Landry, J., Yasinsac, A.: A Risk Assessment Model for Voting Systems using Threat Trees and Monte Carlo Simulation. In: 2009 First International Workshop on Requirements Engineering for e-Voting Systems (RE-VOTE), pp. 55–60 (2009)
25. Sallhammar, K., Knapskog, S.J., Helvik, B.E.: Building a Stochastic Model for Security and Trust Assessment Evaluation (October 2005), http://q2s.ntnu.no/publications/open/2005/Mass_media/2005_sallhammar_BSM.pdf
26. Tipton, H., Baker, P.: Official (ISC)2 guide to the CISSP CBK (2010)

# Denial-of-Service Mitigation
# for Internet Services

Aapo Kalliola, Tuomas Aura, and Sanja Šćepanović

Aalto University, Espoo, Finland
{aapo.kalliola,tuomas.aura,sanja.scepanovic}@aalto.fi

**Abstract.** Denial-of-service attacks present a serious threat to the availability of online services. Distributed attackers, i.e. botnets, are capable of exhausting the server capacity with legitimate-looking requests. Such attacks are difficult to defend against using traditional filtering mechanisms. We propose a machine learning and filtering system that forms a profile of normal client behavior based on normal traffic features and, during an attack, optimizes capacity allocation for legitimate clients based on the profile. The proposed defense mechanism is evaluated using simulations based on real-life server usage patterns. The simulations indicate that the mechanism is capable of mitigating an overwhelming server capacity exhaustion DDoS attack. During attacks where a botnet floods a server with legitimate-looking requests, over 80 percent of the legitimate clients are still served, even on servers that are heavily loaded to begin with. An implementation of the mechanism is tested using synthetic HTTP attack traffic, also with encouraging results.

**Keywords:** denial of service, internet service, filtering, clustering.

## 1   Introduction

Denial-of-service (DoS) and distributed denial-of-service (DDoS) attacks present an increasing threat to service availability on the Internet. Botnets can either exhaust the target server's processing capacity or its network bandwidth. Traditional methods for defending against a DDoS attack are based on manually configured filters. This filtering can either be done at the server itself or pushed to a firewall or a router further in the network.

As botnets have grown larger, it has become possible to overwhelm an online service by using perfectly legitimate-looking requests. These attack requests can be distributed among a large number of bots that make requests similar to those from normal users. It is difficult for a system administrator to define rules for differentiating between legitimate and attack traffic. For this reason, we look for automatic DoS filtering mechanisms which do not require manually configured rules, which work well against DDoS attackers, and which are benign to flash crowds.

The solution we propose builds on several ideas from the literature and uses a combination of machine learning and filtering. Our defense mechanism observes

K. Bernsmed and S. Fischer-Hübner (Eds.): NordSec 2014, LNCS 8788, pp. 213–228, 2014.
DOI: 10.1007/978-3-319-11599-3_13, © Springer International Publishing Switzerland 2014

normal inbound traffic to the server and builds a profile of its distribution. When a DoS attack starts, i.e. when the server is overloaded, this profile is used for prioritizing requests. The assumption is that the attack traffic is not perfectly identical to the normal traffic. By giving priority to requests that most closely resemble the normal traffic, we are able to serve a large fraction of the legitimate clients and drop most of the DoS traffic.

In the learning phase, the system profiles the normal traffic as a set of clusters and their capacities. The clusters can be based on hierarchical traffic features such as IP addresses or request URLs. The most important feature is the client IP address. A filtering policy is created and updated continuously based on the observed normal traffic clusters. When the server comes under an attack, the learning component stops processing the incoming requests and filtering starts. The filtering policy proposed in this paper is based on comparing the amount of traffic in each cluster during normal operation and during the attack. Those clusters where the traffic volume does not increase significantly are the most likely to contain requests from legitimate clients.

DoS attacks vary widely in their level of distribution, bandwidth per attacker host, and attack traffic type and pattern. We therefore analyse the effectiveness of our DDoS mitigation mechanism using a range of different attack models. The simulation results indicate that once the server is attacked, our defense mechanism can retain good quality of service for over 80% of normal users during a request-flooding attack by a botnet, and for 40% to 70% of normal users during an overwhelming SYN flooding attack. Experiments with a prototype implementation also confirm the results.

## 2   Background and Related Work

Defending against denial-of-service attacks has been an area of active research. On a high level, the defense mechanisms can be divided into two main groups: host based and network based.

Network-based mechanisms often require significant changes to the communication mechanism between client and server. For instance in Phalanx by Dixon et al. [5] a massive packet forwarding swarm is set up to withstand botnet attacks. Others require the deployment of new mechanisms to core routers, as in pushback by Ioannnidis and Bellowing [8]. Peng et al. [13] present an overview of network-based defense mechanisms. Some of the host-based methods identify anomalous traffic at routers and communication endpoints with packet inspection [10].

One algorithm proposed for traffic clustering is *hierarchical heavy hitters* (HHH). The HHH algorithms were first presented in one-dimensional form by Cormode at al. [3]. HHH has also been used for DDoS detection by Sekaret al. [15].

Traffic filtering is commonly performed at a firewall near the server. Typically simpler filtering can also be done on routers and switches. The mechanism presented in this paper aims to be fully automatic and simple enough to deploy on any of these network components. Our filtering mechanism can also be considered to bear similarities to priority-queue schemes such as that by Lin et al. [12]. IP-based filtering has also been discussed by Collins [2]. In contrast to work by Collins, our clustering mechanism produces dynamic and equal-bandwidth clusters with a fundamentally different goal for the filtering mechanism.

Overall, our approach to mitigating the impact of capacity-exhausting DDoS attacks combines aspects of host and network based countermeasures. We analyse the traffic reaching the server and use this information to activate a filtering mechanisms on the server itself or further upstream.

# 3   Filtering DoS Attacks

## 3.1   DoS Attacks

In this paper, we aim to filter DoS attacks in which the attacker overwhelms an online server, such as an HTTP server, with an excessive amount of requests. The attack may be executed from a small number of hosts, either inside or outside the target organization, or from a botnet with millions of computers distributed randomly around the Internet. The attacker may mount a brute-force attack to exhaust the CPU power or network bandwidth of the server, or it may intelligently request web pages that require expensive processing from the front-end web server or the back-end database. Consequently, the server must drop most of the incoming requests. Our goal is to be smart about which requests to drop at the server.

An attacker that is unable to exhaust the server capacity with legitimate-looking requests may turn to more primitive attack methods such as packet-flooding and connection-flooding. Most packet-flooding attacks can be filtered by a stateful firewall, which only allows through established connections and the initial packets, such as SYN packets for new TCP connections. This leaves the attacker with the possibility to open millions of connections to the server from botnet hosts or to send SYN packets from spoofed IP addresses. Our secondary aim is to protect against these types of attack by selecting intelligently which SYN packets are dropped at a firewall or upstream routers.

## 3.2   Filtering Defense

The architecture of our defensive system is shown in Figure 1. Inbound requests and connections are tapped into at the web server or in a separate device such as a firewall, router or switch. Depending on the bandwidth of the traffic flow, we can use either random samples or full traces of web requests and network connections. An out-of-band host analyzes the tap data and profiles the normal traffic. The system also monitors the server load and deploys the filter when a DoS attack is detected, i.e. when the server load exceeds 100%. The server may simply drop the filtered request or it may respond with a "Service Temporarily Unavailable" message.

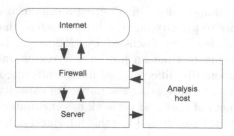

**Fig. 1.** Example of physical architecture elements

For high-bandwidth attacks that involve connection or SYN flooding, the filter needs to be deployed also at the firewall. In the experiments reported in this paper, though, the traffic tap and filter were implemented only on the server itself. We believe this to be sufficient to demonstrate the principle since the filter can be expressed as simple firewall rules. Nevertheless, there may be further implementation and performance details to consider in a high-bandwidth firewall or router, which require further investigation.

The analysis host continuously updates a profile of the normal traffic and prepares to deploy traffic filters based on this profile. The traffic profile and the filter have two components. Firstly, both define traffic classes called *clusters*. These are defined by sets of traffic features such as IP header fields and HTTP request parameters. Secondly, the traffic profile includes the measured *normal request rate* in each cluster, and the filter defines a *capacity allocation* for each cluster. When the filter is active, each cluster is limited to the given capacity and excess requests are dropped randomly.

As mentioned, *attack detection* in this paper simply means detecting when the server load exceeds 100%. No difference is made between DoS attacks and legitimate server overload such as flash crowds. Since some requests must be dropped during server overload, the filtering of legitimate requests causes no further damage. The effect of our filtering policy on legitimate overload is that the regular clients of the service will be favored over new or infrequent ones.

### 3.3 Feature Selection

It is desirable to find traffic features that differentiate legitimate requests from attack ones. The attacker, on the other hand, may try to *mimic* legitimate requests. The mimicking is made easier if the attacker gets feedback of it success, i.e. whether each request was served or dropped, as this enables an *adaptive* attack strategy.

Much of the past research on DoS attack detection uses timing features, such as inter-arrival times [14] and ramp-up behavior [7], to differentiate between an attack and legitimate server overload. These techniques do not, however, help to classify individual requests into legitimate and attack classes. Moreover, it can be assumed that attackers are capable of mimicking such static features of the traffic if defenses based on them are widely deployed.

We considered various features in the request packets, such as IP header fields and HTTP request parameters, and initially expected to select a broad combination of these. Almost all such features can be mimicked by an attacker, especially since the server gives feedback by serving some requests and rejecting others. Finally, we settled for using the client IP address as the only feature. This is because the attacker cannot easily adapt its IP addresses to match the distribution of the IP addresses of the server's legitimate clients. Even a large botnet will lose most of its attack capacity if it uses only the bots that fall into the same subnets as the legitimate clients of the target service. Another advantage of IP addresses is that they are relatively stable. The distribution of application-level features such as the request URL may change much faster than the distribution of client IP addresses.

A SYN-flooding attacker that uses spoofed IP addresses can, in principle, choose any source IP addresses for the SYN packets. Its total capacity will, however, be somewhat limited by ingress filtering [6]. Furthermore, the attacker will not get feedback on the success of each spoofed packet, which will make it difficult to adapt the attack to the filter. It also helps the filtering that, in reality, certain significant classes of attacks, e.g. DNS reflection attacks, send the attack traffic from a small number of addresses.

## 3.4  Clustering

Given one or more traffic features, such as the client IP address, it is not at all obvious how the feature space should be divided into traffic classes. Our approach is to use a data clustering algorithm that automatically extracts some structure from the feature space. This was initially inspired by Liao et al. [11] who mapped packet features into real numbers. However, continuous feature spaces are a poor match for discrete or hierarchical features. In particular, IP addresses are by nature hierarchically allocated and also used in that manner [1]. It is therefore logical to perform the clustering with an algorithm that takes advantage of the hierarchical structure.

From the various ways of clustering the IP address space, we use the *hierarchical heavy hitter* (HHH) algorithm, which produces clusters with roughly equal rates of legitimate traffic. The resulting clusters are in practise IP subnets defined by an address prefix. One subnet may be inside another, in which case the traffic counts of the smaller subnet are not included in the traffic counts of the larger subnet. The filtering operations for these clusters are done by longest-prefix matching and thus can be performed very efficiently with firewall or router hardware. This efficiency is critical because the traffic volumes for the filtering can be very high. An example of the resulting cluster structure can be seen in Figure 2. The bracketed values after the subnet identifier show the legitimate and attacker requests counts in each cluster during a simulation run. As an additional advantage of HHH, the learning itself can be executed at line speed without buffering the training data [4].

The HHH algorithm takes as input a threshold value which determines the minimum size of a cluster as a percentage of the training traffic. For example, if the threshold value is 1%, the output will be at most 100 clusters. As a slight modification to the normal HHH, we always include a top-level cluster (zero-length prefix) for catching all remaining traffic even if its volume does not meet the threshold.

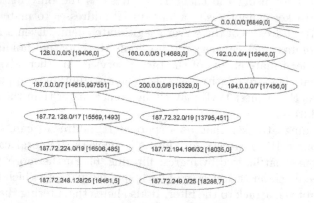

**Fig. 2.** HHH clustering example

The choice of an algorithm that produces clusters with roughly equal normal traffic rates can be argued as follows. IP addresses are un-uniformly distributed over the whole IP address space. This is especially true for IPv6. In order to minimize the number of configurable parameters, we do not want to give any a-priory knowledge about the IP address allocation as an input to the algorithm. Therefore, the only available information about the structure of the IP address space is the distribution of the client addresses during the learning period. By selecting clusters with equal normal traffic volumes, we use the given number of clusters relatively effectively to model the parts of the IP address space relevant to the particular server. It would, of course, be desirable to select the clusters in such a way that they maximally differentiate between the legitimate and attack traffic. Unfortunately, we cannot know in advance how the attacker IP addresses are going to be distributed. The only assumption we are prepared to make is that the distribution of source IP addresses in the attack traffic somehow differ from the legitimate traffic.

## 4    Simulation

### 4.1    System

We simulated a DDoS attack and the filtering defense on a web server that has a certain capacity for serving HTTP requests. The client IP address is used as the only traffic feature. Both the traffic monitoring and filtering implementations take place on the server itself. The main interest in the simulation is to measure the effect of our filtering defense on the amount of legitimate traffic and clients that are served during an overwhelming DoS attack. The simulation is implemented in Python.

Real-life request traces from different web servers are used to generate the legitimate traffic. The graphs shown later are representative results that have been validated using the other data traces as well. The normal traffic data sets are roughly laid out in the following list.

1. *University web site 1*: medium traffic, 3 month period
2. *University web site 2*: low traffic, 3 month period
3. *Small business web site*: medium traffic, 6 month period

The attacker requests are created synthetically with the help of real-life IP source data from honeypot servers. The real-life IP data set contains over 100000 unique IP addresses that are actively attempting to spread malware. While they are almost certainly not part of the same botnet we can surmise that their IP address distribution is reasonable for approximating a large botnet. The relative activity rates of these compromised hosts are also used in modeling the non-homogenous capabilities of bots. The reason for using synthetic attack data is that real-life DDoS attacks are rarely recorded for academic use.

The simulation starts with a *learning period* during which only legitimate traffic is sent to the server. The hierarchical clustering algorithm is applied to the data from the learning period to create the cluster-based profile of legitimate traffic. Synthetic attack traffic is then generated and merged with the legitimate traffic from the next time period. As this data is fed to the simulation, the defense system moves from the learning phase to the filtering phase. It uses the previously constructed profile of legitimate traffic in combination with current measurements of the attack-time traffic to generate a filter for the incoming traffic. The filters are computed following a policy in which *the clusters with the highest ratio of legitimate traffic to attack-time traffic are allocated capacity and the rest of the traffic is dropped*. That is, some clusters are fully served while others are not served at all.

The only configurable parameter in the defense mechanism is the number of clusters $k$. It represents the complexity of the profile which the defender builds of the legitimate traffic during the learning period. It is not always the case that a larger $k$ is better. First, there is the danger of overfitting the training data. That is, a too accurate profile of the legitimate traffic during the learning period will not match well the legitimate traffic during the attack. One goal of the simulations is to determine the best range of $k$ in this respect. Second, the parameter also determines the number of traffic classes in the filter that is deployed during the attack. The filtering platform, such as a firewall implementation, usually can handle only a certain number of traffic classes effectively.

## 4.2    Attack Scenarios and Predicted Outcome

Since we use the IP address as the traffic feature for clustering and filtering, the attack model also focuses on the attacker IP addresses. We consider several different attack-traffic models. The reasoning is that if the filtering works against a comprehensive set of different attack-traffic patterns, it will also be effective against a range of real-life attacks.

In the simulations, we considered the following request-flooding attack types:

1. *concentrated*: high-bandwidth attack from a small number of IP addresses
2. *random*: random source IP addresses
3. *botnet*: simulated botnet based on real-life malicious host data

In the concentrated attack model, a heavy attack originates from only a few IP addresses or subnets, which are not among the regular clients of the server and thus are not present in the training data. A significant portion of real DDoS attacks fall into this category. In this case, the attack traffic falls into relatively few clusters. Most of the legitimate clients are in the other clusters and thus are expected to retain close to 100% service levels.

The random attack model represents a SYN flooding attack with spoofed source addresses. It can also be seen as a rough estimate of the pessimistic scenario where the attack is so massively distributed that each attacker source IP address is used only once or a few times. Many of the spoofed IP addresses will overlap with normal traffic clusters leading to reduced filtering effectiveness.

The third attack model is the most realistic one. We simulate the IP address distribution of a large botnet by using real-life malicious IP source addresses and adjust the flooding-traffic bandwidth from these bots according to observed real-life behaviour. The expected simulation result for the realistic botnet attacker is something between the concentrated and random scenarios.

## 4.3    Simulation Results

In this section, we show the simulation results of the attack models explained above. In addition, we discuss the effect of the learning period on the results.

In Figures 3 and 4, we use one-month datasets from a university web server as the normal traffic. Each dataset contains approximately one million requests with monthly unique IP counts in the order of tens of thousands. The datasets for the learning period and the attack period are from consecutive calendar months. The server load was varied by compressing a longer dataset into a shorter time period. The server load in normal operations prior to attack is indicated with separate lines in the figures. During the attack period, synthetic attack traffic exceeding the normal traffic by a factor of $10^6$ is merged with the legitimate traffic. We measure how well the defense mechanism is able to filter the attack. The metric used for this is the percentage of the normal traffic served during an attack. It should be noted that the unrealistic factor $10^6$ was chosen for demonstration purposes to show that the filtering *algorithm* scales well to any volume of attack traffic.

First, we conducted the simulation with only 10 high-bandwidth attacker IP addresses sending the attack traffic. In this simulation, we served 87-100% of the traffic regardless of server load in normal situation. The cluster count for these percentage values was between 100-10000. These good results are explained by the fact that, with such a low number of attackers, the attack traffic is placed into very few clusters.

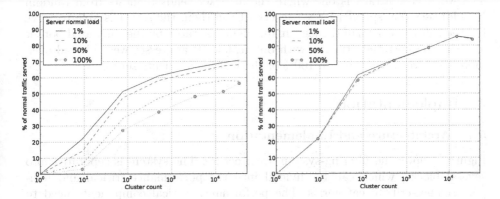

**Fig. 3.** Attack from random source addresses    **Fig. 4.** Attack by simulated botnet

Next, we simulated the attack with random IP addresses. Figure 3 shows the percentage of legitimate traffic served during the attack. The x-axis indicates the number of clusters $k$, i.e. the granularity of the model which the defender builds of the normal traffic. The simulation results for the random (address-spoofing) attacker show that, even under the extreme DoS attack, the server is able to serve between 40% and 70% of the legitimate requests depending on the normal load. It is important to note that the service quality does not degrade equally for all clients. Those clients in the high-priority clusters are served all or most of the time and those in the low-priority clusters (i.e. ones where most attack traffic falls) are not served at all. We also observe that the normal load of the targeted server has a fairly small effect on the effectiveness of the defense.

In Figure 4, the attack traffic originates from a virtual botnet that contains about 110000 bots. The bots are geographically distributed based on real-life malicious hosts, as described earlier. In comparison to figure 3, we observe that the percentage of legitimate traffic served is higher, approximately 80% with manageable numbers of clusters.

We also analyzed the effects of overlearning, learning period duration and model aging to the filtering efficiency. We observed that overlearning can have a negative impact with very high cluster counts, as can be seen in the last data point of Figure 4. The learning period duration had relatively little effect after a number of requests in the order of tens of thousands was received. Model aging in relation to learning period had a significant effect on the filtering efficiency with served traffic percentage dropping from an immediate value of 80% to 40% after the attack duration exceeded the learning period duration by a factor of 2. As the learning periods in real filter deployments are likely to be days or weeks, this would imply that an attack lasting several weeks is needed to degrade the service quality below 50%.

Overall, the simulation results indicate that the proposed clustering and filtering mechanism is effective in mitigating the effects of DoS and DDoS attacks. The worst case attack is one where the attacker sends requests from random IP addresses (i.e. spoofed SYN packets). Even then, the server is able to serve between 40% and 70% of the legitimate clients. Attacks by the simulated botnet and the concentrated attacker with only a few IP addresses were filtered even more effectively, with 80% to 100% of the legitimate clients served.

## 5   Implementation

### 5.1   Architecture and Implementation

Figure 5 shows the filtering-system architecture. The system is separated into several blocks, which can be divided into the performance-critical and non-performance-critical categories. The performance-critical components need to process in real time the requests arriving to the server. In order to not adversely effect the server throughput, these components on the path of the normal traffic to and from the server must be as simple as possible. Therefore, all the CPU and memory-intensive operations are performed on a separate analysis host connected to the traffic handling equipment over socket communications.

Traffic destined for the server is copied to the traffic tap and sent for feature extraction. The data from the tap is used both to create the normal traffic profile and to measure the server load levels. The feature extraction takes the IP addresses from the packets and sends them to feature-set bookkeeping. Both the traffic tap and the feature extraction may drop some data when the server comes under heavy load. This has little effect on the overall traffic profiling and filter generation process as long as the IP packets or HTTP requests are dropped randomly, so that the dropping does not bias the data.

Feature-set bookkeeping maintains a sliding window of data on the traffic features. The data in this window is fed to the HHH clustering algorithm. Our implementation of the HHH algorithm does not take advantage of the various approximation and memory-saving techniques presented in the literature. This is because we wanted to experiment with different variations of the algorithm. However, the slower algorithm is not detrimental in our implementation as the clustering algorithm is not placed in the performance-critical part of the system.

In normal traffic situations, the traffic filter receives empty filter sets from the filter updater and thus permits all traffic. When the server load exceeds a defined threshold, the traffic filter generator rolls back to the previous clean cluster set, gives the clusters a priority order based on which are believed to contain proportionally most legitimate traffic, and blacklists those clusters that exceed the server capacity. The filter is updated periodically to match changes in

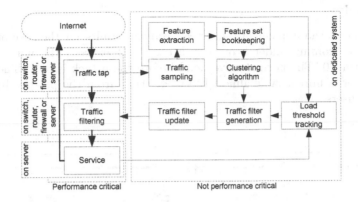

**Fig. 5.** Implementation architecture

the attack traffic. Once the attack subsides, the system observes the return of the incoming traffic to non-overload levels, removes blacklists from traffic filtering, and resumes normal learning operation.

We have implemented the tap and filter as user-space extensions to the iptables firewall. The traffic filters are black and whitelists of address prefixes. The clustering and traffic-filter-generation mechanism is an independent program running on a separate analysis host. The non-performance-critical clustering code is written in Python. The traffic tap could also be implemented as a separate network device, such as a switch, that mirrors the incoming traffic to the feature-set extractor though a monitoring port. Similarly, the filter could be deployed on a separate device. On the other hand, if we decided to use application-level features such as HTTP request parameters for the filters, it would be necessary to tap into that information on the web-server level. Further optimizing the implementation of the tap and filter components using for instance hardware support is left for future research.

## 5.2   Test Setup

In order to test the functionality and performance of the implementation, traffic was fed to the server from two systems running traffic-generation software. One of the client systems generates traffic belonging to the legitimate clients based on data from recorded traffic logs while the other acts as the botnet. The network link between the client systems and the server is uncongested because our experiments are primarily concerned with server capacity exhaustion and not network congestion.

The performance of the clustering and filtering mechanism is evaluated on the client side. Both the legitimate client system and the attacker system analyze responses to their requests and generate reports on served and dropped HTTP requests. These reports are then analyzed and compared with the findings of the simulations.

## 5.3 Results

Figure 6 shows the implementation measurement results for the case of unprotected server coming under a one-day attack that exceeds the normal traffic by the factor 10. The normal server load before the attack is 50%. The unprotected server is unreachable almost the whole time from the perspective of the legitimate users.

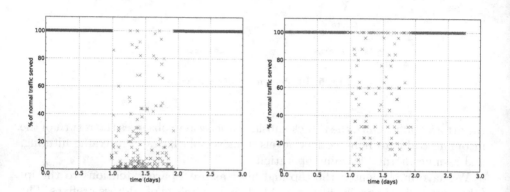

**Fig. 6.** Unprotected server, one day attack **Fig. 7.** Protected server, one day attack

Figure 7 shows the implementation measurement results for the case of a protected server subjected to the same attack as in Figure 6. The protected server remains mostly responsive to the legitimate users, serving an attack-time average of 69.8% of the legitimate requests. As in the simulations, this attacker with random source addresses is the worst case and attacks by a concentrated attacker or by a simulated botnet are filtered better.

## 6    Discussion

The simulation and implementation results show that the DoS defense mechanism proposed in this paper is effective in principle. The simple structure of the longest-prefix-matching filters is also an indication that it can be deployed in real systems.

One fundamental question is whether the local filtering of DoS attacks makes sense compared to distributed approaches. There are two kinds of distributed DoS solutions: network based and server based. The network-based solutions require broad changes to the Internet architecture or protocols and routers, which means that they cannot be deployed today to protect a specific service. The server-based solutions distribute the DoS protection or the online service itself globally, e.g. to a scalable server farm or cloud infrastructure. This kind of an approach is reasonable for large businesses that are able to pay for the higher availability. Small service provides and non-profit services with limited budgets, on the other hand, struggle to meet the cost of such protection. Services that are frequent targets to DoS attacks may even be rejected by ISPs that consider them troublesome customers. Specialized DoS filtering services exist but at a premium price. For these reasons, we believe that there is a need for inexpensive locally-deployed DoS defenses that can mitigate the attacks at least to some extent.

In the sections below, we discuss some of the implementation and security issues that have not yet been answered in the paper.

## 6.1  Implementation Issues

For the reasons explained in section 3, we have used the client IP address as the only feature in the clustering and filtering implementations. Another feature that could be useful in addition to the IP addresses is the TTL field in the IP header, which has been been successfully used for filtering spoofed traffic [9]. If used in addition to the client IP address, it could improve the filtering accuracy against spoofed SYN packets in our system. In a network-based filtering system that protects multiple targets, such as a firewall in front of a data center, the target host may become another dimension for clustering. Application-level features such as the request URL could also be considered but these have the previously mentioned problem of being vulnerable to adaptive attacks.

The hierarchical-heavy-hitter algorithm works very well for one-dimensional hierarchical data. Multi-dimensional versions of the algorithm exist but they produce overlapping clusters, which is not acceptable in our application. HHH also does not work well with non-hierarchical data types such as port numbers. We initially designed algorithms for multi-dimensional clustering but they have not been thoroughly tested and the details are beyond the scope of the current paper.

It is arguable that our filtering strategy is unfair since it completely blocks access to some traffic classes that fall into the same clusters with heavy attack traffic. We believe this to be acceptable because TCP connections and most other network protocol fail anyway when most of their packets are dropped. However, it is trivial to change the filtering policy so that some small capacity is given to every cluster.

In the simulations, we have not given the lengths of the learning period and attack in normal time units such as hours or days. This is because we make no use of the timing of the recorded legitimate requests. Instead, the timing has been adjusted to get the desirable server load. This allowed us to experiment with a wide range of relative time periods and load levels. It would obviously be interesting to test the algorithms with naturally timed legitimate traffic and to observe the effects of natural time periods such as days and weeks on the learning algorithm.

We have also been somewhat vague about how the server overload is detected. In fact, in the simulations, we do not detect the attack but explicitly inform the algorithms to switch to attack mitigation mode. In the implementation, a threshold bandwidth for the traffic tap output was used to trigger the attack response. The traffic threshold, of course, does not accurately tell when the server is overloaded, and a real deployment of the defense system should use some additional metrics. It is not trivial to accurately detect overload of a server because there are many resources, such as CPU, memory, hard disk, back-end database server, local network etc. that could become performance bottlenecks. This is a broader problem for web server management, though, and many ready solutions from that world exist. It remains to evaluate them and choose the right one for our purpose.

The filtering algorithm is based on longest prefix matching, which is also a key part of IP routing. Thus, much work has been done on its efficient implementation in both hardware and software. In the simulations, we have considered cluster numbers of up to $10^5$ because the Internet routing tables are in that order of magnitude. In practice, we would not expect a local firewall or router to be able to handle filter tables of that magnitude with high-bandwidth traffic. The realistic cluster counts are one or two orders of magnitude smaller. As we have seen, cluster counts (and thus prefix counts) in the order of $10^2 \dots 10^4$ already produce good filtering results.

In fact, we also experimented with a filtering implementation based on a DiffServ traffic classifier and scheduler with the hierarchical-token-bucket (HTB) queuing discipline. DiffServ supports at most 16 traffic classes. Nevertheless, it was able to successfully filter attacks from a limited number of IP addresses, with over 70% of the legitimate packets surviving.

Even then, there is the issue that real packet flooding (e.g. SYN flooding) DDoS attacks can reach bandwidths of tens of gigabits per second. While we have shown that the filtering algorithm scales well to almost any attack bandwidth, network hardware that can handle such amounts of traffic and execute prefix matching on every packet is going to be costly. One possibility for future consideration is to use our filtering policy for push-back, i.e. to deploy the filters in upstream routers at the ISP network.

## 6.2   Security Issues

Like in any security system, we need to also consider ways in which the attacker can circumvent the defense. One obvious way is to mount the SYN flooding attack from spoofed source addresses and try to *mimic* the address distribution of the legitimate clients. This requires the attacker to know how the legitimate clients are located in the Internet address space. The major disadvantage of the spoofing attacker is that the attack cannot be adaptive. That is, since the SYN packets are sent from spoofed IP addresses, the attacker gets no feedback on whether a particular address is served or not. Hence, the attacker must resort to manual research on the client-address distribution of the target server. That is possible but not at all as attractive as a fully automated attack, and one might expect many attackers to pass on the tedious work.

In addition to mimicking, another general concern in security systems that learn normal traffic profiles is the *poisoning* of the data. The danger is that the attacker slowly poisons the normal traffic set with malicious requests that remain under the detection threshold. When the actual DoS attack then starts, attack traffic originating from the same IP addresses would be considered legitimate. With our mechanism, this attack is not extremely dangerous: even if some of the clusters contain attacker addresses, those clusters will experience the largest traffic increase during the DoS attack and, therefore, they will be served with the lowest priority. In addition, poisoning the normal traffic forces the attacker to begin his activity well in advance and risks alerting the defender about the attack beforehand. To achieve significant results, the attacker would need to do the poisoning for the majority of the learning period duration and to add a large amount of traffic to the normal traffic. Most attackers however prefer surprise to the risk of being detected early because the detection could alert the defender to take precautionary measures. Forcing the attacker to take such a risk is in itself an achievement.

## 7  Conclusion

While previous DDoS research has developed various solutions to different kinds of DDoS attacks, the problem of mitigating attacks consisting of perfectly valid request traffic has not been exhaustively researched. We have utilized machine-learning algorithms commonly used in data and traffic analysis to create cluster-based traffic profiles and used these profiles to optimize our allocation of server resources to different traffic clusters during the attack.

Our simulation results show that this filtering mechanism is capable of mitigating overwhelming attacks by botnets to such a degree that over 80% of the legitimate client requests are served. Under a SYN flooding attack, the same filtering algorithms enable us to serve 40% to 70% of the normal users. In practice, this would enable many of the regular clients of the service to continue to access it relatively undisturbed even during the attack. As a desirable side effect, the mechanism can also act as protection against flash crowds by favoring the regular users of the service.

Overall, we have presented and analyzed in detail a DDoS mitigation mechanism based on normal traffic profiling and attack-time filtering of traffic. By progressing through simulations on several different attack models to a proof-of-concept implementation, we have demonstrated the effectiveness of our mechanism in mitigating DDoS attacks that are based on flooding the server with valid requests or excessive numbers of connections or SYN packets.

## References

1. Cai, X., Heidemann, J.: Understanding block-level address usage in the visible internet. ACM SIGCOMM Computer Communication Review 40(4), 99–110 (2010)
2. Collins, M., Reiter, M.: An empirical analysis of target-resident DoS filters. In: Proceedings of the 2004 IEEE Symposium on Security and Privacy (2004)

3. Cormode, G., Korn, F., Muthukrishnan, S., Srivastava, D.: Finding hierarchical heavy hitters in data streams. In: Proceedings of the 29th International Conference on Very large Data Bases, VLDB 2003, vol. 29 (2003)
4. Cormode, G., Korn, F., Muthukrishnan, S., Srivastava, D.: Finding hierarchical heavy hitters in streaming data. ACM Trans. Knowl. Discov. Data 1(4) (February 2008)
5. Dixon, C., Anderson, T., Krishnamurthy, A.: Phalanx: Withstanding multimillion-node botnets. In: Proceedings of the 5th USENIX Symposium on Networked Systems Design and Implementation, NSDI 2008 (2008)
6. Ferguson, P., Senie, D.: Network ingress filtering: Defeating denial of service attacks which employ IP source address spoofing. RFC 2827 (Best Current Practice) (May 2000)
7. Hussain, A., Heidemann, J., Papadopoulos, C.: A framework for classifying denial of service attacks. In: Proceedings of the 2003 Conference on Applications, Technologies, Architectures, and Protocols for Computer Communications, SIGCOMM 2003 (2003)
8. Ioannidis, J., Bellovin, S.: Implementing pushback: Router-based defense against DDoS attacks. In: Proceedings of Network and Distributed System Security Symposium, vol. 2 (2002)
9. Jin, C., Wang, H., Shin, K.G.: Hop-count filtering: an effective defense against spoofed DDoS traffic. In: Proceedings of the 10th ACM Conference on Computer and Communications Security, CCS 2003 (2003)
10. Lakhina, A., Crovella, M., Diot, C.: Mining anomalies using traffic feature distributions. In: Proceedings of the 2005 Conference on Applications, Technologies, Architectures, and Protocols for Computer Communications, pp. 217–228. ACM (2005)
11. Liao, Q., Cieslak, D.A., Striegel, A.D., Chawla, N.V.: Using selective, short-term memory to improve resilience against DDoS exhaustion attacks. Security and Communication Networks 1(4) (2008)
12. Lin, C.-H., Liu, J.-C., Jiang, F.-C., Kuo, C.-T.: An effective priority queue-based scheme to alleviate malicious packet flows from distributed DoS attacks. In: International Conference on Intelligent Information Hiding and Multimedia Signal Processing, IIHMSP 2008 (August 2008)
13. Peng, T., Leckie, C., Ramamohanarao, K.: Survey of network-based defense mechanisms countering the DoS and DDoS problems. ACM Comput. Surv. 39 (April 2007)
14. Ranjan, S., Swaminathan, R., Uysal, M., Knightly, E.: DDoS-resilient scheduling to counter application layer attacks under imperfect detection. In: Proceedings of the 25th IEEE International Conference on Computer Communications, INFOCOM 2006 (April 2006)
15. Sekar, V., Duffield, N., Spatscheck, O., van der Merwe, J., Zhang, H.: LADS: large-scale automated DDoS detection system. In: Proceedings of the Annual Conference on USENIX 2006 Annual Technical Conference, ATEC 2006 (2006)

# Spook in Your Network: Attacking an SDN with a Compromised OpenFlow Switch

Markku Antikainen[1], Tuomas Aura[1], and Mikko Särelä[2]

[1] Aalto University, Department of Computer Science and Engineering, Finland
[2] Aalto University, Department of Electrical Engineering, Finland
{markku.antikainen,tuomas.aura,mikko.sarela}@aalto.fi

**Abstract.** Software defined networking (SDN) and OpenFlow as one of its key technologies have received a lot of attention from the networking community. While SDN enables complex network applications and easier network management, the paradigm change comes along with new security threats. In this paper, we analyze attacks against a software-defined network in a scenario where the attacker has been able to compromise one or more OpenFlow-capable switches. We find out that such attacker can in suitable environments perform a wide range of attacks, including man-in-the-middle attacks against control-plane traffic, by using only the standard OpenFlow functionality of the switch. Furthermore, we show that in certain scenarios it is nearly impossible to detect that some switch has been compromised. We conclude that while the existing security mechanisms, such as TLS, give protection against many of the presented attacks, the threats should not be overlooked when moving to SDN and OpenFlow.

## 1 Introduction

In just a few years time, OpenFlow [10] together with software defined networking (SDN) [8] has grown from university labs into a serious challenger of the traditional Ethernet architecture. OpenFlow unifies the control interface of the network equipment, and the SDN architecture provides a uniform network application programming interface making it possible to easily develop, test, and deploy novel networking applications. This change is said to be unparalleled in the history of networking [13].

The core idea behind software defined networking is relatively simple. In SDN, the decision making is moved to a logically centralized element called a *controller*. This differs from traditional networks where the routers and switches function in distributed manner. The implications of moving the intelligence from the switches and routers to the centralized controller are huge.

First of all, the logically centralized controller will have a view over the whole network. This gives it very good capabilities for traffic optimization. Secondly, since the intelligence is moved from the switches and routers to the controller,

K. Bernsmed and S. Fischer-Hübner (Eds.): NordSec 2014, LNCS 8788, pp. 229–244, 2014.
DOI: 10.1007/978-3-319-11599-3_14, © Springer International Publishing Switzerland 2014

the data-plane equipment becomes lighter and cheaper. Thirdly, as already mentioned, the centralized controller removes the need for application-specific control-plane protocols by making it possible to develop new networking applications on top of the application programming interface (API) provided by the controller.

Software defined networking changes the security environment by introducing a centralized decision making point (controller), standardizing the interface between the control and data planes (OpenFlow), and providing a unified API for network management applications. This change creates possibilities for new ways of improving security (see e.g. [5, 11, 15]).

However, the centralization and homogeneous interfaces also creates new security problems. Design and implementation flaws are more likely to have broader impact in SDN than in traditional networking, which has had inherent protection against adversaries in the form of proprietary software, decentralization, and heterogeneity of the network devices [9]. Also, the cost of exploiting vulnerabilities is reduced since the attacker no longer needs to tailor the attacks to the target network's equipment.

This paper analyzes attacks against a software defined network where the attacker has access to one or more OpenFlow switches. We discover that an such attacker can perform a wide range of attacks against the data plane as well as the control plane by only utilizing the standard OpenFlow functionality on the compromised switch. The attacks presented in this paper include eavesdropping network traffic, spoofing the network topology, and man-in-the-middle (MitM) attacks. Furthermore, we describe how, in some situations, it is impossible to automatically detect the existence of such attackers.

The rest of this paper is structured as follows: Section 2 describes the background for our work explaining the fundamentals of the OpenFlow protocol and related work. In Section 3, we describe building blocks for the attacks that can be done with a compromised OpenFlow switch in a target network. After explaining the basic principles of the attacks, we move on to describe more sophisticated control-plane attacks in Section 4. Section 5 discusses how and to what extent the presented attacks can be mitigated. Finally, Section 6 concludes the paper.

# 2   Background

## 2.1   OpenFlow Protocol

OpenFlow is a protocol used to communicate between the network control plane, namely a *controller*, and data-plane elements, namely OpenFlow *switches*. It essentially provides a standard interface for communication between the control plane and data plane. By offering a standard interface for data-plane management, OpenFlow changes the traditional distributed networking model into a centralized one, where a logically central controller makes the forwarding decisions. (The actual controller implementation could be distributed.) The protocol development has been very active — specification for OpenFlow version 1.0 was released in 2009 and, at the time of writing, the most recent version is 1.4.0.

OpenFlow is built around the concept of data *flows*, which are identified by header-field values in the network packets or frames. Commonly used header fields include the medium-access-control (MAC) addresses, the virtual-local-area-network (VLAN) tag, and the Internet protocol (IP) 5-tuple. Each switch has flow tables that contain rules against which the incoming data flows are matched. For each rule, the tables specify one or more actions, such as dropping the packet, forwarding it through a certain interface, or sending it to the controller for processing. The controller can modify the flow tables on each switch either proactively or reactively. Proactive flow-table modification means that the controller simply configures the necessary rules to the switches' flow tables. In reactive flow-table modification, there is a default flow-table entry that instructs the switch to send packets belonging to new flows to the controller for processing. The controller then adds flow-table entries reactively for the new flows as it observes them. The reactive decisions make it possible to use OpenFlow for building complex network applications such as stateful firewalls.

As said, the OpenFlow protocol is used to communicate between a logically centralized controller and OpenFlow switches. The protocol uses a transmission-control-protocol (TCP) connection, which is initiated by the switch. The connection integrity and confidentiality may be protected with transport-layer security (TLS), which provides mutual device authentication between the switch and the controller. TLS can also be used with one-sided controller authentication, in which case the switches are not authenticated. In many current deployments, TLS is not used at all. In fact, there are several OpenFlow implementations (both switches and controllers) that do not yet support TLS [2].

There are two different ways of handling the OpenFlow connections between the controller and the switches. The OpenFlow connections can either use a dedicated control network, or the control-plane connections can be transmitted over the same physical network as the data-plane communication. We refer to these methods as *out-of-band* control and *in-band* control channel, respectively (see Figure 1). Security-wise, the main difference between these two methods is that, in the out-of-band control model, the control traffic may be sent through other OpenFlow switches. As we will see in Section 4, this may enable, for example, man-in-the-middle attacks against the control traffic if some switch on the path has been compromised. Out-of-bad control is less vulnerable to attacks but more expensive because of the need for separate cabling and interfaces. Therefore, it is feasible only in some specific scenarios, such as in data centers where the network covers a relatively small physical area.

## 2.2  Related Work

OpenFlow networks can face security threats from hosts connected to the network, compromised switches, compromised controllers, and from network applications utilizing the network API provided by the controller.

One potential avenue is to attack the control traffic between the controller and the switch. OpenFlow uses TLS for device authentication and to provide confidentiality for the control-plane communication. However, there have recently

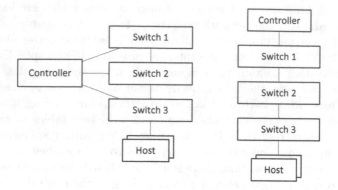

**Fig. 1.** In-band and out-of-band control plane

been several reports about vulnerabilities in SSL/TLS implementations [4, 17] and, even more worryingly, TLS adoption to the OpenFlow devices has been slow. In their recent work, Benton et al. [2] analyzed eight popular OpenFlow switches and controllers, out of which only one controller and two switches provide full TLS support. The situation has improved slightly since the article was published, but there are still several products that lack TLS support.

Another problem is created by the fact that the network administrators often consider TLS a nuisance [2]. Since OpenFlow uses mutually-authenticated TLS, the network administrators must create device-specific certificates (both controller certificates and switch certificates), sign all of them, and finally distribute the certificates to the devices. The tedious key-management required by the mutually authenticated TLS may tempt network administrators to skip some parts of the process. This may mean using TLS to authenticate only the controller, or dropping TLS altogether.

A compromised host may attempt a denial-of-service attack either by flooding the control channel or by filling the flow-tables with garbage [2, 3, 7, 14]. Firstly, the attacker may target the controller by flooding the network with frames or packets that are sent to the controller for processing (*control-plane resource consumption* [14]). These attacks can be mitigated by limiting the rate of packets sent to the controller. Indeed, rate limiting has been part of the OpenFlow specification since version 1.2 [16]. Secondly, the attacker may flood the network with packets that create new flow entries in the flow table of the target switch (*data-plane resource consumption* [14]). The flow table will eventually overflow and some entries have to be evicted, after which the switch will send also legitimate packets to the controller for processing.

The data-plane resource consumption attacks against a switch have been demonstrated and analyzed by Klöti et al. [7]. They not only show that it is easy to mount a denial-of-service (DoS) attack that completely fills the switch's flow table, but also that an attacker can use message round-trip times to identify flows that are suitable for a DoS attack. This further increases the risk of a successful DoS attack. The suggested mitigation strategies for the data-plane attacks include event filtering done by the controller, flow aggregation, and various intrusion detection mechanisms.

Finally, even though SDN is based on the idea of an omniscient controller, it may happen that the controller does not know the state of the network accurately. For example, it is possible that a switch erroneously removes a flow entry (this may be caused by a bug or by an attacker). The only way for a controller to verify the integrity of a flow table is to explicitly query it from the switch. While the this is not a threat in itself, an attacker may use this shortcoming as a part of a more complex attack. One potential fix for this issue, proposed by Benton et al. [2], is to introduce a checksum of the switch state to the *keep-alive* messages, which the controller could then use to monitor the state of the network.

## 3    Attacker Controlled OpenFlow Switch

In this section, we analyze what an attacker can do if it has been able to compromise one or more OpenFlow switches. How the attacker has gotten the access to the switch is outside our analysis — the attacker may have exploited some vulnerability on the switch or reconfigured the switch by accessing it physically. We assume that the switch implements the OpenFlow standard (our analysis covers OpenFlow versions 1.0–1.4.0). Moreover, we assume that the switch has access to the Internet.

### 3.1    Flow-table Modification

We start describing the attacks with a simple case where an attacker can modify the flow tables of a compromised switch. We assume, that the attacker can arbitrarily add, remove, and modify the entries in the flow table of the compromised switch. The attacker cannot, however, do anything else such as extract the cryptographic keys from the switch or change the way how the switch processes control messages sent to it. The possibility of this kind of attacks has been identified at least by Benton et al. [2], but they did not analyze this particular threat in detail.

The ability to modify the flow tables makes a large variety of attacks possible. Figure 2 shows two of these: eavesdropping by traffic duplication and man-in-the-middle attack for a certain flow.

The basic principle of the eavesdropping attack is simple: the attacker adds an entry to the switch's flow table to duplicate certain flows to an IP-address of a computer controlled by the attacker (see Figure 2b). This eavesdropping computer does not need to reside in the same network as the compromised switch; it can be located outside the target network or in the public Internet, as long as there is connection between the compromised switch and the eavesdropping computer for sending the data.

In a similar fashion, the attacker can perform a man-in-the-middle attack for data flows going through the compromised switch. In this case, the compromised

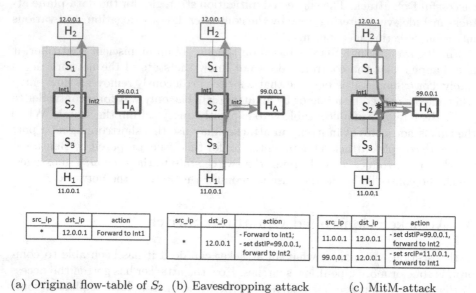

(a) Original flow-table of $S_2$   (b) Eavesdropping attack          (c) MitM-attack

**Fig. 2.** Flow-table of switch $S_2$ when the attacker eavesdrops traffic (2b) or performs a MitM attack (2c)

switch should not duplicate the flow but instead redirect it to the attacker-controlled computer in the Internet. After this, the attacker-controlled computer may modify the packets and send them to the original recipient. Alternatively, the attacker can also send the flow back to the compromised switch and configure it to forward the returning packets to the original recipient (see Figure 2c). In this case, the attacker has to insert another flow entry to the switch for redirecting the flow from the attacker-controlled computer to the original recipient.

For the above attacks to work, the compromised switch and the attacker-controlled computer must be able to send the diverted packets to each other. Since we are interested in attacks that exploit the functionality of a standard OpenFlow switch, this should be done without changes to the switch software or hardware. In the simplest case, the attacker-controlled computer is directly connected to the compromised switch, so that the packets can be forwarded to it directly. When the computer is further away, the traffic diversion can be achieved by modifying the destination IP address of the packet, as shown in the figure. If there is any pair of IP addresses that will cause the data packets to be sent between the compromised switch and the attacker controlled computer, then the two are able to communicate. This is almost certainly the case in Internet-connected networks. For example, if the compromised switch sees any inbound or outbound web traffic, it probably can use the internal client or server IP address from those packets for sending packets to the Internet. When multiple data flows need to be diverted at the same time, some other IP header field can be use for multiplexing the flows.

There are some limits to when the above attack will work. First, the rewriting of source and destination addresses is a optional feature in OpenFlow and not necessarily implemented by all switches. Second, the attacker needs to initially know at least one IP address or flow that it can exploit for the traffic diversion. After that, it can learn more about the target network's IP addresses and flows by momentarily diverting classes of packets and observing them at the attacker-controlled host. Third, if there is a firewall between the SDN-enabled network and the Internet, it will limit the types of packets that can be sent, and rewriting of other fields than the source and destination addresses may be required to get all desired packets through the firewall. A stateful firewall will also make harder for the attacker to set up the traffic diversion. A determined attacker is nevertheless likely find some way through the firewall.

It should be noted, that Figure 2c shows the MitM attack only in one direction, for traffic sent from $H_1$ to $H_2$. If the attacker would like to monitor or modify the traffic also in the opposite direction, it would have to amend the shown flow table accordingly.

As described by Benton et al. [2], it is possible to detect these kinds of attacks if the controller of the network compares the expected state of the compromised switch to the actual state the switch. This means that the controller must store information about the network state and periodically query the flow tables from the switches. However, querying the complete state of the network is a relatively heavy operation. Spontaneous changes in the switch state also create a challenge: for example, if a switch loses connection to the controller it may drop all the entries in its flow tables. Nevertheless, it is possible, for an intelligent control software to identify switches that are in an invalid state.

The attack detection would become much more difficult if the attacker was able to change the way in which the compromised switch reports its flow tables to the controller. This attack, however, would be non-trivial and would require implementation-specific information on the compromised switch. Furthermore, we found a much easier way to avoid detection, which will be discussed in the following section.

## 3.2   Control-channel Hijacking

Eavesdropping and MitM attacks become more interesting when the attacker can not only modify the flow tables of a compromised switch but can also reconfigure the switch to use a different controller. We call this kind of attacks *control-channel hijacking*. The term should not be confused with an attack where the attacker compromises the controller of the target network. Instead, we assume only that the attacker can reconfigure the switch to use a different controller than the one it should.

In this attack, we assume that the attacker can change the SDN controller used by the compromised switch. We also assume either that the switch does not use a certificate for authenticating itself or that attacker is able to compromise its cryptographic credentials (i.e. the private key for TLS). Note that this is

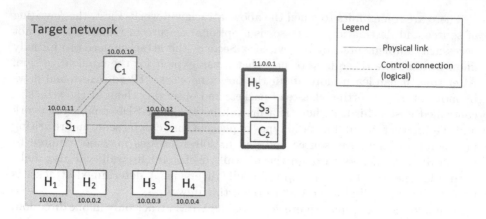

**Fig. 3.** Proof-of-concept topology for control-channel hijacking. The nodes with strong red lines (including the virtual switch $S_3$ and controller $C_2$) are controlled by the attacker.

different from replacing the switch with an arbitrary malicious computer: we are only relying on the capabilities that a normal SDN switch has.

Control-channel hijacking is more serious than the case discussed above where the attacker could only modify the flow table of a switch. This is because, when the attacker can change the controller for a switch, it can also more easily spoof control traffic to the target network's controller. The attacker can set up a controller application on its own machine somewhere on the Internet and change the compromised switch to use this malicious controller. By altering the flow table of the compromised switch in the way already explained in the previous section, the attacker can forward all control traffic from the target network's controller to the malicious controller. This way, the attacker's controller can spoof any messages to the target controller. The attacker may, for example, fool the target controller to think that the compromised switch is in a different state than it really is. Because of this, the control-channel hijacking attack may be very difficult to detect.

In an abstract sense, the compromised switch and the malicious controller in this attack achieve the same capabilities as a general-purpose computer that is placed inside the victim's network at the location of the compromised switch: it can manipulate the traffic going through the switch in any way it wants. Of course, the compromised switch is also capable of doing normal data-plane forwarding if the attacker wishes so. In any case, the attacker is able to escalate the attack from being able to replacing the controller for the compromised switch to the equivalent of replacing the compromised switch with a malicious computer. The effects of the attacks are summarized in the three top rows of Table 1.

We built a proof-of-concept implementation of this attack with the Mininet network emulator. The topology is shown in Figure 3. The network has three switches $S_{1..3}$ out of which $S_{1..2}$ reside in the target network and $S_3$ is a virtual switch running at the attacker's host $H_5$. Both switches in the target network have two hosts attached to them. The attacker-controlled computer $H_5$ hosts a virtual (malicious) controller $C_2$ that controls the compromised switch $S_2$. $H_5$ also hosts a virtual switch $S_3$ that emulates the real switch $S_2$, as if it was uncompromised and operated in the normal way, and communicates with the target controller $C_1$. The purpose of $S_3$ is to make the target controller think that it still has control over all its switches.

As discussed already in the previous section, there are some topological re quirements for this attack. First of all, it must be possible for the compromised switch to forward traffic to the Internet. Alternatively, the attacker controlled host may reside in the target network. The latter may be possible, e.g., in a data-center where the tenants cannot be trusted. In our proof-of-concept topology, this means that $S_2$ must be able to send traffic to $H_5$ and back. As discussed earlier, it is likely that such routing is possible by substituting some pair of source and destination IP addresses.

One way the target controller can still get a hint about the control-channel hijacking is to observe the latencies of the OpenFlow messages. Because all Open-Flow messages from $C_1$ to $S_2$ are forwarded to the attacker-controlled node $H_5$, which may be remote, the replies will have higher latency that usual. However, careful data analysis will be needed to differentiate between high latencies caused attacks from those caused by legitimate reasons.

At the more theoretical end of defense mechanisms, active traffic shaping and latency measurements could be used to analyze the network in detail. For example, in a larger network, there might be non-compromised switches between the compromised switch and the attacker-controlled computer. In our proof-of-concept topology this would happen if the compromised switch were $S_1$ instead of $S_2$. In that case, if the controller suspects that a switch has been compromised, it can start delaying classes of data-plane traffic. If delaying the data plane traffic also affects the latency of the OpenFlow messages sent to the compromised switch, it can conclude that the suspected switch is compromised. However, this would affect the performance of the network detrimentally even when there is no attacker present.

## 4 Attacking the Control Plane with a Compromised Switch

Next, we move on to describe what kinds of control-plane attacks are possible when the attacker has compromised one or more OpenFlow switches in the target network. The capabilities of the attacker are largely determined by two factors: how TLS is used to protect control-plane communication, and whether the network uses in-band or out-of-band control channels. Additionally, some attacks are only possible if the attacker can perform control-channel hijacking instead of only being able to modify the flow-table of the compromised switch. We consider all of these cases. Our focus is on attacks against control-plane traffic confidentiality and integrity. Denial-of-service attacks, such as flooding and packet dropping, are analyzed only briefly.

As discussed in Section 3, the compromised switch can be used to replicate the data going through it for traffic eavesdropping. It is also likely that the attacker can perform MitM attacks on the traffic going through the compromised switch by rerouting the packets to an external attacker-controlled computer. Additionally, the attacker may choose to drop certain packets at the switch. These three, eavesdropping, man-in-the-middle attacks, and packet dropping, are the main building blocks for the more complex attacks we now present.

We have summarized the attacks in Table 1. The tables show how well the attacks work depending on how TLS is used to protect the control-plane communication and whether the network uses in-band or out-of-band control channels. The attacks can be categorized into three groups: control-plane eavesdropping, state and topology spoofing, and denial-of-service attacks. We describe the attacks in this order.

## 4.1  Eavesdropping Control Plane Communication

The attack against control-plane traffic confidentiality does not differ much from the attacks where the attacker eavesdrops the data-plane traffic. This is because the compromised switch treats all traffic that is not destined to itself as data-plane traffic. Thus, a compromised switch can be used to eavesdrop the control-plane traffic going through it in the same way as it can be used to eavesdrop data-plane traffic.

Requirements for the control-plane eavesdropping are relatively easy to understand. As said, the attacker can eavesdrop all unencrypted control-plane traffic that goes through the compromised switch. This means that the attacker can eavesdrop the control-plane traffic of all downstream switches in the tree formed by control flows and rooted at the controller — unless TLS is used. If the control-plane uses TLS, the attacker can only see the encrypted packets. This is the case also when TLS is only used to authenticate the controller.

Additionally, it is possible to eavesdrop the control-plane traffic sent to the compromised switch if the attacker can perform control-channel hijacking for the compromised switch. As explained in Section 3.2, TLS does not prevent this if attacker is able to extract the cryptographic keys from the compromised switch.

As seen in Table 1, the out-of-band control channel will (ideally) protect against eavesdropping as effectively as TLS. The reason for this is simple: since the control traffic is sent over dedicated lines, no control traffic goes through the compromised switch. However, is the out-of-band control network does not provide adequate isolation between the switches, that could lead to new attacks.

## 4.2  State Spoofing and Topology Spoofing

The compromised switch can be used to attack the integrity of the network state. More specifically, the attacker can spoof the state of some switches to the controller. We call this a *state-spoofing attack*. Additionally, if TLS is not used with OpenFlow, or if is used only to authenticate the controller, the attacker

Table 1. List of attacks analyzed in this paper

| | Flow-table modification | | | | Control-channel hijacking | | | |
|---|---|---|---|---|---|---|---|---|
| | No TLS | Controller authentication | Mutual authentication | Out-of-band control channel | No TLS | Controller authentication | Mutual authentication | Out-of-band control channel |
| Eavesdrop control data with packet duplication | | ✓ | ✓ | ✓ | ✓ | ✓ | ✓ | ✓ |
| MitM attack by diverting traffic | | ✓ | ✓ | ✓ | ✓ | ✓ | ✓ | ✓ |
| Spoof the state of the compromised switch e.g. to avoid attack detection | | | | | ✓ | ✓ | ✓ | ✓ |
| Eavesdrop control traffic of the compromised switch | | | | | ✓ | ✓ | ✓ | ✓ |
| Eavesdrop downstream switches' control traffic | | | | | ✓ | | | |
| Spoof downstream switches' state | | | | | ✓ | | | |
| Topology spoofing: add bogus switches to the network | | ✓ | | ?1 | ✓ | ✓ | | ?1 |
| Empty downstream switches' flowtables (DoS) | | | | | ✓ | | | |

1 Depends on the control-network implementation. This and many further attacks against uncompromised switches may be possible if the control network does not provide adequate isolation between switches.

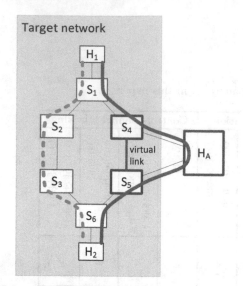 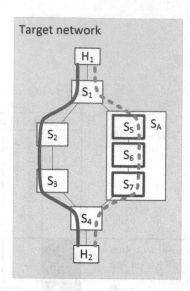

(a) Topology spoofing with virtual links     (b)  Topology  spoofing  with  virtual switches

**Fig. 4.** Topology spoofing in two ways. The dotted green line depicts the original shortest-path between $H_1$ and $H_2$, and the solid red line depicts the shortest path after topology spoofing.

can create bogus virtual switches to the network. By adding bogus switches to the network, the attacker can launch a *topology-spoofing attack*.

In the state spoofing attack, the compromised switch lies to the controller about its own state, or about the state of some other switch that communicates with the controller through it (i.e. a downstream switch). The attacker may, for example, lie to the controller about the contents of the switch's flow table, traffic statistics, or even about which interfaces the switch has. The attacker may do this in order to hide its own activities or in order to otherwise alter the behavior of the controller.

As mentioned, the attacker can spoof the state of any switch that communicates with the controller through the compromised switch unless TLS is used. This highlights the importance of deploying TLS if the network relies on in-band control channels. It should be noted that, even if TLS is not used to authenticate the switches (i.e. only the controller has a certificate), it still provides protection against MitM attacks on the control-plane traffic going through the compromised switch to the downstream switches.

However, if TLS is not used to authenticate the switches, the attacker can create bogus virtual switches to the network. This attack may be used to change the network topology which the controller observes. In this topology-spoofing attack, the attacker creates virtual nodes or links to the network and thus changes, for example, the way in which packets are routed in the network. We identified two ways for an attacker to exploit topology spoofing. Firstly, the attacker may add virtual links between compromised switches in order to attract traffic to those switches. This is shown in Figure 4a where the attacker adds a virtual link between two compromised switches $S_4$ and $S_5$. If the network uses shortest-path routing, this causes some of the traffic sent between $H_1$ and $H_2$ to be forwarded through the compromised switches, thus enabling a man-in-the-middle attack on those flows.

Alternatively, the attacker may want to add bogus switches to the network in order to make certain paths longer. Figure 4b shows this. The attacker creates three virtual switches with the compromised switch $S_A$, thus making the controller-observed path $H_1 - S_1 - S_5 - S_6 - S_7 - S_4 - H_2$ longer than the alternative. This strategy may be used, for example, in order to create congestion to switches in the alternative path or to reserve bandwidth for the attacker's own use.

### 4.3  Denial of Service

The attacker may also launch a wide range of different denial-of-service attacks with the compromised switch. As discussed in Section 2, a control-plane DoS attack may target either the controller or the OpenFlow switches. A DoS attack against the controller can be done for example by flooding it with forged *packet-in* messages. Depending on the controller logic, processing carefully crafted packets may require considerable amount of processing. However, since this attack is highly dependent on the controller's logic and its implementation, a detailed analysis of this kind of attacks is not possible without making many assumptions about the controller.

DoS attacks against OpenFlow switches would be more interesting since they can be analyzed with much fewer assumptions. However, DoS attacks are not the focus of this paper and we refrain from discussing them in detail. We just give one rudimentary example of a DoS attack: if the attacker can do a MitM attacks against the control-plane communication between a switch and the controller, it can rather trivially flush the flow-tables of the switch. This attack can be used to knock out any OpenFlow switch. Thus, using TLS may actually give protection against some DoS attacks. It must be noted, however, that other DoS attacks are possible, at least if some switch has been compromised.

## 5  Discussion and Future Work

While OpenFlow is very expressive giving the controller a possibility to implement complex network applications, the same expressiveness also allows a wide range of attacks against the network. One of the more interesting possibilities we have described in this paper was that an attacker who is able hijack the control channel of a switch can launch a wide range of attacks and avoid detection by spoofing the switch state to the honest controller.

Our results, summarized in Table 1 show that using (mutually isolated) out-of-band control channels significantly reduces the possibilities for the attacker. This is not surprising: since no control traffic goes through the compromised switch (apart from the control traffic destined to the switch itself), the attacker can only alter the behavior of the compromised switch itself.

It can also be seen in Table 1 that TLS gives the same level of protection against the analyzed attacks as the out-of-band control channel. Also, slightly surprisingly, using TLS only to authenticate the controller (instead of mutual authentication) also gives protection against most of the analyzed attacks. It has been argued that mutually authenticated TLS creates a heavy burden for the network administrators in the form of key management [2]. Our analysis show that, in some cases, it may be possible to simplify the key management by dropping the mutual authentication from the TLS without completely sacrificing the network security.

It should be noted that there are other threat vectors against a software-defined networks that have not been analyzed in this paper. For example, the attacker could try to compromise the controller or a network application running on it instead of compromising individual switches. In fact, the logically centralized controller would be the most obvious target for an attack. However, for this same reason, a lot more attention has been paid to the security of the controller than to the individual switches. Our results should be seen as a reminder that the controller is not the only security-critical element in SDN.

The relevance of our research could be questioned by saying that similar attacks to the ones described in this paper are also possible against traditional Ethernet networks. However, traditional networks are often heterogeneous or make use of proprietary protocols, thus making the attacks more expensive to implement. Moreover, OpenFlow has actually been proposed as a solution for many well-understood Ethernet security problems, such as address resolution protocol (ARP) poisoning and spanning tree protocol (STP) root attacks [6]. Finally, compromising an Ethernet switch requires hacking of the software or hardware on the switch while, as shown in this paper, a compromised OpenFlow switch does not necessarily require software of hardware modifications: the attacker can control the compromised switch by misusing its standards features. Thus, we believe our analysis to be relevant for practical network security.

We acknowledge that this paper only scratches the surface an does not fully analyze all of the possible consequences and limitations of the suggested attacks. We believe that even more serious cascading attacks may be possible. In particular, the topology-spoofing attack, which was briefly presented in Section 4.2, should be analyzed in different network topologies. We intend to continue our work by analyzing this attack in a more systematic manner following, e.g., what has been done for Bloom-filter-based forwarding [1, 12].

# 6    Conclusion

The goal of this paper is to analyze attacks against a software defined network in a scenario where the attacker has compromised one or more OpenFlow switches.

We describe how a compromised switch can be used to perform eavesdropping and MitM attacks against both data and control-plane traffic. Furthermore, we built a proof-of-concept implementation of a control-channel hijacking attack that disguises the state of a maliciously acting switch from a controller that tries to monitor it. The attacks presented in the paper show that ill-protected networks are particularly vulnerable to control-plane attacks done with a compromised switch.

Software-defined networking is becoming increasingly popular, and for a reason. It simplifies network management and enables novel applications. However, SDN also changes the security environment of the networks. The new threats should be taken into account when starting the migration towards software-defined networks.

**Acknowledgments.** We would like to thank Timo Kiravuo for his valuable comments.

# References

1. Antikainen, M., Aura, T., Särelä, M.: Denial-of-service attacks in Bloom-filter-based forwarding. IEEE/ACM Transactions on Networking (to appear), Preprint online at http://ieeexplore.ieee.org/stamp/stamp.jsp?arnumber=6616021
2. Benton, K., Camp, L.J., Small, C.: OpenFlow vulnerability assessment. In: Roccedings of the Second ACM SIGCOMM Workshop on Hot Topics in Software Defined Networking, HotSDN 2013, pp. 151–152 (2013), Extended version online at http://homes.soic.indiana.edu/ktbenton/research/openflow_vulnerability _assessment.pdf
3. Dillon, C., Berkelaa, M.: OpenFlow (D)DoS mitigation. Technical report (February 2014), http://www.delaat.net/rp/2013-2014/p42/report.pdf
4. Georgiev, M., Iyengar, S., Jana, S.: The most dangerous code in the world: Validating SSL certificates in non-browser software. In: Proceedings of the 2012 ACM Conference on Computer and Communications Security, pp. 38–49 (2012)
5. Khurshid, A., Zhou, W., Caesar, M., Godfrey, P.: Veriflow: Verifying network-wide invariants in real time. ACM SIGCOMM Computer Communication Review 42 (October 2012)
6. Kiravuo, T., Särelä, M., Manner, J.: A Survey of Ethernet LAN Security. IEEE Communications Surveys & Tutorials 15, 1477–1491 (2013)
7. Kloti, R., Kotronis, V., Smith, P.: Openflow: A security analysis. In: NPSec 2013, Eighth Workshop on Secure Network Protocols (October 2013)
8. Koponen, T., Casado, M., Gude, N., Stribling, J., Poutievski, L., Zhu, M., Ramanathan, R., Iwata, Y., Inoue, H., Hama, T., et al.: Onix: A distributed control platform for large-scale production networks. In: Proceedings of the 9th USENIX Conference on Operating Systems Design and Implementation, OSDI 2010 (2010)
9. Kreutz, D., Ramos, F.M., Verissimo, P.: Towards secure and dependable software-defined networks. In: Proceedings of the Second ACM SIGCOMM Workshop on Hot Topics in Software Defined Networking, HotSDN 2013, New York, USA, pp. 55–60 (August 2013)
10. McKeown, N., Anderson, T.: OpenFlow: Enabling innovation in campus networks. ACM SIGCOMM Computer Communication Review 38, 69–74 (2008)

11. Porras, P., Shin, S., Yegneswaran, V., Fong, M., Tyson, M., Gu, G.: A security enforcement kernel for OpenFlow networks. In: Proceedings of the First Workshop on Hot Topics in Software Defined Networks, HotSDN 2012, p. 121 (2012)
12. Särelä, M., Rothenberg, C.E., Aura, T., Zahemszky, A., Nikander, P., Ott, J.: Forwarding anomalies in Bloom filter-based multicast. In: IEEE INFOCOM 2011 (April 2011)
13. Shenker, S., Casado, M., Koponen, T., McKeown, N.: The future of networking, and the past of protocols. Open Networking Summit (ONS) 2011 presentation, http://www.opennetsummit.org/archives/apr12/site/talks/shenker-tue.pdf
14. Shin, S., Gu, G.: Attacking software-defined networks: a first feasibility study. In: Proceedings of the Second ACM SIGCOMM Workshop on Hot Topics in Software Defined Networking, pp. 165–166 (August 2013)
15. Shin, S., Porras, P., Yegneswaran, V., Fong, M.: FRESCO: Modular Composable Security Services for Software-Defined Networks. In: NDSS Symposium 2013. Internet Society (February 2013)
16. The Open Networking Foundation. OpenFlow Switch Specification Version 1.2 (December 2011)
17. US-CERT. OpenSSL 'Heartbleed' vulnerability (CVE-2014-0160). Alert TA14-098A (2014)

# Security in Healthcare and Biometrics

# Patients' Privacy Protection against Insurance Companies in eHealth Systems

Liangyu Xu and Armin B. Cremers

Institute of Computer Science, University of Bonn, 53117 Bonn, Germany
xul@iai.uni-bonn.de, abc@iai.uni-bonn.de

**Abstract.** To preserve fraud detection, in most current eHealth systems, the health information of patients is fully disclosed to the insurance companies which cover the expenses of the patients' health care. However, such disclosure might infringe on the privacy of the patients. In this paper, we propose a novel pseudonym scheme and corresponding signature scheme for the billing process, in order to protect the privacy of patients against insurance companies while enabling the latter to check the truthfulness of the bills.

**Keywords:** privacy, eHealth, pseudonym, signature, DLP.

## 1    Introduction

With the development of the information technology, healthcare activities are becoming more and more paperless [1], i.e., many of the patient related records and communications are carried out through eHealth systems [2] using computers and internet. EHealth systems can definitely improve the efficiency and quality of health care [3]. E.g., eHealth systems enable doctors to access the patients' previous health records more quickly and comprehensively, which can help to improve the speed and precision of diagnosis on the patients, thus increasing the popularity of eHealth in many countries and areas   [4] [5].

Given the ease of duplicating and distributing data in information systems eHealth systems, in particular, are confronted with patient privacy issues [6]. Thus, in many countries there exist laws and regulations on protecting the data and communications in eHealth systems. For example, the U.S. enacted the Health Insurance Portability and Accountability Act (HIPAA) [7]; the European Union issued the Privacy Directive [8]; New Zealand has Health Information Privacy Code [9]. The privacy of the patients has different connotations in different procedures. E.g., when storing the patients' health records in a server or in the cloud [10] privacy protection may refer to encrypting the data in the records by a proper scheme and distributing the key to decrypt them to the persons who are intended to be able to access the data; when preparing health records for secondary use [11] (e.g., medical research) privacy protection may mean to remove the identifiers of the patients in order to make use of the data anonymously [12].

K. Bernsmed and S. Fischer-Hübner (Eds.): NordSec 2014, LNCS 8788, pp. 247–260, 2014.
DOI: 10.1007/978-3-319-11599-3_15, © Springer International Publishing Switzerland 2014

This paper will focus on the patients' privacy in the billing procedure as part of eHealth systems [13]. In many countries, people have health insurance covering the expenses of their health care served by the healthcare providers (e.g. practitioners, hospitals, pharmacies). Especially in most European countries, the health insurance is mandatory to most residents, e.g. through some statutory insurance company or public health fund [14]. The insurance companies receive and pay the bills from healthcare providers (where the healthcare providers bill the insurance companies directly on behalf of the patients), or the patients (where the patients receive the bills from the healthcare providers and afterwards send the bills to the insurance companies to get reimbursed).

The bills usually indicate some important information about the patients' illnesses, e.g., the operations and the medicines administered to the patients. This private information will be completely disclosed to the insurance companies who receive the bills. The insurance companies know whom the bills come from and which patients the bills are for as the identities of both the healthcare providers and patients are directly enclosed in the bills. One important reason why the insurance companies hold such information is that the insurance companies may need to detect fraud. Some malicious patients who are not covered by health insurance or limitedly covered might steal the information of other people to cheat the insurance companies to get invalid benefits [15]. The insurance companies have to confirm that the bills are for the customers who are insured by them through checking the identities of their customers. The insurance companies can also conduct some statistics on the patients' healthcare information for the benefits of patients such as in the assessment of new treatment approach or medicines, where the identities of the patients are not necessary and are often removed (de-identified). In many current eHealth systems, the patients' private health information with their real identities is fully disclosed to the insurance companies due to such reasons. Although the insurance companies announce their promises to keep the privacy of the patients under the restraining of laws, the patients may still doubt that the insurance companies might use their health information for some present or future purposes without their consents. Furthermore, as the health information of the patients is stored in the servers operated by the insurance companies, there exist risks that the data may be stolen by skilled attackers by conquering these servers or malicious insiders. So in this case, the health information of the patients may also be disclosed to some unintended persons. In this paper, we revise the billing procedure in many eHealth systems and propose a novel pseudonym scheme and corresponding signature scheme for the billing process. Technically, it protects the identities of the patients in the bills against the insurance companies, and at the same time, the insurance companies can validate that the bills are for the customers insured by them. Our solution excludes any trusted party that could imitate the patients or discover all the private information (e.g. disease history) of the patients.

The remainder of the paper will be constructed as follows: Section 2 gives a general review of some related work; Section 3 presents a simple billing model and a revised billing process for ordinary activities in eHealth systems by using traditional digital signatures and pseudonym signatures; a concrete pseudonym and signature scheme design will be presented in Section 4; some special issues and remarks will be discussed in Section 5and a conclusion is given in Section 6.

## 2     Related Work

To protect the privacy of the patients, many researchers propose to use pseudonyms to hide the patients' identities. In [16], such a pseudonym scheme is used to index the patients' healthcare records. The pseudonyms are stored at two trusted parties, and they are used to store and retrieve the health records in a central server. However, this solution would require the patients to store much information in the smart cards, and the existence of trusted parties places disclosure risk on the patients' privacy. In [17], a general pseudonym scheme is proposed for generating pseudonyms for one user (possessing a secret) and using the credentials issued by one organization at other organizations without revealing the user's identity. Each user's pseudonym is generated based on the user's secret with the organization's participation. They minimize the dependency on a trust party, and the security relies on the user-only known secrets. In [18], a pseudonym scheme is reported to enable the patients to store and manage their health records in a cloud environment. The pseudonym scheme protects the privacy of the patient against outside attackers properly. However, it is not clear how the patients can keep their privacy against the insurance companies.

In [19], a novel delegate signature scheme was proposed to protect the privacy of the patients' prescriptions. The delegates sign the prescriptions instead of the patients to avoid the disclosure of the identities of the consignors i.e. patients. They may also be used to protect the identities of the patients against insurance companies in the billing procedure. However, it requires that the delegates to be fully trustworthy.

There are some existing technologies to protect the identities of users under a common business model. The U-Prove [20] and Identity Mixer [21] are two representative products in the market. In these technologies, the users firstly register at a trusted party (issuer) and get credentials. The users can use the credentials at other service providers (verifiers) without leaking (or partially revealing) any information about the users' identifiers. These technologies are very useful when the users want to buy some commodities from untrusted merchants without letting the merchants know their identities. However, in the eHealth systems there are more roles including (but not limited to) patients, healthcare providers and insurance companies, and the business procedure is much more complicated than that in a common business model. It is not easy to set up such a trusted issuer in eHealth systems. Furthermore, the insurance companies need to master the real identities of the patients when they sign the insurance contracts with the patients. However, they are not expected to know the identities of the patients when they receive and pay bills for the patients. So these current anonymous technologies to protect the identities for users seem to be hard to apply in eHealth systems.

Anonymous payment [22] is also a popular technology used in bill systems. The bills and payment are transported through a trusted third party (e.g. a bank). Customers pay the bills through the trusted party to merchants anonymously without revealing their identities (e.g. bank account) to the merchants. The trusted third party who holds the identities of the customers is responsible to keep the privacy of their purchases. However, in eHealth systems, the patients whose privacy needs to be protected do not pay to the insurance companies for their health care. In some cases when the patients pay the bills from healthcare providers, the patients do not need to protect the privacy against these billers.

Secure multi-party computation [23] is also a popular technology to protect the participants' privacy in a system without a trusted third party. It enables multiple participants to compute the value of a function with their own private inputs, while protecting their private inputs from being known by other participants. In this paper, the content of the bills are not intended to be protected against the insurance company, but the identity information of the patients related to the bills is what we considered as private. We want to prevent the insurance company from knowing the concrete identity information in the bills. We are not sure how to utilize the secure multi-party computation in such situation to our knowledge. However, we are considering using secure multi-party computation to enable the healthcare providers to query the insurance coverage of the patients anonymously from the database of the insurance companies in Section 5.

In this paper, we would like to discuss the necessity and possibility of protecting the identity information of the patients against the insurance companies especially in billing procedure. We address the privacy problem in such a complicated business model without introducing a single trusted party in our solution. Nevertheless, we require some doctors in the eHealth systems to be trustworthy in some critical processes, and this is usually the case in practice (refer to Section 5 for more discussion about this issue).

# 3    A Refined Billing Procedure

## 3.1    A Simple Billing Model

The billing process is usually complicated and differs in different implementations of eHealth systems. In some eHealth systems (e.g. in German statutory health insurance systems), the healthcare providers (e.g., practitioners, hospitals, pharmacies) send the bills to the insurance companies directly to get paid. The patients are not involved in the billing procedure directly. In contrast, some private insurance companies reimburse the bills sent from the patients who pay firstly the bills from the healthcare providers. There are even separate billing companies (consolidators) in some eHealth systems. Some bill collectors who work with healthcare providers and insurance companies deal with the billing on behalf of them. To simplify the interpretation of our scheme, we model a simple billing procedure shown in Figure 1. This billing model is a simplified version of many nation-wide statutory eHealth systems [24, 25]. We remove some intermediate roles (e.g. bill collectors, banks) in order to describe clearly the essential problem that the privacy of the patients is confronted with in the billing procedure. We are not going to examine the technical details of a practical billing system, as the scheme proposed in this paper does not bear much on those technical details, but rather concerns the general procedure of most billing systems and could be applied in such billing systems in the eHealth world. Some more discussion about adopting our scheme for other billing models is presented in Section 5.

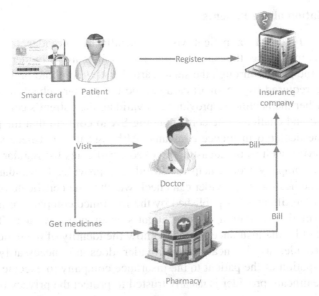

**Fig. 1.** A Simple model of billing procedure

A patient firstly registers at an insurance company. In the registration, the patient usually needs to provide the real identities and some other information to the insurance company, e.g. the employer information. The patient and/or the employer need to pay the premium to the insurance company according to the business model of the current health insurances.

The patient gets a smart card from the insurance company. The smart card can be used for many functions, e.g. storing some important medical information of the patient. For the billing function, the smart card needs to store the publicly known tokens (company name, billing address) of the insurance company. The smart card also stores a certificate issued by the insurance company to the patient. Along with the certificate, a secret private key (SK) which is only known by the patient is stored in the protected memory of the smart card. On the smart card, a photo of the patient may be also imprinted. For our refined billing procedure, we require the smart card to store a master secret key (MSK) generated and only known by the patient. The MSK is also stored in the protected memory of the smart card and used for generating the pseudonym of the patient and signing on bills. The smart card may also be set a PIN (only known to the patient) for authenticating the patient to avoid abuse of the smart card.

Each healthcare provider also needs to get a certificate (Cert_h) from a trusted authority with self-known private key (HSK) which is not depicted in the Figure 1 for simplicity. The trusted authority could be the health department of the government which confirms the healthcare providers' qualifications by issuing them the digital certificates in which information like healthcare categories and identities of the healthcare providers can be enclosed. The private key HSK needs also to be stored in the protected memory of a smart card issued to the healthcare provider with an authenticating PIN.

## 3.2     Validation of the Patients

As shown in Figure 1, a patient visits a healthcare provider (e.g. a doctor or pharmacy) taking along the smart card. The healthcare provider can check the validation of the patient through the smart card. Firstly the photo on the smart card or the PIN code required by the smart card can be the primary check by the healthcare provider. Further the healthcare provider can validate the patient's certificate stored in the smart card and challenge the corresponding SK to confirm that the patient is truly insured by the declared insurance company. Although it is not necessary, an online certificate service such as broadcasting revoked certificates list regularly provided by the insurance company would help the healthcare provider to validate the patients effectively. The healthcare provider can check whether the certificate of the patient is in the revoked certificates list published by the insurance company or not, in order to further confirm the validation of the patient's insurance coverage. The validation process will not let the insurance company know the identity of the patient visiting the healthcare provider as the healthcare provider does not necessarily provide any identity information of the patient to the insurance company to execute the validation check. The healthcare provider is usually trusted to protect the privacy of the patient.

## 3.3     The Format of Bills

A bill from a healthcare provider has to list all the services or drugs that a patient has taken. This is certainly the first basic information the bill should contain. The healthcare provider's tokens (e.g. the bank account information) should also be included. Another part is the signatures of the patient ($Sig_p$) and the healthcare provider ($Sig_h$). The patient's signature includes two parts. The first part is the traditional digital signature by using the secret private key SK corresponding to the patient's certificate issued by the insurance company. The patient's certificate should not be attached into the signature, as not to allow the insurance company to know the identity of the patient directly from the certificate. So this traditional patient's signature would be simply the encrypted (by using SK) value of digest of data to be signed. However, the healthcare provider needs to keep both the certificate and the signature of the patient in a local storage. The other part of the patient's signature is the signature corresponding to the pseudonym which will be detailed in section 4. The traditional digital signature of the healthcare provider by using HSK and the certificate ($Cert_h$) are the last necessary parts of the bill.

As illustrated above, a bill should at least format as following where "||" means concatenation.

```
B = Services/Drugs List || Tokens of healthcare provider
Sig_p = Sign_SK(B) || Sign_MSK(B)
Sig_h = Sign_HSK (B || sig_p)
Bill = B || Sig_p || Cert_h || Sig_h
```

## 3.4    Verification of Bills

The insurance company receives a bill from a healthcare provider. The verification process should be executed to confirm the bill is from a valid healthcare provider and for a customer who is insured by this insurance company. By checking the validation of the certificate and the signature of the healthcare provider, the insurance company can easily confirm the bill is from a valid healthcare provider. Secondly, the insurance company needs to check the validation of patient's signature corresponding pseudonym. The validation of the patient's signature corresponding to the pseudonym indicates that the signature does come from a customer that is insured by the insurance company. I.e., the bill is for one insured customer. However, the validation process does not disclose any information about whom the patient is exactly. The insurance company pays to the healthcare provider according to the tokens of the healthcare provider enclosed in the bill after confirming all the validations of the bill.

As the certificate of the patient is not enclosed in the traditional signature by the patient's secret private key (SK), the insurance company will not be able to verify this traditional digital signature by SK. Thus the insurance company could not know the identity of the patient from the signature of the patient. However, this signature reserved in the bill enables the insurance company to conduct necessary investigation on the bill in the future. Please refer to the discussion Section 5 for more explanation.

# 4    The Proposed Pseudonym and Signature Scheme

## 4.1    Initialization

When a patient registers at an insurance company, the patient gets a smart card with publicly known tokens which encloses some numbers $\lfloor g, p, q \rfloor$ generated by the insurance company as the following. The insurance company chooses a k-bits (k is usually no less than 160 bits) prime integer $q$, and another prime number $p$ (the size of $p$ is usually not less than 512 bits) which satisfy $q|(p-1)$. By $Z_p^*$ we denote a multiplicative group modulo $p$. The insurance company finds $g \in Z_p^*$, to be of order $q$ modulo $p$. Then $g$ is the generator of the subgroup $G_q$. The insurance company initializes the patient's smart card by embedding the numbers $[g, p, q]$ into the smart card. The insurance company just needs to generate these numbers only once, as all the patients insured by this company will have the same numbers in their smart cards.

After getting the smart card, the patient chooses randomly from $G_q$ a number MSK which is stored into the protected memory of the smart card. MSK is chosen and only known by the patient. The process of choosing MSK can be optionally done at the patient's own device or a trusted family doctor's computer.

According to the difficulty of the discrete logarithm problem [26], given $g, h \in G_q$, such that $h$ was selected from $G_q$ uniformly at random, it is hard to compute an integer $x$ such that

$$g^x = h \bmod p.$$

The complexity to find such $x$ is no less than $O(\sqrt{q})$ [27]. For ease of notation, we will sometimes drop the "mod $p$" part of the arithmetic expressions in $G_q$.

## 4.2    Generation of Pseudonym

The patient computes his own pseudonym $PID = g^{MSK} \bmod p$. The computation can be done at the patient's own device or a trusted family doctor's computer. The $PID$ of the patient is sent to the insurance company with the help of a doctor. When the patient firstly uses the smart card at a doctor, the doctor sends a message including the patient's pseudonym $PID$ to the insurance company. Optionally, the message could be sent by the trusted family doctor. The message further includes the signature on the $PID$ by using the doctor's secret key HSK and certificate $Cert_h$. So the message sent from the doctor to the insurance company is defined as,

```
MSG = PID || Sign_HSK(PID) || Cert_h.
```

Before sending the message, the doctor needs to validate the patient's certificate stored in the smart card and challenge the corresponding SK to confirm that the patient is insured by the declared insurance company. The message does not contain any identity information about the patient. So the insurance company is not able to know whom the pseudonym $PID$ belongs to. However, by validating the certificate and the signature of the doctor on $PID$, the insurance company can confirm that the $PID$ does come from a doctor with the certificate $Cert_h$. The doctors are usually assumed as trustworthy in most processes in eHealth systems. However, there exist rare scenarios that a doctor might be doing fraud. A corresponding countermeasure is proposed in the discussion Section 5.

## 4.3    Generation of Signature

A patient signs the basic information B in a bill by using the following algorithm.

```
H = Hash(B)
Patient chooses a random number r in G_q.
y = r + H*MSK mod q
σ = [g^r, g^y, y, PID]
```

The output $\sigma$ is the patient's signature on B based on the pseudonym $PID$. As the signature is generated by the patient's master secret key MSK which is only known by the patient, nobody else can generate a valid signature except the patient himself. The security of the signature is based on the one way property of the hash function and the difficulty of discrete logarithm problem. The difficulty of forging the signature of the patient is equal to find the second pre-image [28] of the hash function or to solve the discrete logarithm problem which are neither feasible. It guarantees that attackers can not steal any patient's information for malicious usage without getting the master secret key MSK of the patient.

We notice that the signature σ only includes the pseudonym and some variables computed from the secret MSK without any identity information of the patient. What is more, to deduce the patient's identity information (i.e., to find out MSK) has the same difficulty as solving the discrete logarithm problem.

## 4.4  Verification of Pseudonym and Signature

The insurance company has stored all the pseudonyms *PID*s of the insured customers sent from the firstly visited doctors or the trusted family doctors. The *PID*s may be stored in a table in the database operated by the insurance company. Once the insurance company receives a bill from a healthcare provider, it extracts out from the bill all the sections as shown in section 3.3, and executes the following procedure to verify the bill is for an insured customer by this insurance company.

```
Checks whether PID from the bill exists in the database,
if not, returns NO.
else
    H' = Hash(B)
    Checks whether g^y ?= g^r PID^{H'},
    if not, return NO,
    else return YES.
```

It is clear that if the customer has ever submitted his pseudonym to the insurance company and signed the bill by his master secret key MSK, the insurance company can easily confirm the bill is for one of its insured customers by checking that $g^y$ is euqal to $g^r PID^{H'}$. However, the insurance company is not able to know whom the patient is except that the patient's pseudonym is *PID*. Further the insurance company is not able to gather any useful information to deduce the identity of the patient, because the difficulty of successful deduction of the identity of the patient has the same complexity as solving the discrete logarithm problem.

We notice that the verification procedure does not need the randomly generated number r ($g^r$ is what was enclosed in the signature σ) in the generation procedure of the signature. Thus neither the patient nor the insurance company needs to store the number r.

# 5     Discussion

## 5.1  Trustworthiness of the Healthcare Providers

In the initialization procedure as indicated in section 4.1, we suggested a patient without necessary knowledge or resources to find a trusted doctor to help set the patient's master secret key MSK and to generate the pseudonym *PID* of the patient. In practice, a patient usually has a family doctor who is considered fully trusted in keeping the privacy of the patient. It is reasonable to assume the patient could find such a trusted doctor to assist with these matters.

Although all the registered healthcare providers holding a valid certificate are assumed to be trustworthy in keeping the privacy of the patients in practical eHealth systems as the registered healthcare providers are publicly known and such privacy protection is guaranteed by law and public monitoring, we nevertheless do not expect that all the healthcare providers a patient will visit are trustworthy in obeying the designed billing procedure. A dishonest healthcare provider might commit a fraud to get invalid payment from the insurance company. The healthcare provider may send a forged message including an invented patient's pseudonym to the insurance company. I.e., the healthcare provider could invent a nonexistent patient with an arbitrary master secret key MSK'. We suggest that the parameters such as $g$ are only known to the insurance companies, and they are embedded in the protected memory of the smart cards (even not directly accessible to the patients). So it is not easy for a dishonest healthcare provider to invent such a nonexistent patient without knowing these parameters.

However, it might be disputable to keep these parameters as secret only known by the insurance company, because patients may still worry that an insurance company uses different parameters for different customers to trace their healthcare activities. So it would be better to let these parameters be publicly known to everybody. In this case, a dishonest healthcare provider might be able to invent easily such a nonexistent patient. Regarding this situation, we required in each bill sent to the insurance company, the patient signs the bill with the SK in a traditional digital signature way except excluding the certificate of the patient from the signature. The healthcare provider who sent this bill has to save the bill enclosing both the certificate and the traditional signature of the patient at a local storage (refer to Section 3.3 for detail). The insurance company can be authorized to select some bills to check with the healthcare providers in order to avoid such fraud. The healthcare providers are required by the insurance company to provide the certificates of the corresponding patients in the bills. With the patient's certificate, the insurance company can verify the patient's traditional digital signature in the bill and finally confirm the bill is for one of its insured customers. As the certificates of the patients are issued by the insurance company, any dishonest healthcare provider cannot generate valid certificates and valid signature. So, in the end, the fraud behavior of the dishonest healthcare provider could be detected.

Instead of requiring the healthcare providers to store the complete bills (with patients' certificates) at local storage, an alternative way is to enclose the encrypted patient certificate into each bill sent to the insurance company. A healthcare provider encrypts the patient's certificate by the public key in the $\text{Cert}_h$, and encloses this encrypted certificate along the patient's traditional digital signature into the bill. The healthcare provider does not need to store the bill any more. Once the healthcare provider is asked by the insurance company to verify the bill, the healthcare provider decrypts the encrypted patient certificate in the bill by using the corresponding HSK. The insurance company can finally check which customer the bill is for by validating the patient's traditional digital signature with the certificate.

## 5.2    Adapting to other Billing Models

Our simple billing model presented above does not consider the fact that different patients may be covered to different ranges by the insurance company. In practice, before a healthcare provider sends a bill to the insurance company, the healthcare provider may need to check whether the expenses in the bill are covered by the insurance company or not. A simple way is to enable the healthcare provider to query the insured range of the patient online from the insurance company by using the secure multi-party computation. The secure multi-party computation enables the healthcare providers to query the insurance coverage range anonymously from the database of the insurance companies. The insurance companies do not know what the healthcare providers have queried but the healthcare providers can get the answers from such anonymous queries. Another practical way may be storing a statement of the coverage range made and signed by the insurance company in the patient's smart card.

In many billing systems, healthcare providers and insurance companies may use bill collectors as agents to deal with the billing. In this case, the healthcare providers and insurance companies can issue sub-certificates to the bill collectors to execute our scheme proposed in this paper.

In the billing model of some private healthcare systems, a bill from a healthcare provider is firstly sent to a patient and the patient pays the bill to the healthcare provider. Later the patient sends the bill to the insurance company to get reimbursed. In this case, the patient needs to add the personal tokens (e.g. bank account information) into the bill and sign it using the MSK and pseudonym. It might be a little difficult to protect the identity against the insurance company unless the patient's tokens in the bill are anonymous and the patient can send the bill to the insurance company and get reimbursed in an anonymous manner (e.g. sending bills from an anonymous email address or a trusted agent and get reimbursed through anonymous payment provided by a trusted bank).

We noticed that, in practice, there are many more billing models which may not be so obviously amenable to our proposed privacy protection scheme. It is interesting to examine whether they are suitable to apply our scheme or not. However, our current major purpose of the proposed scheme is to protect the privacy of patients in some selected billing systems. Besides our scheme, we believe that there are other solutions for other concrete billing models.

## 5.3    The Loss of the Smart Card

When a patient's smart card was lost, the patient gets a new smart card with new certificate and SK from the insurance company. At the same time the insurance company will revoke the certificate in the lost smart card. The patient then generates a new pseudonym (he may use the old MSK or a new MSK) and goes to a trusted doctor to register the new pseudonym with the insurance company. The patient can then use the new smart card in a normal way.

In some rare scenarios, the smart card and even secret keys and PIN of a patient may be stolen by an attacker. The patient needs to report this to the insurance company in order to revoke the certificates as soon as possible to avoid the abuse of the lost smart card. After that, the new smart card issued by the insurance company recovers the patient's normal healthcare activities.

## 5.4    Shortcomings

Our scheme does not anonymize the kind of healthcare providers the patients have visited and the frequency of treatments. The insurance will still learn that the patient account X is frequently billed by a gynecologist, an abortion clinic, or a neurologist. It seems to be difficult to avoid this situation. As the insurance companies could not know the identities of the patient account X, the knowledge does not infringe the patient's privacy directly. However, such knowledge could enable the insurance companies to do some data mining and analysis to decrease the range of the candidates for the account X.

## 6    Conclusion

This paper addresses the privacy protection of patients by advocating a strict "need to know" principle to be maintained by insurance companies. To our knowledge, privacy problems regarding the insurance companies so far have not come up in eHealth industry and research. We argue that it is not necessary for the insurance companies to possess the full health information with the patients' real identities, especially they do not need to know the real identities of the patients holding the health information in the bills in most ordinary cases. Under a simple billing model, we have designed a refined billing procedure combining a traditional digital signature and a novel new signature scheme based on pseudonym in order to protect the identity information of the patients against the insurance companies. The proposed solution enables the insurance company to verify the validation of bills without knowing the identities of the patients thus providing more extensive privacy.

In future work, we are going to examine some major billing systems in practice to evaluate the feasibility of our scheme when implemented in such real systems. We also need to investigate whether the actors are willing to adapt their work processes.

**Acknowledgements.** We would like to thank Dr. Adrian Spalka who raised many challenges and comments from the viewpoint of practical eHealth systems to this paper. Also we appreciate Jan Lehnhardt for discussing with us about the details of the scheme and revising this paper. We also would like to express our thanks to the four anonymous reviewers who supplied many beneficial comments to improve the quality of the final version of this paper.

# References

1. Jha, A.K., DesRoches, C.M., Campbell, E.G., Donelan, K., Rao, S.R., Ferris, T.G., Shields, A., Rosenbaum, S., Blumenthal, D.: Use of electronic health records in US hospitals. New England Journal of Medicine 360(16), 1628–1638 (2009)
2. Oh, H., Rizo, C., Enkin, M., Jadad, A.: What is eHealth?: A systematic review of published definitions. World Hosp. Health Serv. 41(1), 32–40 (2005)
3. Zandieh, S.O., Yoon-Flannery, K., Kuperman, G.J., Langsam, D.J., Hyman, D., Kaushal, R.: Challenges to EHR implementation in electronic-versus paper-based office practices. Journal of General Internal Medicine 23(6), 755–761 (2008)
4. Jha, A.K., Doolan, D., Grandt, D., Scott, T., Bates, D.W.: The use of health information technology in seven nations. International Journal of Medical Informatics 77(12), 848–854 (2008)
5. Bisbal, J., Berry, D.: An analysis framework for electronic health record systems. Methods Inf. Med. 50(2), 180–189 (2011)
6. Haas, S., Wohlgemuth, S., Echizen, I., Sonehara, N., Müller, G.: Aspects of privacy for electronic health records. International Journal of Medical Informatics 31, e26–e31 (2011)
7. U.S. Department of Health and Human Services. Health Insurance Portability and Accountability Act (HIPAA), http://www.hhs.gov/ocr/privacy/
8. Fromholz, J.M.: The European Union Data Privacy Directive. Berk. Tech. LJ 15, 461 (2000)
9. King, A.: The New Zealand Health Strategy. Ministry of Health Wellington (2000)
10. Fernández-Cardeñosa, G., de la Torre-Díez, I., López-Coronado, M., Rodrigues, J.J.: Analysis of cloud-based solutions on EHRs systems in different scenarios. Journal of Medical Systems 36(6), 3777–3782 (2012)
11. Hersh, W.R.: Adding value to the electronic health record through secondary use of data for quality assurance, research, and surveillance. Clin. Pharmacol. Ther. 81, 126–128 (2007)
12. Pommerening, K., Reng, M.: Secondary use of the EHR via pseudonymisation. In: Studies in Health Technology and Informatics, pp. 441–446 (2004)
13. Sofsian, D.: An Introduction to Medical Billing, http://www.e-healtharticles.com/Detailed/1449.html
14. Saltman, R., Busse, R., Figueras, J.: Social health insurance systems in western Europe. McGraw-Hill International (2004)
15. Ahuja, R.: Protecting Your Identity in an e-Health World (2013), http://journal.heinz.cmu.edu/2013/02/protecting-your-identity-in-an-e-health-world/
16. Li, Z.-R., Chang, E.-C., Huang, K.-H., Lai, F.: A secure electronic medical record sharing mechanism in the cloud computing platform. In: 2011 IEEE 15th International Symposium on Consumer Electronics (ISCE). IEEE (2011)
17. Lysyanskaya, A., Rivest, R.L., Sahai, A., Wolf, S.: Pseudonym systems (Extended abstract). In: Heys, H., Adams, C. (eds.) SAC 1999. LNCS, vol. 1758, pp. 184–199. Springer, Heidelberg (2000)
18. Xu, L., Cremers, A.B.: A Decentralized Pseudonym Scheme for Cloud-based eHealth Systems. In: International Conference on Health Informatics, pp. 230–237. SCITEPRESS (2014)
19. Yang, Y., Han, X., Bao, F., Deng, R.H.: A smart-card-enabled privacy preserving E-prescription system. IEEE Transactions on Information Technology in Biomedicine 8(1), 47–58 (2004)

20. Microsoft, U-Prove, http://research.microsoft.com/en-us/projects/u-prove/
21. IBM, Identity Mixer, http://idemix.wordpress.com/.
22. Camenisch, J., Piveteau, J.-M., Stadler, M.: An Efficient Electronic Payment System Protecting Privacy. In: Gollmann, D. (ed.) ESORICS 1994. LNCS, vol. 875, pp. 207–215. Springer, Heidelberg (1994)
23. Yao, A.C.: Protocols for secure computations. In: 2013 IEEE 54th Annual Symposium on Foundations of Computer Science. IEEE (1982)
24. Duennebeil, S., Leimeister, J., Krcmar, H.: Business Models for Electronic Healthcare Services in Germany. In: Critical Issues for the Development of Sustainable E-health Solutions, pp. 271–291. Springer (2012)
25. Kolachalam, S.: eHealth in Australia. In: International Telemedicine and eHealth (2006)
26. McCurley, K.S.: The discrete logarithm problem. In: Proc. of Symp. in Applied Math. (1990)
27. Lim, C.H., Lee, P.J.: A key recovery attack on discrete log-based schemes using a prime order subgroup. In: Kaliski Jr., B.S. (ed.) CRYPTO 1997. LNCS, vol. 1294, pp. 249–263. Springer, Heidelberg (1997)
28. Rogaway, P., Shrimpton, T.: Cryptographic hash-function basics: Definitions, implications, and separations for preimage resistance, second-preimage resistance, and collision resistance. In: Roy, B., Meier, W. (eds.) FSE 2004. LNCS, vol. 3017, pp. 371–388. Springer, Heidelberg (2004)

# Segmentation and Normalization of Human Ears Using Cascaded Pose Regression

Anika Pflug and Christoph Busch

University of Applied Sciences Darmstadt - CASED,
Haardtring 100,
64295 Darmstadt, Germany
anika.pflug@cased.de,
christoph.busch@hig.no
http://www.h-da.de

**Abstract.** Being an emerging biometric characteristic, automated ear recognition is making its way into forensic image analysis for law enforcement in the last decades. One of the most important challenges for this application is to deal with loosely constrained acquisition scenarios and large databases of reference samples. The research community has come up with a variety of feature extraction methods that are capable of handling occlusions and blur. However, these methods require the images to be geometrically normalized, which is mostly done manually at the moment.

In this work, we propose a segmentation and normalization method for ear images that is using cascaded pose regression (CPR). We show that CPR returns accurate rotation and scale estimates, even for full profile images, where the ear has not been segmented yet. We show that the segmentation accuracy of CPR outperforms state of the art detection methods and that CPR improves the recognition rate of an ear recognition system that uses state of the art appearance features.

**Keywords:** ear recognition, biometrics, normalization, segmentation, appearance features.

## 1  Introduction

In the last decade, ear recognition has evolved towards a promising new biometric trait that can help to extract more information from half profile and profile images. Building on the work of Iannarelli [7], the shape of the outer ear is widely regarded as unique and persistent. The research community has evaluated a large number of different types of features. Traditionally, the most important application of ear recognition systems is forensic images analysis on images from surveillance cameras, where subjects are usually unaware of the image capture process. Based on ear features, several cases could be cleared, such as a series of robberies at gas stations [6].

Another anticipated application of ear recognition is automatic border control. Both scenarios, law enforcement and airport security, require a stable and reliable

K. Bernsmed and S. Fischer-Hübner (Eds.): NordSec 2014, LNCS 8788, pp. 261–272, 2014.
DOI: 10.1007/978-3-319-11599-3_16, © Springer International Publishing Switzerland 2014

normalization algorithm that is capable of rotating and scale the ear image to a well-defined reference orientation. Having normalized images allows us to use all kinds of appearance features, such as LPQ and HOG for describing the ear structure. The normalization should also be tolerant to smaller pose variations and partial occlusions.

When working with CCTV footage, the ear is often small and blurry which makes landmark detection a complicated problem. Some landmarks, and sometimes even the whole ear region may be occluded when a subjects is not co-operative. We also know these problems Landmark-based approaches for face recognition in the wild. For this particular problem, feature selection methods using random forests are successfully applied. In [15] landmark candidates are selected from an image and then selected during a voting process. A major challenge in ear normalization is, that accurate landmark localization is a difficult problem as such. The extraction of landmarks is prone to errors, because many approaches, such as ASM for example, depend on proper initialization and requires a large training set. Unlike the face the ear does not have a symmetry axis to support landmark positions.

In [16], Yazdanpanah and Faez normalize previously cropped ear images by using edge information. A similar approach is also proposed by Wang [13], where the outline of the outer helix is extracted from the convex hull of a binary image that describes the outer helix and other elevated parts of the ear. In both approaches, the authors are using the axis that connect the two points with the largest distance and rotate the image, such that this axis is vertical. However, these approaches require that the ear has been located exactly and that all edges in the image actually belong to the ear. Gonzalez et al. propose to use an active shape model for locating the outer helix and then also use two farthest points on this line for normalization [5]. Both approaches require that there are no occlusions in the image and that the outer ear has already been located by a previous detection step. For a more in-depth discussion and comparison of recent advances in ear biometrics, please refer to the survey of Pflug and Busch [11].

We propose to estimate the orientation of the ear by using cascaded pose regression (CPR) [4]. This algorithm uses an abstract elliptical model for pose estimation, which fits well to the shape of the outer ear. CPR locates and normalizes the outer ear in profile images, such that a texture descriptor will have a stronger performance. CPR segments the ear region and rotates the cropped image in a way that the superaurale is oriented vertically (see Fig. 1). Working with normalized images enables a higher recognition performance with texture-based features and a more accurate landmark detection with Active Shape Models and Active Appearance Models.

The main contributions of this paper are (1) Segmentation of the outer ear in pre-cropped full profile images and (2) rotation normalization of the ear region. The normalization experiments are conducted on three different publicly available datasets.

The remainder of this paper is organized as follows: in Section 2 Cascaded Pose Regression (CPR) is briefly outlined. In the subsequent section we first

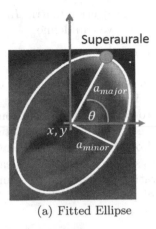

Superaurale

$a_{major}$

$\theta$

$x, y$

$a_{minor}$

(a) Fitted Ellipse

(b) Normalized Ear

**Fig. 1.** Illustration of the CPR-based geometrical normalization of ear images. We fit a ellipse that encloses the ear, and rotate the whole image such that the major axis of the ellipse is vertical.

report on the detection performance for full profile images and compare the performance with existing state of the art approaches for object detection. The experimental results on the performance gain from normalizing the ear image with CPR are presented in Section 4. The paper is concluded with final remarks and future work in Section 5.

## 2   Cascaded Pose Regression

Cascaded Pose regression (CPR) was proposed recently by Dollar et al. [4]. This algorithm is capable of estimating the pose of a roughly located object in an image by using a cascade of weak fern regressors with local features. In their work, Dollar et al. show that CPR converges fast and performs well with small training sets. They also show that CPR can be applied in different contexts, such as pose estimation of mice, fish and facial landmark detection [2]. What makes CPR particularly interesting for normalizing ear images is the fact that it is not relying on any symmetry constraint or other kinds of higher semantic information. It is solely using local brightness information for estimating a transformation matrix between a given state of the descriptor and the trained model. We will only briefly outline the main ideas of CPR in this selection. For more details, please refer to the original paper by Dollar et al. [4].

In the beginning of the estimation process, the model is initialized at a random position in the image. In our case, the model is describes by the parameters of an ellipse, with center coordinates $x, y$ (see Fig. 1). With respect to this coordinate system, we pick a fixed number of pose indexed control point features [9]. A control point feature $h(p_1, p_2)$ is defined by the difference between two gray scale values at two locations $I(p_1)$ and $I(p_2)$ in the image $I$.

For each pose $\Phi$, we can define an associated $3x3$ projection matrix $H_\Phi$, that express $p$ in homogeneous coordinates. Based on this, we can define

$$h_{p_1,p_2}(\Phi, I) = I(H_\Phi p_1) - I(H_\Phi p_2) \tag{1}$$

The algorithm iteratively optimizes the projection matrix, such that the differences between a pair of two pose indexed features is minimized.

During model training, the algorithm learns to predict the orientation of a given object by minimizing a loss function $L$ between the current orientation $\Phi_i$ and a defined ground truth orientation $\Phi_i^T$ based on the pose indexed features. The loss function models the sum of differences of all pose indexed features between the current pose and the previous iteration. Let $d()$ be the function that computes the difference between two sets of pose indexed features. Then the loss function $L$ can be written as

$$L = \sum_{i=1}^{N} d(\Phi_i^T, \Phi_i) \tag{2}$$

In this equation, $i$ refers the $i$'th stage in the cascade. The training in each stage is repeated until the error drops below a target value $\epsilon \geq 1$, which reflects that the error in the previous iteration was either smaller or as large as in the current iteration.

$$\epsilon = \sum_{i=1}^{N} d(\Phi_i^t, \Phi_i) / \sum_{i=1}^{N} d(\Phi_i^{t-1}, \Phi_i) \tag{3}$$

A stage in the cascade consists of a fern regressor [9] that is taking a randomly chosen subset of features and then samples random thresholds. The fern regressor is created by randomly choosing a given number of elements $S$ from the vector of pose indexed features and them samples $S$ thresholds randomly. We chose the best fern regressors in terms of training error from the pool of $R$ randomly generated ferns. It may happen that CPR gets stuck in a local minimum and hence fails to estimate the correct orientation. To prevent this, the regressor in initialized $K$ times and the solutions are clustered. CPR then returns the orientation with the highest density.

For normalizing ear images, we use a single part elliptical model that roughly encloses the outline of the ear. By doing this, CPR can make use of the rich and distinctive texture information inside the ear region. The elliptical model is defined by a set of pose indexed features that are used for optimizing the position of the model in the image as briefly described above.

A particular pose of the ear is defined by a given set of ellipse parameters $x, y, a_{major}, a_{minor}$ and $\Theta$, where $x, y$ are the coordinates of the ellipse center, $a_{major}, a_{minor}$ are the lengths of the major and minor axis of the ellipse and $\theta$ denotes the skew. When fitted to the ear, the major axis of the ellipse is cutting the lobule and pointing towards the superaurale and the minor axis of the ellipse encloses the tragus region. Fig. 1 shows an example of how the ellipse is placed.

Following the recommendations in [4], we choose the parameters of our trained model as follows: The number of cascades is set to $T = 512$, the number of ferns

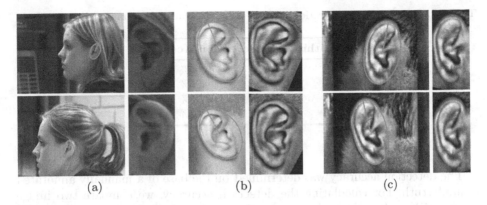

(a)                    (b)                    (c)

**Fig. 2.** Examples for fitted ellipses in original database images from UND-J2 (a), AMI (b) and IIT-Kanpur (c) along with cropped and normalized ROIs

is $F = 64$, and the number of pose-indexed features is chosen to be $R = 512$. The regressor is initialized for $K = 50$ times.

Based on the ellipse parameters of a fitted model, we can segment and normalize the ear region. This is done by rotating the image about the center point of the ellipse in a way that the major axis of the fitted ellipse is horizontal. The rotation angle $\rho$ can be directly inferred from the orientation of the ellipse, denoted as $\theta$. This is also illustrated in Fig. 1.

$$\rho = 90 - \theta \tag{4}$$

After rotating the ear into the defined pose, the ear region is cropped by using the enclosing rectangle of the fitted ellipse. When the major axis of the ellipse is rotated to be vertical, differences in scale can be removed by resizing the ROI in a way that the major axis of all ellipses have the same length. The width of the ROI is adjusted accordingly such that the aspect ratio is preserved.

In Fig. 2, we see pairs of example images with the fitted ellipse in the original image and the cropped region of interest (ROI). There are two pairs from the same subjects and from each database.

## 3  Detection from Profile Images

In this experiment, we determined the segmentation performance of our CPR model on full profile images. Using the UND-J2 [14] database, we compared the segmentation accuracy of cascaded pose regression with HOG features, Haar like features and LBP. We used the Implementations of OpenCV 2.4.3. Each of the four detectors was trained with 400 images of the UND-J2 database. The remaining 1377 images were used for evaluation. We are aware, that a selection of 400 images is a rather small training set for Haar-like features, LBP and HOG detectors. This is done on purpose, to highlight the fact that CPR gives exact estimations of the orientation of the outer ear, even with a small training set.

**Table 1.** Comparison of detection rates of different features on images from UND-J2

| Algorithm | Detection Accuracy |
|-----------|-------------------|
| HOG       | 77.05%            |
| LBP       | 99.05%            |
| HAAR      | 98.32%            |
| CPR       | 99.63%            |

The detection accuracy was determined on the base of a manually annotated ground truth. For calculating the detection accuracy, we compare two image masks with each other and compute the overlap $O$ of these two regions. We consider a detection as being successful if the overlap between the ground truth and the detected region is larger than 50%. This constraint is set in accordance to related work on ear detection, such as in [10], in order to be comparable. Both of these works are using left profile images from the UND collections as well. Let the ground truth region be denoted as $G$ and the detection region be denoted as $R$. Then $O$ can be written as

$$O = \frac{2|G \cap R|}{|G| + |R|} \tag{5}$$

The results of this experiment are summarized in table 1. CPR segmentation clearly outperforms HOG and Haar-like features. The detection accuracy of LBP and CPR are similar, however, the detection accuracy of CPR is still slightly better than LBP.

In contrast to cascaded detectors, CPR does not only provide information about the location of the ear, but at the same time, gives an estimate of the axis between the tragus and the superaurale for normalization. Moreover, the segmented ear regions from CPR are more accurate than the ROIs of cascaded detectors. This means that the segmented region contains only a small portion of the ear's surroundings.

## 4    Normalization

### 4.1    Experimental Setup

In the second series of experiments we evaluate the impact of CPR normalization on the recognition performance of local texture descriptors. All of these descriptors are vulnerable to pose and scale variation We hence expect an increase in recognition performance for each of these methods, when the image is normalized prior to feature extraction.

Further, we expect the performance improvement to be independent to the texture descriptor and the projection technique. In other words, we expect the EER and the rank-1 recognition rate in a configuration where CPR normalization was used to be better than in the same configuration in a reference system, where the image was not normalized. The ear recognition system for obtaining the performance indicators is outlined in Fig. 3. We apply 10-fold cross validation for obtaining the performance indicators in each of the configuration.

Configurations with normalized ears use the cropped and normalized ROI, that is returned from CPR. The reference system, is using manually cropped ear regions for UND-J2. For AMI and IITK, we used the complete images for computing the reference performance (see Fig. 2. The performance indicators for normalized images were operating on the output ROIs from CPR (see Fig. 2).

The recognition experiments were conducted on UND-J2, AMI and IIT-Kanpur databases with the following partitioning:

**UND-J2:** The UND-J2 database is an image collection with 2D and 3D left full profile images, however, only the 2D images are used in this evaluation. The ground truth image of UND-J2 have been cropped manually. Samples, where the ear detection using CPR failed, have been removed from the evaluation set in order to keep the segmentation error and the recognition error separated. We used all subjects with at least 6 samples that have not been used for CPR training. Five of these samples were used for training, and one sample was used for testing. In consequence we were using 583 images for training and 117 images for testing.

**AMI:** The AMI database is a collection of close-up, high resolution ear images. It consists of 8 samples per subject in total, whereas the first sample shows the right ear and all other samples show the left ear of each subject. For left ears, each sample was captured from a slightly different pose and distance. The first 30 subjects have been used for training CPR. For the remaining 67 subjects, we used sessions 2 until 6 for training and session 7 for testing. This implies that we have 335 training images and 67 testing images.

**IIT-Kanpur:** The IIT-Kanpur database contains ear images that have been collected on different days with a fixed distance between the subject and the camera. There are slight variations in the pitch pose. The first 50 subjects have been used for training CPR. For the remaining subjects, we used sessions 1 until 3 for training and all remaining images for testing. Hence, the training set contained 225 images and the testing set was composed of 81 images from 74 different subjects.

## 4.2   Texture Descriptors

For texture description, we apply three different state of the art texture descriptors, which are Unified Local Binary Patterns (uLBP), Local Phase Quantizaton (LPQ) and Histograms of Oriented Gradients (HOG).

**Unified Local Binary Patterns (uLBP):** uLBP [8] encodes local texture information on a pixel level by comparing the grey level values of a pixel to the grey level values in its neighborhood. The size of neighborhood is defined by a radius around the pixel $g_j$, which is at least 1 (for a neighborhood having 8

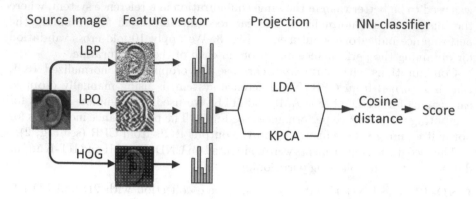

**Fig. 3.** Experimental setup showing all appearance features and projection schemes

pixels). Every pixel $q_i$ within the radius that has a larger grey level value than the center pixel is assigned the binary value 1, whereas all pixels with a smaller grey level value are assigned the binary value 0.

The binary values in the neighborhood pixels are concatenated to form a binary string corresponding to the center pixel. Only those binary strings which have at most two bit-wise transitions from 0 to 1 (or vice-versa) are considered - there are 58 such strings. This binary string is then mapped to a value between 0 and 58.

The uLBP-based ear descriptor is computed by first sliding a window of a predefined size and overlap (step size in pixels) in the horizontal and vertical direction over the LBP image. From each sub window a local histogram with 59 bins is extracted (the first 58 bins correspond to the uniform binary strings, and the 59-th bin corresponds to the rest).

The final descriptor is the concatenation of each local histogram. For a window size of 20×20 pixels and an overlap of 10 pixels, this results in a feature vector of dimension 3776.

**Local Phase Quantization (LPQ):** The concept behind LPQ [1] is to transform the image into the fourier domain and to only use the phase information in the subsequent steps. Given that a blurred image can be viewed as a convolution of the image and a centrally symmetric point spread function, the phase of a transformed image becomes invariant to blur. For each pixel in the image, we compute the phase within a predefined local radius and quantize the image by observing the sign of both, the real and the imaginary part of the local phase. Similar to uLBP, the quantized neighborhood of each pixel is reported as an eight digit binary string.

Given an image, the LPQ value is first computed for every pixel. Next, local histograms with 265 bins are computed within a sliding window. We move this sliding window, with a given overlap between two neighboring windows, in horizontal and vertical direction over the image and concatenate each local histogram. With a 20×20 window size and an overlap of 10 pixels, this results in a 16.384 dimensional feature vector.

**Histogram of Oriented Gradients (HOG):** Computation of the HOG [3] descriptor involves five steps, which are the gradient computation, orientation binning, histogram computation, histogram normalization and concatenation of local histograms. The algorithm starts by computing the local gradient by convolving a $3 \times 3$ region (HOG cells) with two one-dimensional filters $(-101)$ and $(-101)^T$. The local orientation at the center of each HOG cell is the weighted sum of the filter responses of each pixel.

The local orientations within a larger sub-window, denoted as block, are then quantized into bins in the $[0, 2\pi]$ interval. Subsequently, the image is divided into blocks of equal size and a local histogram of quantized orientations is extracted. Subsequently, the local histogram from each block is normalized with the L2-norm. Finally, all local histograms are concatenated to form the HOG descriptor for the image. The HOG descriptor with block size of $8 \times 8$ pixels and 9 orientation bins has 5184 dimensions.

## 4.3   Feature Subspace Creation

The feature subspace for each of the descriptors is created with one of four different projection techniques. We apply the widely used LDA as representative for linear projection method. Additionally, we use KPCA [12] to have a non-linear technique. Finally, the most likely identity for each probe image is the reference image that has the smallest cosine distance to the projected probe image in the feature subspace. Parts of the source code for this experiment are based on the PhD Face recognition Toolbox.

## 4.4   Results

In Table 2 the rank-1 recognition rates and the EERs are summarized for all possible combinations between texture descriptors and the two dimensionality reduction techniques. As the numbers show, CPR normalization improves the performance all pipeline configurations using LDA and with each of the databases. Compared to the reference configuration, the EER is improved up to 3% in each of the databases. The improvement is of course dependent on the degree of pose variations in a dataset. Because the poses in UND only vary slightly, we have larger pose variations in IITK and the AMI datasets. The ear images in IITK vary in rotation and the images in AMI contain rotation and scale variations (see Fig. 2)Consequently, there is more potential for CPR to correct variations of scale and rotation, as well as to accurately segment the ROI. Examples for successfully corrected variations, are shown in Fig. 2.

When using KPCA for creating the feature subspace, we obtain high error rates However, the error rates as well as the standard deviation between the error rates from different cross-validation attempts are high for these configurations.

**Table 2.** Detection rates with normalization (CPR) and without normalization (GT) for selected recognition pipelines. EER and rank-1 recognition rate are given in percent and are represented as tuples of the form *EER // Rank-1*.

| | LDA | | KPCA | |
|---|---|---|---|---|
| | CPR | GT | CPR | GT |
| **UND-J2** | | | | |
| uLBP | 2.58 // 93.35 | 3.43 // 90.94 | 23.36 // 38.86 | 29.93 // 22.28 |
| LPQ | 3.23 // 91.51 | 4.50 // 82.28 | 17.02 // 55.44 | 22.22 // 36.08 |
| HOG | 1.76 // 95.70 | 3.05 // 91.14 | 26.87 // 19.43 | 32.66 // 5.44 |
| **AMI** | | | | |
| uLBP | 1.85 // 93.4 | 4.32 // 86.1 | 39.02 // 19.30 | 28.40 // 26.1 |
| LPQ | 0.40 // 97.2 | 5.19 // 85.2 | 40.53 // 16.0 | 25.98 // 42.1 |
| HOG | 0.68 // 98.10 | 5.21 // 82.2 | 22.99 // 43.1 | 28.44 // 19.9 |
| **IITK** | | | | |
| uLBP | 0.26 // 99.72 | 1.67 // 97.22 | 11.84 // 72.64 | 16.88 // 70.41 |
| LPQ | 0.02 // 99.72 | 3.28 // 94.03 | 8.01 // 85.28 | 18.76 // 61.1 |
| HOG | 0.18 // 99.72 | 1.48 // 95.83 | 6.01 // 86.25 | 23.22 // 35.27 |

Based on our observation, we conclude that KPCA is not a suited for the texture descriptors in our experiment. The recognition performance of all configurations using LDA yields EERs below 3,5% in all databases. On average, the lowest error rates were achieved with HOG. However, LPQ and uLBP perform similarly on all datasets.

Another factor that may also have influenced the performance of images, that have been normalized with CPR is, that CPR is capable of cropping the region of interest more accurately than other segmentation techniques, such as those used in the previous section. Hence, the feature vector contains less information for the surroundings of the ear compared to the ground truth in AMI and IITK. The region around the ear contains some information, which helps to increase the performance in datasets, which have been collected in a short period of time. However, we expect that these features are subject to changes in hairstyle, clothes and jewelry and hence are rather a soft biometric, than a permanent features. For real life applications, we assume that a more accurate segmentation will result in better recognition performance.

## 5   Conclusion

In this work, we have shown, that an ear image can be normalized without the need for symmetry or landmark extraction. We have provided experimental evidence showing that cascaded pose regression improves the performance in two ways. With CPR it is possible to detect and normalize the outer ear from profile images with only one processing step. The ear region can be segmented accurately to make sure that the feature vector only contains information about the ear and not about its surroundings. In addition to this, CPR also extracts information to compensate differences in rotation and scale, while being robust to minor occlusions.

We have shown that the performance improvement, which can be achieved with CPR in independent of the capture scenario by using different datasets. The performance improvement is also independent to the texture descriptor. Motivated by our results, we plan to train multi-part CPR models for landmark detection in the future.

**Acknowledgments.** This project is funded by the Federal Ministry of Education and Research (BMBF) of Germany in the context of the research programme for public safety and security. Anika Pflug is supported by the COINS Research School of Computer and Information Security.

# References

1. Ahonen, T., Rahtu, E., Ojansivu, V., Heikkila, J.: Recognition of blurred faces using local phase quantization. In: 19th International Conference on Pattern Recognition, ICPR 2008, pp. 1–4 (December 2008)
2. Burgos-Artizzu, X., Perona, P., Dollár, P.: Robust face landmark estimation under occlusion. In: ICCV (2013)
3. Dalal, N., Triggs, B.: Histograms of oriented gradients for human detection. In: IEEE Computer Society Conference on Computer Vision and Pattern Recognition, CVPR 2005, vol. 1, pp. 886–893 (June 2005)
4. Dollar, P., Welinder, P., Perona, P.: Cascaded pose regression. In: CVPR (2010)
5. Gonzalez, E., Alvarez, L., Mazorra, L.: Normalization and feature extraction on ear images. In: 2012 IEEE International Carnahan Conference on Security Technology (ICCST), pp. 97–104 (2012)
6. Hoogstrate, A., Heuvel, H.V.D., Huyben, E.: Ear identification based on surveillance camera images. Science & Justice 41(3), 167–172 (2001)
7. Iannarelli, A.V.: Ear identification. Paramont Publishing Company (1989)
8. Ojala, T., Pietikainen, M., Maenpaa, T.: Multiresolution gray-scale and rotation invariant texture classification with local binary patterns. IEEE Pattern Analysis and Machine Intelligence 24(7), 971–987 (2002)
9. Ozuysal, M., Calonder, M., Lepetit, V., Fua, P.: Fast keypoint recognition using random ferns. IEEE Transactions on Pattern Analysis and Machine Intelligence 32(3), 448–461 (2010)
10. Pflug, A., Back, P., Busch, C.: Towards making hcs ear detection robust against rotation. In: 2012 IEEE International Carnahan Conference on Security Technology (ICCST), pp. 90–96 (October 2012)
11. Pflug, A., Busch, C.: Ear biometrics: A survey of detection, feature extraction and recognition methods. IET Biometrics 1(2), 114–129 (2012)
12. Scholkopf, B., Smola, A., Müller, K.-R.: Kernel principal component analysis. In: Advances in Kernel Methods - Support Vector Learning, pp. 327–352. MIT Press (1999)

13. Wang, S.-Z.: An improved normalization method for ear feature extraction. International Journal of Signal Processing, Image Processing and Pattern Recognition 6, 49–56 (2013)
14. Yan, P., Bowyer, K.: Biometric Recognition Using 3D Ear Shape. Pattern Analysis and Machine Intelligence 29, 1297–1308 (2007)
15. Yang, H., Patras, I.: Sieving regression forest votes for facial feature detection in the wild. In: 2013 IEEE International Conference on Computer Vision (ICCV), pp. 1936–1943 (December 2013)
16. Yazdanpanah, A.P., Faez, K.: Normalizing human ear in proportion to size and rotation. In: Huang, D.-S., Jo, K.-H., Lee, H.-H., Kang, H.-J., Bevilacqua, V. (eds.) ICIC 2009. LNCS, vol. 5754, pp. 37–45. Springer, Heidelberg (2009)

# Poster Papers

# Dynamic Enforcement of Dynamic Policies

Pablo Buiras and Bart van Delft

Chalmers University of Technology, Sweden

**Abstract.** LIO is a dynamic information-flow control system embedded in Haskell that uses a runtime monitor to enforce noninterference. The monitor is written as a library, requiring no changes to the runtime. We propose to extend LIO with a state component, allowing us to enforce not only noninterference but also information-flow policies that change while the program is running.

Enforcement mechanisms for information flows in software frequently aim to achieve the *noninterference* security property. This property states that no change in sensitive (secret) inputs to the system should affect non-sensitive (public) outputs, which captures the idea that secrets should not be leaked.

LIO [3] is a Haskell runtime monitor that enforces noninterference. Over time, LIO has been successfully extended to prevent information leaks via certain covert timing channels. The security condition has, however, not yet been generalised, even though it is generally accepted that noninterference is too strong a requirement for most applications.

There are several canonical examples of applications that necessarily violate noninterference. A password checker needs to allow for some interference from the password database to the user to signal whether the login attempt was successful or not. Information purchase applications require noninterference on confidential information to hold only until the price for that information has been paid. Yet other applications might need to introduce additional noninterference constraints over time, for example on the information flow from strategic documents to a manager who is demoted while the system is running.

To allow for the enforcement of such dynamic policies, we propose to extend LIO with a state component which records that part of the system state relevant to determine the current policy that needs to be enforced. In the following we briefly summarise how LIO works and how we propose to extend it. For now we consider only the original sequential LIO library, leaving support for extensions such as concurrency to future work.

*Labelled IO.* LIO leverages Haskell's monadic encoding of side-effects to provide security. In Haskell, input/output operations are provided by the IO *monad*, an abstract data type used to express sequencing of effectful computations. The LIO monad provided by the LIO library is intended to be used as a replacement for this type. It provides a collection of operations similar to IO, but enriched with security checks that prevent unwanted information flows. LIO computations

K. Bernsmed and S. Fischer-Hübner (Eds.): NordSec 2014, LNCS 8788, pp. 275–276, 2014.
DOI: 10.1007/978-3-319-11599-3, © Springer International Publishing Switzerland 2014

carry the type LIO l a, where l is an arbitrary security lattice of labels specified by the code using LIO and a is the type of the result of the computation.

The LIO library uses a *floating-label* approach to the dynamic enforcement of information-flow policies, which is based on mandatory access control. The LIO monad uses its state to keep track of a *current label*, $L_{cur}$. This label represents, in a coarse-grained way, the least upper bound over the labels on which the current computation depends. All the (I/O) operations provided by LIO take care to appropriately validate and adjust this label. Consider a standard two-point lattice (Low $\sqsubseteq$ High) and a computation starting with $L_{cur}$ being Low. When this computation reads a file labelled High, $L_{cur}$ is raised to High and writing to Low files is prohibited by the LIO monad from that moment onwards, independent of what would actually be written to these files.

*Stateful LIO.* We propose for LIO computations to carry the type LIO s l a, where s is the type of the state component for LIO to use in its enforcement. That is, when writing to a file with label $l$ we now check whether $L_{cur} \sqsubseteq_s l$. The LIO library exports functionality to update this state $s$, so the outcome of this check for the same $L_{cur}$ and $l$ can vary depending on the current value of $s$.

As the relation between labels can now change arbitrarily over time, the labels lose their lattice structure and a least upper bound can no longer be computed. Therefore $L_{cur}$ is modified to contain the *set* of labels of all the information on which the current computation depends. When performing a sensitive operation like writing to a file, the $\sqsubseteq_s$ check is performed for each label in $L_{cur}$ individually.

*Encodings.* We can now present various policy change mechanisms as restricted interfaces to Stateful LIO. Clearly, we can regain the original noninterference by simply not exporting the operations to update the state component.

We can export an explicit declassify function, by using a boolean value as the state component and having the ordering among policies as usual except that High $\sqsubseteq_{true}$ Low holds but High $\sqsubseteq_{false}$ Low does not. An operation p can now be declassified by calling declassify p which sets the state to *true*, performs p and then resets the state to *false* before returning.

We can also encode policy languages that allow for much more policy change, such as Paralocks [1] (in which the state component becomes a set of open locks) or non-disclosure policies [2] (where the state tracks the set of flow-relations).

# References

1. Broberg, N., Sands, D.: Paralocks – Role-Based Information Flow Control and Beyond. In: Proceedings of the 37th Annual ACM SIGACT-SIGPLAN Symposium on Principles of Programming Languages, POPL 2010 (2010)
2. Matos, A.A., Boudol, G.: On declassification and the non-disclosure policy. In: 18th IEEE Workshop on Computer Security Foundations, CSFW-18 2005, pp. 226–240. IEEE (2005)
3. Stefan, D., Russo, A., Mitchell, J.C., Mazières, D.: Flexible Dynamic Information Flow Control in Haskell. In: Proceedings of the 4th ACM Symposium on Haskell, Haskell 2011, pp. 95–106. ACM, New York (2011)

# Availability by Design

Roberto Vigo, Flemming Nielson, and Hanne Riis Nielson

DTU Compute, Technical University of Denmark, Denmark
{rvig,fnie,hrni}@dtu.dk

Availability is "the property of being accessible and usable upon demand by an authorised entity" [1], and its absence is termed Denial-of-Service (DoS) or unavailability. DoS typically occurs when the resources of a target server are exhausted, preventing a given service to be offered to clients and often leading to the paralysis of an entire system, with a domino effect. Our proposal aims at preventing such effect through a defensive programming style.

Despite availability has received lesser attention than confidentiality and integrity, with which it forms the so-called CIA properties [2], DoS attacks to systems of public concern occur increasingly and have become infamous on the Internet, the distributed system *par excellence*. Besides active attackers, limited resources or optimistic assumptions about the environment can be source of unavailability, suggesting that cryptography is not the ultimate solution.

We claim that the absence of first-class constructs supporting DoS considerations in existing programming frameworks is one determining factor of a great many availability threats. Promoting unavailability to be a first-class citizen of a language not only raises the awareness in developers, but also leads to devise more precise analyses. To this end we proposed the Quality Calculus [3,4], a process calculus in the $\pi$ calculus family that is equipped with the notion of absence of communication and lacking information.

As availability concerns naturally apply to distributed communicating systems, we find it fruitful to study the problem in process algebraic settings, where DoS is defined as the absence of expected communication and acceptance of improper information. The first trait corresponds to classic network-level DoS (expected data are not received), while the second accounts for the migration of availability attacks up the ISO/OSI stack. Indeed, whether we receive nothing or something we cannot use, the effect is the same.

The main novelty of the Quality Calculus is a binder specifying the inputs to be performed before continuing. In the simplest case it is an input guard $t?x$ describing that some value should be received over the channel $t$ and should be bound to the variable $x$. Increasing in complexity, we may have binders of the form $\&_q(t_1?x_1, \cdots, t_n?x_n)$ indicating that several inputs are *simultaneously* active and a quality predicate $q$ that determines when a *sufficient* combination of inputs has been received to continue. Moreover, input patterns can be used to specify what sort of data an input is willing to accept, as in $t?x[p]$.

As a consequence, when continuing with the computation some variables might not have obtained proper values, as the corresponding inputs might have not been performed. To model this we distinguish between data and optional data, much like the use of option data types in programming languages like

K. Bernsmed and S. Fischer-Hübner (Eds.): NordSec 2014, LNCS 8788, pp. 277–278, 2014.
DOI: 10.1007/978-3-319-11599-3, © Springer International Publishing Switzerland 2014

Standard ML. If $c$ is the message received by an input, then the corresponding variable is bound to some($c$), while in case the input is not received but we continue anyway the variable is bound to none. Whenever accessing an input variable, then, the calculus obliges to inspect its content through the construct case $x$ of some($y$): $P_1$ else $P_2$, executing $P_1$ if $x$ carries some($c$) or $P_2$ otherwise. In this sense, at every point of the computation we know what data we have and what we have not.

The calculus is complemented by a number of verification aids, including two static analyses and an executable specification of the semantics, that facilitate the work of the developer by pointing out where and why DoS might occur, in terms of reachability of program points and combination of values for the inputs. The analyses are implemented as Satisfiability and Satisfiability Modulo Theories problems (the latter not yet published), and thus can exploit the scalability of modern off-the-shelf solvers.

We deem that our investigation leads to a shift in the mind-set. Existing literature on availability zeroes in on mechanisms to detect and avoid DoS attacks on the target side. This is a challenging task, as the detection process itself can be frustrated by the ongoing attack. Moreover, unavailability has a great many sources that are not encompassed by active countermeasures to DoS. We advocate instead for a world in which components are aware of being part of a system and are determined to operate even if their ideal partners become unavailable and do not provide expected information, perhaps because such partners are undergoing a DoS attack. The overall perspective is then lifted from a self-centred, muscular approach to a more realistic view which admits the existence of DoS and tries to circumvent it.

The spirit of our proposal is thus to cope with the effect of DoS through a pessimistic approach to programming. Nonetheless, it is not always possible to follow alternative plans, and therefore ongoing work is focusing on quantitative considerations, to ensure that potential sources of DoS do not impact the behaviour of the system with respect to given contracts. Finally, another line of development concerns studying the portability and effect of our approach to availability on real programming languages.

# References

1. ISO: ISO/IEC 7498 - Part 2: Security Architecture
2. Gollmann, D.: Computer Security, 3rd edn. Wiley (2011)
3. Riis Nielson, H., Nielson, F., Vigo, R.: A Calculus for Quality. In: Păsăreanu, C.S., Salaün, G. (eds.) FACS 2012. LNCS, vol. 7684, pp. 188–204. Springer, Heidelberg (2013)
4. Vigo, R., Nielson, F., Riis Nielson, H.: Broadcast, Denial-of-Service, and Secure Communication. In: Johnsen, E.B., Petre, L. (eds.) IFM 2013. LNCS, vol. 7940, pp. 412–427. Springer, Heidelberg (2013)

# Pareto Efficient Solutions of Attack Trees

Zaruhi Aslanyan and Flemming Nielson

DTU Compute, Technical University of Denmark, Denmark
{zaas,fnie}@dtu.dk

Nowadays IT systems rarely work in isolation; they rather cooperate with each other, communicating in an interconnected world. In this growing global computing environment security has become one of the main issues. The continued integration and cooperation of distributed components creates new security problems. Formal methods are necessary to face the complexity of these new scenarios and to study their security properties and threats. Attack trees are a well-known formal yet graphical approach for describing threats on systems and representing the possible attacks.

The first graphical representation for analysing the safety of a system, called fault trees, was introduced in early 1980's. Fault trees represent a failure of a system in terms of the failure of its components [1]. Inspired by fault trees researchers adopted a similar approach to security.

In 1991, Weiss presented threat logic trees as a formal attack modeling technique [2]. Later, in 1999, Schneier introduced attack trees as a tool to evaluate the security of complex systems in a structured, hierarchical way. Attack trees allow to analyse the possible attack scenarios and reason about the security of the whole system in a formal, methodical way, based on varying attacks [3].

The root of an attack tree represents a goal of the attacker. The sub-trees of a node in the tree refine the goal of the node into sub-goals. The leaves of the tree are the basic actions to be executed by the attacker. An internal node shows how the sub-trees have to be combined in order to achieve the overall goal of the attacker. Standard attack trees combine sub-trees either conjunctively or disjunctively, thereby limiting their expressiveness. They do not consider the fact that the absence (negation) of some action might lead to an attack.

Traditional literature on attack trees focuses on single (mainframe) computers and describes threats they are subject to. Most approaches model the attacker's behaviour on such systems by considering one-parameter attack trees and analysing a particular aspect of an attack, such as feasibility or cost. The analyses are performed by assigning values to the basic actions and traversing the tree from the leaves to the root. Different analytical methods suggested different functional operators for computing the value from child nodes to the parent node, based on the type of refinement. However, the study of single computer systems is no longer adequate for dealing with the challenges of a global computing environment. Various extensions of attack trees with multiple parameters have been studied. In most multi-parameter models, values characterizing basic attacks are propagating to the root relying on local decision strategies. In case of incomparable values, however, this approach may yield sup-optimal results.

K. Bernsmed and S. Fischer-Hübner (Eds.): NordSec 2014, LNCS 8788, pp. 279–280, 2014.
DOI: 10.1007/978-3-319-11599-3, © Springer International Publishing Switzerland 2014

In order to overcome the limitation in expressiveness of the standard model, we introduce negation as a refinement operator. The extension makes attack trees more flexible and allows to model and analyse a wider range of attack scenarios, including the cases of unrecoverable and conflicting actions. For instance, cutting a communication wire might be unrecoverable, and after having cut a wire we might not be able to communicate with a given device.

Moreover, for analysing complex scenarios with more than one-parameter, we present an evaluation technique that considers basic actions (leaves) characterized by more than one dimension (e.g. probability and cost). In order to deal with such a scenario our technique optimizes all the parameters at once, thus computing different aspects of an attack and handling multiple objectives. Furthermore, as different objectives may conflict with each other, we consider the set of Pareto optimal solutions to face the analysis of incomparable values.

In particular, we study the problem in the settings of a Boolean and a probabilistic semantics for attack trees. For each such semantics, we first consider the problem of feasibility of the attack, and then we extend our technique to compute optimal attacks in presence of multiple costs.

We illustrate the developments on a home-payment system. A home-payment system allows people, who may have difficulties leaving their home, to pay some services such as care-taking or rent. The payment is performed through the remote control of a television box thanks to a contact-less payment card. The card is protected by password to authenticate the owner when a transfer is initiated. The attack scenario that we consider is to steal money from the card-holder by forcing him/her to pay fake services. With our evaluation technique, we have computed the minimum cost of the tree corresponding to the attack scenario in the Boolean and probabilistic cases. In particular, the probabilistic evaluation deals with conflicting parameters, as we want to maximize the probability while minimizing the cost of attacking the system. The result of the evaluation represents the Pareto frontier, each point describing a probability of success with the corresponding cost.

In future work we plan to interpret negation refinements as defender's actions and consider attack-defense trees [4]. We plan to relate an attack-defense scenario with game theory and study the interaction between attackers and defenders as a two player game.

# References

1. Vesely, W., Roberts, N., Haasl, D., Goldberg, F.: Fault Tree Handbook, vol. 88. Systems and Reliability Research, Office of Nuclear Regulatory Research, U.S. Nuclear Regulatory Commission (1981)
2. Weiss, J.D.: A system security engineering process. In: Proceedings of the 14th National Computer Security Conference, pp. 572–581 (1991)
3. Schneier, B.: Attack Trees: Modeling Security Threats. Dr. Dobb's Journal of Software Tools 24(12), 21–29 (1999)
4. Kordy, B., Mauw, S., Radomirović, S., Schweitzer, P.: Attack–Defense Trees. Journal of Logic and Computation (2012), http://logcom.oxfordjournals.org/content/early/2012/06/21/logcom.exs029

# Verification of Stateful Protocols
## Set-Based Abstractions in the Applied π-Calculus

Alessandro Bruni, Sebastian Mödersheim, Flemming Nielson,
and Hanne Riis Nielson

Technical University of Denmark
{albr,samo,fnie,hrni}@dtu.dk

An ideally designed security protocol should not be state-dependent. In practice however real applications require a certain amount of state for different reasons: encryption keys need to be updated periodically to prevent attackers from learning valid ones, messages are signed with timestamps in order to avoid replaying them after they are no longer valid, etc. Specialised protocols that need to run with bandwidth and real-time constraints may rely solely on state mechanisms to provide their claimed security properties, such as MaCAN and CANAuth, two proposed protocols for automotive that we recently analysed [1].

We propose an extension of the applied π-calculus with support for potentially infinite sets of values. With this extension we are able to analyse protocols with unbounded number of sessions, where security and authenticity properties rely on the use of counters and timestamps, or databases of keys.

We extend the calculus of ProVerif [2,3], a widely used verification tool, which over-approximates its analysis by abstracting away state information translating processes into Horn clauses. The abstraction approach taken by ProVerif simplifies the state exploration, and allows verifying secrecy and authenticity properties over an unbounded number of sessions in many concrete protocols, but is unable of modelling the following simple protocol:

$$A \rightarrow B \; : \; \{Msg, Counter\}_{Key}$$

Alice sends to Bob a message, signed with a counter and a shared key. Bob checks whether the counter is new by comparing it with the ones already observed, and accepts only fresh messages. Injective correspondences in ProVerif cannot prove its freshness, because there is no injective relation between the session identifiers of the processes for A and B. Encoding the protocol is also non-trivial as the applied π-calculus does not have a global non-monotonic state.

StatVerif [4] presented an extension of the applied π-calculus that added a global synchronised state, allowing the analysis of stateful processes. However we were not able to encode sets of values without generating terms of ever-increasing size, which lead to non-termination of the analysis. The authors suggested the need for further abstractions in such cases.

Our analysis applies the set-membership abstraction, as proposed by AIF [5], while translating the protocol description into Horn clauses. Values in the process algebra are mapped to their membership class, a term $\mathsf{val}(x, x_{s_1}, \ldots, x_{s_n})$ that abstracts the sets to which $x$ belongs. Our particular encoding allows a

K. Bernsmed and S. Fischer-Hübner (Eds.): NordSec 2014, LNCS 8788, pp. 281–282, 2014.
DOI: 10.1007/978-3-319-11599-3, © Springer International Publishing Switzerland 2014

$$M, N ::= x \mid a \mid f(M_1, \dots, M_n) \qquad \text{variables, names, constructors}$$

$$
\begin{aligned}
P, Q ::={} & 0 \mid \; !P \mid \; P_1 \mid P_2 && \text{nil, replication, parallel composition} \\
& \mid \overline{M}\langle N \rangle.P \mid M(x : T).P \mid (\nu\, a : A)\, P && \text{output, typed input, restriction} \\
& \mid \mathsf{let}\; x = \mathsf{g}(M_1, \dots, M_n) \;\mathsf{in}\; P \;\mathsf{else}\; Q && \text{destructor application} \\
& \mid \mathsf{if}\; M \in s_i \;\mathsf{then}\; P \;\mathsf{else}\; Q && \text{set membership test} \\
& \mid \mathsf{enter}(M, s_i).P \mid \mathsf{exit}(M, s_i).P && \text{set membership transitions} \\
& \mid \mathsf{lock}(s_i).P \mid \mathsf{unlock}(s_i).P && \text{acquire/release set lock}
\end{aligned}
$$

**Fig. 1.** The process calculus

compact representation of potentially infinite values, while still distinguishing two different values in the same class, increasing the precision of the analysis.

The calculus is presented in Figure 1. As in ProVerif, we have terms $M, N$ which are either variables, names or constructor applications. Constructors are generally accompanied by destructors defined as rewrite rules that describe cryptographic primitives, for example $\mathsf{dec}(\mathsf{enc}(msg, key), key) \to msg$ defines the behaviour of symmetric key cryptography.

Processes $P, Q$ are the usual stuck process, replication, parallel composition of two processes, output, typed input, restriction and destructor application. The distinguishing feature of our calculus is the ability to track values in sets: the set membership test allows us to check whether a term $M$ is in a set $s$, while $\mathsf{enter}(M, s)$ and $\mathsf{exit}(M, s)$ respectively transition to a state where $M$ is in set $s$ and $M$ is not in set $s$. Finally we use finer grained locks than StatVerif to increase the precision of our analysis.

By lifting the set-membership abstraction to the applied $\pi$-calculus we reduce the abstraction gap required in the verification of security protocols that rely on mechanism such as key databases, counter or timestamps to ensure security and authenticity properties.

## References

1. Bruni, A., Sojka, M., Nielson, F., Nielson, H.R.: Formal Verification of the MaCAN Protocol. To appear in The 11th International Conference on Integrated Formal Methods. LNCS (to appear, 2014)
2. Blanchet, B.: An efficient cryptographic protocol verifier based on Prolog rules. In: IEEE Computer Security Foundations Workshop. IEEE Computer Society (2001)
3. Blanchet, B.: From Secrecy to Authenticity in Security Protocols. In: Hermenegildo, M.V., Puebla, G. (eds.) SAS 2002. LNCS, vol. 2477, pp. 342–359. Springer, Heidelberg (2002)
4. Arapinis, M., Ritter, E., Ryan, M.D.: Statverif: Verification of stateful processes. In: 2011 IEEE 24th Computer Security Foundations Symposium (CSF). IEEE (2011)
5. Mödersheim, S.A.: Abstraction by set-membership: Verifying security protocols and web services with databases. In: Proceedings of the 17th ACM Conference on Computer and Communications Security. ACM (2010)

# Improvement Proposal for the CryptoCloak Application

Dijana Vukovic[1,2], Danilo Gligoroski[1], and Zoran Djuric[2]

[1] Department of Telematics, NTNU, O.S. Bragstads plass 2B, Trondheim, Norway
[2] Department of Computer Science and Informatics, Faculty of Electrical
Engineering, Patre 5, Banja Luka, Bosnia and Herzegovina

**Abstract.** Since July 2013, huge effort was invested into spy-resistant
application development. Different initiatives were organized world-wide
by EFF[6] and similar organizations to fight for the Internet as it is used
to be (e.g. "The day we fight back", "Reset the Net", etc.). CryptoCloak
is an application for privacy protected chat communication. Encrypted
communication is masked with dynamic cheap chat conversation. In current version of this application, Diffie-Hellman key exchange is done in
clandestine manner - instead of sending uniform sequence of numbers,
sentences are sent. It produces huge overhead. In this paper, one proposal
for its improvement is given.

## 1  Introduction

Internet surveillance exists for a long time, but people became more aware of it
after Snowden affair started[7]. Revelations about NSA partnership with leading
companies in the Internet communication area appeared (e.g. Microsoft, Google,
Skype, etc.). The fact that the NSA had an access to the private communication
of individuals is a huge violation of privacy. Surveillance, as a close observation of a person or a group, can be justified in the case that observed person
is under suspicion, or in the case that surveillance can help in preventing crime
or terrorism. Considering the simple definition of privacy as "the right to be
left alone", conclusion is - the surveillance can be a big threat to the privacy.
"Surveillance/privacy" issue led to developing tools for anonymous communication over the Internet. The most popular chat application with this purpose are:
Cryptocat[1] and Telegram[2]. Our approach implemented in CryptoCloak application was for the first time presented on BalkanCrypt Workshop[3]. The main
idea was use of solid and secure cryptoalgorithms to provide secure chat communication, but do it in the clandestine way - instead of sending encrypted information, mask them with cheap chat. Cheap chat - sentences such as: "Hello!",
"How are you?", used in everyday chat communication, are the cloak for hiding
encrypted information. CryptoCloak application is written in Java programming
language. Major disadvantage in the current version of CryptoCloak is: to ac-
complish successful key exchange using cheap chat it takes around 30 minutes[4].
Second chapter gives an overview of proposed improvement for the CryptoCloak
application. At the end, some notes and comments on the current state of CryptoCloak project is given.

K. Bernsmed and S. Fischer-Hübner (Eds.): NordSec 2014, LNCS 8788, pp. 283–284, 2014.
DOI: 10.1007/978-3-319-11599-3, © Springer International Publishing Switzerland 2014

## 2   An Improvement Suggestion for the CryptoCloak

To speed up the current key exchange process in CryptoCloak, parameters $a$ and $b$, needed for Diffie-Hellman key exchange can be sent as an e-mail message. It can be implemented the way is shown in Figure 1. Using the same algorithm from previous version[4], parameters will be converted into array of sentences, and, instead of sending these sentences via chat communication, they will be sent using legitimate e-mail account from well-known and secure e-mail server. When the particular parameter is received, it will be transformed into its real value, and the key will be calculated. The same process will be executed on both sides, Bob's and Alice's, and after successful Diffe-Hellman key exchange, they can start AEC-CBC encrypted communication. User can send/receive e-mail message over/from different accounts. If we split communication this way, it will be efficient and harder to follow. This technique will be similar to the the one the Tor[5] uses - based on twisty, hard to follow routes. Although, this

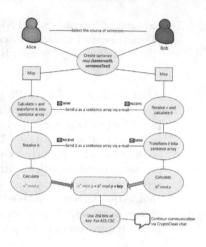

**Fig. 1.** CryptoCloak improvement

provides exposure diversification - if communication is intercepted, it will still be hard to determine from where the message is sent or who is the sender.

*Notes and Comments.* Suggested improvement is in an implementation phase. In further versions, threat model has to be created, the perfect forward secrecy has to be proven, and a way to cope with cryptanalysis techniques has to be given.

## References

1. Cryptocat, https://crypto.cat/
2. Telegram, https://telegram.org/
3. Vukovic, D.: The CryptoCloak Project. BalkanCrypt Kickoff Meeting and Workshop, Sofia, Bulgaria (2013)
4. Vukovic, D., Gligoroski, D., Djuric, Z.: On privacy protection in the Internet surveillance era. In: SECRYPT 2014, Vienna, Austria (accepted for publication, 2014)
5. Tor project - About, https://www.torproject.org/about/overview.html.en
6. Electronic Frontier Foundation - About, https://www.eff.org/about
7. Edward Snowden and the NSA files – timeline, http://www.theguardian.com/world/2013/jun/23/edward-snowden-nsa-files-timeline

# Process Tracking for Forensic Readiness

Yi-Ching Liao and Hanno Langweg

Norwegian Information Security Laboratory, Gjøvik University College,
Teknologivn. 22, 2815 Gjøvik, Norway
{yi-ching.liao,hanno.langweg}@hig.no

**Abstract.** We summarize our research on process tracking for forensic readiness, including the state-changing activities of processes, cost-benefit analysis of process tracking, and the architecture for process tracking. We consider the privacy and admissibility issues as future work.

**Keywords:** forensic readiness, process tracking, kernel tracing.

## 1  Introduction

Forensic analysis suffers from insufficient logging of events, and current system loggers do not record enough information for incident analysis and replay. Similar to flight data recorders preserving performance parameters for aircraft accident investigation, comprehensive process tracking can provide precise, timely, complete, and dependable information for incident investigation and replay. Moreover, the collected traces can recover the traceability links between the incident and the person or action accountable for the incident.

## 2  The State-Changing Activities of Processes

Without identifying the state-changing activities of processes, it is impossible to know when to track and what to log. To answer the question: "What are the state-changing activities of processes?", we evaluated the existing process tracking systems from the perspectives of forensic analysis and forensic readiness, including the logging method, the tracing granularity, the replay boundary, and the implementation method [1]. We found that most process tracking systems for security aim at the process-level granularity, which is insufficient for determining the root cause of incidents. On the other hand, the instruction-level tracing can provide fine-grained information for incident analysis and replay, but the cost of process activity tracking can be quite expensive. To strike a balance between the forensic effectiveness and efficiency, it is essential to evaluate the soundness, completeness, and cost of process activity tracking.

## 3  Cost-Benefit Analysis of Process Tracking

To meet the two objectives of forensic readiness [2]: maximizing the usefulness and minimizing the cost, it is important to perform cost-benefit analysis of process tracking. Since kernel tracing systems can provide more dependable and

K. Bernsmed and S. Fischer-Hübner (Eds.): NordSec 2014, LNCS 8788, pp. 285–286, 2014.
DOI: 10.1007/978-3-319-11599-3, © Springer International Publishing Switzerland 2014

comprehensive process activities for incident investigation and forensic analysis, to answer the question: "How effective, efficient, and expensive is comprehensive process activity tracking?", we conducted a cost-benefit analysis of three kernel tracing systems: strace, SystemTap, and LTTng [3]. We discovered that LTTng can provide system-wide tracing with lower performance and storage overhead. On the other hand, strace and SystemTap can provide better flexibility for tracing evolving intruder tactics and hacking techniques through dynamic instrumentation. For cost-benefit trade-off, it is necessary to design the architecture for flexible and adjustable process tracking.

## 4    The Architecture for Process Tracking

Security incidents or digital crimes must occur with system resource usage. Since system calls cause state transitions of resource usage, they are at the proper level of granularity for process tracking. To answer the question: "Which architecture facilitates process activity tracking?", we presented a resource-based event reconstruction prototype that corresponds to different phases of digital forensics framework, and conducted a feasibility study by assessing the applicability of existing open-source applications to the proposed prototype [4]. By regarding system resources as an evidence source and system calls as digital events, the proposed prototype can enhance the capability of an organization for gathering, preserving, protecting, and analysing digital evidence.

## 5    Future Work

Since kernel traces may contain personal information and aggregating traces from various hosts can raise serious privacy concerns, to protect the confidentiality of personally identifiable information, we need to answer the question: "What are privacy implications for users of systems that support comprehensive traceability?" by conducting privacy impact assessments. Moreover, to ensure that the collected traces are admissible as evidence, we will answer the question: "How does comprehensive traceability affect evidence gathering and the legal process?" by conducting security and vulnerability assessments.

## References

1. Liao, Y.C., Langweg, H.: A Survey of Process Activity Tracking System. In: 6th Norsk Informasjons Sikkerhets Konferanse, pp. 49–60 (2013)
2. Tan, J.: Forensic Readiness, pp. 1–23. @ Stake, Cambridge (2001)
3. Liao, Y.C., Langweg, H.: Cost-Benefit Analysis of Kernel Tracing Systems for Forensic Readiness. In: Proceedings of the 2nd International Workshop on Security and Forensics in Communication Systems, pp. 25–36. ACM, New York (2014)
4. Liao, Y.C., Langweg, H.: Resource-based Event Reconstruction of Digital Crime Scenes. In: IEEE Joint Intelligence and Security Informatics Conference (to be published, 2014)

# Computationally Analyzing the ISO 9798–2.4 Authentication Protocol

Britta Hale and Colin Boyd

Norwegian University of Science and Technology – NTNU

As it is widely agreed that authentication protocols are difficult to design correctly, standardized authentication protocols are very useful for practitioners. Among the protocols available from a variety of different standards bodies, some are widely deployed, such as the well known TLS and SSH protocols. Among its 9798 series of standards, the ISO have standardized a suite of authentication protocols, yet like most standardized authentication protocols, these are not defined in a fully formal way. Effectively, among other possible undesirable consequences, this can lead to uncertainty about how to correctly implement the protocols securely.

With the goal of providing computational proofs for one of the 9798–2 protocols which have so far been lacking, we focus on ISO 9798–2.4 (9798-2, section 6.2.2 Mechanism 4 of the standard [2]) which is shown below. Notationally, $Text_i$ is an optional text field, $\mathcal{E}_K$ an "encipherment function" between $A$ and $B$ [2, p. 4], $I_B$ an optional unique distinguisher, and $R_i$ a random nonce.

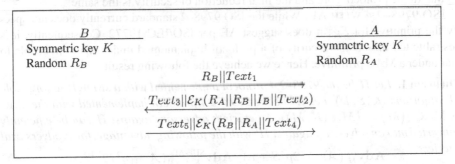

**Fig. 1.** ISO 9798–2.4 Protocol

CHOICE OF CRYPTOGRAPHIC PRIMITIVES. ISO 9798–2.4 protocol makes use of an encipherment algorithm with a shared symmetric encipherment key and requires that it is able to detect "forged or manipulated data"[2, p. 4]. Authenticated encryption (AE) is recommended for implementation. However, any formal definition or technical description of such properties is missing from the standard and it is observable that entity authentication can be achieved without use of encryption at all. Thus, aiming to obtain security under maximal efficiency, we show in our computational security proof that a message authentication code (MAC) algorithm can be safely implemented.

COMPUTATIONAL SECURITY. Focus in the computational security proof is on the protocol core – the optional fields in the protocol are not considered. In the Bellare–Rogaway '93 model [1], principals possess matching conversations if and only if they accept. Correspondingly, adversarial advantage, $\mathbf{Adv}_\Pi^{MA}(E)$, is defined as the probability that the adversary can succeed in persuading an oracle to accept without a matching

K. Bernsmed and S. Fischer-Hübner (Eds.): NordSec 2014, LNCS 8788, pp. 287–288, 2014.
DOI: 10.1007/978-3-319-11599-3, © Springer International Publishing Switzerland 2014

conversation. If $p$ the number of principals, $S$ the number of sessions, $1^k$ the security parameter, and $q$ queries allowed to $\mathcal{A}$, and $E$ runs in time $t$ and asks $q$ queries, then

$$\mathbf{Adv}_{\Pi}^{\mathrm{MA}}(E) \leq 2p^2 S \cdot \mathbf{Adv}_{\Pi}^{\mathrm{MAC}}(F) + \frac{q^2}{2^{k+1}}.$$

Moreover, $F$ runs in time $t_F \approx t$ and asks $q_F = q$ queries.

ROGAWAY–STEGERS FRAMEWORK. While the analysis above demonstrates security of the ISO 9798–2.4 protocol core it omits the optional text fields, an important aspect of the original protocol. Rogaway and Stegers [3] introduced a model that addresses this issue by splitting the protocol into two parts: the partially specified protocol core (PSP) and the protocol details (PD), whicht selects content for the text fields. Yet, since there is no restriction on the data that is sent in these fields, it is necessary to consider that data choice could weaken the protocol. Allowing the adversary itself to choose the optional text fields models this weakness. Essentially, the Rogaway–Stegers framework under this assumption requires that mutual authentication is satisfied in addition to requiring that matching session IDs (in our implementation, matching conversations) imply matching AD. Thus, we capture the optional fields of ISO 9798–2.4 while applying the Rogaway–Stegers framework in its first application to a standardized protocol.

Discriminately, data fields fall into two categories, with the authenticated associated data (AD) being of salient concern. Of the ISO 9798–2.4 protocol's text fields $T_l$ for $l \in \{1, \ldots, 5\}$, only $T_2$ is authenticated and guaranteed received by the protocol, and hence is the only AD. Succinctly, the proof of security, when AD is considered, builds on that of the protocol core and the final reduction of security is the same.

ISO 9798–2.4 WITH AE. While the ISO 9798–2 standard currently does not specify the primitive for $\mathcal{E}_K$, it does suggest AE per ISO/IEC 19772. Consequently, it is desirable to know if the security of a protocol implemented under AE is traceable to that under a MAC primitive. Hence we achieve the following result.

**Theorem 1.** *Let $\Pi$ be the 9798–2.4 protocol implemented with a strongly unforgeable AE algorithm $(\mathcal{K}, \mathcal{E}, \mathcal{D})$. Let $\Pi'$ be the 9798–2.4 protocol implemented with the MAC as $\mathrm{MAC}_K(M) = (M, \mathcal{E}(K, M))$. An efficient adversary against $\Pi$ can be efficiently converted into an adversary against $\Pi'$ with the following advantage, for $n$ adversarial queries:*

$$\mathbf{Adv}_{\Pi}^{\mathrm{AE}}(\mathcal{A}) \leq (2p^2 S + n) \cdot \mathbf{Adv}_{(\mathcal{K}, \mathcal{E}, \mathcal{D})}^{\mathrm{SUF\text{-}AE}}(\mathcal{A}) + q^2/2^{k+1}.$$

Ultimately, these results underscore the security of ISO 9798–2.4, a real-world mutual authentication standard – demonstrating a notable improvement to the standard's current requirements while also validating security in the computational model.

# References

1. Bellare, M., Rogaway, P.: Entity Authentication and Key Distribution. In: Stinson, D.R. (ed.) CRYPTO 1993. LNCS, vol. 773, pp. 232–249. Springer, Heidelberg (1994)
2. ISO: Information technology – security techniques – entity authentication – part 2: Mechanisms using symmetric encipherment algorithms. ISO ISO/IEC 9798-2:2008, International Organization for Standardization, Geneva, Switzerland (2008)
3. Rogaway, P., Stegers, T.: Authentication without Elision: Partially Specified Protocols, Associated Data, and Cryptographic Models Described by Code. In: Proceedings of the 2009 22nd IEEE Computer Security Foundations Symposium, pp. 26–39. IEEE Computer Society (2009)

# Differential Privacy and Private Bayesian Inference*

Christos Dimitrakakis[1], Blaine Nelson[2],**, Aikaterini Mitrokotsa[1], and Benjamin I.P. Rubinstein[3]

[1] Chalmers University of Technology, Sweden
[2] University of Potsdam, Germany
[3] The University of Melbourne, Australia

We consider a Bayesian statistician ($\mathcal{B}$) communicating with an untrusted third party ($\mathcal{A}$). $\mathcal{B}$ wants to convey useful answers to the queries of $\mathcal{A}$, but without revealing private information. For example, we may want to give statistics about how many people suffer from a disease, but without revealing whether a particular person has it. This requires us to strike a good balance between utility and privacy. In this extended abstract, we summarise our results on the inherent privacy and robustness properties of Bayesian inference [1]. We formalise and answer the question of whether $\mathcal{B}$ can select a prior distribution so that a computationally unbounded $\mathcal{A}$ cannot obtain private information from queries. Our setting is as follows:

(i) $\mathcal{B}$ selects a model family ($\mathcal{F}_\Theta$) and a prior ($\xi$).
(ii) $\mathcal{A}$ is allowed to see $\mathcal{F}_\Theta$ and $\xi$ and is computationally unbounded.
(iii) $\mathcal{B}$ observes data $x$ and calculates the posterior $\xi(\theta|x)$ but does not reveal it. Instead, $\mathcal{B}$ responds to queries at times $t = 1, \ldots$ as follows.
(iv) $\mathcal{A}$ sends a query $q_t$ to $\mathcal{B}$.
(v) $\mathcal{B}$ responds $q_t(\theta_t)$ where $\theta_t$ is drawn from the posterior: $\theta_t \sim \xi(\theta|x)$.

We show that by choosing $\mathcal{F}_\Theta$ or $\xi$ appropriately, the resulting posterior-sampling mechanism satisfies generalised differential privacy and indistinguishability properties. The intuition is that robustness and privacy are linked via smoothness. Learning algorithms that are smooth mappings—their output (*eg.* a spam filter) varies little with perturbations to input (*e.g.* similar training corpora)—are robust: outliers have reduced influence, and adversaries cannot easily discover private information. Consequently, robustness and privacy may be simultaneously achieved and perhaps are deeply linked.

Our results [1] show that mild assumptions are sufficient to obtain a differentially-private mechanism in the Bayesian setting. As a first step, we generalise the definition of differential privacy [2] to arbitrary dataset spaces $\mathcal{S}$. To do so, we introduce the notion of differential privacy under a pseudo-metric $\rho$ on the space of all datasets.

* This work was partially supported by the Marie Curie Project ESDeMUU grant No: 237816 and the FP7 STREP project BEAT, grant No: 284989.
** Blaine Nelson is now at Google, Mountain View.

K. Bernsmed and S. Fischer-Hübner (Eds.): NordSec 2014, LNCS 8788, pp. 289–290, 2014.
DOI: 10.1007/978-3-319-11599-3, © Springer International Publishing Switzerland 2014

**Definition 1 (($\epsilon, \delta$)-differential privacy under $\rho$.).** *A conditional distribution $P(\cdot \mid x)$ on $(\Theta, \mathfrak{S}_\Theta)$ is ($\epsilon, \delta$)-differentially private under a pseudo-metric $\rho : \mathcal{S} \times \mathcal{S} \to \mathbb{R}_+$ if, for all $B \in \mathfrak{S}_\Theta$ and for any $x \in \mathcal{S}$, then $P(B \mid x) \leq e^{\epsilon\rho(x,y)} P(B \mid y) + \delta\rho(x,y) \; \forall y$.*

Our first assumption is that the $\mathcal{F}_\Theta$ is smooth with respect to some metric $d$:

**Assumption 1 (Lipschitz continuity)** *Let $d(a, b) \triangleq |\ln a/b|$. There exists $L > 0$ such that, for any $\theta \in \Theta$: $d(p_\theta(x), p_\theta(y)) \leq L\rho(x, y), \qquad \forall x, y \in \mathcal{S}$ .*

As it can be hard for this assumption to hold uniformly over $\Theta$, we relax it by only requiring that $\mathcal{B}$'s *prior* probability $\xi$ is concentrated in the smoothest members of the family:

**Assumption 2 (Stochastic Lipschitz continuity)** *Let $\Theta_L$ be the set of $L$-Lipschitz parameters. Then $\exists c > 0$ such that, $\forall L \geqslant 0$: $\xi(\Theta_L) \geqslant 1 - \exp(-cL)$ .*

One consequence of either of those assumption is that the posterior is robust, in the sense that small dataset changes result in small changes in the posterior:

**Theorem 1.** *If $\xi$ is a prior on $\Theta$ and $\xi(\cdot \mid x)$ and $\xi(\cdot \mid y)$ are the respective posterior distributions for datasets $x, y \in \mathcal{S}$, then the posterior KL-divergence satisfies: $D\left(\xi(\cdot \mid x) \parallel \xi(\cdot \mid y)\right) \leqslant O(\rho(x, y))$, with linear terms depending on $L, c$.*

Consequently, one way to answer queries would be to use samples from the poster distribution. In fact, we show that such posterior-sampling mechanisms are differentially private:

**Theorem 2.** *Under Assumption 1, the posterior is $(2L, 0)$-differentially private under $\rho$. Under Assumption 2, the posterior $\xi$ is $\left(0, \sqrt{\frac{\kappa}{2c}}\right)$-differentially private under $\sqrt{\rho}$.*

As the adversary performs more queries, he obtains more information about the true dataset. Finally, we bound the effort required by an adversary to be $\epsilon$-close to the true dataset:

**Theorem 3.** *The adversary can distinguish between data $x, y$ with probability $1 - \delta$ if $\rho(x, y) \geqslant O(\frac{\ln 1/\delta}{n})$, with a linear dependency on $L$ or $c$.*

We have shown that both the privacy and robustness properties of Bayesian inference are inherently linked through the choice of prior distribution. Such prior distributions exist for example in well known conjugate families. There is also a natural *posterior sampling* mechanism through which differential privacy and dataset indistinguishability can be achieved.

## References

[1] Dimitrakakis, C., Nelson, B., Mitrokotsa, A., Rubinstein, B.: Robust and private bayesian inference
[2] Dwork, C., McSherry, F., Nissim, K., Smith, A.: Calibrating noise to sensitivity in private data analysis. In: Halevi, S., Rabin, T. (eds.) TCC 2006. LNCS, vol. 3876, pp. 265–284. Springer, Heidelberg (2006)

# Event Invitations in Privacy-Preserving DOSNs*
## Formalization and Protocol Design

Guillermo Rodríguez-Cano, Benjamin Greschbach, and Sonja Buchegger

KTH Royal Institute of Technology
School of Computer Science and Communication
Stockholm, Sweden
{gurc,bgre,buc}@csc.kth.se

The most common form of Online Social Networks (OSNs) are run in a logically centralized manner (although often physically distributed), where the provider operating the service acts as a communication channel between the individuals. Decentralization has been proposed to reduce the effect of these privacy threats by removing the central provider and its ability to collect and mine the data uploaded by the users as well as behavioral data.

One of the standard features of OSNs is the handling of event invitations and participation, i. e., a call for an assembly of individuals in the social graph for a particular purpose, e. g., a birthday celebration, demonstration, or meeting. There is usually metadata related to each event, such as date, location and a description. An implementation of this feature must provide security properties, e. g., that a user can verify that an invitation she received was actually sent by the organizer. Furthermore, it must support certain privacy settings. For example, an organizer could choose that only invited users learn how many other users were invited and that only after a user has committed to attend the event, she learns the identities of these other invited users.

Realizing this in a decentralized scenario is non-trivial because there is no Trusted Third Party (TTP) which all involved users can rely on. This is a problem especially for privacy properties where information shall only be disclosed to users with a certain status. In the example above, a neutral, trusted broker could keep the secret information (the identities of invited users) and disclose it only to users who committed to attend the event. This would guarantee fairness to both the organizer and the invited users. It becomes more challenging to implement this without a central TTP and still allowing different types of information about the event to be shared with different groups of users in a secure way.

In our proposal for a privacy-preserving decentralized implementation of the event invitation feature, as depicted in Figure 1, we divide the users of the Decentralized Online Social Network (DOSN) into the organizer of the event, the invitees, those who confirmed attending the event (attendees) and the remaining users. We assume basic functionality of popular OSNs to be available in a decentralized manner, such as user search or user messaging. We also assume

---

\* A full paper on this work will be presented at the Privacy and Identity Management for the Future Internet in the Age of Globalisation - 9th IFIP WG 9.2, 9.5, 9.6/11.7, 11.4, 11.6 and Special Interest Group 9.2.2 International Summer School, Patras, Greece, September 7-12, 2014.

K. Bernsmed and S. Fischer-Hübner (Eds.): NordSec 2014, LNCS 8788, pp. 291–292, 2014.
DOI: 10.1007/978-3-319-11599-3, © Springer International Publishing Switzerland 2014

that users are identified by a public key and the ability to verify the identity of other users via some sort of Public Key Infrastructure, which can be realized in a decentralized manner. Moreover, we rely on a distributed storage featuring access right management, e. g., that a certain storage object is only writeable by a specific user, and "append-only" storage objects, where new data can be appended, but existing data cannot be modified or removed without notice.

We describe and formally define two basic and five more complex security and privacy properties for the event invitations feature in DOSNs, such as invitee/attendee identity privacy (who learns the identities of the invitees/attendees), invitee/attendee count privacy (who learns the count of invitees/attendees), and attendee-only information reliability (availability of information exclusive to the attendees).

We also describe privacy enhancing tools, such as storage location indirection (to control not only who can decrypt an object but also who can see a ciphertext), controlled ciphertext inference (to allow a controlled information leak, e. g., about the size of an encrypted object to parties not able to decrypt the content) and a custom "commit-disclose protocol" to disclose a secret only to users who committed to attend an event. Using these tools together with standard cryptographic primitives, we discuss and propose a TTP-free architecture and decentralized protocols to implement the event invitation feature in a DOSN and analyze the usability and privacy implications. The suggested protocols cover all of our defined properties, considering 20 different parameter combinations for the tunable privacy properties.

The results can be applied in the context of Privacy-Preserving DOSNs, but might also be useful in other domains such as Working Environment and their corresponding collaborative-specific tools, i. e., groupware.

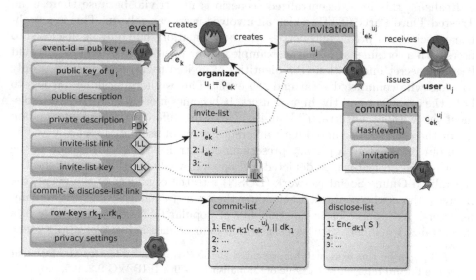

**Fig. 1.** Overview of system components and actions between stakeholders

# Attacks on Privacy-Preserving Biometric Authentication

Aysajan Abidin, Elena Pagnin, and Aikaterini Mitrokotsa

Chalmers University of Technology, Gothenburg, Sweden
{aysajan.abidin,elenap,aikmitr}@chalmers.se

**Abstract.** Biometric authentication based on facial image, fingerprint, palm print, iris, retina, or veins are becoming increasingly popular. However, compromised biometric templates, indeed, may lead to serious threats to identity and their inherent irrevocability makes this risk even more serious. Because of such serious privacy implications the need for *privacy-preserving biometric authentication protocols* is of utmost importance. Recently, Yasuda *et al.* [1,2] proposed two efficient privacy-preserving biometric authentication using packed homomorphic encryption based on ideal lattices and on ring learning with error. We review these protocols and analyse their security against *malicious* internal adversaries.

Yasuda *et al.* [1,2] have proposed two packed homomorphic encryption schemes based, respectively, on ideal lattices and on ring-LWE (ring-learning-with-errors). Let $vE_1(\cdot)$ be the type 1 packed encryption, and $vE_2(\cdot)$ the type 2 packed encryption. Let $A$ and $B$ be bitstrings of length $N$. Then, $ct_H = CvE_1(A) + C'vE_2(B) - 2vE_1(A)vE_2(B)$ corresponds to an encryption of the Hamming distance between $A$ and $B$, for suitable chosen constants $C$ and $C'$. In particular, $vE_1(A)vE_2(B)$ provides an encryption of the inner product between $A$ and $B$. Both protocols involve three entities (a client server $C$, a computation server $CS$ and an authentication server $AS$) and are composed of three phases:

– **Setup Phase:** $AS$ generates the public key pk and the secret key sk for the SHE schemes, and distributes only pk to both $C$ and $CS$.

– **Enrolment Phase:** $C$ generates a feature vector $A$ from the client's biometric readings, computes $vE_1(A)$, and sends it with client's ID to $CS$, who then stores $vE_1(A)$ and ID in its database $DB$.

– **Authentication Phase:** $C$ generates a feature vector $B$ from the client's fresh biometric readings, computes $vE_2(B)$, and sends it with the client's ID to $CS$. Then, $CS$ retrieves the template $vE_1(A)$ corresponding to ID from $DB$, computes $ct_H$ and sends $ct_H$ to $AS$. Subsequently, $AS$ decrypts $ct_H$ with the secret key sk to obtain the Hamming distance $HD(A, B)$. Finally, $AS$ returns the authentication result YES (resp. NO) to $C$ if $HD(A, B) \leqslant \tau$ (resp., otherwise), where $\tau$ is a pre-defined threshold.

We briefly describe the attack algorithms that could be employed when $C$ (Algorithm 1) and $CS$ (Algorithm 2) are malicious. Note that Algorithm 1 can also be employed by a compromised $CS$. In the attack algorithm descriptions, $C \xrightarrow{A} CS$ denotes $C$ sends $A$ to $CS$.

K. Bernsmed and S. Fischer-Hübner (Eds.): NordSec 2014, LNCS 8788, pp. 293–294, 2014.
DOI: 10.1007/978-3-319-11599-3, © Springer International Publishing Switzerland 2014

**Algorithm 1** Center search attack

**Input:** $B = B_1, \cdots, B_N$ (fresh)
**Output:** $A = A_1, \cdots, A_N$ (reference)
**for** $i = 1$ to $N$: **do**
$\quad D \leftarrow \overline{B}_1, \ldots, \overline{B}_i, B_{i+1}, \ldots, B_N$
$\quad \mathcal{C} \xrightarrow{\mathsf{vE}_2(D)} \mathcal{CS}$
$\quad \mathcal{CS} \xrightarrow{\mathsf{ct}_H} \mathcal{AS}$
$\quad$ **if** rejected **then**
$\quad\quad$ break
$\quad$ **end if**
**end for**
**for** $i = 1$ to $N$: **do**
$\quad \mathcal{C} \xrightarrow{\mathsf{vE}_2(D_1,\ldots,\overline{D}_i,D_{i+1},\ldots,D_N)} \mathcal{CS}$
$\quad \mathcal{CS} \xrightarrow{\mathsf{ct}_H} \mathcal{AS}$
$\quad$ **if** accepted **then**
$\quad\quad A_i \leftarrow \overline{D}_i$
$\quad$ **else**
$\quad\quad A_i \leftarrow D_i$
$\quad$ **end if**
**end for**

**Algorithm 2** Cheating attack

**Input:** $\mathsf{vE}_1(A)$
**Output:** $A = A_1, \cdots, A_N$
**Initialise:** $A = 0_1 0_2 \cdots 0_N$
**for** $i = 0$ to $N - \tau$: **do**
$\quad D \leftarrow 1_1 \cdots 1_{\tau+i} \, 0_{\tau+i+1} \cdots 0_N$
$\quad \mathcal{CS} \xrightarrow{\mathsf{vE}_1(A)\mathsf{vE}_2(D)} \mathcal{AS}$
$\quad$ **if** rejected **then**
$\quad\quad$ break
$\quad$ **end if**
**end for**
$i' \leftarrow \tau + i; \; A_{i'} \leftarrow 1$
**for** $i = 1$ to $i' - 1$: **do**
$\quad D \leftarrow 1_1 \cdots 1_{i-1} \, 0_i \, 1_{i+1} \cdots 1_{i'} 0 \cdots 0_N$
$\quad \mathcal{CS} \xrightarrow{\mathsf{vE}_1(A)\mathsf{vE}_2(D)} \mathcal{AS}$
$\quad$ **if** accepted **then**
$\quad\quad A_i \leftarrow 1$
$\quad$ **end if**
**end for**
**for** $i = i' + 1$ to $N$: **do**
$\quad D \leftarrow 1_1 \cdots 1 0_{i'} \cdots 0 1_i 0 \cdots 0_N$
$\quad \mathcal{CS} \xrightarrow{\mathsf{vE}_1(A)\mathsf{vE}_2(D)} \mathcal{AS}$
$\quad$ **if** rejected **then**
$\quad\quad A_i \leftarrow 1$
$\quad$ **end if**
**end for**

We reviewed two recently proposed privacy-preserving biometric authentication protocols and presented two attack algorithms. The center search attack (Algorithm 1) enables to recover a reference biometric template using a fresh acceptable template. The second attack (Algorithm 2) allows the recovery of reference templates of arbitrary users. Both attacks require a number of authentication attempts that is linear in $N$ (*i.e.* the length of the biometric template) to fully recover a reference template.

**Acknowledgements.** This work was partially supported by the FP7-STREP project "BEAT: Biometric Evaluation and Testing", grant number: 284989.

## References

1. Yasuda, M., Shimoyama, T., Kogure, J., Yokoyama, K., Koshiba, T.: Packed homomorphic encryption based on ideal lattices and its application to biometrics. In: Cuzzocrea, A., Kittl, C., Simos, D.E., Weippl, E., Xu, L. (eds.) CD-ARES 2013 Workshops. LNCS, vol. 8128, pp. 55–74. Springer, Heidelberg (2013)
2. Yasuda, M., Shimoyama, T., Kogure, J., Yokoyama, K., Koshiba, T.: Practical packing method in somewhat homomorphic encryption. In: Garcia-Alfaro, J., Lioudakis, G., Cuppens-Boulahia, N., Foley, S., Fitzgerald, W.M. (eds.) DPM 2013 and SETOP 2013. LNCS, vol. 8247, pp. 34–50. Springer, Heidelberg (2014)

# Author Index